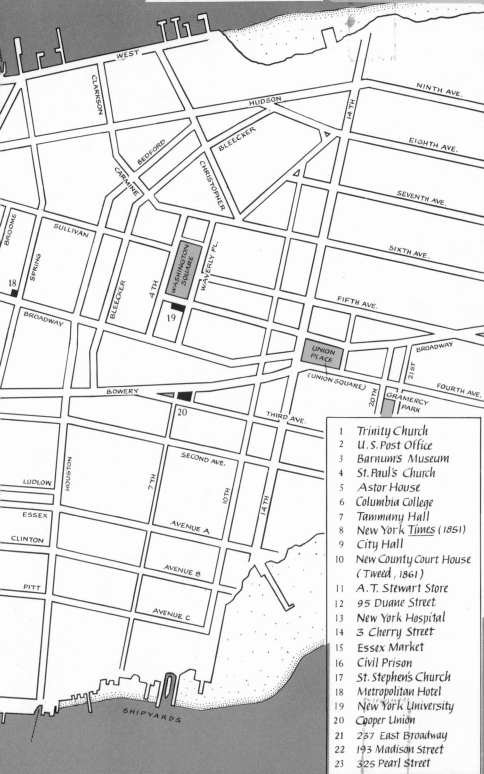

1 Trinity Church
2 U. S. Post Office
3 Barnum's Museum
4 St. Paul's Church
5 Astor House
6 Columbia College
7 Tammany Hall
8 New York Times (1851)
9 City Hall
10 New County Court House (Tweed, 1861)
11 A. T. Stewart Store
12 95 Duane Street
13 New York Hospital
14 3 Cherry Street
15 Essex Market
16 Civil Prison
17 St. Stephen's Church
18 Metropolitan Hotel
19 New York University
20 Cooper Union
21 237 East Broadway
22 193 Madison Street
23 325 Pearl Street

TWEED'S NEW YORK

LEO HERSHKOWITZ was born, raised and educated in New York. He is currently Professor of History at Queens College, City University of New York, where he teaches New York City and State history. His interests in the city's neglected records and archieves led directly to this volume as well as to numerous other publications on various aspects of city life.

TWEED'S NEW YORK
Another Look

LEO HERSHKOWITZ

ANCHOR PRESS/DOUBLEDAY

GARDEN CITY, NEW YORK

1977

Library of Congress Cataloging in Publication Data

Hershkowitz, Leo.
Tweed's New York.

Bibliography: p. 379.
Includes index.
1. New York (City)—Politics and government—To 1898.
2. Tweed, William Marcy, 1823–1878. 3. Statesmen—
New York (City)—Biography. 4. New York (City)—
Biography. I. Title.
F128.47.H54   974.7′1′040924 [B]
ISBN 0-385-07656-8
Library of Congress Catalog Card Number 76–5338

To Herbie and Henry

AUTHOR'S NOTE

There are several episodes which come to mind that relate to the writing of this volume. Some time ago, authorities in the comptroller's office informed the author that certain records were to be destroyed. As usual there was no interest in their preservation by other agencies, public or private. Fortunately Queens College provided space, as well as moral and financial support, and these papers were brought to that institution's Historical Document Collection. They were a literal treasure-trove, containing as they did a good portion of the financial history of the City of New York. There were well over a million documents dating back to 1701. In hundreds of dusty boxes were records pertaining to the Tweed period. Here were bills, vouchers and warrants from and to contractors Garvey, Keyser, Ingersoll; financial accounts of Tweed, Connolly, Hall, Sweeny; records of investigation committees, including those of the Pinkerton National Detective Agency, records of funerals, parades, costs of entertaining visiting dignitaries. Just about every penny the city spent for a service was there in bills, receipts and notes. None of this material had been used or seen since the day they were folded and tied into bundles. Often when early documents were opened for the first time, sand used for blotting ran out and the script sparkled as light caught particles imbedded in heavy black ink. This was the start of this book, the realization that in this vast uncharted sea no one had gone before. There were new continents to be discovered.

Next to Texas. Publicity caught the notice of Mr. and Mrs. Richard M. Tweed in Borger, Texas, a little town outside of Amarillo, and these kind and generous people offered the hospitality of their home and the use of valuable family papers. The time spent with the Tweeds was a rewarding and very pleasant experience. Dick and Holly's interest and help are greatly appreciated. Unhappily Dick died just prior to publication. As in the case of the comptroller's records, few have seen the letters of William and his brother Richard. These provided needed family background material.

I must also acknowledge the assistance and courtesy extended to me at the New-York Historical Society, where Tom Dunnings and Reynold J.

Yuska in manuscripts are ever ready guides to the perplexed. A note of appreciation to Albert K. Baragwanath, Librarian and Curator of Prints, Museum of the City of New York. My thanks also to the staffs of the New York Public Library, especially the Manuscript Division, Columbia University, Butler Library, Library of Congress and National Archives, Washington, D.C., and to Mr. Norman Goodman, New York County Clerk, Mr. Vincent Caruso in the County Clerk's office, James H. Sheridan, Assistant Deputy Executive Officer, Supreme Court Criminal Term, Sidney Barkan, Court Clerk I, Criminal Term, and Arthur Vidockler, Chief of Administrative Services, comptroller's office. All have opened many doors to me, and their help and cooperation are gratefully noted. My thanks also to President Joseph S. Murphy, Vice-President Nathaniel H. Siegel and Dean Albert M. Levenson, all of Queens College, for their many courtesies. To William Asadorian, librarian-archivist, Historical Documents Collection, who has always been unstinting with his help, a special word of appreciation. Julius M. Bloch, Department of History, Queens College, a cohort of mine in establishing the Collection, Sam Pinzer and the Paul Klapper Library staff have all been most cooperative. Thanks also to Ann Goldweber for research assistance. I am indebted to Lena Meyers, who has spent many days typing this manuscript. I would also like to express my appreciation to Loretta Barrett, Editorial Director of Anchor Press, for her encouragement and advice and the help given me by the staff at Anchor, especially Pamela Tyler, Angela Cox and Molly Friedrich.

Finally, I wish to express my gratitude to my wife, Marcia Berger Hershkowitz, whose knowledge of law was indispensable, whose advice and editing skills could not be duplicated, and who helped more than anyone—and to my children, Herbert Berger and Henry Learned, who allowed me use of the family Ping-Pong table for the period of this writing.

Leo Hershkowitz

CONTENTS

V: THE LAW

Injustice is relatively easy to bear;
what stings is justice.

H. L. MENCKEN

"A book," I observed, "might be
written on the injustice of the just."

ANTHONY HOPE

MYTH

William M. Tweed, the notorious "Boss" Tweed, is one of the great myths of American history. His ugly features, small beady eyes, huge banana-like nose, vulturish expression and bloated body are the personification of big-city corruption. Thomas Nast, political propagandist and executioner of *Harper's Weekly*, has made them a triumph of the caricaturist art. Tweed's deeds, or rather misdeeds, as fashioned by historians and the like, are perhaps even better known. They have been told and retold in countless textbooks, monographs, biographies, articles, reminiscences, and have become an American epic whose proportions with each recounting become more fantastic, more shocking. Here are fables of monumental robberies of the New York City treasury, of fraud, deceit, treachery, of monstrous villainies, of carpets, furniture and of courthouses. Like fables, they are largely untrue, but like most legends, they perpetuate themselves and are renewed and enlarged with each telling.

The myth has become so much a part of history and Tweed such a convenient reference for the after-dinner speaker, pulp writer, or simply something to frighten little children with, that if there wasn't a Tweed, he would have to be invented, and he was.

Tweed is a fat, urban Jesse James without any saving graces. James is a western Robin Hood, a sort of criminal St. Francis. Tweed's patron saint is an eastern St. Tammany, refuge for the greedy, vulgar, corrupt—in short, consummate—politician. Tweed is the essence of urban rot, malodorous, the embodiment of all that is evil and cancerous in American municipal and political life. The monster lives. In a recent tax-evasion case, the prosecution charged a defendant with failure to report income allegedly obtained illegally. During the course of the trial, an enlarged Nast cartoon of "Boss Tweed" was produced to illustrate the similarity of crimes. The jury voted for conviction. Interestingly, the United States Court of Appeals reversed the verdict partly because the court felt use of the cartoon had prejudiced the jury. Eternally threatened plans to destroy the "Tweed Courthouse" (the name itself is an example of the myth) still standing behind New York's City Hall caused many New Yorkers to ask that the building be spared as a monument to graft and a reminder of the necessity of rooting out piggish politicians who take their slops at the public trough. Almost miraculously, the building, though supposedly built by corrupt politicians and contractors, is one of the finest examples of Italian Renaissance design in the country. It has not collapsed into a pile of plaster and sawdust, as critics predicted it would.

A popular cast-iron bank depicts an oily-faced tuxedoed figure, supposedly a banker, greedily swallowing the pennies of innocent children. What really "sells" the bank is calling it "Boss Tweed," even if one has nothing to do with the other. The myth is so salable and so deeply rooted that it is as American as "apple pie" or "Mother." A noted TV station produced a "documentary" on Tweed. When told that a mass of evidence exists that questions the "facts," representatives of the station offered an opinion, without pausing even to look at the material, that they wished all such records were destroyed. What price integrity as long as the legend lives, and it does so with abandon.

When political leaders think of New York, the vile image of Tweed taught them with their earliest history lessons returns to mind and appeals on behalf of the city fall on deaf ears. When Congress or the state legislature meet to debate New York's future, Tweed like some ghoulish specter rises up and beckons an end to discussion.

The myth is outrageously simple. Tweed was born in New York. Big, strong, ambitious and ruthless, he climbed out of the streets, and leaped like a snarling "Tammany Tiger" on unsuspecting citizens. Through fraud, deceit and intimidation, he was elected to various city and state offices, and even served a term in Congress. Tweed yearned for bigger and better things. He met kindred souls whom he placed in strategic places as members of "The Ring" to pillage the city treasury, conquer the state and finally the nation. By using the simple device of padded or fictitious bills for items not delivered or not needed, millions were stolen. The county courthouse, the "Tweed Courthouse," became the symbol and center of the operation. Subservient members of "The Ring" were Peter B. ("Brains") Sweeny, city chamberlain; Richard B. ("Slippery Dick") Connolly, city comptroller; A. Oakey Hall ("The Elegant One"), mayor; and John T. ("Toots") Hoffman, mayor and governor. Hoffman would hopefully become President to serve Tweed better. An army of poor, unwashed and ignorant were also recruited. These were recent Irish and German immigrants, whose largely illegal votes were cheaply bought in return for jobs given away at City Hall or a turkey at Christmas. Judges were necessary to stay the hands of the law, so added to the conspiracy were George G. Barnard, John H. McCunn and Albert Cardozo. Misguided though willing contractors like Andrew Garvey, "Prince of Plasterers"; James H. Ingersoll, the "Chairmaker"; John Keyser, the "Plumber"; and numerous others were awarded contracts, but kicked back up to 75 per cent to Tweed and "The Ring." Tweed received the lion's or rather "Tiger's" share of perhaps 50 to 200 million dollars at a time when an average workman received two to three dollars a day.

The fable continues that this monumental looting was halted by courageous, honest men. There were Democrats like Samuel J. Tilden, who on the strength of his attacks against "The Ring" became governor and presidential candidate. Honest Republicans like George Jones, editor of the *Times*, combined to disgrace "The Ring" with the help of Nast and *Harper's Weekly*. Indictments were handed down against Tweed, who was found guilty and sentenced to the penitentiary. Finally, like most of the others of "The Ring," he fled the country. Recognized in Spain by a sailor, or someone or other who just happened to be an avid reader of *Harper's Weekly*—the myth is never clear on details—and was quite familiar with the Boss's features, he was returned to prison to die a lonely but deserved death, a lesson to evildoers.

With great delight, happy historians, political activists, popularizers, drooled over juicy tidbits like carpets and plumbing and people named Dummy and Cash, never bothering to look at dust-gathering records, or even those quite dust-free. It would seem that research would interfere with exorcising the devil or prevent the development of some interesting theories. One theory concerned the failure of adequate communication in an evolving, increasingly complicated metropolis. It was a lack of such communication as seen in a decentralized and chaotic government which explains the emergence of Tweed and the "Big Pay-off." Others see Tweed emerging from the schismatic web of Tammany politics to seize and consolidate power by "pulling wires," hiring professional toughs and modernizing control within Tammany.

Lord James Bryce, a hostile critic of American urban government, in his classic *American Commonwealth* found Tweed the end product of "rancid dangerous Democracy." The scornful Englishman felt that "The time was ripe, for the lowest class of voters, foreign and native, had now been thoroughly organized and knew themselves able to control the city."

This voting mob was ready to follow Tammany Hall, which he concluded "had become the Acropolis of the city; and he who could capture it might rule as tyrant." Bryce found Tweed's unscrupulousness matched by the crafty talents of others, creating a perfect blend of flagrant corruption. But the essential ingredient was democracy and failure to follow traditional leadership. It was such democracy which allowed a Falstaff-like Tweed to emerge as a hero; a "Portuguese Jew" like Albert Cardozo who was born in New York to "prostitute" his legal talents for party purposes; or a Fernando Wood, Tweed's predecessor in Tammany, to become a major figure from such small beginnings that he was "reported to have entered New York as the leg of an artificial elephant in a travelling show." Bryce thus denounced Tweed and a form of government that had little if any respect for birth or breeding, but rewarded the mean, the base-born for their audacity and treachery.

It all sounds so plausible, but does it help Tweed emerge from behind Thomas Nast's leering cartoons? The problem with Tweed and the myth is that it is all so much vapor and so little substance, and what has been written has not dispelled shadows; only deepened them. So little has been done to obtain even basic information about the man, and what is known is generally wrong. Perhaps never has so much nonsense been written about an individual.

A few questions to start. Was it possible for one man or even a group of men to plan such a vast swindle involving hundreds if not thousands of officials, clerks, laborers, contractors, and hope to succeed? If Tweed plotted such an operation which supposedly involved bribing the state legislature, coercing judges, muzzling the press, aborting the gossip of bank officers and city auditors, he must have been a genius, a Houdini, Machiavelli, Napoleon rolled into one. Such a mind surely would have withstood the trivial intrusion of a hundred brash reformers. Yet he was shaken from his lofty perch, tumbled into prison and hounded to death. All this was done without organized resistance and in literally the twinkling of an eye. Tweed had such "power" that he was thrown out of his party without a word spoken in his behalf, even before he was found guilty of anything. There was, except for counsel, no one to defend him, no congressman, senator, assemblyman, no one in authority. "The Ring" was so strongly forged that it shattered at the slightest pressure, its component parts flying about with no other thought than every man for himself. If "The Ring" was supposed to be a strong political or financial alliance well led and directed, then it like "Boss" Tweed was simply a figment of historical imagination, a pretty bit of caricature.

At no time did such a "Ring" dominate New York City politics, let alone the state or national scene. Supposed "Ring" members rarely had much to do with one another, socially or otherwise. Sweeny was a friend of Victor Hugo's, Hall aspired to make a mark in the theater, Tweed aspired to office, Connolly had Connolly. There was little to bind the so-called "Ring." Except by an accident of history that they served in various city posts at the same time, there is little to relate one with the other.

Even the dreaded "Tammany Tiger" was a paper one. Certainly in Tweed's day Tammany did not dominate New York politics. Perhaps it never did. The city was and is a complex, competitive system of diverse interest. It was then and is now too heterogeneous, too much made up of various groups, classes, outlooks, beliefs for any part or let alone one person to control. New Yorkers' cosmopolitanism and tolerance have a tragic price.

The city cannot send representatives to Washington or to Albany who can express the single-minded view of smaller, simpler communities. Its large immigrant population creates suspicion: is New York an American city? A rural backwater has more political clout than all of the city when it comes to power on national or state levels.

Partly this is in consequence of an age-old struggle between the city and the farm, an eternal tug of war between the city in its search for greater self-government and rural conservative interests who find New York a threat to themselves and their entrenched power. There were some deeply rooted animosities. Cities are not natural. God made the earth, trees, animals and man. Cities are man-made. Natural things are pure, innocent and obedient to order, while man is sinful, evil, disobedient, whose works like cities are suspect. There may be a Garden of Eden, but there is no City of Eden, only Sodom and Gomorrah. This kind of morality underlines economic and political selection. It is served by the Tweed myth, since the horrors of municipal corruption and Tammany bossism plainly demonstrate the impossibility of the city even governing itself. It is in a deeper sense an implied failure of man governing himself apart from some external power. As New York cannot be given greater home rule, it must even be more closely regulated and watched by the state; so too man must observe a higher authority.

To make matters worse, New York also destroys its political talent, its best lost in the heat of murderous combat. It was a rare aspirant indeed who could emerge from his trials to become a national figure of any permanence. Alexander Hamilton and Aaron Burr were testimony to this. De Witt Clinton and Edward Livingston were further examples of early casualties. By mid-nineteenth century, no New York City politician had any voice in national or state affairs. Fernando Wood, potentially a great politician and a champion of the city's interest against the state rural lobby, was destroyed by bitter intra-party fighting. William Tweed might have provided the city with a voice and he too was destroyed, but in such a way that the city too suffered in countless ways—not the least of which forever identified the metropolis as a spawning ground for corruption and filth. Why then pay it any attention? Why spend money on the sewers? Tweed was and is a convenient stick with which to beat the city over the head, preferably at regular intervals. In many ways, the tragedy of New York is that Tweed did not succeed, that a strong unified political force was not created, that the paper tiger was not real.

As for Tweed, there remain the stories. There is no evidence that he created the "Tammany Tiger" or ordered it to be used as his personal symbol. The clawing, snarling, toothed tiger was Nast's idea, part of the image he wished to create. It was plastered on Tweed and Tammany and sold. What politician would use such a symbol to win votes or influence people, except a madman or a cartoonist like Nast?

One of the universally accepted myths is that of Tweed's reactions to the July 1871 disclosures exposing "The Ring." He is supposed to have snarled like his tiger to a group of cowering reporters, reformers and the public at large, "What are you going to do about it?" Again, what politician, especially in this country, would make such an asinine statement, no matter how sure he was of his position? It was certainly not Tweed's style, and if he made "The Ring," he was not that stupid. In truth, the phrase was never used by Tweed, but invented by Nast as a caption for a June 10, 1871, cartoon a month before Tweed and "The Ring" made headlines. Reporters asked Tweed that question after the deluge and his troubles with the law. It was never Tweed's question. It was all "Boss," all Nast and all nonsense.

Tweed was no saint, but he was not the Nast creature. He was more a victim than a scoundrel or thief. Characteristically, Tweed was intensely loyal, warmhearted, outgoing, given to aiding the underdog and the underprivileged. But he was also gullible, naïve and easily fooled. If he were a real "Boss," he should have been able, like Sweeny and others, to avoid inundating calamity. He was a good family man, and there simply is no scandal to report so far as his personal habits are concerned. Even his bitterest enemies could find nothing. He was not an intellectual, he was not at home with a Sweeny or an Oakey Hall, but found a close friendship with Jubilee Jim Fisk, the brilliant short-lived Roman candle and bon vivant.

Why then Tweed? First, he was what he was. In his prime, he reportedly weighed close to three hundred pounds. A "slim" Tweed would not be as inviting a target. Point one, for dieters. His features could be easily exaggerated by someone like Nast, and he was enough in the public eye for the *Times* and *Harper's*. He was ambitious, but not ruthless. He had money, but not enough to throw a scare into or buy off his opponents. He had power, but not enough to withstand attacks by newspapers, law, rivals and supposed friends.

Further, and much more importantly, he represented the interests of New York. He had established legislative programs which opened schools, hospitals, museums, programs tailored to meet the needs of a rapidly expanding constituency. His identification with the interests of the city was enough for the traditional rural-suburban leadership to seek his destruction. He provided a means for Republicans from President U. S. Grant on down to those in the local level to make people forget the corruptions in Republican circles, like the Whisky Ring, Indian Ring or Crédit Mobilier—all schemes to defraud millions from the government—but see instead the balloon-like figure of Tweed, Tammany and the defeat of Democratic opposition. National Democrats like Horatio Seymour and the inept "Sammy" Tilden could point to Tweed and gain cheers and votes for their efforts to "delouse" the party. If there ever was a scapegoat, its name was Tweed.

The Tweed story does not need exaggeration, lies, half-truths, rumors to make it interesting. It is in itself an incredible story. Debunking the myth is part of it, but there is much more. There are bigots like Nast, George T. Strong and others who saw in Tweed an outsider threatening their position by his supposedly championing the "drunken-ignorant Irish," the overly ambitious German-Jewish immigrants and those seeking to change the status quo. That he sought to provide answers to the increasing complications of urban life did not help. Tweed never traveled in upper-class society. With all his apparent success, he was never able to wash away the tarnish of the Lower East Side. Moreover, there are some of the most incredible trials and abuses of the judicial process on record. There are hand-picked judges and juries, not as might be expected by Tweed, but by the prosecution. The misuse of grand jury indictments should become legendary.

Tweed was never tried for or found guilty of graft or theft, the crime Tweed stands accused of by history. He was convicted after some strange, improper, even illegal judicial proceedings, which were in many ways worse than anything Tweed supposedly committed, of a misdemeanor—failing to audit claims against the city. Hall was tried three times on the same charge and was not convicted. Connolly and Sweeny were never tried.

Tweed died in prison after having spent some four years there, and he would have remained longer but for his death—only one of these years was he in a penitentiary, on the misdemeanor conviction. The remaining years he spent in the county jail because he could not raise an exorbitant bail in a civil suit. The manipulation of the law by those sworn to uphold the law was a real crime. Then add the threatening, tampering with, and intimidation of witnesses, as well as the use of informers and agent provocateurs. Under these conditions, Snow White would have been hanged for loitering to commit prostitution.

The threat to individual liberty by an unbridled omnipresent legal system is rarely as clear as in the Tweed case. The innocent and guilty are too often given the same even-handed justice.

Couple this with yellow journalism and abuse of power by the press and Nast. Horace Greeley in his bid for the presidency in 1871 complained that he did not know whether he was running for that office or the penitentiary. Tweed was as much a victim of irresponsible journalism. Tweed, too, was "hot copy." He was also tried and convicted by newspapers in a too often repeated process in which rabid reporters and editors became judge and jury and headlines substitute for trial and district attorneys, while editors scratch each other's backs for the sake of publicity—where an indictment is often all that is necessary to make a point, sell papers and win votes.

What follows then is a story of the unmaking of a myth—an account of a tragedy that was and is New York's, of a city and a man, and of those who would destroy both.

I

Roots and Branches

1

Cherry Street

Cherry Street, obscure and almost forgotten, is one of the dark, dingy passages crisscrossing the Lower East Side of New York. Old Brooklyn Bridge casts its arched shadow through the seasons and over darkened tenements and warehouses. A drab grayness is all-pervasive. Yet, the street has a special claim to fame—George Washington lived there and William M. Tweed was born there.

Originally part of the area known as Sackett's Orchard, Cherry Garden or Cherry Hill, it was a pleasant suburban neighborhood dotted with small farms and country houses set on gently rolling ground. There were woods and numerous small streams. "Manhattan," the Indian word for "Island of Hills," is aptly named. By 1744, the gradual pressure of urban growth and real estate speculators caused a commissioner to be appointed to see to the opening of Cherry Street.

In 1754, Cherry Hill was fortified in preparation for a French and Indian attack. The following year, the road was laid out and graded at least for a short distance. It was really an extension of Queen Street, now known as Pearl Street, a main thoroughfare fronting the East River. Close to wharves and mercantile houses, yet distant from the noise and traffic of the lower city, it was a good residential area. William "Boss" Walton, a prosperous merchant, built a most elegant, three-story mansion of yellow Holland brick surrounded by gracious gardens on Pearl Street, just below St. George, later Franklin Square. The Walton house reportedly so impressed the British Parliament, that it was cited as proof of the extravagance of colonists and their ability to support taxation. Unfortunately demolished in 1881, it might be looked on as the house that began the Revolution. In 1784 it became home of the Bank of New York, the first such institution in the state.

Other merchants also built homes. Walter Franklin's at 3 Cherry

3

Street was another showplace and became for a time the residence of George Washington when the city served as the new nation's first capital in 1789–90. This building was torn down in 1856. So goes New York history. After the war, John Hancock lived at number 5, as president of the Continental Congress. De Witt Clinton was a resident at number 9. Samuel Leggett, one of the wealthiest New Yorkers and the first to have gas illumination—this in 1824—lived at number 7. Numbers 3 and 5 Cherry Street were later used by Richard Tweed as location for his chairmaking establishment, while his son William was born in 1823 at number 1. The yellow brick building was demolished in 1862 and the site became a coalyard.[1]

By the year of William Tweed's birth, the quality of life along Cherry Street had altered. Nearby, wharves were constructed, small businesses and tradesmen began to congregate and the population expanded as a more genteel life slipped by. Cherry Hill was another example of a rapidly changing New York. Still, it was an area of considerable history and Tweed would add to it.

Tweed is not an early New York name, and appears only at the end of the eighteenth century. William's father Richard was born on April 10, 1791, probably on Rutgers Street. Both father and son had most of their children baptized as Episcopalians, either at St. Stephen's or at Trinity. A contemporary gossip remarked that Richard regularly attended the Baptist church of "Dr. Cohen" (Dr. Stephen F. Cone) on Broome Street. If he did, it is possible William was raised initially as a Baptist. His notice of baptism and that of his older brother Richard are not in extant church records. There is also mention of the Tweeds' being Quakers. Religion seemed a small matter to the "Boss," who called himself a "tolerationalist" having no religious affiliation.[2]

Seemingly of Scottish ancestry, William Tweed would on occasion wear a "Scottish cap" when on the campaign trail. The New York *Times* at one point, undoubtedly to harass Tweed, asserted the family was of Irish background but, as usual, gave no evidence. Others said Tweed was of Jewish origin because of the length of his nose.[3] With this kind of reasoning, a man with a long neck would be a giraffe.

Richard Tweed learned the art of chairmaking from fellow New Yorker George W. Skellorn, who later became keeper at City Hall, where he could sit on rather than make chairs. Still the trade was profitable. Furniture- and chairmaking was an old business and in the beginning of the nineteenth century a particularly good one for some. Thomas and Gilbert Ash and the famed Duncan Phyfe could scarcely keep up with the demand for their product, especially from the southern market. Windsor chairs were specially sought after in Latin America.[4] A man working hard, with a little luck, could make out well enough. By 1817 Richard established residence and shop at 1 Hague Street, a small no longer existing lane, just off Pearl Street and close to Chatham Square.

In about 1816 Richard, a "fine-looking man and always in good spirits," married Eliza Magear, possibly the daughter of Thomas Magear, a laborer. She was born April 30, 1793. Two boys followed: Richard Jr. in 1818, William M. on April 3, 1823; and two daughters, Ann and Eliza.

It has always been believed that Tweed's middle initial M. stood for Marcy in honor of William L. Marcy, a Jacksonian Democrat who became governor of New York in 1831 and who reportedly coined the politicians' credo "to the victor belongs the spoils." But Marcy was an unknown at the time of Tweed's birth. Though there is no known example of Tweed spelling out his initial, it surely stood for Magear, his mother's maiden name; both his son and grandson were baptized William Magear. Marcy was surely tacked on by newspapermen as a clever thought, a nickname befitting a "corrupt" politician. It would be like Peter "Bismarck" Sweeny, or John "Toots" Hoffman. History gave it a stamp of approval in Tweed's case without the quotes.[5]

Like most New Yorkers, the elder Tweed moved about a great deal. Roots are never planted too deeply in city streets. The Richard Tweeds left their Hague Street address, and in 1822 moved to 24 Cherry Street. The business address was at number 1. In 1823 both business and residence were there.

In the late 1830s Tweed Sr. joined brushmakers Joseph C. Skaden and Daniel Berrian, Jr., and by 1843 the firm of Daniel Berrian & Co. was started at 240 and 357 Pearl Street and he temporarily gave up his chairmaking business. However, he returned to his original occupation by 1847, rejoining his son, Richard Jr., at the old shop at 5 Cherry Street. He remained a chairmaker until his death on May 18, 1860.[6]

William grew up together with his brother, as did most boys, fighting, playing and attending the local public school and amid the cries of street vendors, neighing horses and clattering carriages, learning the means and manners of his father's trade. He made a lifelong friend of Charlie Devlin and some others like Dr. James Wood, who later started a famous anatomical museum at Bellevue Hospital.

His brother Richard Jr. married Margaret Michaels Sands, daughter of grocer Benjamin Sands, on October 3, 1843. William Tweed always referred to his sister-in-law as Aunt Maggie, or more formally as Aunt Margaret. There was a great attachment between the two. Soon after his marriage, Richard Jr. left his father's home, then at 237 East Broadway, and moved to 37 Attorney Street. Almost a year later on September 18, 1844, William M. Tweed married Mary Jane C. Skaden, born March 14, 1825,

daughter of brushmaker Joseph C. Skaden, his father's partner. The ceremony was held at St. Stephen's, then at the corner of Chrystie and
Broome streets. Boston-born Reverend Dr. Joseph J. Price officiated as he
did at most family affairs. He would also deliver William Tweed's funeral
service. The newly married couple moved in with the Skadens at 193
Madison Street, where they stayed for two years. Business and marriage
prospered; children arrived.

Their first child, born November 14, 1845, was William Magear Jr.
He was followed by Richard on January 8, 1848. Then came several
daughters: Mary Amelia, born August 17, 1849; Lizzie C. on March 19,
1851; Josephine S., April 30, 1852; Isabel M., January 25, 1854; Jennie,
June 8, 1857; Adele, January 23, 1862. Finally, more sons, Charles Cornell,
July 10, 1863, and George Young, August 18, 1867. Thus, the Tweeds had
four sons and six daughters. All lived into adulthood except Isabel or
Isabella, who died within her first year, and Adele, who died three days
after her birth.

William was a concerned and devoted parent and he went through
the usual pattern of child raising. Late in 1846, both his wife and first-
born son, William Jr., contracted a bad case of whooping cough, but the
crisis passed by March 1847, and he happily reported their health had returned along with the prosperity of his business, for the Mexican War had
filled the South with money and "it is contrary to the nature of them to
keep it still." He also wrote that on May 1, New York's traditional moving
day—a time when seemingly everyone packed their bags and went to find
different lodgings—he intended to leave his father-in-law's house for the
first time since his marriage, "going on my hook for a year, at least." Spur
for the decision seemed to have been too devoted attention given his son
by doting grandparents. "If I don't [move] the folks will pet my boy to
death—for they think he is the greatest child that was ever born and cannot do wrong. So that if my wife corrects him, they all say oh, oh, too bad
—good boy, and so make him worse than ever. He is a great big fat fellow
and is about as good as the average young uns."[7] Such was Tweed's experience with the universal in-law syndrome. He moved to 35 Vandewater
Street.

Shortly after his marriage and sometime in 1845 or 1846 he opened
brush shops at 206 and 357 Pearl Street with his father and father-in-law.
He remained in brush manufacturing until 1852 when he took up the family chairmaking business. His brother Dick had always wanted William
to work with him "at the Headquarters Tweed Chair Establishment Store,
5 Cherry Street, Factory at 12 Ridge Street, old chairs repaired, painted
and rebuilt, a liberal allowance made to shippers," which was Richard's
way of humorously describing his enterprise. In 1848 he extended his

6

brother another invitation to return to the "Old-Flea Patch."[8] This was finally accepted, and in 1857 the firm of William M. Tweed & Brother was opened at 325 Pearl Street next to of all places Harper Brothers, the conservative Republican publishers. Tweed filed for bankruptcy within four years. Perhaps his lack of success at selling oak and Windsor chairs to and in the city, resulted from his attention to other matters.

There was a world changing about him, horizons were being stretched. There was a city and country ever expanding. There were things to do, people to meet and William, friendly and gregarious, sought opportunity. What did a small business have to offer an ambitious young New Yorker? He tested the water slowly.

By 1846 he was an active member of the National Lodge 30, International Order of Odd Fellows (I.O.O.F.). Odd Fellows were and are a benevolent society founded in the early nineteenth century. Grand Lodge, New York, was formed in 1823. Tweed characteristically often expressed himself in terms of helping others, and saw such an opportunity now and joined. The I.O.O.F. was a growing institution with several prominent members, a fact noted by Tweed, who worked diligently in his new organization. He proudly informed his friend, Henry L. Davis of Oswego, that along with Judge John W. Edmonds and Mayor Andrew Mickle, there were "any quantity of other large Fish in active membership in our Lodge." Other members included David T. Valentine, city clerk and compiler of the famed manuals; Albert Cardozo later justice of the Supreme Court; and Benjamin J. Lossing, a noted historian. The order was interdenominational and attractive to members of the lower and middle classes since opportunity to join the more exclusive clubs like Yacht, Union, Bread and Cheese or Salamagundi was very limited. The order provided a degree of social acceptance for the unacceptable.

Tweed wrote a number of interesting letters—some of the very few Tweed letters extant—to Odd Fellow Davis, detailing his concern with lodge affairs, which provide some insight into his character and ambition. In October 1846, he happily told Davis of an interesting experience in regard to an application of a penniless young Odd Fellow from Ohio for a loan to proceed to a job awaiting him in Oswego. A motion was offered allowing $10, but it required a unanimous vote. The motion fell by one. Tweed acted quickly and "Upon its being declared lost, I lost my temper and talked pretty plain to some who upheld the single voter and finally coaxing and threatening succeeded in getting the sum of ten dollars voted for the relief of the Brother." In gratitude, a Past Grand (P.G.) from Ohio and various members thanked Tweed, whose name was becoming known to other Odd Fellows. The man had a presence. Tweed also reported other lodge news, including the election of Isaac Ammerman as

Permanent Secretary. Tweed informed Davis that Ammerman had failed in business during 1845, but being of the "never give up school," would die a rich man. "He doesn't know the meaning of the word Pride where there is money to be made honestly," Tweed concluded. Ammerman had married a cousin of Tweed's and was the "best of husbands." Later on Eliza A. Davis, possibly the daughter of his friend Henry, married Tweed's eldest son, William M. Jr. Surely the lodge abetted, even if unwittingly, their romance.

And there was also I.O.O.F. politics. He wrote of opposition to a re-forming convention which he hoped had "burnt itself out." God grant it may do so, continued Tweed, "for our Glorious Institution is too much needed in a country like ours to be ruthlessly assailed by Political Hacks and Worn-Out Demagogues." Loyalty and purpose were deeply felt.

Tweed worked his way up the lodge ladder. A delegate to the annual convention of 1846, he was by 1860 a Past Grand and attended annual services through 1865. He remained with I.O.O.F. until 1875. In that year, buried deep in prison, he was suspended for non-payment of dues.[9]

Another fraternal order also attracted Tweed, for on October 23, 1851, he was initiated as a first- and second-degree Mason into the still extant Palestine Lodge, 204. And on November 6, 1851, he was raised to Master Mason. Though in 1858 he was reported as unaffiliated, his membership was restored on October 10, 1861. He remained in the order until his death.[10] Young Tweed's interest in Odd Fellows and Masons was shared by an attraction to politics and early letters to Davis reveal a different Tweed —in complete disagreement with what has been written about him.

Politics was a national persuasion. In 1821 after years of movement toward political democracy, what amounted to universal malehood suffrage became part of the state constitution. The number of appointed officials was reduced while those chosen by ballot increased. In 1834, New York City for the first time elected its mayor. Offices were available, votes were free, the stakes high. The march of democracy was now sung by the voice of the people—not always in tune. The charter or municipal election then held for three days in April witnessed outbreaks of violence. Riots and improper voting procedure and intimidation were the order of the day. Those who held that democracy meant confusion and worse had their fears borne out by events. People should not be allowed more power, but rather less, for the proof was in the pudding. There were stonecutters' riots, anti-abolition riots, riots against Irish Catholics. The panic of 1837 led to bread riots. There emerged bitter hostility against newly arrived immigrants, most of whom came from Ireland and Germany. There were more anti-Irish riots in 1844.

One thing was certain, the world was changing, the city was changing, and not to everyone's liking. Philip Hone, selected mayor in 1826 by the Common Council, a "gentleman" mayor, a patrician by persuasion and a merchant and landowner by profession, was appalled by the crowds that stormed his home on Broadway when he, as was the custom, invited visitors to his inauguration. In the past, such occasions were small intimate affairs. Now they were ugly, uncontrollably democratic. Tweed and other newcomers were a reminder of the dangers of democracy. Elected officials increased their distance from the public. The early Presidents of the United States, Washington, Adams, Jefferson, members of a social aristocracy, received visitors in person, often at home. Andy Jackson, hero of the poor, the symbol of the new democracy (and notice it is Andy—would anyone think of calling George Washington Georgie, or Thomas Jefferson Tommy), remained behind a barrier of protocol. Democracy breeds its own form of contempt and its own contradictions.

As government became increasingly representative, politics became increasingly a ladder for lower classes to achieve power. Politicians were no longer supposedly men of duty persuaded by inner conviction, but increasingly those without principle who saw in politics a vocation, a job, a chance to make money, at least critics like Hone so observed. Of course, the bought and paid-for "sellout" was not only a spawn of democracy; he could be found in all manner of government and in all times. But democracy with its code of faith, honor, equality and honesty was shaken by what it spawned, especially disturbed if its ideals were violated.

Tweed was, like most of his contemporaries, a political animal. He voted for the first time in 1844, for in April of that year he turned twenty-one, the requisite age. It was an angry time. James Harper, member of Harper Brothers, publishers, successfully ran for the office of mayor on the Native American ticket. It was a contest in which violent hatred of Irish Catholics and immigrants in general was the keynote. Native Americanism was an outgrowth of a traditional anti-Catholic bigotry built on nativist fear of competition from immigrants and was an attempt on the part of conservatives to control or maintain the status quo. Part of the nativist appeal, which would heighten during the next decade, was not only to the bigot and reactionary, but also to those who saw the movement in terms of "protecting" American ideals and aspirations and so guarding the hard-won but threatened position of the middle and working classes; these, made up of individuals like Tweed, formed the majority of the party. As a member of the lower echelon of society, Tweed sought status and opportunity; entrenched parties represented a vague conspiracy to deny him both. Nativism in many ways was an early form of populism, and New Yorkers had seen it all before.

In 1836, Samuel F. B. Morse, artist and inventor of the telegraph, ran

9

as a nativist for the mayoralty. Rumors were abroad that every Revolutionary War veteran would be fired and "dirty Irish" worshipers of the "Whore of Babylon" (the Pope) would be hired. These hysterical fears were fanned into flames by professional Protestant bigots, such as Morse, who reminded Americans that Catholicism was a secret, dark conspiratorial religion, unlike the open, clear, pure Protestant American ministry. Could in fact a Catholic become an American citizen? Could he really abjure loyalty to a foreign prince like the Pope? Wars of Reformation and Counter Reformation were still very much alive, if not always in deed, then in the heritage of strong pent-up emotions. If economic, religious threats did not disturb, then the "fact" that the immigrant voted the Democratic ticket was enough for others to seek some means of controlling the consuming Jacksonian tide before the entire nation was engulfed. Fanaticism and bigotry are very much a part of American history and are partly underwritten by the Constitution. Only a native-born citizen can be elected President. In the 1830s, difficulties with Mexico, the attack by Catholics on the Alamo and the killing of Protestants like Davy Crockett were reminders that it "could happen here." Obscene "literature" like Maria Monk's fictitious, pornographic libel, *Awful Disclosures*, dealing with the sexual misadventures of a novice in a Montreal nunnery, added to fear and superstition as hatred boiled over into the streets.

Despite traditional New York tolerance and forbearance, Harper and his followers won out, cheered on by the votes of pseudo-patriots, conservative Whigs and young Tweed. The latter liked nativist candidates and, at least, some of nativism's sentiments. When Harper was defeated in 1846, an unhappy Tweed wrote that "Nativism with its one idea is dead." His evaluation was premature; nativism would re-emerge with even greater strength. It would cost him.

Yet despite his flirtation with the nativist movement, Tweed considered himself a maverick Democrat, a "Loco," a descendant of radical Democrats, who as Locofocos or Equal Righters in 1835 gored the Van Buren Albany regency and Tammany Hall and sought to break the monopoly of party dictatorship. There were no Locofocos in 1846, but the name was applied by the movement's opponents to the entire Democratic Party as the party of chaos and disorder. Nativism was also a way dissidents could attack the Establishment. A youthful Tweed could not stomach regular Democrats, and in 1846 cast his ballot for the unsuccessful Whig ticket, though voting Whig went "against the grain." In these early years, Tweed did not belong to the Democratic Party, and was not sure where he belonged. Thoughts whirred about in his head. He desired relief from campaign oratory. He mused sadly that politics was the "only thing I get crazy on." It was all too much.[11]

Tweed interested himself in a new pastime—the Fire Department. He seems to have first joined a company in 1839. Why? Several suggestions might be made. He was young, only sixteen. Fire companies, all voluntary, enjoyed the attention of an often admiring public, especially the ladies. The figure of the brave, bold, strong young gallant in his uniform of helmet, boots, colored shirts and gallowses (suspenders) was the epitome of manhood. Firemen, dashing through the street dragging their hand-pumped machines, followed by shouts of small boys, barks of dogs and admiring ladies, not necessarily in that order, stirred the blood and imagination. Many firemen gained great reputations and achieved social recognition. Everyone knew the heroes of the department, Chief engineers like Cornelius V. Anderson, Thomas Franklin, Zophar Mills, James Gulick, or individual firemen like "old Mose," who accomplished legendary deeds. The department offered honor and excitement, not only in fighting fires, but also as it was rumored in starting fires and in frequently fighting firemen of rival companies. Exemption from jury or militia service and a place on the social ladder, especially if one of the elite companies offered an appointment, were additional inducements. James Lenox, Fletcher Harper, brother of James, William A. Macy, Mayors Gideon Lee and Daniel F. Tiemann, restaurateur Lorenzo Delmonico and Robert and Peter Goelet, members of the elusive but very wealthy landowning family, were in the ranks. While politicians, rich men, professionals answered the alarm, most members were of the poor and middle classes. Tweed was one of them.

It was not all fun and games. Fire, a dread fear for New Yorkers since New Amsterdam days, was never as real as in the middle 1800s. In 1835, a disastrous conflagration virtually destroyed all of the city's business district and was partly responsible for the panic of 1837, as well as an increased interest in fire insurance. In 1845, another such fire leveled more of the lower city. A hideous death awaited many department members. New Yorkers learned to tread carefully in regard to fire and to appreciate the importance of the Fire Department as the first if not only line of defense.

The eleven years Tweed spent in the department had considerable consequence in his future career. Little is known of his early fire-fighting days, except for a few incidents related by Tweed and others. Writing to his friend Davis on October 1, 1846, Tweed recounted an incident of "learning mean men [how] to be generous," again illustrative of many qualities characteristic of the later man. A member of Tweed's company who decided upon marriage also tried to escape "doing the honors" at a bachelor's party. There were thoughts of retribution. The culprit was told that a "splendid serenade" was planned for an evening concert and the unsuspecting invited several "female acquaintances" to sleep at his home. At

1 A.M., a "splendid Flutist" and several good singers were sent to wake up the recalcitrant member. When it was certain he was stirring, "twenty-five instruments from the Fishermans Tin Horn at the Conk Shell embracing drums, triangles, trombones, accordions, dinner bells, sleigh bells, tambourines, etc. joined in the chorus and kept it up for over an hour." The noise was too much. A messenger was sent with a flag of truce suing for peace, "but it was too late to trust unless he paid the invading Army their expenses and a champagne supper—being Commander in Chief of the invading forces, [I] would listen to no other tunes and on those terms peace was finally declared." That, concluded a happy Tweed, "was my first effort at learning mean men how to be generous." Tweed was especially tickled because the man didn't know who sent for or who were the twenty-five members of the "Cast Iron Band."[12] In ways like this, Tweed became known in the department. By January 1, 1849, Tweed and others formed Engine Company 6. Various names for the company were debated—Black Joke, Franklin, Americus. The latter name won, and the company moved into quarters on Gouverneur Street. Notices were sent out alerting members to attend a parade in honor of visiting Baltimore Friendship Fire Engine Company at City Hall Park. Members of Americus proudly displayed their new Philadelphia-style engine glistening with fresh paint and highly rubbed brass fittings. A contemporary painting of the double-deck engine shows a panel of the center box decorated by two female figures—no tigers. However, there remains a panel from Americus Engine supposedly painted by Joseph Johnson in 1851 which shows a snarling toothed tiger. But another picture of the new firehouse depicts over the main doorway a large eagle and shield. Over two small side doorways are small carved rather benign tiger or lion heads. If Americus Engine adopted the tiger image, it was a central motif. It remained for Thomas Nast to take the seemingly innocent unheralded figure and make it into the dread "Tiger." There is little evidence to show that Tweed wanted the tiger as a symbol. Even if he had, he was not the most influential of the new company.

It was not until August 1850 that Tweed was elected foreman of the company and then for only a short time. At the time of his election, Tweed was presented with a trumpet and a gold watch. The trumpet and the frontispiece of his helmet still exist.

Tweed's career as foreman was short-lived, though lively. Joseph Johnson, who succeeded him later remembered him at the company's first ball, given in July 1849. Tweed, wearing a blue coat with brass buttons, was "young and good looking then, with dark brown hair and clear, gritty eyes. He was a tip-top dancer and never wanted a partner." A number of balls were given during Tweed's tenure in office, including those at Niblo's Garden—the entertainment center of the city. For Tweed, his grandest moment undoubtedly was a triumphant tour the company made of Philadelphia, Baltimore and Washington during April 1851. There was also an earlier visit to Montreal and Quebec. With the men of Americus dragging their glittering engine up Pennsylvania Avenue headed by Tweed bearing his silver trumpet, they made a stirring sight. At the White House, Tweed introduced the "Big Six" boys to President Millard Fillmore, and gave a brief speech. When asked why he didn't talk longer, Tweed remarked that he let the "boys' looks speak for them." Someone suggested, "Wouldn't any seventy-five young men in red shirts look as well," to which Tweed replied, "Does Croton Dam look like Niagara Falls—not by a damned sight."[13]

Days as foreman of Big Six were happy, proud and short-lived, but life in the department had its drawbacks. If its members were admired, they were also often considered bands of toughs and worse. On several occasions, the Common Council heard charges of larceny, riot, murder and rape brought against firemen. On the other hand, firemen argued that they were often attacked and that theft of equipment was common. Still official censure was quick in coming. On September 3, 1850, Chief Engineer Alfred Carson presented a lengthy report to the council and made several suggestions to improve efficiency. He condemned the outrageous rowdyism of street gangs, "desperate fighting men," such as the "Short Boys," "Old Maid's Boys" or "Rock Boys," who attacked firemen, beating some almost to death, and destroyed apparatus. He complained that if any were arrested, they were usually released quickly to continue their attacks, and that the police, often themselves ex-convicts, were too lenient. He gave examples. Engine Company 19 on the way to a fire were set upon by one hundred "demi-devils" who broke their engine and beat the men. Engine Company 6, Americus, was attacked on August 19, 1850, as were Hose Company 14 and 26, by banditti who also robbed and beat defenseless citizens and "violated helpless and chaste females." But firemen too were among street gangs and were sometimes the worst offenders. Carson ended his report with a personal criticism of Tweed as illustrative of so many department wrongs. Firemen of Hose Company 31 had accused Tweed of having his men attack their company with "axes, barrels and missles" while they were running to a fire. There was no room in the department, Carson felt, for such shocking behavior. Action was taken and Tweed was expelled and Americus suspended for three months. This was really something of a slap on the wrist. Perhaps the council was not too sure of the charges, since real breaches of discipline usually resulted in dismemberment of the company involved. Americus was left intact. Later,

Tweed's dismissal was changed to three months' suspension because of his eleven years of "long and active service" and his reputation as a peaceable and well-disposed citizen.[14] Nevertheless, he never returned to the department.

Thus came to an end Tweed's fire-fighting career. It would not be the last time he would feel the reprimand of authority. He would meet Carson again.

2

Freshman Politician

Tweed began his search for public office in the fall election of 1850.
He was picked by Democrats to run as assistant alderman of the Seventh
Ward. There were certain advantages in Tweed. He was strong, good-look-
ing, and at twenty-six ambitious, vigorous and someone who had attracted
public attention, even if not always favorably. He also was a businessman
and came from a respectable family. There were, on the other hand, drawbacks. He was not an experienced politician. His fight with Carson and
the stigma of the chief engineer's report could cost votes. Tweed was also
not a regular Democrat, not a member of Tammany, and his sympathy
with nativists and Whigs was possibly known. Still 1850 was not a good
Democratic year. Whigs were in the ascendancy, especially after the success of Henry Clay and Daniel Webster in pushing through Congress
their compromise bill on the disposition of western territory, averting for a
time a North-South crisis. Someone was needed to run—taken all in all,
why not Tweed?

The Common Council was composed of a Board of Alderman and a
Board of Assistants. It dated back as an institution to 1653 when the city
became a municipality and members were known as burgomasters and
schepens. In 1664, following English conquest, a Board of Aldermen was
created. In 1686, under the Dongan Charter, the city was divided into
wards and a two-chamber council created. It was a legislative body making
necessary laws and ordinances, passing on expenses of government and issuing reports and surveys. The council also had a quasi-judicial function
with its members originally sitting on the Mayor's or Common Pleas
Court, and by mid-nineteenth century, sitting as paid judges in certain
criminal courts. In addition, mayor, recorder and aldermen also made up a
Board of Supervisors who audited and examined claims drawn on the city,
and reviewed tax matters. Councilmen received expense accounts of four

dollars a day and were elected for a two-year term, while assistants served for one. The mayor was also elected for a two-year term. The boards sitting in open session chose their president and other officers. The assistants had the sole power to impeach city officials, and the aldermen, the sole power of trial. Membership in the council had through the years attracted the elite of New York society. De Witt Clinton, Nicholas Bayard, Egbert Benson, John Cruger, Philip Hone, Peter A. Jay, Robert Lenox, Philip Livingston, Fredrick Philipse, James, Cornelius and Nicholas Roosevelt, Philip Schuyler, Cornelius Steenwyck and Olaf Stevenson Van Cortlandt were among distinguished officeholders. A number of these became mayors, while others were elected to Congress. Clinton was nominated to run for President of the United States. Livingston signed the Declaration of Independence. Most of the 1850 membership, however, were not particularly distinguished and being a member of the council was not a particularly sought-after position. In fact, fewer and fewer well-known or influential figures were attracted to the office. No longer were there Van Cortlandts, Clintons, Beekmans and the like, but rather tradesmen, small-business men, recent immigrants and relative unknowns became increasingly present. The day of the gentleman politician gave way to the day of the commoner. The council became an avenue to position for the ambitious and unknown, but increasingly it was associated with graft and corruption, a view perpetuated in large part by the popular press.

When Tweed ran for office, Caleb S. Woodhull, a lawyer, was mayor, and those sitting in the council included Joseph Jamison, a saddler, James Kelly, baker, James E. Wood, coal dealer, and Dennis Mullins, glover. The alderman from the Seventh Ward was Morgan Morgans, a founder, while John B. Webb, a boat builder, was the assistant alderman. The revolution in American politics and society which had taken place the last fifty years was as much in evidence in the composition of the council as anywhere else. It was a triumph of the petit-bourgeois. It was a place which afforded small men great influence and prestige. It was a place for William Magear Tweed.

The campaign was a rather lackluster one. Democratic party stalwarts, like Virginia-born Isaiah Rynders and Elijah Purdy, the "War Horse," were in the field, but not with much enthusiasm. Party rallies were few, and those usually conducted by Whigs. As expected, Democrats lost heavily. Fernando Wood, a future mayor, lost that office to Ambrose Kingsland. Both were merchants. Tweed was beaten by incumbent John Webb by a vote of 1,222 to 1,577.[1] Although losing, he reduced Webb's majority from the year before. Defeat was ascribed to the state of national politics and the assumption, true or not, that "black legs," grogshop characters, bullies and scoundrels were representative of the party. Such references might well have been meant to include Tweed, especially by those who remembered his departmental dismissal. Riot and chaos associated with the democracy took their toll.

Despite this loss, Tweed had taken a first step toward a political career, weak and insecure as it was. New Yorkers of the Seventh Ward had another chance the following year to vote for Tweed when he was nominated for alderman. This time he had a better opportunity since there was now a third candidate in the field running against Tweed and Webb. Joel Blackmer, president of the Seventh Ward Temperance Alliance, upholding the "purity" banner, split the opposition, since most of his votes came from those who would otherwise have voted for Webb. There is nothing to show that Tweed had anything to do with the Blackmer candidacy. It was his fortune that the dry issue was pressed by his enemies.

The New York *Times*, whose career would be so involved with that of Tweed, printed its first copy on September 18, 1851. Founded principally by Henry J. Raymond, as editor in chief, Fletcher Harper, brother of James, and Vermont-born George Jones, the paper was from the first a rabid anti-Tammany journal. Raymond particularly had political ambitions and waged war on the city in general and on Tammany and urban corruption in particular—the three in the publisher's mind being synonymous. The crusade was also very good for circulation, though it did great harm to the image of the city. But in this instance the paper was useful to Tweed. The *Times* unfurled the reform banner upon news of the passing in Maine of a strict prohibition law, by asking New Yorkers to follow the lead of the "blessed" town of Portland, the center of down east dry-dom. By early October 1851, "Friends of Temperance," such as the merchant and Whig William E. Dodge and former mayor James Harper, formed the New York City Temperance Alliance, aimed at "purifying" elections by removing intoxicating liquors from polling areas and enforcing existing laws banning Sunday liquor traffic. Eventually, the sale of liquor at any time would be prohibited.[2]

The movement brought together nativists, Whigs, do-gooders, anti-Catholics, anti-immigrants, Fundamentalists and assorted sour apples— generally the most conservative anti-urban, anti-democratic elements. Abolitionists too were attracted to anything marked reform. It was, in many instances, a marriage of convenience, but a useful tool with which to claw at the "degraded" opposition. The image of a drunken, besotted Democrat, usually seen as an Irish alderman, opposed to a clean-thinking, clean-living Whig or later Republican, was a picture presented often and early in many forms and disguises. The later attack on Tweed by Thomas Nast, paid propagandist for *Harper's Weekly*, was a part of this legacy.

The message was repeated often for those who at first did not understand. At a meeting of the Sons of Temperance, a criticism was made of the Common Council and "some part of our judiciary [which] have been too long under the influence of rowdyism." Examples were given. At primary elections, peaceful citizens were attacked by drunken thugs—one had an eye pushed out, another his head bruised, and a police captain had his jaw broken. Arrests were made, but few were imprisoned. A call was made for proper sober men to preserve peace, property and order. Readers of the *Times* were constantly reminded of riot and mayhem and liquor. A shocked audience was informed of an assault on a barkeeper at the Florence Hotel by Tom Hyer and "Big Bill" Poole, both noted pugilists and "bully-boys." They held the man by his hair and beat his head, causing the loss of an eye, because he refused them more than two drinks. Such was demon rum. At least that was what the *Times* said.[3] Anti-temperance people were quick to answer. The reformer denied individuals freedom of choice, not only of drink, but also of thought. If drink is denied, why not political freedom? Where does censorship end? To finish the equation and pointing to the presidential elections of 1852, the right of property, including the slaveowner's right to his slave, was also upheld. The issue was tailor-made for Democrats who could strike at the alliance of temperance and abolition and appeal to the southern vote, immigrants and believers in individual liberty.[4] It was a useful gambit.

The fall elections were animated but peaceful. Democrats regained control of the city. Tweed defeated Webb by forty-eight votes, 1,384 to 1,336. Blackmer received 206, enough to give Tweed the victory.

With elections over, New Yorkers forgot the fuss of politics and the drudgery of everyday life when Lajos, more popularly Louis, Kossuth, Hungarian patriot, hero of his people's fight against Russian invasion, was received at Castle Garden on December 7, 1851. Public celebration had a long-standing tradition. In provincial New York, the King's birthday and other such occasions were cheered before the flames of public bonfires. There was a huge parade in 1788 following news of the state's ratification of the Constitution. An extravagant reception, full of pomp and circumstance, greeted General Lafayette in 1824. In the following year, New Yorkers could be seen at and see the festivities celebrating the completion of the Erie Canal, and then in 1842 at the completion of the Groton Water Works project.

New Yorkers wore their hearts on their sleeves, they were naïve, vigorous, flamboyant, expansive, sociable, happily letting off steam, yelling, shouting encouragement to one and all. It gave them a chance to show off their city with its numbers, its richness, its accomplishments. They enjoyed being host for the nation's guests. New York was a giant advertisement for the country. Those who proudly welcomed foreigners waved

the flag of American freedom and liberty as a symbol of help for the oppressed and downtrodden of Europe. That it all had a circus-like atmosphere disturbed few. The spirit was the thing. Slowly, of course, this time
would pass. Though New York is still the world city, hosting the UN, and
parades of ethnic groups are still held, it is not as it was. New York is now
a quiet city, the shout and noise are gone, but while it lasted, there was a
glorious tumult in the streets.

It was in this spirit that Kossuth was welcomed ashore, even though
George T. Strong, arch-conservative lawyer, acidly noted in his diary that
most of those who cheered the "man of genius" had no more knowledge
of Hungary and its institutions than they had of "Entomostracrus fos-
sils."[5] He was probably correct. Despite Strong, a tremendous procession
formed, including twelve regiments of state militia, City Guards, City
Rifles and Irish volunteers. Music, noise, clattering of horses, rattling of
metal against metal, flags, colors were the order of the day, all at city expense. In a barouche drawn by six bay horses rode Kossuth and the mayor.
In others were governors, senators, congressmen, state senators and as-
semblymen, various state and city court officials and city councilmen. Kossuth pleaded with the crowd to have the United States and England prevent Russia from marching into Hungary—loud cheers and huzzas were
the answering cry. He fit into the American mood of opposition to tyranny.
The search for personal liberty and freedom were catch phrases taught
Americans from birth. Put this together with a chance to see a good parade
or show and it was an unbeatable combination.

On the twelfth, the city again honored the Hungarian "freedom
fighter" at a dinner at the Irving House. The huge banquet included
twelve pastries and sixteen confectionery plates. On December 16, the
press wined and dined Kossuth at the Astor House. The Democratic
Republic General Committee representing the Tammany Society had its
opportunity to wine and dine Kossuth, also at the Irving House the following day. Present were young mercurial Daniel E. Sickles, descendant of
an old Dutch family, and William M. Tweed. Sickles in a short address
told Kossuth that there were many examples of large contributions of
money made to the "noble cause of Hungary." He went on, however,
"Few can emulate these and only a few." Kossuth surely steeled himself
for what was to come: "but there are millions in the United States whose
hearts and hopes and prayers are with you. These cannot give thousands,
or hundreds or tens, but they can and will give their dollar." And as a symbol of this multitude, Sickles grandly announced, "I take this opportunity
to offer as my contribution to the Treasury of Freedom, a gold dollar,
fresh from our free mines of the Pacific." It was a gift from a "money-
making people in its noblest instinct and its truest ambition."[6] Whether

Kossuth expected more from the "munificent" Tammany sachems is doubtful. But a dollar? Well, at least the words of Tammanyites were with the fighters for Hungarian freedom, if not their money.

Many, including Strong, objected to the "clap-trap" about Kossuth; surely the United States could and would do nothing to aid the Hungarians, despite the rhetoric. They were right. It cost the city some $16,000 properly to entertain the Hungarian and his escort, and this brought about considerable debate in the council. Whig Alderman Oscar Sturtevant was particularly angered over the piecemeal presentation of the bill done in order to "fool" the council.[7] Tweed was being introduced into the wiles of city government by masters.

3

The Caldron

If Tweed felt he had stepped into a "soft" job he was mistaken. He was now in the center of a maelstrom of politics in the cockpit of the biggest city in the country. Municipal headaches were perennial and relief was not to be found in a simple aspirin or something ilke Sands Sarsaparilla, one of the many contemporary cure-all patent medicines. It was a place to learn and perhaps a place to leave. Criticism of councilmen was constant and always bitter and vicious. They were at least incompetents and at worst drunken thieves. Tweed remained on the Board of Aldermen for one term and never returned.

Introduction to city government was at first largely ceremonial. The first meeting of the new Board of Aldermen was held on January 5, shortly after noon. Mayor Ambrose C. Kingsland, a dealer in oil, leaning on the arm of the former Board President Morgan Morgans, a founder, entered the council chamber, called the Board to order and administered the oath of office to each member. Tweed repeated, "I do solemnly swear that I will support the Constitution of the United States and the Constitution of the State of New York, and that I will faithfully discharge the duties of Alderman according to the best of my ability." Tweed's career as a politician was on its way.

David T. Valentine, who is linked with the publication of the very useful and valuable *Manual of the Common Council*, commonly called *Valentine's Manual*, a kind of documentary history and "green book," a yearly project, never continued after 1870, one of the casualties of the "Ring" disclosures, was reappointed city clerk. Twenty aldermen sat in the chamber within City Hall, in circular fashion, with Abraham Morse of the First Ward to the right of the president, who sat on a bench facing the group. Following in numerical order were representatives of the various wards. Tweed thus occupied the seventh desk. Kingsland gave the annual

21

message to the Board and invited guests. It could have been written one hundred years earlier or one hundred and fifty years later. In his address, the mayor asked for vigilance in keeping the city clean, free from crime and violence. He outlined a program for street improvement including the rounding of corners of streets crossing lower Broadway and the replacement of cobblestones with some form of smooth surface. He expressed disappointment with the pavement which had been laid on lower Broadway. Kingsland also suggested a crash program of extending street lighting, especially at wharves and piers in order to prevent accident and thievery. Finally, he concluded with a financial summary and laudatory comments about the Fire Department and its "gallant members," surely meant to offset the Carson report. Having heard the message and congratulated the mayor, the Board recessed till 5 P.M. Most Board business, as with many other city agencies, was transacted after five o'clock, thus giving its members time to attend to their daily jobs and affairs. City government was still a part-time avocation and continued so until after the Civil War.

When the Board reconvened, Richard T. Compton was named president. A respected electee and iceman, Compton read a short but prophetic message asking party interest to be set aside for the good of the whole and that economy be the watchword as aldermen were the "treasurers of public property . . . Failing in this we may well be assured that we will be held to a strict accountability for the misuse of power vested in us." Did the freshman alderman from the Seventh Ward pay heed to this warning or was his head full of the excitement and triumph of the moment? Tweed was a teller in the Compton vote, and soon after, he, together with Aldermen Daniel F. Tiemann and Sylvester Ward, was appointed to a committee to hear testimony on the paving of Broadway.[1]

Street surfaces were a vexing and eternal problem and a solution was of high priority. Two types of composition pavement were available. One was that of Horace P. Russ, who with George W. Reid, was proprietor of the Richmond Granite Quarry in Staten Island. The other competing firm was that of John Perine. Both companies were given contracts to pave parts of Broadway and some adjacent streets. During the construction, clouds of dust and dirt were created, but by far the greatest nuisance was the blocking of traffic. Citizens were accustomed to constant sewer construction, repairing of gas and water pipes, and somehow as always endured delays. Impatient but accepting New Yorkers were assured that eventually the results would be worth the bother. The *Times*, unlike Kingsland, found the Russ pavement much better than the Perine, "the worst pavement known in our city." It complained that construction, especially by Perine, was behind schedule and threatened to become perpetually so. Something should be done. Quickly the Board of Assistants ruled

that Perine pay a fine, as he was in violation of his contract. This was at
first overruled by the aldermen, by a vote of eight to seven. Tweed voted
in the minority. The *Times*, irate as always, hastened its attacks on
Perine and the refusal of the Board to cancel the contract. "Is there no
end to this evil?" asked Raymond as he looked to redress at the ballot
box. The Russ-Perine squabble continued for a number of years, and gradually was forgotten, but the problem of street paving and traffic remained
a permanent one.[2]

The newspaper took little notice of what was right with New York.
That there was crime, dirt, noise, was no question, though often these
were found in no greater degree than in other cities in the country or on
the continent. New York was certainly a healthier place in which to live
than many. Disease, filth were less in the city than in London or Paris.
Visitors, though aware of crowded and dirty streets, were astonished by
the vitality of New York and of its people. Broadway was incredible and
its impressive stores and hotels were "more like the palaces of kings than
places for the transaction of business," commented an Edinburgh publisher. Fifth Avenue with its imposing dwellings was thought to be "the
most magnificent street in this continent," if not yet "the finest [street] in
the world." The greatness of New York could be seen amid the forest of
masts found along wharves and piers; in shop windows bursting with the
goods of all the continents; in its busy shipbuilding facilities which supplied so many of the great clipper ships like the *Sea Witch, Young
America, Challenge*; in its manufacturing industries; in its banks and other
commercial institutions. If it was not yet the first city in the world, it was
rapidly becoming so. But the goodness and greatness of New York was lost
on the *Times* and other such critics. That most people lived, worked and
played in its streets, offices, homes without hindrance, without being murdered or assaulted, but on the contrary enjoyed a quality of life not found
in too many other areas, was lost to the *Times*. There were things wrong,
but nothing was quite as bad as the *Times* made it out to be. But objec-
tivity was not that paper's forte; a sense of imagination, an open vision
free from the narrow confines of prejudice and vote-getting were sadly
lacking. Walt Whitman, viewing the same New York at the same time,
saw Manhattan and soared with it,

> City of hurried and sparkling waters! city of spires and masts!
> City nested in bays! my city![3]

All this was lost to the *Times*. It saw only meanness; it saw what it
wanted to see; it looked through its glass darkly. But it was comforted in
what it saw. Its editorials created a world apart and often quite different

23

from reality, and it would continue to do so, certainly through Tweed's lifetime.

Confusion, crime and disorder were constant headlines. "Violence perpetrated in any given round of twenty-four hours is startling," wrote Raymond. "The streets at night are infested with ruffians of all description. They hang around corners . . . they move about in gangs, men and boys together, abusing and sometimes hitting the quiet passerby . . . There is no security for life and limb in the present disorderly state of things." The paper, as always, demanded reform of the "worst governed city in the world," better police protection, cleaner streets, free from filth, garbage, dead rats, cats, dogs, reeking gutters.

"Day after day we record murders, by stabbing and shooting, perpetrated on peaceable citizens, without any ostensible cause save the diabolical thugs. Man or woman cannot appear at night, in some locations, without being subject to the attacks or insults of the ubiquitous gang," and on it went. Other New Yorkers cited the need for vigilante committees to enforce the law.[4]

Young men were warned to save themselves from moral and physical disease, barrooms and unemployment. "Turn your face from the City . . . look to that great empire of the West." "Do anything, but do it in the country where you have God and not Satan for fellow workman," shouted Raymond from his pulpit.[5] In July in an editorial entitled "Wanted—Fresh Air," the atmosphere of New York was described as being filled with "abominable gases" caused in part by "bone-boiling" and other noxious industries. The creation of a park was advocated to preserve God-given nature in the man-made pigsty of a city. The daily implored, "Let us infuse a little more country into our City."[6] Return law, order and God to New York, and if this did not work, hand the city over to San Francisco type vigilantes, fight terror and evil with more terror and evil. Tweed was thus witness to the endless war waged by the *Times* against what it felt were the imperfections of government. Raymond constantly and hysterically sounded the alarm bell of reform as he focused his spotlight on wrong and sold papers. He seemingly never questioned whether his diatribes were just or not; he rarely provided evidence or named names.[7]

Tweed was appointed to three regular committees—Law, Ferries, and Repairs and Supplies. He was also named to a special committee to look into a suitable location for a new potter's field. The *Times* took the occasion of a visit by that group to Randall's and Blackwell's islands, to find a site, to criticize the extravagance of the outing. At Blackwell's Island, dinner was served and champagne was "very liberally administered." Yet, the paper observed, despite expenditure of money in frolic, nothing was accomplished. It was a "fair specimen of the manner in which the legislature of our city discharge their duties. This is the only one of the many devices by which our City Government is made at once the most costly, the most inefficient and the most corrupt government on this side of the Atlantic." The editorial was also a "fair specimen" of the kind of criticism unleashed, usually without much proof, but with much ardor.

There were others.

In March, objection was raised to other expenses. The sum of $603.80 was too much for a trip to Albany, supposedly to discuss laws affecting New York. It was only an excuse for ten or twelve councilmen anxious for a spree to rob the city. If they do anything in Albany, it is to smuggle provisions into the charter to enable them to "thrust their itching fingers into the City Treasury . . . They can outdo Dick Turpin for ingenuity with which to plunder the public better than any other legislative body in the United States, except Congress." It costs more to run New York City than it costs to run any one of sixteen states, concluded the editorial. A June 4 editorial was headed "Our City Government—Its Corruption and Imbecility." This deluge of vituperation, all of it innuendo, stirred a reply. Alderman Sturtevant angrily demanded a more responsible press and one which would make specific charges instead of unsupported allegations. James Gordon Bennett's *Herald* also defended the council from "unfounded" charges. The unperturbed *Times* responded that it was accountable only to a "higher Tribunal," the people, and it would not be backed into a libel action by printing specific charges. It dismissed the *Herald* as a "corporation organ," which is "turned regularly" by the city at only $3,000 a year. Raymond reasoned that the city had a corporation counsel and controlled judges and courts, and he would not permit his newspaper to fall into a trap and allow its resources to be wasted by legal fees. He would not give details or name names. With that curious logic, Raymond's war on New York continued.

In a series of articles, "Evenings with the Aldermen," *Times* readers were alerted to unintelligible reports, frequent and early adjournments usually to attend Democratic caucuses, and other such abuses of office by aldermen. Raymond blamed money received by councilmen for attracting the needy and corruptible while the "best class of our citizens cannot afford the time for such office." Who should serve?[8]

The *Times*, through innuendo, smear, playing upon prejudices and fears, thus sounded trumpets of hysteria. It really did not matter if the city was destroyed in the process. On one hand it asked for change, and on the other sought to destroy any faith New Yorkers might have for their city even if it did change. Again typically, the *Times* rarely named names or gave specifics; headlines were enough. Even if there were truth to their charges, had the paper the right to serve as judge and jury? The Constitution which underscored freedom of the press also provided due process of law for citizens. But behind the barricade of headlines, Raymond threw his mud pies hoping to strike an errant target but too often simply dirtying all about him.

Despite the war of words, the two years Tweed spent on the council were relatively routine. Though debate did at times become bitter, Tweed did not too often become involved. The bulk of argument was carried on by more active members. His interest was directed to his various committees, but these accomplished comparatively little. Most of his work was for his constituents; for example, he was able to have a resolution passed directing that gas lighting of the East River waterfront between Catherine and Grand streets, as well as on Gouverneur Street from Grand Street to the East River, be installed as soon as practicable. It was also agreed that a liberty pole, a relic of past political campaigns, be removed from in front of the Seventh Ward Hotel on Madison Street.[9]

Though not a member of the committee, Tweed was interested in Fire Department affairs. It was more trouble.

In the meeting of the Board of May 5, Alderman Ashael A. Denman read an article from the *Fireman's Journal* which charged the council with expending nearly the entire Fire Department appropriation for the year in a fourteen-week period. The *Journal* saw in this a conspiracy to remove Alfred Carson as engineer by creating enough new companies to have them vote Carson out of office. Denman wanted an investigation. At this point, Tweed leaped to his feet on a point of order. He angrily stated that the *Journal* had particularly singled him out for its abuse, but noted that the *Journal* had such a reputation that the charge could do no harm. Alderman Wesley Smith concurred with Tweed. Denman tried to continue his reading. Tweed and several others again objected. Denman commented that he meant no harm to anyone and was merely trying to see if the allegations were true. His motion to hear a report from Carson was finally passed. Again, Tweed lost, though it amounted to little.[10] Still, where was Tweed the Tiger?

There were more difficulties. Franchises to operate and provide transportation presented one of the thorniest of issues. The need for mass transportation in the ever growing city was unquestioned. Problems arose over where, when, whom, and how. A horse-drawn railroad in one area was inconvenience and expense to persons living somewhere else. A low bidder could be given the franchise for operating a ferry, but would he provide satisfactory service? A contract might include a performance bond, but would that cover time lost in fulfilling the contract? What of influence-peddling and bribery? A good example of such problems was that raised by a group of entrepreneurs asking permission to construct a horse-driven railway along Broadway from the Battery to Manhattanville at the top of the island. On July 17, the *Times* reported favorably on the project, but ten days later rejected the idea because it would snarl Broadway's traffic. A railway on Sixth Avenue, it felt, would be sufficient. By November, after months of behind-the-scene maneuvering and arguing, the Board issued a report in favor of granting the franchise to the Broadway Railroad Company. There were thirty investors in the group including among them Jacob Sharp, a dealer in "round and square" timber, who had gained a reputation for questionable practices in gaining franchises; Peter Barr Sweeney, still spelled with an *e* before the *y*, a sharp-faced, shrewd lawyer; Gershon Cohen, customhouse officer and member of Tammany; and John O'Sullivan, a flamboyant, chauvinistic newspaper editor. The report was adopted 15 to 4, Tweed in favor. However, Mayor Kingsland, like the *Times*, rejected the proposal and vetoed the resolution. Alderman Sturtevant moved for further debate. The required ten days having elapsed since the veto, this was agreed to even though an injunction had been issued against the construction of the line. Angry words followed from those who warned the members that their personal liberty was in danger if they overrode the veto. At that point, Tweed asserted that the people of the Seventh Ward had elected him as their representative with the right to think for them, and this was not given to Justice William Campbell of the Superior Court who had granted the injunction. Campbell could order the executive to obey the order, but he could not order the council; no one could do this. The people were the seat of power, not the judiciary. Shades of Jefferson. Sturtevant, the Whig, followed by injecting a class issue. Those with carriages needed no railway and were opposed, while those without, the poor, were in favor. He supported the proposal and suggested it would be an improvement removing non-rail stages clogging Broadway. Tweed continued in the same vein, expanding on the benefit gained by the working classes, mostly his constituents. He ended his remarks by criticizing that "portion" of the press which always impugned the actions of the council. "Public opinion as expressed by them," he continued, "was only the echo of the dollars of the property holders." Debate on the franchise continued, and the mayor's veto was overridden by a vote of 15 to 3. It still left the injunction.

Later Tweed was quoted as actually saying, "We know the nature of a $50 bill when it is wisely employed and the echo that it will produce." The *Tribune* sarcastically concluded that Tweed certainly knew the value of any number of fifties, otherwise how could he have been elected. Trouble with newspapers began early for Tweed.[11]

Tweed had one more run-in on the last day of the session. The Law committee, of which he was a member, issued a report recommending among other things more room and money for the corporation counsel, Henry Davies. Alderman Bryce raised objection, noting that the city's attorney made thirty-five to forty thousand dollars per year for fees and emoluments. He argued also that it was necessary for the city to save money. Tweed agreed, but denied the size of Davies' income. Tweed reasoned that he could not make that much, since he never tried very hard to obtain the office. Bryce backed down. Well, it was surely at least $10,000 and that was enough to make any man a rich one in the Seventh Ward. Sturtevant sided with Tweed in the debate, only to be accused of switching party allegiance and becoming a Democrat. The report was defeated by one vote.

The alderman pot had more pepper in it. As an alderman, Tweed was obliged to sit on occasion on the bench of the Court of General Sessions together with another alderman and the recorder, the county attorney. An assistant district attorney, who acted as prosecutor before the court, was A. Oakey Hall. Hall, a graduate of New York University, was born Abraham O. Hall, but soon after graduation became Oakey and dropped the Abraham. Just why is not known. These were probably Tweed's first encounters with Hall.

Stories of robbery, false pretenses, prostitution and burglary were among those before Tweed and the court. One important case heard involved the Apollo Association, chartered in 1840 to promote the "fine arts." By 1844, its name had been changed to the American Art Union. The organization supported contemporary artists, such as William Sidney Mount, Henry Inman and Jaspar Cropsey, by distributing their works through a lottery held on Christmas Day. James Gordon Bennett, editor of the Herald, charged in his paper that the better works were being sold to a small handful of persons including Henry J. Raymond and Charles P. Daly, later a Supreme Court justice, so that the majority of the members of the Union were denied an opportunity to purchase. Twenty-one persons who had been accused by Bennett swore out a complaint for criminal libel, and the case came before Aldermen Tweed and Compton and Recorder N. Bowditch Blunt. They dismissed the charge. Tweed's and Compton's failure to uphold Raymond surely did little to ingratiate them and the council with the Times, and it was in the Times that the council and Tweed had their bitterest enemy.

Thus, Raymond had another ax to grind as he now derided decisions of General Sessions. He informed his readers that one of the councilmen, unnamed, who sat between May and June discharged fifty-three persons charged with drunkenness, rowdyism and assault. Members of the Court should be professionals, not "amateur Nestors."[12] What would Raymond have said if his suit against the Apollo Association had been upheld?

Fortunately, there were pleasanter activities, such as innumerable invitations to attend various kinds of dances, parades and such. To the affable Tweed, it was catnip. Accepted by him were invitations from Charles King, president of Columbia College, to attend examinations; Eagle Fire Company Number Thirteen to attend their Twelfth Annual Ball; and that of the Carlisle Light Guard. Carrying out his "responsibilities" obviously had its reward in the abundance of food, drink and good company. Such occasions probably did much to swell the figure, if not the image, of the emerging "Big Bill."[13]

He also attended upon an ever increasing flow of visiting dignitaries, such as Kossuth, as well as various Cuban and Irish dissidents, whose arrival was recognition that New York was the surrogate capital for the country, and that it even then served well as something of a world capital, a meeting place useful to settle the unsettled state of international politics. Traditionally, New York was a base for revolutionary activity. Its usefulness as a port and its polyglot population was such that a revolution in any part of the world could find compatriots and sympathy in the city, and made it a natural haven and center of political adventurism. The 1840s and 1850s also coincided with the raucous spirit of expansion. Concepts of "manifest destiny" and "Young America" included the sweeping away of Old World ideas. The future belonged to the young and the strong and to the United States. New Yorkers were found in filibustering South American expeditions of the early nineteenth century and with the Texan revolutionaries of 1835–36. Many joined the "Texan" army, some were at the Alamo. The city was used as a depot and medical and financial center, often with the tacit approval and connivance of Democratic Washington. In the 1840s, increasing attention was drawn to Cuba and Ireland.

Beginning in 1850, General Narciso López led two expeditions to Cuba made up of Cuban exiles and mostly southern Americans, each similar to the later Bay of Pigs affair. All was disaster. Many were killed or taken prisoner by Spanish authorities. López was executed. Partly due to public clamor in the United States and in order to avoid a possible war with the United States, Spain allowed American prisoners to leave Cuba. George Strong, while somewhat sympathetic to Cuban independence, thought that the movement was made up of those who had a "lust after other people's productive coffee-estates."[14] This kind of cynicism was expressed by others.

When the ship *Prentice* arrived in New York in March 1852 carrying returning "liberators" from Cuba, Alderman Tweed presented a resolution to the council to help the destitute "unfortunates." Tweed's suggestion was immediately criticized as a politician's handout meant only for public consumption and votes. Generally, the objections came from the Whig opposition, who saw the resolve as an attempt to gain public sympathy and then support for a principal plank in the Democratic Party platform. Cuban annexation was high on the list of the pro-southern administrations of Pierce and Buchanan. All this was not lost on Whig Alderman Denman, a Tweed adversary, who pointed out that the returnees were not soldiers, their expedition was not sanctioned by Washington. Moreover, the council had no authority in the matter, it was a national question. Private, not public, funds should be tapped. Expenses like that incurred in the Kossuth affair were not to be repeated. Sturtevant also jumped on the Tweed proposal. "Why does not the gentleman of the Seventh" asked the alderman, "raise his voice in favor of those in our immediate vicinity and whose only crime is that of poverty?" Those men (the returnees), he continued, "are nothing but pirates. They broke national laws and now beg for assistance." He expressed surprise that Tweed would champion their cause. Tweed replied by restating his earlier position, but the motion was defeated by a narrow margin of nine to eight. Surely, Tweed and the filibusters were surprised by the lack of public support. If Tweed counted on a Kossuth affair, he was mistaken. It was a negative, non-partisan vote, Whigs and Democrats splitting evenly. Strict party voting was, in fact, a rare occurrence in council deliberations.

Leaders of the filibuster expedition, John O'Sullivan and a Major Schlessinger, a former captain in the Hungarian Army, and others were tried in March and April of 1852 by the federal government for conspiracy, but the case was dismissed after the jury could not agree on a verdict.[15] It was not the end of similar attempts in years following, as Spanish-American relationships constantly bordered on war.

Now for the Irish. In June, shortly after the Cuban incident, Thomas Francis Meagher, the "illustrious Irish exile," was tendered the hospitality of the city at a dinner given at the Astor House. At the occasion, numbers of councilmen, perhaps including Tweed, raised their glasses in toasts given to liberty and freedom. There were numerous speeches sympathizing with the people of Ireland against British brutality. However, Meagher received no money, not even a "Tammany dollar," and little public support. Ireland unlike Cuba could not be annexed and made part of the Union.[16]

If New Yorkers missed the parading and show of the Kossuth festival, they were to have two regal and magnificent state funerals, those of Henry Clay and Daniel Webster. These were occasions when Gothamites could share in the Victorian celebration of the pageant of death. There had been some elaborate funerals in the past, such as Andrew Jackson's, but those of Clay and Webster, and later of Lincoln, were the most dramatic ever seen in the city. In all these affairs, the council played a prominent role. It was another chance for members to be seen and noted.

Henry Clay, the "Great Compromiser, Harry of the West," perennial Whig runner for the presidency, died June 29, 1852, in Washington. He was seventy-six years old. The council met the following day and began preparations to carry out the funeral obsequies of the renowned politician. As usual, a Committee of Arrangements was formed. It included Tweed and seven others. The remains arrived in New York on July 3, as an elaborate procession formed, led by the mayor, the council and an honor guard of Washington Greys in addition to the Clay Festival Association and Whig and Democratic committees. The procession marched slowly in the bright sunshine up Broadway to City Hall. There the hearse stopped and the coffin was brought into the Governor's Room, where it remained through Independence Day. It was also the seventy-sixth year of the nation's independence. Perhaps one hundred thousand persons streamed past the coffin; the holiday-like atmosphere was appropriately muffled and flags were draped in mourning. At two in the following morning, the Committee of Arrangements and others escorted the coffin aboard the steamboat *Santa Claus*. The quiet light of the full moon, tolling bells and muffled drums underscored the solemnity of the scene. The band played "Auld Lang Syne." At 11 A.M., the boat covered with black and gray cloth left the pier for Albany and finally Kentucky with Clay's son Thomas and his grandson Henry aboard.

Incredible as it may seem, the same scenes were re-enacted a few months later at the death of Daniel Webster. The great orator died on October 24 and official obsequies were held in New York on November 16. The council again established a committee, but without Tweed. The city again made ready. On the day of the event, black and gray were again made official colors and signs were spread above Broadway—"He was not for a day, but for all time"; "Honor to the good, the just and the free"; "Webster, the great statesman"; and "Webster being dead, yet speaketh." Among the pallbearers was Richard Tweed standing in for his brother William. There were the same military divisions, bands, societies, politicians, businessmen as had taken part in Clay's funeral. Harvey B. Dodworth's band also provided the proper musical accompaniment as they had for Clay.[17]

All the festivities and pageants provided a breathing space from the daily grind. For Tweed, as with many other New Yorkers, the work and effort of the year culminated with the fall elections. Raymond was there to remind his newspaper readers of what they had learned. There was the huge city debt, crime and the villainy of the Common Council. He repeated that most councilmen enter office poor, but leave comparatively rich in a year or two by selling their votes. He cited the example of one man, as usual not identified, who entered office with one dollar and left with twenty to thirty thousand dollars. The paper demanded a separation of power within the city, with councilmen being limited to simple duties and having nothing to do with the granting of contracts or sitting as justices. Whigs, to accomplish this, needed votes. In response, a City Reform League met in September to help restore responsibility in government. It continued its activity even after the November elecion.[18]

The year 1852 was, of course, a presidential year and many important state offices, including the governorship, were also at stake. As early as August, furious debate spilled over into violence in many of the wards, mainly between factions of Democrats: "Hunkers" or "Hard Shell" Democrats, generally conservative; and "Barnburners" or "Soft Shell" regular Democrats or Tammanyites. The issues, never very clear, were a carryover from the bitter days of the 1844 Democratic nominating convention battle between Martin Van Buren and James Polk. "Softs" backed the state and national party on issues such as slavery, limited canal building within the state and limited federal aid to localities. "Hards" equivocated on the question of slavery, desired more expenditures on canals and internal improvements, and were not willing to accept regular party leadership. The basic difference was really one of control of Tammany and patronage. The plumage was only part of the bird.

One of the first major Democratic meetings occurred early in September, when Tammany sponsored a large park meeting. At hand were Lewis Cass and Stephen Douglass, who in their florid oratory asked for annexation of Cuba and attacked the English for their treatment of Ireland. Stressed also was the hope that "Hard Shells" and "Soft Shells" would find a unity of purpose.

By late September, Democratic nominations were in. "Soft" Tweed was selected to run for Congress from the Fifth Congressional District, which included the Seventh and Thirteenth wards plus Williamsburg in neighboring Brooklyn. Opposite Tweed on the Whig ticket was Joseph Hoxie, merchant and a well-known figure. If Tweed were elected, he would not take his seat until December 1853 and could finish his term as alderman. But if the *Times* was right, that councilmen got rich in office, it could cost Tweed money to give up the seat. Why the party chose Tweed again is not clear. He was a doubtful runner. He still was not a member of Tammany, plagued by an image of being the bully as depicted by Carson, carrying a less than brilliant record. On the plus side, however, he was considered an energetic man with a "fine personal appearance." Now twenty-nine, he was described as having a "large and robust frame . . . His habits are good, particularly in carefully avoiding, as he does, the use of tobacco and inebriating liquors, which is the case of so many of our great men." These qualities were a considerable advantage, felt the *Herald*. The paper also thought that his experience in trade would aid him in any legislative contest, and expected that a fair proportion of his leisure hours would be passed in the library and in study.

On the ticket with Tweed was County Cork-born Richard Barrett Connolly as Democratic nominee for county clerk. During the campaign, a series of enthusiastic ward meetings were held, some in the park, some at halls and clubhouses, all aimed at getting out the vote, Hard and Soft, behind Franklin Pierce. Tweed did not appear too often at meetings. He did attend one in the Thirteenth Ward along with marching bands and fireworks. There he gave the major speech, after being introduced amid cheers and applause. At first, he reminisced about the fact that the meeting was being held close to where he had been born and went to school— "those merry and useful days at the Academy—the happiest period of our lives." He talked about being a captain of juvenile companies of militia and fire, not dreaming he would become a foreman of an actual fire company or one of the "humble leaders of a great political party." He did not wish public office, Tweed continued, but still, once in office, he would do his best for all of his constituents, regardless of party, in Congress, as he had done in the council. As for himself, he stated that since his youth, "the principles of integrity, generosity and charity were implanted in my bosom . . . Has anyone known me to commit a mean or dishonorable action?" Tweed asked the crowd. Their response was "No, no, no." Tweed asked them to repeat their answer. He continued, "The admonitions of those nearest and dearest to me always were never to commit an act which I might be ashamed of thereafter." These words, Tweed promised, would "ever be uppermost in my thoughts." Dwelling on his past, he recalled that all of his ancestors for more than a century had cherished democratic principles and that he would uphold their principles to help the poor and carry on the tradition of Thomas Jefferson, the "real author" of the Declaration of Independence and "Father of the American Constitution." As to the last odd statement, Tweed admitted that Jefferson was in France at the time of the Constitutional Convention, but his spirit was in Philadelphia, foiling the efforts of Alexander Hamilton, "founder of the Whig Party," to create a government based on monarchial tenets. He ended with plaudits for General Franklin Pierce, who like General Andrew Jackson would uphold the country's commercial interests and show the world that the "great American flag shall be respected by all nations . . ." Then the bands played "Yankle Doodle" and "Hail, Columbia" as fireworks blazed in glory and "cries went up to heaven for the election of Tweed and Pierce." It was not much of a speech, but still it worked.

Tweed defeated Hoxie by a vote of 5,476 to 4,241, although he ran behind the state and national candidates in his ward. The victory was celebrated at a grand festival held at Tammany Hall on November 15. Seymour and Grand Sachem John Van Buren, son of the "Little Magician," were among three hundred other guests attending. Speeches were made, toasts were offered as Shelton's American Brass Band played "The Star-Spangled Banner" and "Yankee Doodle," by now Tweed's victory song.[19]

4

"Abyss of Barbarism"

As Tweed waited to take on his congressional duties, he had an opportunity to attend the opening of the first World's Fair ever to be held in the United States. The center of the "Exhibition of the Industry of All Nations" was the Crystal Palace, a huge glass and iron dome modeled after a similar building erected earlier in London. The event was meant to show the world American genius and to exhibit to Americans the accomplishments of Europe. Built next to the Forty-second Street Reservoir, at a site now occupied by Bryant Park, the Palace enabled New Yorkers to relax and gaze at the wonders before them. This was what New York was all about. The Palace was another example of New York's vibrance, its growth, its importance—what was positive about Manhattan. It was New York lifted above the pebbles and puddles, the irritants that so engrossed the *Times*.

The exhibition officially opened July 14, 1853, with President Franklin Pierce and a host of dignitaries including many members of Congress in attendance. The President landed at Castle Garden at about 10 A.M. and was met by Mayor Jacob Westervelt and members of the council including Tweed and a huge throng which packed the Garden. Pierce congratulated citizens of the Empire City for building in only a few years one of the most important cities of the world. He marveled at the speed of its progress and its patriotic devotion to American rights and liberties. In the evening, a "Great Complimentary Dinner" was held at the Metropolitan Hotel. Attorney General Caleb Cushing and Jefferson Davis, Secretary of War, were the featured speakers.[1]

Crystal Palace was on everyone's lips. It was a grand love affair for New Yorkers. There were Crystal Stables, Crystal Ice Cream Parlors and Crystal Fruit Stalls. The streets were filled with vendors selling banners, illuminations and pictures. This pleasurable excitement, however, was not transferred to the *Times*. To the daily, it was only so much gaudy show. Only drunkenness and thievery were the realities of New York. Its editorials complained of the "army of vagabonds," the thousands of young faces in the city streets "all with the harsh lines of depravity stereotyped upon them," middle-class youths who spent their time in saloons, houses of ill repute, affecting a "feminine air and spending the hard earned money of their fathers." Added to this were other editorials dealing with the "peddling of immoral books," and the fact that "No one can have alighted from a stage to get into a ferry boat, or travel in a railway car, or even linger at the door of a hotel, without being accosted by a class of ragged boys, with low, cunning features, who offer pamphlet novels for sale," including such "filthy publications . . . as the 'Mysteries of the Count of London,' 'The Monk Knight of St. John,' the 'Belle of the Bowery,' etc., etc." The selling of the corruption to young girls and boys should be swept away by "outrages of public decency."

New York of all the Western world is most noted for the insecurity of life, Raymond continued. "During nine hours of the twenty-four there is no safety for sober citizens in the streets. Remain within doors, and bolt the shutters against housebreakers," he advised, for this "is the dictate not of unmanly fear but of respectable prudence." Further the police are too stationary and don't patrol the streets, they are not visible. High-crime areas have few policemen, while safer neighborhoods have more than they need. City Hall Park is attended by only one policeman. No wonder the *Times* concluded a "poor fellow was murdered there the other night." Crystal Palace, indeed.

"The air of our streets requires a throat of brass and lungs of sole leather or gutta-purcha. Flesh and blood go down before it," the journal continued. "The dust is everywhere, you cannot escape . . . You cannot shut it out. Doors and windows are not a hindrance . . . Look at the number of inflamed eyes you meet in a walk. Intemperance is not the cause of it. It is dust and nothing but dust." The *Times* demanded clean streets and ridding the city of pestilence and filth of all sorts, including dead horses. Everyone understood the problem, everyone except city officials, especially the Common Council. The irritation of the *Times* was not reduced by the summer temperature. In one week in August, 150 deaths were reported attributed to heat, as well as liquor. Adulterated milk added to the death toll, especially among infants.

A hundred Crystal Palaces could not help New York, but the creation of a "Middle Park, recapturing God's earth" and allowing the city to breathe fresh air might. It was a cause close to the *Times*'s heart. There were two proposals before the Common Council. One included a park at Jones' Wood, an area between Sixty-sixth and Seventy-fifth streets from

Third Avenue to the East River, and the other a central park, an area between Fifth and Eighth avenues between Sixtieth and 106th streets. The
Times suggested that both be included in one large area. The council and
the state legislature after due deliberation, weighing real estate values as
well as ecological considerations, opted for a central park in a slightly altered form. Tweed in the council went along with the majority view.[2]

Still whatever the council did was not enough as the journal continued its war on that body with mounting ferocity. Earlier in the year, the
Times had supported a bill debated in the legislature to amend the charter, which would "serve to throw the keen scented plunderers off the track
for a season." The state legislature on April 12, 1853, approved a new charter for the city subject to a referendum. By its terms, the City Council was
to consist of a Board of Aldermen with one alderman elected every two
years from each ward, and a Board of Councilmen consisting of sixty men
elected in as many districts for one year. It was hoped that a system of
checks and balances would thus be restored, and the judicial and appoin-
tive power of the aldermen was to be greatly reduced. Aldermen could not
sit on any court. Expenditure of money was limited in cases of celebrations
or parades to specific occasions—Washington's Birthday, July 4 and November 25 (Evacuation Day, celebrating the British departure from New
York in 1783)—unless voted upon by a three-fourths vote of each body. A
Board of Audit was created to supervise the expenditure of money. Stiff
fines and prison terms were the penalty for influence peddling and
improper spending.[3]

On June 5, a great city reform meeting was held in support of the
new charter. Judge Aaron J. Vanderpoel of Kinderhook, New York, and
head of a prestigious law firm gave the major address. It was a denunciation of the "hungry hordes of fat contractors and job sellers" who feed on
the city treasury, the army of harpies who live by their wits, instead of
their labor, by electing city officials to do their bidding. Russ paving contracts were an outstanding example of such corruption and he backed the
new charter since it reduced the power of the Board. Sixty new councilmen, he felt, could not be "bribed but in battalions." He asked Hard-
shells, Soft-shells, Hunkers, Barnburners, Democrats, and Whigs, Wooly
Heads (pro-abolitionists) and bald heads to unite against a common
enemy. Daniel Sickles of Tammany, willing to be part of the popular denunciation of the council, supported charter changes, but warned that citizens held the ultimate responsibility in seeing to it that responsible men
were elected to office. Legislative gimmickry was not enough. In all the
speechmaking that night no city official was singled out or a specific deed
mentioned.[4]

The referendum was held June 7, 1853, and the charter overwhelm-

ingly approved. It was an example of reform triumphant, shouted the
Times, as it looked hopefully forward to furthering the cause in the fall.
Meanwhile under the baleful eye of the reformers, aldermen carried on
city business. Tweed, in office, tended to be more active in 1853, if not
more successful. He sponsored a resolution to have the Chief of Police
keep "suitable books" on amounts of "donations" received by policemen,
but the resolution was defeated.

In September, he became involved in a bitter debate with Alderman
John Doherty, who accused Street Commissioner James Furey of wrongdoing in regard to street paving contracts. It was impudence and "Billings-
gate"—misrepresentation and falsehood, not substantiated facts—charged
an angry Tweed. The Board backed Tweed in the affair 14 to 1. On the
other hand, Tweed, who had sponsored and helped carry a motion to increase policemen's salaries from five hundred dollars per annum to six hundred, was reversed when Mayor Westervelt vetoed the bill much to the
plaudits of the *Times*, who thought that aldermen voted the increase
merely to court votes.[5]

Tweed also found himself grist for the *Times* mill when it rekindled
its attack on the Broadway Railroad Company as a "speculative" scheme
to be paid for by the city treasury and impractical in relieving Broadway
traffic. A list of shareholders was published. These included a number of
persons acting as "masques" for such aldermen as Jacob F. Oakley,
Whelan Morse, Oscar W. Sturtevant, Richard F. Compton and William
M. Tweed, "a gentleman," who, it sarcastically reported, "was never more
startled in his life than when, upon waking one fine morning, he found his
name among those of the proposed grantees of the franchise." The *Times*
gave no proof for its allegations, and whether these aldermen were in fact
shareholders is not known. Surely the *Times* did not know. The proposed
railroad was not approved.[6]

The growing temperance battle was brought to the aldermen by a petition from the City Temperance Alliance asking the Board to "grant no
licenses whatever for the sale of wines, spirits or liquors, or any intoxicating drinks," in order to end the abuses of the "corner grocer" and the
proliferation of licensed and unlicensed liquor shops. The *Times* again
demanded a "Maine" law for New York to prevent the plague of drunken
licentiousness that helped make New York the least civilized city in the
world—an "abyss of barbarism," whose air is "laden with snatches of
drunken songs, fragments of filthy language, or incoherent shouts from
those who were too drunk to articulate." The journal asked, "Is the entire
city drunk?" Young men, old men, women and children were all involved
in an eternal "Saturnallia" and yet the city government did nothing, ex-

cept imbibe in the "aldermanic beer garden." The petition was rejected, but the cause remained.[7]

By September, leaders of woman's rights also active in city affairs met and joined forces with temperance advocates at a World's Temperance Convention held at Metropolitan Hall. Susan B. Anthony was secretary and Thomas W. Higginson of Massachusetts, president. Included as vice-presidents were P. T. Barnum, the showman, Horace Greeley and Lucretia Mott.

Resolutions passed at the convention pledged to work for total abstinence, to end the liquor traffic, to label drunkenness a crime and to "end the reign of Satan among Christians." The movement, now allied with woman's rights, was also joined by two others—the vegetarians and the nativists. The former created a New York Vegetarian Society and on Sunday evening, September 4, 1853, while the rest of the city drank or ate itself into "Satan's arms," held a festival at the Metropolitan Hall. Greeley talked about temperance, socialism, anti-slavery and woman's rights. Vegetarianism helped these other great social reforms. He proposed a Vegetarian Hotel and Eating House where liquor and tobacco would be prohibited in favor of a pure, morality. Shortly afterward, a two-day woman's rights convention was held at the Broadway Tabernacle. Lucy Stone, Lucretia Mott, Susan B. Anthony, William Lloyd Garrison and women from around the country sought greater property and political rights, especially the right to vote. Probably the highlight of the convention was the appearance of Sojourner Truth, a "colored lady of some sixty winters" whose presence linked the anti-slavery movement with woman's rights.

In fact, an anti-slavery meeting was also held on September 4, the same day as the Temperance Convention, and at the same place. It was attended by some fifteen hundred people including a hundred "colored persons." Garrison and Lucy Stone spoke, not always to the plaudits of the assemblage. Radical abolitionism was still abhorrent to many. Both addressed themselves to the need for Christian graces, liberty and freedom. They stressed the immorality of slavery.[8]

It was a busy time for reformers, a busy time for all New Yorkers. There were causes to be fought for, ills to be corrected, and almost everyone seemed to have the perfect solution and could provide necessary leadership. It was a dangerous time; the moralists were abroad. A revitalized nativism, basically anti-Irish-Catholicism, so long a part of the heritage of hatred, was linked to the reform movement by the members' natural hostility to Democrats. On July 4, 1853, pent-up hostilities and repressions were released as vicious fighting between native Protestants and Irish Catholics broke out in the Ninth Ward. The National Guard finally quelled the rioting. Though denounced by the Hibernian Society and Protestant groups, violence remained a popular pastime—a way to solve problems. To the nativist, all immigrants were Irish Catholics, ignorant, poor, depraved and besotted creatures. Later Thomas Nast was "cleverly" to illustrate this "truth." On the other hand, to many immigrants, all New Yorkers were nativists or Orangemen.

But patriotism was in and nativists prospered. On September 22, a large meeting was held at busy Metropolitan Hall to support the action of Captain Duncan H. Ingraham in aiding the escape from the clutches of Austrian authorities of a Hungarian patriot, Martin Koszta, who was brought to New York and made an American citizen. At the meeting American defense of liberty and justice was honored, while foreign countries that sought to infringe on that liberty were condemned. An offshoot of the meeting was a large demonstration held in the park on December 14, partly in support of Koszta, then in New York, but mostly in criticism of Mayor Jacob Westervelt for the arrest of an anti-Catholic agitator, a "street angel," Reverend Parsons, while rabble-rousing during a street demonstration, he had cursed Bishop John Hughes, the "Pope of New York," and Catholics as threats to American freedom and morality and an ever present danger to American independence. Americans, shouted Parsons, must not hold their tongues after seeing the hordes of pauper immigrants flooding the city, most in the service of Jesuits and the Pope; "trust none but Americans on guard to-night." This brand of Americanism contained some curious contradictions. Hungarian, Cuban and Irish demands for independence brought sympathy even if in an indirect way from the nativists. Supporting such political movements, which were essentially Catholic, while being extremely anti-Catholic was a difficult balancing act often attempted, but never quite accomplished. It didn't make much sense, but the movement was not supposed to. One thing was certain, there was a chill wind blowing through the country. Black storm clouds gathered even as Tweed rode to Washington.[9]

5

A Term in Congress

The congressman-elect took his seat in the first session of the Thirty-third Congress as part of New York's thirty-three-man delegation on December 5, 1853. Six were representatives from the city. This was in keeping with the population—3.5 million in the state, 630,000 in the metropolis. Included in the state's delegation were Reuben F. Fenton, a future governor, and Rufus W. Peckham, future member of the Court of Appeals and brother of Tweed's nemesis, Wheeler H. Peckham. It was not a distinguished Congress. Even so, Tweed was a very small fish in the very big ocean of national politics, a neophyte member of an ever changing and very weak New York City delegation. Characteristically, too, this contingent quarreled as often as they agreed, which also did little to strengthen their position.

The first days in Washington were hectic and exciting. In addition to finding a residence—Tweed settled for the Willard Hotel on Pennsylvania Avenue—and such mundane things as eating places, clothing stores, transportation, there was the business of seating in the House, rules and procedures, new friends and perhaps new enemies. Tweed was apppointed to the Committee on Invalid Pensions, Thomas A. Hendricks of Indiana, later vice-presidential candidate, chairman. Russell Sage of New York was also a member.

Tweed's tenure in office was uneventful. He interested himself mainly with private bills generally relating to pensions and city affairs. On December 20, 1853, he introduced a bill presented many times before by other congressmen to establish a United States mint in the city. He had advocated this idea while alderman. Interest in such an establishment was great, and Congress had in fact allowed for it in 1791, but the idea never got off the ground. The city was willing to grant land and exempt such a structure from taxation, but still nothing was done. It was a good illustration of how powerless New York was. Referred to the Committee on Ways and Means, Tweed's effort died there. Tweed also tried during the second session to present a report on building post offices in New York. Others objected to the reading and again Tweed and the city were stymied. Facing the Congress and the country were more important issues, slavery, northern industrial capitalism versus southern agrarianism, generally, and specifically, admission of the new territories Kansas and Nebraska. Senator Douglass had introduced his ill-conceived bill at the beginning of the session. It terminated the Missouri Compromise and opened the road to civil war. The Democratic Party position was now that of Douglass' "popular sovereignty." Let the people of a territory as in Kansas decide as to whether they would be free or slave. But what then of balance and compromise? There was fire in the sky. Could the nation's leaders steer a course around the impending storm? Tweed had a hand on the wheel, but a small hand indeed. He stayed close to the party line. New York City's relationship to the South was an intimate one. Many of its commission merchants lining the wharves and streets of lower Manhattan were factors for southern plantation owners. They sold cotton for their clients and bought furniture and household goods—like that made by Tweed—for them. Southerners often visited the city during the summer, sent their children to New York schools and became friends with New Yorkers. The metropolis was probably as much like a southern community as could be found along the northeastern seaboard. It was a segregated city. Blacks attended separate "colored schools," theaters, churches and public transportation were segregated. Perhaps 1 per cent of the population, some twelve thousand in all, their political power was practically nil. Besides, they were virtually disenfranchised, having to meet stiff property qualifications. In 1855, only five voted. Their future was made more difficult with each passing year as hundreds and thousands of immigrants arrived at Castle Garden and crowded into the streets. The struggle for jobs, housing and social amenities heightened racial differences and deepened social antagonism. Poor agrarian Irish vying for menial jobs were in the center of anti-Negro agitation.

For Democrats, by now the traditional champion of the immigrant, there was a traditional aversion to the black. The old New York-Virginia alliance going back to the days of Jefferson and Clinton was still strong. New York City politicians saw little to gain in opposing their southern counterparts. When Tweed on May 10, 1854, arose on the floor of Congress to speak for the Kansas-Nebraska bill, it was Tammany, commission merchants, theater operators, Irish immigrants and the national Democratic Party speaking. It was a stereotyped speech. He believed the Missouri Compromise dividing western free from slave territories was unconstitutional. It was in violation of "Supreme Law" because it "encroaches on the rights of the South, to have an equal share with the North in the enjoyment of our dominion." He was in favor of the bill which allowed Kansas admission as a slave state, since the people of Kansas having made that choice, should "control their own institutions." It was as close to a speech Tweed would make in Congress.

In the second session which began on December 7, 1854, he took part in a debate on a Trans-Pacific Railroad bill as a "friend of the bill." After considerable debate, the bill was passed 109 to 97, Tweed in favor. When the House voted to reconsider, Tweed was in the minority. The bill was sent to committee and eventually was passed in revised form. In sum on the floor of Congress he presented a less than heroic figure. But this was in keeping with being a freshman congressman from New York City. Tweed never spoke of his sojourn in Washington. He was happier at home; in Washington the ball park was too big. He had his family, his brushes and chairs, his friends in New York. Anyway, he was not renominated.[1]

6

Know-Nothings

Back in New York, where was Tweed to go? His aldermanic seat gone, his term in Congress over at the end of the year and his political future in doubt, he did not take an active part in deliberations, and he was definitely not a key figure in the Democracy. Somehow amid the swirl of confusion about him Tweed sought to find a secure position or be swept away by time and tide. He barely managed to survive.

Certainly, nothing had changed in Tweed's absence, especially in regard to the *Times* crusade. This was the same.

Editorials lividly if not happily told of a rising murder rate, of attacks by knife and bullet on helpless citizens and even policemen. They recommended reform of the prison system, specifically in keeping young prisoners away from hardened criminals. New Yorkers also read of the case brought against Anna Lohman, the notorious Madame Restell, allegedly an abortionist who made profit from the results of the lost "virtue" of young, pretty and innocent girls. Seldom found guilty, although hunted and finally hounded to death, Restell, born in England in 1812 as Anna Trow, was a fixture on the New York scene for many years as an adviser to those having "female complaints," much to the annoyance of the medical profession. Madame Restell, guilty or not, and she seemed to have harmed no one, was still another object lesson, if that was necessary, of dangers of city life and the need for eternal vigilance. She committed suicide at her home at 657 Fifth Avenue on April 1, 1878, by slitting her throat while in a bathtub. The Committee for the Suppression of Vice, which had long sought the "female physician," using her to obtain support for a depleted treasury, could now rest easy—so could Restell.

This committee was headed by a veritable inquisitor, Anthony Comstock, a haunted, driven man dedicated to the eradication of vice, particularly in the form of prostitution and obscene literature. He was obsessed

44

with pornography and carried satchels full of such matter to show to intimates. A good deal of these wares consisted of advertisements for contraceptives or pictures of nude women. He visited prostitutes disguised as a "client," had them undress, then ordered arrests. He liked to draft counterfeit letters, invent fictitious circumstances in order to inveigle his prey. Restell was caught in his web when she fell for a trumped-up story involving his "wife" and her "desperate" need for Restell's assistance supposedly in the form of an abortion-inducing drug. Comstock had a long career; the anti-pornography laws bearing his name were an indication of his power. Judges and district attorneys waited on his every word on puritanism revived.[1]

For those like Comstock and the *Times*, there was a need for such revivalism—a little witch-hunting cleanses the soul. There was so much to be told. Look at young men, especially the sons of the rich. Fathers amass fortunes, but allow their offspring to become "useless drones." How can America be sure of its future? The *Times* lamented, "We cannot expect great statesmen, or generals, or masters of finance of youths that have wrecked their constitutions ere they have ceased to be boys, and whose minds are familiar with the vices of maturity before their joints have been well knit, or their cheeks lost their down." Deplored also were riotous outbreaks among students at "our most respectable colleges." Student unrest was traced to the failure of parental authority and insensible teachers. What of the state of public schools, where 150,000 students registered, but only 50,000 regularly attended school? It was a danger and a tragedy. Poor children, barefoot and worn, sell matches and radishes on street corners, others become criminals. Absenteeism should be ended and authority restored. The need for law and order was obvious.[2]

But how could this be done when the municipal administration was "universally despised as unprincipled, corrupt and audacious to the last degree"? The *Times* relished the thought of the sentencing of Alderman Sturtevant to a fifteen-day prison term for his contempt of the decision made by Justice Campbell in the Broadway Railroad franchise case, and hoped this would bring a more responsible government. This sentence was one of very few meted out to any of the "Forty Thieves," a popular expression or better a canard for the Common Council.[3] Unsuccessfully, aldermen fought the wave of criticism. In October, State Senator Thomas J. Barr, a former alderman, brought a libel suit against Henry Erben, an organ dealer. Erben had called Barr a corrupt member of a corrupt board. Even after anti-Catholic remarks were also traced to Erben, the jury disagreed.[4] Encouraged, critics continued flailing like windmills and hoping to strike a target as November rolled around.

Electioneering was confused and complicated as ever. Whigs, nativists,

45

known also as Know-Nothings, and temperance advocates paraded behind the uplifted and uplifting anti-urban banners of purity and Americanism, while Democrats, as usual, Hards, Softs and in-betweens, fought over party preference behind the banners of Pierce, Douglass and popular leaders of various factions who came out of the woodwork at election time. Tweed remained on the fringe, mentioned but rarely heard. He was given an outside chance at the mayoralty, but insiders correctly felt it was an office "he won't get."

Still there was a chance. Literally, a hundred names were in the air; almost the same number of factions were at hand.

By October, decisions had been reached. Tammany Softs overwhelmingly nominated Fernando Wood for the mayoralty. His victory was made easier when at the Democratic meeting a brief letter from Tweed dated October 9 was read: "I am not a candidate for the nomination of Mayor during the present canvass." Tweed probably realized he could not win and might as well bow out gracefully. Wood was closer to the scene, a much more popular figure than Tweed, considered more able and not tainted with Common Council "corruption." Whatever the reason, the strategy worked, factions united. Still, the episode could have left Tweed with a bitter feeling toward Wood.

With little to look forward to, Tweed now resurrected an errant hope that he could retain his congressional seat. Maybe as a reward for his withdrawal, he received a tentative nomination a few days later. Those in the know, however, felt Tweed would have to "work diligently, or he may be crowded out." Feelings such as these again proved correct. He was not even allowed the chance "to work diligently." By October 20, Tweed was replaced by Abraham J. Berry as Soft congressional candidate.

Tweed then received, probably as a bone, the last in the cupboard, the Tammany nomination for his old seat as alderman from the Seventh Ward. Charles Fox ran against him as a Whig and Know-Nothing. William D. Murphy, secretary of Olive Street Baptist Church, and John Murphy ran as Hard and Independent, respectively.[5] It was not going to be easy.

One of the more interesting aspects of the electioneering was the flowering of the colorful "street angels," an apt name for Bible-carrying evangelists such as Father Parsons and including one well-known itinerant, Mr. Orr, popularly known as "Angel Gabriel." He used the pavements and the Bible to malign Irish Catholics, and by inference all Democrats. Frequently the street angels were themselves attacked. In September, a young man named Mills, another called Paul and one called Moses went at Catholics with an ardent furiosity. They fanned the air like bellows in a foundry in directing contempt toward foreigners not willing or able to ac-

46

cept Protestant Americanization for themselves or their children. On September 5, a riot broke out in Newark. Two people were killed, and a Catholic church was sacked by a Protestant mob. In New York, a parade by members of the American Protestant Association was attacked by or themselves attacked Irish Catholics and a full-fledged and dangerous melee ensued. Still street preaching continued at a faster pace. Police readied themselves for another Astor Place riot, an event which occurred in 1849 after an anti-English, anti-foreign mob was stopped by the militia only after the loss of many lives. Know-Nothingism, bigotry wrapped in the American flag, was a dangerous political development, but a popular one. Tweed, who years earlier had found nativism attractive, did not join in this movement, but others did. More than "street angels" spoke out against Tammany Hall and "putrid foreign elements," or found nativism was "composed of men who pay their debts and don't drink bad rum."[6]

There were statistics to give support to those clamoring against immigrants. In 1845, New York City's population was 371,323. Of these 134,656 were foreign-born, 96,581 coming from Ireland and 24,416 from the German states. Ten years later the city's population almost doubled, reaching 629,904, but the foreign population was now more than half of the total, at 322,460. Of these 175,735 were Irish and 95,572 German, growing at a greater rate than the Irish. What added to the unease in the city over the immigrant tide—over 300,000 newcomers entered the port in 1854—was the fact that while foreigners were half of the population, they constituted 75 per cent of the inmates at the almshouses, workhouses and the city prisons and state penitentiary. They also lived in crowded tenements, dark basements—the poorest areas of the city. To add to the dreary picture, as of May 1854 the city licensed 6,571 taverns. New York received ten dollars a license. For every 115 persons, there was one tavern. As of February 1855, 5,540 taverns were licensed, the poorest wards, the Fourth and Sixth, having the greatest number. It was clear to nativists and temperance advocates that the hated enemy was the "besotted Irish immigrant and Tammany Hall revelers."[7] The alliance of nativism and temperance worked, aided by Democratic Party schism. Tweed's fate was predictable. Tweed had 1,167 votes to Fox's 1,390; 669 votes went to Hard William D. Murphy; independent reformer John Murphy had 350 votes. The Hard vote cost Tweed the election, just as it did Horatio Seymour, who ran for governor.

Years later, at the time of Tweed's death, Fox recalled the campaign as a very exciting one conducted with unusual energy. Democrats had attempted to "count" Fox votes on election night, but he marshaled his friends in strong force and at midnight marched to the "Hook," Tweed's stronghold, and frightened the inspectors into "decency." Where was history's all-powerful Tweed? Anyway, could Tweed really have changed the results? The times were against it and wasn't the story told after Tweed's death just that, a story?[8]

Tweed's old congressional seat went to a Know-Nothing, Thomas R. Whitney. Soft Abraham J. Berry, Tweed's replacement, ran a poor last. Could Tweed have done much better? Possibly, but only if Hards and Softs united. Fernando Wood barely defeated his Know-Nothing opponent and only because there was a reform candidate in the field.

Several conclusions seem clear. Again, Tweed, while a force in the party, was only a minor one. Political power, omnipresent power, did not exist at least as held by a single party. This was true for Tammany, Know-Nothings, Whigs and reformers. New York politics was again distinguished by its fractured quality, divided among various groups, cliques, interests. It was like a three-ring circus, in the 1854 election a five-ring circus, though Tammany had one of the larger rings. Combination and coalition was the road to success. Tweed's defeat was not necessarily a personal one. Four of the six incumbent representatives were defeated or were not renominated. Again, this was in the nature of the New York political game—something like musical chairs. So intense were political contests, so lacking was party discipline, few city congressmen or even state legislators ever succeeded themselves. Shifting political sands move quickly and are not a secure base on which to build personal power. In New York's case, it was a disaster, as few of its politicians could build enough seniority in national or state office to have the city and its interests taken seriously. The cosmopolitanism of New York, its "melting pot" quality, ensured political weakness. Obviously, the struggle for power and some kind of political unity was essential to Tammany as it was to the city and to Tweed.

7

A Small Victory

A cold, wet New Year welcomed the new mayor's administration. It was not a cheerful time. New Yorkers were warned of hall thieves—men who enter a home on a pretext and if left alone for a moment make off with hats, overcoats or gold-headed canes. "Our windows should grow tighter and our doors more secure, as the times grow harder," was a warning sentiment. Poverty and crime whistled through New York streets like a chill wind. Raymond suggested organizing an Emigrant Employment Society and moving paupers into the interior of New York and the nation in a kind of "go West, young man." If this did not work, then "sturdy beggars" should be compelled to work. Why should those who work support the idle and indolent? The ever growing number of immigrant poor dramatized virulent anti-foreign sentiment, while fear of violence and the harangues of street angels made New Yorkers tread carefully.[1]

Yet, Mayor Wood, tall and handsome, made a good impression. His forthright inaugural and his demand for good government struck a responsive chord. He demanded the highest devotion to duty from each individual in the police force. He asked reports on all uncleaned streets, houses of prostitution, public places which kept open on the Sabbath, gambling dens, street encumbrances and in short, any violations of city ordinances. Police were asked to rid the streets of drunks, loiterers, beggars and all manner of nuisance. He also outlined a proper fiscal program promising to end expenditures not "purely devoted to the public want." He promised to curb the entry of criminals and paupers from foreign countries.

Wood began a "Black Book" where complaints received from citizens would be noted and acted upon. Hundreds of notices of theft, nuisances and the like were processed. It was a mixed bag. One R. Platt complained of boys who played ball on Sundays in Franklin Square and of others who congregated on Broome Street, especially on Sunday, and insulted the passers-by, "even ladies." J. H. Maynard told Wood of the "loafers" on Fourteenth Street and Irving Place and the theft of a "very valuable cow." James Turner complained of a bookseller from whom he purchased an obscene book, entitled *The Mysteries of Venus; or the Amatory Life and Adventures of Miss Kitty Pry*. A police raid netted a collection of books of a "truly revolting nature." These were presented in the mayor's office to alert Wood to the evil of pornography. A grand jury, whose foreman was James Harper, met with Wood and lauded his intention to enforce law, especially those referring to the observance of the Sabbath. Pleased by the meeting and approval of his position, Wood pledged increased devotion to law and order. If he proved negligent, he expected "unflinching and vigorous impeachment." Shortly afterward, the *Times* took pleasure in sturdy blows dealt by Wood and police against saloonkeepers and gamblers. Other proposals by Wood, however, ran up against opposition. Streetsweeping machines like those operating in London were utilized. They looked like threshers on which brooms were installed in an endless chain. A number of men went before the machine clearing more difficult obstruction. Innocent as it was, workingmen, "Huge Paws," denounced the "degrading" invention which deprived honest men of their jobs. A mass meeting held in the park on August 1 held political overtones. Congressman Mike Walsh and other Hards were among the leaders criticizing the police-like character of the administration. One faction's appeasement is another faction's treason. It is a law of the city, as Wood quickly found out. The machines were destroyed.[2]

The cleanup of the city was particularly directed against "Nymphs of the Pave." During one day in May, about sixty streetwalkers were hauled into court. The youngest was sixteen, the oldest forty-eight. Most were less than twenty-one. Thirty-four were from Ireland, sixteen born in the United States. Some of the women arrested claimed they were innocent seamstresses, or servants, walking quietly to their jobs. One girl swallowed laudanum after protesting innocence, saying she would rather die than live disgraced.

This raid was the result, at least in part, of the *Time*'s morality drive and the demand that the "indecent parade of miserable women" through the city be stopped. The irate paper found that "From Chambers Street to Canal, at night, these public pests flaunt their gay clothing and painted faces under every lamp facing even honest females without quailing, and stand upon every corner tempting youth to their ruin." A little booklet, "Guide to the Harem or Directory to the Ladies of Fashion in New York and various other cities for 1855," written by an "old man of twenty-five," probably one Charles DeKock, rated the attractions of "houses," most along Mercer Street, for prospective visitors. Sex and what to do about it occupied almost everyone, some not enough. Police were seen talking and laughing with the "nymphs," instead of making arrests. But at the same time, the *Times* condemned the periodic arrest of prostitutes—men and women—for the express purpose of lining the pockets of lawyers or bail bondsmen. Such practices corrupted the law and law enforcement and should be abolished.

Wood's reform program had many objectives, one to keep Albany away from City Hall and preserve home rule. Secondly, if Wood could reform the city, leaders of the community, the Astors, Lorilards, Lenoxes, Harpers, might support him and his ambitions. Despite his party affiliation, Wood was held in high regard, and was often characterized as a "bold, fearless" leader, the "right sort of man" to bring good government to New York. He was better than any charter amendment. For a time during the honeymoon, the *Times* even attacked the state legislature. In one instance, it decided the legislature was helping the gas monopoly "grind the poor and pay the rich" through higher and higher prices.[3] The *Times* asked for an investigation. It didn't happen.

Several events occurred in the city which served to remind New Yorkers that some deep-rooted problems remained even with the best of mayors. One was the sensational murder of Bill Poole, known as the "Stanwix Hall" homicide. Poole, a popular figure, was a pugilist, a nativist and altogether a New York character. He died on March 8, 1855, at age thirty-three as the result of a saloon brawl which took place in February. One Louis Barker had allegedly shot him. Poole reportedly murmured "I die a true American" just before his end. He became a martyred hero. A gambler, whose friends were the "dregs of society," Poole received a funeral which was as sensational as his death. Six thousand persons and fifty-five carriages joined members of the William Poole Association and Order of United Americans on a procession down Broadway past draped buildings to Greenwood Cemetery and interment.

Stanwix Hall, a saloon with hotel attached, was often visited by local toughs. The affair started when Irish-born John Morrissey, a pugilist, later congressman and saloonkeeper extraordinary, and Poole met late in February in the hall. Morrissey sneered at Poole, "You are a pretty American fighting son of a bitch." Poole put his finger to his nose. Words followed and Morrissey produced a five-barreled pistol. Police broke up the ominous scene. Soon after, Morrissey and his friends, including Barker, pursued Poole. When he returned to the hall, the quarreling continued, and Poole was shot. Dr. John M. Carnochan, later Tweed's physician, found Poole had been wounded several times and had a pistol bullet in his heart. Morrissey, Louis Barker and a number of others were present at the shooting. A coroner's jury heard detailed accounts of the event. Witnesses were vague and confused, but after lengthy deliberation, the coroner's jury accused only Barker of murder. A number of others were considered accessories. Morrissey was accused of assault with intent to kill.

After a long chase sponsored and paid for by the city, ending in the Canary Islands, Barker was returned to New York. He as well as others were indicted. A. Oakey Hall was now district attorney. The long trial produced conflicting testimony, but it was clear Poole also had a pistol, and possbily had wounded Barker. No one was really quite sure who did what to whom, except that Poole was dead. The jury disagreed over the verdict and all concerned were set free. The Poole murder, one of those unsolved crimes, pointed up at least to the reformer the low state of morality and the high state of crime and corruption in the city. Wood's star began to fall.

A trial of P. T. Barnum in May for allegedly violating the person of a married woman who had visited his museum on Ann Street did little to clean up the moral atmosphere even though the case was dismissed as an extortion attempt.[4] There was much to be made from reform. Everyone got into the act. In September, the Aldermanic Investigation Committee of Malpractice in the Police Department headed by John Briggs went into action. It was essentially a trifling affair, though the hurrah was great. Witnesses were asked if drapery used in the Clay funeral was privately appropriated and whether politics entered into certain department appointments. Nothing was uncovered. However, later in the month, six members of the council were arrested for bribery and corruption involving the funeral. Interestingly, James Harper provided $2,500 bail for Alderman Samuel H. Moser, one of those indicted. Two councilmen resigned their office. The accused went before Justice James Roosevelt in Oyer and Terminer. Hall was the prosecuting attorney. During the trial, the grand jury handed down other indictments against City Judge Sidney H. Stewart, also basically for bribery and conspiracy. After a very involved battle, a lot of smoke, no fire, all were freed as the jury could not agree.[5] Innocent or not, the entire affair left city government open to more suspicion. One result was that Hall made a name for himself, though he was not particularly successful in court. A graduate of New York University and student for a year at Harvard Law School, a Whig by persuasion, he considered himself a legal scholar and frequently asked for reform of the criminal justice system. He also often lectured on such literary subjects as "The Proper Study of Mankind Is Man." Hall's name was increasingly before the public.[6] New Yorkers also found other names coming before them.

On May 17, 1855, Jews' Hospital, presently Mount Sinai, was opened at Twenty-eighth Street between Seventh and Eighth avenues. The event was celebrated by a large audience and distinguished guests. A synagogue located in a wing of the building was used for the opening ceremonies. A message was received from President Pierce. Lieutenant Governor Henry J. Raymond delivered a short speech on charity and benevolence. Albert Cardozo, then a young lawyer, commented on religious and political freedom. It was one of his first public appearances.[7]

The opening of the hospital was a sign of a changing New York. Not everyone liked the changes. What seemed a horde of inundating immigrants was a threat that one or a dozen hospitals could not avert. Some of these brought with them "alien" philosophies, such as those expounded by Karl Marx, while Catholics brought new reminders of papal conquests. Surely, these were times, as never before, for street angels and reformers to step forward and save the country. Again meetings, bonfires and torchlight parades reminded a free people to be constantly vigilant "against the insidious wills of foreign influence."

Then there was liquor. The "Maine (or Prohibition) Law" which was to take effect in New York July 4, 1855, brought plaudits from the *Times*, as it railed against Irish and German liquor dealers and inebriated Democratic politicians. Fernando Wood, while questioning the efficacy of the "Act for the Suppression of Intemperance, Pauperism and Crime," looked to the ballot box for its defeat. Until then he promised to uphold that law as he would any other. Others, however, felt morally committed. Lieutenant David Porter, commander of the United States storeship *Supply*, with agreement of the crew, shipped out without the traditional rum aboard. His "praiseworthy experiment will afford convincing proof that rum is not necessary to Jack's comfort or health," noted the *Times*.

There were other reactions. Liquor dealers meeting in April at Tammany Hall heard Isaiah Rynders rant as only he could at the mixing of politics and religion. Temperance, he insisted, was an individual decision and in many cases the use of liquor was a religious necessity. William Tweed appeared, but rarely, at such meetings. For Democrats, the temperance issue was almost too good to be true. Outside of the liquor issue, there was little unanimity among them. As in the past, Tammany and the Democratic Party was held together by spit and very little glue.[8] Liquor could be a very good bond.

The Democratic county convention to name candidates for city and state office held in the "Old Coal Hole," Tammany Hall, in October was, as usual, a head-butting affair. Tweed was called to preside and took the "seat of honor amidst the cheers and groans of the members." Perhaps no one else wanted the job of trying to control the noisy floor. It was impossible. Each faction broke off and selected its own slate of candidates. At least, Tweed did gain some recognition for his fruitless efforts. He was mentioned as a possible candidate for sheriff, as a Soft Tammany

Democrat. Thomas J. Barr, Peter Sweeney's father-in-law, a Hard Shell, was to be his opponent. In the end, and as usual, Tweed did not get the nomination for sheriff or any other position. It was just as well, as Know-Nothings and Whigs swept into office, winning the race for sheriff and comptroller, together with fourteen of twenty-two council seats. The 1855 election was a notable victory for the anti-Democrats, continuing the trend of the preceding year. While Whigs and nativists were a potent force, it was still the inability of Democrats to unite which contributed most to their defeat.

Suddenly the tide changed. As quick as the rise of Know-Nothingism, so fast was its decline. Temperance, too, quickly lost its impetus. As anticipated, the "Maine Law" was declared unconstitutional by the New York Court of Appeals, as the ever growing and menacing issue of slavery crowded the Know-Nothings off the front pages. That group gradually was swallowed up by the newly established Republican Party, which included in its fold Whigs and reformers. For Democrats, political schism was not as easily solved. For Tweed, political oblivion continued to be his lot, with his time spent at his chairmaking business and with his family. There was a small opening politically when Tweed attended a two-day state convention in Syracuse on July 29–30, 1855. He was named a secretary at the meeting. Calls to unite against bigotry and fanaticism were cheered, committees were established and balloting taken for nomination for governor. At an informal ballot, Wood emerged as a leading candidate. However, Wood's name was withdrawn, despite the loyalty of city delegates who stood as a block behind him. Augustus Schell, a former port collector, although receiving more votes than Wood, also exited, Sweeney making the announcement. Horatio Seymour, unable to capture the city votes bowed out as nondescript Amasa J. Parker was nominated for the office. Democrats were so divided that the best candidates were left by the wayside. The city again was the loser. Tweed's role on the first day was limited to calling the roll during voting. On the second day, he was more active, as were events at the convention. Hard John Cochrane asked for an amendment on the method of choosing the electoral ticket. Tweed objected to the suggestion that a committee from each congressional district settle the state electorals. He was not willing to give his right of choosing an elector to any man. However, after some debate, the amendment was carried. Perhaps to mollify him, Tweed was put on the Electoral Committee representing the Fifth Congressional District.

While the convention passed resolutions supporting the national slate, such unity was not apparent on the city level. Cochrane attempted by a change in rules to deny Wood renomination for mayor, but Wood survived the challenge. Tweed was mentioned as a possible candidate, but his candidacy was not seriously considered by anyone. It was not expected that he could carry even the Seventh Ward if he somehow managed to run against Wood. Tweed really was of no matter. There was a more serious challenge now, when ex-alderman James E. Libby, who aided by John Cochrane and Sweeney at a "Custom House convention" vowed to gain the mayoralty from Wood. They charged Wood with being angry because of his defeat for the gubernatorial nomination and now hatching a secret scheme using illegal means, such as employing city policemen, to defeat his enemies. Woodites answered that Cochrane, the heart of the opposition, was a nephew of the hated abolitionist Gerrit Smith and secretly committed to that party.

Before the schism became more serious, an accommodation was reached between Cochrane and Wood. Cochrane received a congressional nomination with Wood's approval and Wilson Small, corporation counsel and a Cochrane supporter, was chosen chairman of Tammanyite's Democratic-Republican Committee to replace Lorenzo Shepard, who had recently died. In return, Cochrane backed Wood. Libby was left high and dry to run as an independent. At the nominating convention, Tweed received five votes for the mayoralty nomination to Wood's one hundred and the latter's nomination was made unanimous. Tweed had seen this before.

Unreconciled Hards like Sweeney, Barr and Smith Ely, Jr., remained unconvinced by the supposed unanimity for Wood's candidacy. The Cochrane "deal" and what seemed an obvious "indecent" abuse of power by Wood—as when at a Wood ratification meeting in Tammany Hall a small but noisy Libby faction was forcibly thrown into the street by exuberant "shoulder hitters"—stirred protest against the mayor.

Such protests came at a bad time for Democrats, especially as there was a new but strong Republican Party to contend with. Though denounced as "Nigger Worshippers" and "trouble makers," they had won the support of Raymond, Greeley, Oakey Hall, David D. Field and a host of the most influential men in the city, Democrats included. Opposition to the extension of slavery, the threat of rebellion and mob rule as an outgrowth of the "peculiar institution," the alliance of the Democracy with immigrants and corrupt leadership with the slavocracy—these were the principal reasons for joining the new Republicans. The party's standard-bearer, army officer and explorer John C. Frémont, was a resident of New York.

These were confusing but stirring times—music, banners, parades, speeches and fights filled the streets as New Yorkers went to the polls. Buchanan with 42,000 votes carried the city comfortably over Frémont, who had 18,000, and Millard Fillmore, the ex-President, who received

20,000 as the Know-Nothing candidate. Amasa Parker carried the city but lost the state. Sickles and Cochrane were elected to Congress as Democrats regained control of the city. Wood defeated the Know-Nothing Isaac O. Barker, his principal opponent, 35,000 to 25,000. The Seventh went heavily for Wood. Way down on the list was Libby—so much for the challenge. Charley Fox, probably much to Tweed's satisfaction, was defeated. For Tweed, too, there was a victory of sorts. He was elected for a two-year term to the Board of Education. Of so little import was the job that the political affiliation of the members were not listed on returns, as it was of "no consequence." The same could be said of the Board itself. It was a minor post and a minor victory, but Tweed was alive and kicking —though barely. Interestingly, elected to the Board at the same time were attorneys Andrew H. Green and Nelson J. Waterbury. They would have a chance to know each other.

There was a rumor that Richard B. Connolly, now city clerk, would be a candidate for clerk of the House of Representatives, but this it was felt would be denied him in "consequence of an imperfection of voice, that would prevent his being heard or understood at any considerable distance from his person." Perhaps this imperfection, not often noted, kept Connolly from expanding his political horizon.[9]

8

Panic

Re-election as mayor was one thing, carrying out the duties of office was something else. Wood was forever plagued with eternal divisions in the party and new difficulties with the Republican-controlled state government. Wood's regime lost its steam and direction, the final blow being a severe economic disaster toward the end of 1857. Wood might have wanted reform, might have wished for an end to crime and corruption, but both continued unabated; as Wood's desire for a greater city fell apart so did his hopes for political advancement.

The Republican-controlled legislature on April 15, 1857, passed a bill establishing a five-member Board or Commission of Police to be appointed by the governor with the approval of the Senate to direct police activities in a new Metropolitan police district including the counties of New York, Brooklyn, Richmond and Westchester. This so that it would not seem to be directed only against New York, which it was. The mayors of New York and Brooklyn were named ex officio members of the Board with the power to suspend policemen for misconduct. Only the Board could try the accused. A new Metropolitan Police Force, modeled in part after those in London and Paris, where heads of state made appointments to police, was thus created. The cities of Brooklyn and New York were taxed to raise necessary funds, but would have little say in the operation of the department.

This law was reportedly the brain child of District Attorney A. Oakey Hall operating from "Parlor headquarters of the Republican junta" in the Astor House. The purpose of the reform in addition to more efficient police work was obviously to contain Wood's power and the city's independence and especially to reduce Democratic control.

That the aim of the new law was Republican control of the city was also evident. There was opposition. What was needed was not more state

57

boards, but a charter giving the mayor and Common Council greater power, suggested the cross-eyed James G. Bennett, as he sided with Wood, who had fought the bill in the legislature as a violation of the rights of the city.[1]

On April 21, on the city's application, former corporation counsel Henry E. Davies, now justice of the Supreme Court, issued an injunction restraining the commissioners from assuming jurisdiction over the existing Municipal Police. Wood also received the support of Police Chief George Matsell and most police captains. He informed them that he intended to carry on and execute all his duties as mayor including his police power—at least until the court decided otherwise. Still the new Commissioners of Police met, elected Simeon Draper, a long-time merchant and Republican, as president and awaited developments. The lines were drawn. Diarist Strong acidly felt it was a struggle "between two gangs" over who would control the plunder. Bennett heatedly charged the "nigger-worshipping, spoils seeking legislature," with denying the people of the city a voice in their own interest. The commissioners impatiently dismissed Matsell. George Walling, another career policeman, was put in his place as new policemen were appointed, others dismissed. Members of the council and Board of Supervisors argued and argued, tempers were strained.

By May after long legal debate before three justices of the Supreme Court, it was determined that the state did have "supreme authority" over the executive functions of the municipality. Councilmen nevertheless supported Wood and the "ancient" right of the city to establish a police force. The colonial Dongan and Montgomerie charters were read and reread as people in the streets argued constitutional issues involving state government versus municipal authority as the case went to the Court of Appeals. Sixty municipal policemen were dismissed on June 9 by the commissioners, who were assuming complete control. On the other hand, Wood also dismissed several policemen, leaning toward the Metropolitans. The police had to choose as to their loyalty. The old Locofoco and now police surgeon Dr. Stephen Hasbrouck refused to report to the commissioner's office on White Street. Municipal policemen ate at Tammany Hall.

Then an incident. On June 16, Daniel D. Conover, whom Strong referred to as a "dirty politician," was appointed by the state as street commissioner to fill the vacancy created by the incumbent's death. Wood, claiming the power to appoint such an officer, named another to the post. Wood's municipal policemen "hustled the governor's appointee out [of City Hall] neck and heels by manifestations of physical force." Conover applied to Justice Murray Hoffman of the Superior Court for an order of arrest against Wood and those who would not let him take possession of his office. Wood refused to accept the order. The warrant was then delivered to the Metropolitan Police for service. Fifty Metropolitans were assembled as loud cheers for Fernando Wood were given by a large but still just curious crowd. Everyone marched to City Hall. The scene became ugly. Every door was guarded. The iron gates around the historic building and park were closed. Ranks of Municipals ringed the hall. Metropolitans moved through shouting crowds, growing increasingly hostile, toward the back steps of the building. They were met by some two hundred Municipals aided by "a miscellaneous assortment of suckers, soaplocks, Irishmen and plug-uglies, officiating in a guerilla capacity." Clubs flashed, fists and feet flailed, as combatants tumbled about the steps. More Municipals arrived. The crowd hemmed in the beleaguered White Street forces. The Metropolitans broke, many managed to find refuge in City Hall, while the mob gleefully chased others through the park. Gangs such as "Plug Uglies" and "Dead Rabbits" had a field day in one of the most bizarre scenes in the city's history. No one was killed though many were seriously hurt. After the noonday riots, the warrant, now held by Sheriff James C. Willet, was given quietly to Wood. Wood accepted it, reasoning that it was delivered by a city officer. He would not accept process from a state officer. It was a face-saving explanation. Major General Charles W. Sandford of the New York State militia had announced that he would have used troops to bring Wood in if that had become necessary.

Wood's counsel applied for a writ of habeas corpus. Hearings were held before Abraham D. Russell in General Sessions. Despite Hall's objections, the writ was granted and the mayor freed. The *Herald* thought the incident and resultant legal battles examples of the "long chain of frauds, acts of violence, tricks and rascalities . . . which the Albany oligarchy was using to gain the city's money." Nevertheless, on July 2, the Court of Appeals by a 6 to 2 vote held the Municipal Police Act constitutional. Chief Judge Hiram Danio, a Democrat, wrote the majority opinion. It was a curious one upholding the state's authority as the source of police power, Danio noted that such specific legislation might not be constitutional if applied to one city, but when applied to several, it became clearly constitutional. He found another way out by stating that the "true remedy for unwise legislation is provided for in the constitution by the frequent renewal of the Legislature."[2]

If Metropolitans celebrated, others thumbed their noses and fists at the new law and order. Beginning on July 4, at least three major riots occurred. In the "Bloody ould Sixth Ward," Dead Rabbits and Bowery Boys revived an old feud, as police from the Sixth, Seventh, Thirteenth and Eighteenth wards were called to quell the fights. The area around Mott, Mulberry, Bayard and Elizabeth streets in the Bowery, the present-day

Chinatown, was for two days the scene of a whirling mass of stones, brick-bats, clubs and finally gunshots. Simeon Draper appealed to Sandford for military assistance. Police were helpless. Barricades and bloodshed were the order of the day. Casualties for these riots conservatively were estimated at eight killed and forty-three wounded.

A few days later, on July 12, Germans of the Seventeenth Ward attacked Metropolitan Police after long-simmering tempers reached a boiling point with the alleged killing by police of a German immigrant, one John Miller. Germans held a mass protest meeting of three thousand at the time of Miller's funeral, under a banner reading "Victim of the Metropolitan Police." There was an ugly mood. Mutterings of revenge were heard. Police made themselves scarce. Slowly tempers cooled, but the Metropolitans kept away from Avenue A and Twelfth Street, the heart of the German area. With the military on the alert and feeling against police brutality and the Metropolitans high, like Gilbert and Sullivan's bobby, the New York policeman's lot was not a happy one.[3]

If the state had not interfered, would the riot have occurred? Possibly not, but the riots were a disaster to Wood and his ambitions. They hardened opposition to the city self-government and to Wood's leadership. Of course, the *Times* argued, as always, that violence, murder and crime were such that some outside control was necessary. A gruesome incident emphasized the "truth" of this view. Sometime during the evening of January 30, 1857, Dr. Harvey Burdell, a dentist who lived at 31 Bond Street, was murdered. His body, covered with blood from at least fifteen deep knife wounds, was discovered by an apprentice. Burdell had been strangled, as well as viciously stabbed. Obviously, someone did not like him. For months New Yorkers read of the details. A one-thousand-dollar reward was offered for the capture of the murderer. A clairvoyant was called in to aid the coroner's jury at their inquest. The finger of suspicion pointed to a Mrs. Cunningham, who resided in the house on Bond Street with two daughters and two sons. Two men, both residents, named Echel and Snodgrass, were also thought involved. The noted Whig and Know-Nothing Daniel Ullman also lived in the house. Mrs. Cunningham was supposedly the secret wife of Burdell. A grand jury indicted Mrs. Cunningham and Echel for the murder and Snodgrass as an accessory on February 14. District Attorney Hall tried the case in the Court of Oyer and Terminer, but after a sensational and lurid trial, the Victorian kind, the accused were found not guilty, much to the approval of all who attended the hearings. In August, Mrs. Cunningham went through a sham accouchement, and asked for Burdell's estate, alleging her "baby" was his. She went before the surrogate, but he decided against her, and Burdell's estate became public property. His murderer or murderers were never found.

The murders of Sarah Bloom, a young girl with "long blonde hair," and of another young girl bludgeoned to death in Richmond were added to the list of unsolved crimes. The *Times* warned women to "stay at home nights, nor stray with anyone not known well. The New York murderer must be guarded against more cautiously than a wild beast. He is more brutal than the English ruffian, more treacherous than the Irish murderer, more vindictive than the Spanish Navo, more cowardly than the Asiatic assassin." There was still more. New Yorkers also read of a serious prison revolt at Sing Sing. Guards were beaten, and many prisoners attempted escape. The fortress of law and order was under heavy siege; strong hands were needed to man the ramparts. Many looked for a return to the "good old days" of peace and quiet. It was 1857.[4]

The police riots, the failure of Wood and even the Metropolitans to solve the crime problem took on an added measure of importance when in September a financial panic brought on by overspeculation began and brought with it fear of more social disaster. Hundreds of businesses failed, banks went under and tens of thousands became unemployed. Given the unrest in New York, this was all that was needed. Debate followed and causes were examined, but for the poor something other than debates was wanted. A Workingmen's Association was founded. Signs saying simply "Work" in English and "Arbeit" in German were paraded through the city and carried at large protest meetings at City Hall and Tompkins Square. City government was called upon to carry out public works programs or face the horror of mob rule; Central Park benefited. Legislation fortuitously passed in April 1857 now allowed thousands to be engaged in building its lakes, roads and structures. Since the park provided an excellent safety valve, the council approved appropriations for $250,000 for use in construction.[5]

Wood's troubles with the state were intensified by unrest within the Democracy. The Libby faction often met in the offices of Peter Sweeney to develop plans to replace Wood. Although other Democrats moved to form new coalitions, Wood continued to maintain control of city patronage, while "Sweeney and Company" could count on federal appointments in the post office, customhouse and the like. Wilson G. Small, chairman of the Democratic-Republican General Committee and a Wood adherent, attacked the use of federal patronage, and Daniel Sickles, in particular, for "illiberal and unfair" manipulations. He pointed out that John A. Kennedy, the brother of Tammanyite William D. Kennedy, was Republican Thurlow Weed's right-hand man in the Emigrant Department at Castle Garden, and that most Libbyites, like Kennedy, flirted with "Black Republicans" and sought to embarrass Wood. John Kelly, calling Sickles and sachem Isaac Fowler traitors, charged them with siding with the Republican Seward in order to get Fowler the postmaster's job. Wood was finally outmaneuvered by the combination of Fowler, Sweeney and Libby, with possible aid, it was suspected, from Republicans like Seward and A. Oakey Hall. A schism was there, and Wood lost control of the party. Democrats met in Syracuse in September 1857 to determine the ticket in the off-year election. Woodites shared with Libbyites in representing New York City. Debate in the convention centered on the nomination for the Court of Appeals. Woodites were anxious to defeat Judge Danio, who was backed by the Sweeney group. Despite Wood's anger, Danio was renominated. To many in the city, it was a blow at an independent judiciary, as well as an obvious defeat for Wood and his fight for an independent municipality. Wood had lost a round, but not necessarily the war.

But in October the mayor lost even more control when at a lengthy meeting held at the hall, nominations for various positions went to those opposing him. The meeting, which went past midnight, also finally produced six nominations for the Board of Supervisors. Though the title was an old one, charter revisions passed in April, in fact, created a new Board which assured Republican representation, but divided the municipality into two segments consisting of city and county governments. Also, legislative control of at least a part of the city's finances was obtained. It would have a fateful effect upon Tweed's future and, while a pretty piece of party expediency, it was harmful to New York. Tweed, now a member of the Democratic-Republican General Committee, Tammany's steering assembly, although not yet officially a member of the Tammany Society, was one of the nominees. For Tweed, who except for the Board of Education post had been out of office for a year, it was an opportunity to come out of the darkness. The Board of Supervisors, at this time composed of twelve men representing both parties equally, was a watchdog committee overlooking the finances of the county. The Board was half elected and half appointed, the latter from a list of defeated candidates. A vote of the majority of the Board was necessary to pass on county expenditures. Supervisors served without pay. It was an important job, but not a sensitive one. It was mostly an honorary reward for service.

Despite his reversals, Wood received the nomination for mayor. He remained popular with many members of the Democracy. Among them was Thomas Francis Meagher, the Irish patriot, who declared that only the "professional friend of the negro and the mortal enemy of the Roman Catholic" was opposed to Wood. But also nominated for office were Wood's opponents Peter B. Sweeney for district attorney and George G. Barnard for recorder. Democrats achieved victory in state contests held in

November, electing all their candidates to state office, but the municipal election held December 1 was a different matter. Daniel Tiemann, who had been a Hard Democrat, ran as a Republican Whig for mayor and was successful as he received the support of unreconciled Libbyites like Sweeney, Fowler and Tilden. The selection of Tiemann was supposedly Hall's idea. Wood's promise, which had shone so brightly, was now tattered and dull, though the Democracy put on the usual display of bands and fireworks in support of its "Champion of Municipal Rights" and the "Workingmen's Friend."

While Wood was defeated much to the delight of the Libbyites, Democrats still controlled the council and numerous city offices. Peter Sweeney defeated Daniel Ullman for district attorney, and their six candidates for supervisors, Tweed included, were elected. Interestingly though, Tweed had the lowest vote of any Democrat—about one thousand less than his peers. He also ran behind Wood and Tiemann in his own Seventh Ward.[6] Tweed's name was obviously not a household word.

9

The Bible

The hot potato of city government was now Daniel Tiemann's, and it was more than he had bargained for. A change in administration did not lessen the difficulty of running the growing but beleaguered metropolis. With increasing population and greater pressures upon existing services, the mayor's office was no picnic. The need for good housing to overcome the fast-spreading blight of slums and squalid tenements, for parks, schools, police and fire protection and means of mass transportation made life for those in public office generally a less than pleasing one. Added to the burdens of officials was the universally accepted stereotype of the corrupt politician leading a corrupt city. Daily charges of fraud filled the air; it was catnip to the press. In February 1858 barbs were aimed at Charles Devlin, earlier appointed street commissioner by Republican Governor John King. Devlin, however, was denied office as an investigation of the Street Department was held. Allegations were made that money was paid for uncompleted work and that contractors were paid for inflated bills. For example, the flagging of Fifty-fourth Street should have cost $100, but a bill was submitted for $325. By April 12, Devlin officially gave up the battle for the office. Wise man.

James B. Smith, a clerk in the comptroller's office, was next. He was arrested and tried in General Sessions before Recorder Barnard. The comptroller of the Finance Department, Azariah C. Flagg, said Smith defrauded the city by manipulating books. Smith, basically responsible for adjusting claims for work done for the Street and Croton Aqueduct departments, was held by Barnard in $5,000 bail on a count of forgery. Eventually, Smith was cleared, but a point had been made; evil lived well in New York. The Board of Aldermen held its own hearings on frauds involved with paving and flagging city streets. While examples of padding were frequent, the looseness of record keeping and auditing also became clear as a pattern emerged of poor supervision and unchecked fraud. The Board issued a report warning of improper bookkeeping, destruction of vouchers and warrants and "extreme disorder" prevailing in the comptroller's office. It found that assessments were never collected, and in addition, overpayments were made for work performed. As an example, a surveyor found 35,000 cubic yards of earth were removed for a street opening, yet the contractor was paid for removing 60,000 cubic yards. The Board recommended reorganization of the Finance and comptroller's departments. This would be repeated in some twenty years. The *Herald* and *Times*, undoubtedly buoyed by the report, campaigned anew against rising taxes and deteriorating services. It cost $8 million a year, "a pretty large sum for a city so miserably mis-governed as this," and still there are "dirty streets, rampant rowdyism, scarcity of water and no parks."[1]

The *Times's* obsession with extravagance in public expenditure was at times extreme. It disapproved a gift of fifteen hundred dollars to Dr. W. T. G. Morton, discoverer of ether used as an anesthesia. It was a betrayal of public trust for the governors of the almshouse to scatter money in this way. "Why not give money to the descendants of Jenner or Harvey?" Raymond lauded president of the governors Washington Smith for his refusal to sign the check.[2]

Violence in the city, as well as in the country, of course remained a favorite subject of discussion. John Morrissey again made news when he defeated John Heenan, the "Benicia Boy," for the "Championship of America." A reported quarter of a million dollars was waged on the test. Bloodletting had its reward and sold newspapers. Though the *Times* found the spectacle, which was held in Canada, a "triumph of brutality," it hypocritically gave a long account of the entire affair, gore and all.[3]

Then there was another kind of "brutality." In November, policeman Robert Cairnes while taking into custody one Hollis, "a man of desperately bad character," was struck by his captive, who then broke loose and ran away. Cairnes followed; Hollis was caught by a passer-by. The policeman came up and shouted, "You will get away from me, will you?" and shot him in the back. Hollis died within minutes. "Was it murder?" The *Times* held that while the power of the police was great, that power had responsibility. Escape is not punishable by death, without trial, evidence or sentence. Hollis should not have been killed. Moreover, there was another issue. The police have no right to act as judge and jury in trying to catch escapees or in making arrests. After citing examples of the use of guns by police, the *Times* maintained that police were not using pistols for self-defense, but to stop men from running away; "they are considered substitutes for swift feet and long arms." True, they dealt with a "savage set of ruffians," but they have training, numbers and clubs. If that was not

65

sufficient, let the law remedy the situation. Surely, the death during the year of four police officers illustrated the difficulty of the job, but also the uselessness of firearms. An interesting point of view.

Cairnes was held in $10,000 bail, but the grand jury dismissed the complaint and endorsed the action of the policeman as being "perfectly proper." Some felt that Hollis was a noted villain and rejoiced in his death. If he had been arrested for assault, he would have probably been set free by some magistrate. It was dangerous logic. To the *Times*, such sentiment clearly demonstrated the bankruptcy of law and order and local government. There is no other country in the world where an officer or justice could make and execute law, and where public morality was so degraded as to approve this course of action. Cairnes was not to blame as much as conditions within the city, but the public must see the danger of giving every policeman the power of an absolute monarch armed with a pistol and the right to take life instantly without benefit of jury or law. But overall, social values in the city must change, government must become respected. Law, not anarchy, must be allowed to prevail. The *Times*'s reasoning was fruitless. Violence and the arming of policemen continued as a matter of course.[4]

Tweed commenced his turn as supervisor during the storm lashing against city government. Supervisors first met on January 4 in City Hall and commenced the year's business by electing Tammany sachem Elijah F. Purdy as president. Tweed was one of the tellers. He was placed on a committee to revise rules. The Board met infrequently, did routine work and raised at this time little comment.[5] Tweed's role was minimal. This was not the case with the Board of Education, which now found itself in the middle of a bitter issue involving the role of religion in public education. Tweed reached for his other hat.

Created in 1842, there were forty-four non-paid Commissioners of Common Schools, two from each ward. William Tweed and Daniel Coger represented the Seventh Ward. Tweed was on two standing committees, Normal Schools and School Furniture, the latter of some use to him, as he sold a few chairs to the city. There were about one hundred primary schools plus three colored primary schools. Several thousand teachers and clerical workers supervised 150,000 pupils.

The Board first met in 1858 on January 15, and elected William H. Neilson president. In a brief address, he asked greater attention be given to hiring of teachers, as too much trouble resulted from using the young and inexperienced. The *Times* had its own message and warned of the past delinquency of the Board, which was composed of people "utterly unfitted by ignorance, or degraded and immoral character for the post." It warned of extravagance in a budget of over $200,000, and charged members with enriching themselves at public expense. The Board, the *Times* continued, was made up of opportunists, fanatics and corrupt politicians "selling their friends and their principles for the smallest mess of pottage." They were "second, third and fourth class hacks who should be in the pupils' seats rather than directing them." The journal wanted the Board to be appointed by the mayor rather than elected.

However, the explosive issue proved to be not extravagance or ignorance, but the Bible and nativism. The practice of reading daily portions of the Bible in public schools had not been enforced so that many schools omitted that procedure. On November 14, a pro-Protestant Bible convention asked that the Board direct mandatory daily reading. Chief opponents to the readings, done from the King James Version, were Roman Catholics, who the *Times* felt had always been opposed to the system of free education and were creating an issue to destroy the public school system. The paper observed that Democrats had elected Irish Catholics as officers in many of the ward schools and it objected to putting the system under the control of its "open and armed enemies." Bible reading, the Protestant version, was a good moral practice and not offensive to any Christian.

The *Times* now riveted its attention to upcoming elections for the Board. Tweed received special scrutiny and was labeled a thoroughgoing partisan of Tammany who was believed to be of Irish descent, though a native of the city, a supposition in the case of ancestry that was untrue but was in keeping with what the *Times* passed as fact. It found Tweed's position as a supervisor and member of the Board of Education an "obnoxious impropriety" since Tweed would be in a position to revise on one Board what was passed by another. Tweed, as a member of a Committee on By-Laws, helped draft a compromise report issued on November 27 on the question of Bible reading. This suggested that control over reading be left to local officials, since there was no law which authorized the Board to require it "against the wishes of the local authorities," although it recommended that such a practice was "healthful moral training" and should be continued "without vote or comment." But the whole Board issued its own report signed by Tweed and twenty-eight others, which directed reading of the Bible in all schools. It said nothing of local control.

Tweed was defeated for re-election. William D. Andrews, owner of an iron yard on Henry Street, strongly in favor of compulsory recitation, was put in his place. Possibly Tweed's defeat was a result of his backing off on the Bible issue, but the four other members of the committee, who took the same position, won. Still, only four of twenty-two Tammany Democrats won their contests, including Andrew H. Green. The remaining victors were five Woodites, one anti-Tammany Democrat, four Republicans and seven Know-Nothings plus one independent Democrat. Twenty-two members of the Board were holdovers. For Tweed, it was still another setback. The elections reflected the dissension and weakness within the Democracy which obviously hurt Tweed in his bid to retain what was essentially a minor post.[6]

Although Tweed did comparatively little while a member of the Board, during later years when he became state senator and one of the leaders of Tammany he was able to accomplish a great deal toward the modernization of the school system and the execution of "reforms unequalled during the nineteenth century." These included aid to parochial schools, founding a normal college, prohibition of corporal punishment, health inspection, introduction of German as a required subject in grammar schools, salary increases for teachers and at least an attempt to modernize curriculum. In pushing through these programs, Tweed came under severe criticism, a criticism which helped provide a proper atmosphere for his ultimate destruction. With the fall of Tweed, much of his enlightened policy was abolished including the prohibition of corporal punishment. But this was in the future.[7]

The party was split in previous years, but now it was completely disorganized. All the old factions—Wood, Libby, Shell—were again at each other's throats. What made things even more difficult was the national inability to solve the crucial slavery issue. This indecision was reflected in ward politics. For example, Wood and Tammany again both sent their delegations to the state conventions held in September in Syracuse. "Warhorse" Elijah Purdy had his delegation seated while Wood and his group were thrown out of the convention. It did not heal party schism.

At the county convention in October, the fighting continued.

Sickles, now close to Tammany, called Wood a "prude recreant," while Wood held Sickles responsible for conducting a filthy campaign against him. The bitterness was deep. The chief office to be nominated by the convention was county clerk. Tweed received a few votes, but the overwhelming number of votes went to John Clancy, a newspaperman and alderman. Tweed again had lost. Thrown another bone, he was renominated as a member of the Board of Supervisors, a nomination which was tantamount to election under the electoral procedure for the Board.[8]

Tweed had a chance to forget his problems when he attended the wining and dining of the Philadelphia Hibernian Engine Company No. 1, as it visited New York on November 21 and 22. Members of Americus Engine Company No. 6 wearing silver badges of identification, without snarling tigers, were the hosts. The Philadelphians visited workhouses at Randall's Island and fire stations in the city. They visited Williamsburg and returned to a dinner at Mozart Hall. Tweed presided at the cheerful affair. Toasts were made to the President and to each other. It was the kind of event that perhaps had Tweed wishing he had remained a fireman.[9]

10

The Visitors

Occasionally there is in history a year when significant developments and odd twists and turns occur together. Such a time was 1776, and again 1859. Darwin published his *Origin of Species*, John Brown raided the arsenal at Harpers Ferry and the forces of European nationalism were abroad. New York was also caught up in powerful currents and strange events. Blondin, the fantastic aerialist, crossed Niagara Falls on a tightrope. Dan Sickles shot and killed Philip Barton Key, son of Francis Barton Key, in a duel. Sickles also supposedly seduced his own mother-in-law. Paul Morphy, America's first chess champion, was welcomed in New York after a triumphant tour through Europe which gained him immortality, as sales of chess sets zoomed. It was a passing fancy as an eccentric Morphy quickly faded into oblivion along with the sale of sets.

Finally, and anticlimactically, Tweed became a member of Tammany. On September 5, 1859, he and twenty-one others were admitted to the society. The event attracted no attention, it raised no eyebrows, but for Tweed it was a significant step. He had traveled his own tightrope and had made the big ball team. It was his time of decision. It was so for others. Interestingly a month later on October 4, Albert Cardozo became a member. Sweeney had been inducted on November 22, 1856. Connolly was an old-timer, having become a member on October 21, 1839.[1] Officially part of the Tammany Society now, Tweed would be expected to deliberate on the direction of the Democracy, partake of patronage and generally have a voice in its affairs. Though a step up the ladder, this ladder had many loose rungs and was a very slippery perch. Since 1789, the society, originally a benevolent organization, had a long and very tempestuous history marked principally by intra-party squabbles and lack of discipline. Surely the careers of De Witt Clinton and Fernando Wood were testimony that Democrats, let alone Tammany, did not always control the city

—rivals, Federalists, Whigs, Republicans, Know-Nothings were many and influential. Newspapers like the *Times, Herald, Tribune* fed on the foibles and mistakes of Tammanyites and the society was rapidly becoming, if not already so, deservedly or not, a name synonymous with corruption and political bossism. While it had a degree of patronage from Democratic Presidents and the few Democratic governors, outside the city it had little power. Though Tammany spoke for many immigrant groups, especially Irish and German, issues such as Bible reading, temperance and nativism affected personal allegiance. One thing could be said of Tammany—it was not the solely dominant political party in the city. It was not so in 1859 or at any time back from its founding. It probably was not so even after 1859. New York City was too diverse, too big, too cosmopolitan to be governed by a single entity even if that entity was one-minded, which Tammany was not. New York might have been helped by a real Tammany machine.

Certainly, however, Tweed's political career in the city could be advanced by his membership in the society, even if it did not ensure him success. Why did Tammany want him? He had been a fireman, alderman, congressman and member of the Boards of Supervisors and Education, but he lost often enough to question his talent. He had not taken much part in party debate. He was something of an unknown quality. Still, he was experienced and had a certain amount of popularity. No scandal, except for the Carson incident, was attached to his name. He seemed honest, hard-working and loyal. He did not complain. Why not sign him on the team? There was need for staunch adherents, especially in view of the turbulence of the times.

And the times were threatening and foreboding. Slavery, states' rights and national union, talk of dismemberment of the country crowded closer to New York. Most politicians hoped that the slave question would disappear. Certainly this was true of Tammany Democrats. But it did not. The question was debated in the streets and in the newspapers. What of the slaves? Were they like "Uncle Tom," benign and loyal, or were they animals and cannibals? The latter view was most popular. Illustrative of a strident Negrophobia was a series of articles on the subject appearing in the *Herald*. One such was entitled "Pauperism among the Colored Population of New York" in which Bennett hoped "We trust our readers are not yet tired of the almighty nigger" and would be willing to read on. With the exception of a few merchants, like the restaurateur and oysterman Thomas Downing, he found the city's 10,807 blacks lived on charity or in almshouses, because they were inferior to whites. He noted also that the crime rate was double among blacks, but such crimes as embezzlement or forgery, which require a "high degree of intellectual development," were rare among them. The *Herald* placed a good deal of the problem on the shoulders of the abolitionists and "black Republicans," who sought more than could be accomplished. These strident anti-Negro editorials were used as a political weapon, not only in stirring up anti-Negro sentiment—feelings which were always close to the surface—but also in fostering pro-southern anti-Republican sentiment.[2]

While New Yorkers pondered race relations and prepared for the fall presidential elections, their interest was caught up in matters more spectacular, at least for the moment. Mayor Wood, once again in City Hall after surviving another difficult campaign, took up the old cudgels on behalf of home rule. He derided the numerous city departments which were self-directed and responsible to no one—a situation due, he felt, mainly to state interference. Wood also detailed in his inaugural a plan to reduce city expenditure and to increase revenue.[3]

But his plans for curtailment had to be altered, as groups of foreign dignitaries arrived to visit Gotham. Anyhow it took New Yorkers' minds off themselves even if it was expensive.

New York had witnessed many spectacles in its history—Lafayette, Kossuth and Jenny Lind, the "Swedish Nightingale," were among overseas visitors given the kind of reception only the city could offer. One of the most elaborate was that given for a group of Japanese headed by Crown Prince Tateish Onojero. They had arrived in the United States earlier in the year and visited Washington, Baltimore and Philadelphia, and then came to New York, the "capital of the country," on June 16, 1860. Preparations had been going on for weeks. Hotels were decked out, bands hired, halls made ready, entertainers waiting in the wings. It was to be a celebration in honor of "American diplomacy" and the "opening of the doors of the immense Treasury of the Far East." The Japanese, more commonly referred to as "Japs," arrived at the Battery during the day and were greeted by members of the council, detachments of police, the Veterans of 1776 and the War of 1812. Every house top, balcony, doorstep, lamppost was crowded with people. An exaggerated one half million, the time-honored estimate, waited to see the procession, and especially "Tommy," as the crown prince was affectionately referred to. A great favorite and center of attraction, "Tommy" was about seventeen years old and four feet high. Like the others, Morita Okataro, Governor of the Imperial Treasury, and Sinme No-Kami, Japanese Ambassador to the United States, he was dressed in colorful native costume. They ate food cooked by Japanese chefs. The excitement of the visitors as they gazed at their strange hosts was reciprocated by a vast army of New Yorkers. The procession proceeding from the Battery up Broadway to the park was huge. Policemen, militia, bands and hundreds of carriages, including those carrying "Tommy" and his party, paraded by. Ladies threw flowers. Banners, flags and bunting, colors of all hues bedecked the metropolis. At City Hall, Mayor Wood with city officials and their wives in attendance welcomed the Japanese, dressed in spotless "talmas" and "pyjamas." Also in attendance were Japanese and Dutch interpreters, the Dutch having been the first Europeans allowed into Japan, predating Americans by over two hundred years. Governor Edwin D. Morgan and Mayor Wood greeted the guests to the great City of New York which the mayor noted was like the Japanese city of Yedo (later Tokyo), with which it had special ties. Commodore Matthew Perry lived and died in New York, and Townsend Harris, first American representative to Japan, resided in New York. Wood desired ties of trade, amity and brotherhood. Ambassador No-Kami responded by stressing hope for lasting peace and friendship between the two nations. That evening and for days after, officials sat at sumptuous feasts and drank innumerable toasts. Crowds followed "Tommy" wherever he went. The *Herald* ran an article on the military power of "Japs" which it considered formidable.

It was a costly affair for the city. The bill at the Metropolitan Hotel, now run by Simeon Leland, came to $57,000, which included supper for nine thousand guests at three dollars a person, Brandy, champagne, sherry and "segars" consumed most of the rest of the cost. There were other charges totaling $7,854, generally to cover carriage hire.[4]

Following hard on the heels of the Japanese was the arrival on June 28 of the greatest ship then built, and the largest to be built for decades, the *Great Eastern*, a product of English shipyards and the somewhat eccentric engineer Isambard Brunel. Another English product, the Prince of Wales, Albert Edward, later Edward VII, son of Queen Victoria, arrived at Castle Garden on October 11 and again the fabled one half million filled rooftops and lampposts to view a splendid military spectacle, as bands and banners colored Broadway. The visit was held as "one of the wonderful events of the age" and an example of the "Entente Cordiale" with England. He was welcomed by the mayor and the Common Council at Castle Garden. Flags of all nations decorated the outside and interior of the Garden. The largest banner was a huge green flag with the Hibernian harp in the center. The prince visited the Free Academy, later City College, its library and classrooms. On the afternoon of October 12 he was hosted by Wood at a sumptuous dinner. Among the honored guests were ex-President Millard Fillmore, Archbishop John Hughes, Charles O'Conor, John Jacob and William B. Astor. Working politicians, such as Tweed, were absent.

One out-of-state traveler who visited New York in the early part of the year delivered an address at Cooper Union on February 27, but he received little of the attention accorded foreigners. New Yorkers loved spectacle and pomp and the prosaic Abraham Lincoln did not stir the imagination, not just then.[5]

And there was serious business. Democrats attended the Charleston, South Carolina, convention beginning on April 21, 1860. Both Mozart and Tammany Hall delegates were present. Tammany did what it could to prevent as usual the seating of the Woodites, who generally had the support of those Southerners opposed to the candidacy of Stephen Douglass. The convention adjourned without a candidate or platform. The next month, May 12, Tammany stood with Douglass at the nomination at the Baltimore convention which urged defeat of Abraham Lincoln to ensure a "government of the white man."

On the second of July, an "old fashioned gathering of the Democracy" was held in support of the "Little Giant." Many dignitaries were present to hear the florid campaign ranting and to see rockets and Roman candles light up the night sky. Present were ex-congressman George Jones of Tennessee, Senator Pugh of Ohio and John Forsyth of Alabama. A large number, about seventy-five, vice-presidents were chosen. At the bottom of the list was Tweed. Isaac Fowler, Grand Sachem of Tammany, was missing. Accused of stealing $155,000, he was in Cuba, safe from pursuing agents. Tammanyites recovered quickly from the news, and two days later, on the fourth, met at the hall to hear John T. Hoffman give the traditional reading of the Declaration of Independence and laud William D. Kennedy who had replaced Fowler.

On September 17, Douglass himself was given a royal banquet before thirty thousand persons, in Jones' Wood. The Illinois senator arrived shortly after two to cheering crowds and the playing of "Hail, Columbia." August Belmont was chairman of the barbecue meeting, and a whole group of the usual faithful, Sweeney, Connolly, Kelly and Tweed among them, were present. Belmont, Douglass and vice-presidential candidate Hirschel V. Johnson made speeches in support of themselves and party unity.

Wood and Mozart Hallers held their own convention, despite efforts of the "muscular shoulder hitters" of Tammany to disrupt such proceedings. These meetings centered on selection of candidates for city office rather than on support of a presidential candidate. Though Wood tended to support Kentuckian John C. Breckinridge, a more pro-southern politician, he finally went along with the Tammanyites, behind Douglass. Unity ended here as Woodites nominated George G. Barnard for Supreme Court and John J. McCunn for city judge, in opposition to Tammanyites. Wood himself received the nomination for congressman. He had had enough of being mayor.

Democrats in the city, united under Douglass, were able to poll 62,000 votes for their presidential candidate, compared to Lincoln's 33,000 votes, although Lincoln carried the state and the nation. The Republican gubernatorial candidate, Edwin D. Morgan, also won. Wood did win his congressional race, defeating Tammany's John Cochrane, but John Hoffman, Tammanyite, captured the recorder's post. McCunn and Barnard won judicial positions.[6]

Tweed took little if any part in any political business. He did not run for office, made no recorded speeches, rarely attended political meetings. To say, as do so many historians and biographers, that he was at this time a political force, powerful and respected, is simply not borne out by any evidence. The most he could manage was an appointment as a commissioner of deeds by a resolution adopted 15 to 1 by the Board of Aldermen. He spent most of this year in obscurity, taking care of his family and attending to affairs raised by his father's death. Although he had the esteem of some members of the business community who noted that he was a successful entrepreneur and a credit to the community, this reputation did not necessarily extend to the political community.[7]

II

Civil War

11

Lincoln's New York

The storm broke. In December 1860, South Carolina dissolved ties with the Union. Other states followed. On February 4, 1861, the government of the Confederate States of America was established. The effect in New York of the secession was to turn it rapidly from a traditional pro-southern city to an ardently patriotic one, fully the rival of any in support of the Union. For some, however, deep sentiments were hard to change.[1]

An example of the remarkable turnabout in attitude was the ardor and vigor, even if sometimes somewhat reserved, with which New Yorkers greeted President-elect Abraham Lincoln when he visited the metropolis on February 19. A year before he had been all but ignored, and when not ignored, vilified. The Japanese and the Prince of Wales were by far the eye-catchers in 1860—Lincoln was a mere country bumpkin. It was different now. "Honest Abe" arrived with his family and various aides including the popular young New Yorker Colonel Ephraim Elmer Elsworth. Lincoln was tired. He didn't share the excitement as did his son Bob, "Prince of Rails." Lincoln towered above all, his face and forehead furrowed by a thousand wrinkles, "his hair unkempt, his new whiskers, as if not yet naturalized, his clothing illy arranged." However, he appeared as a "man of immense power" and "natural talent." All asked him, "What will you do?" His consistent reply, "Nothing inconsistent with the Constitution."

On the trip down from Albany, Lincoln passed Sing Sing and the prisoners saluted. Ladies of Tarrytown waved handkerchiefs. "Old Abe" ordered the train stopped for a moment to allow orphan children at Dobbs Ferry a chance to see him. As the train neared New York his hair and beard were quickly brushed, his clothes straightened. The party arrived at 3 P.M. at the new depot of the Hudson River Railroad Company on Thirtieth Street between Ninth and Tenth avenues. The day was bright and warm. A group of Metropolitans led the procession as it headed toward Astor House. It was not like some of the earlier parades. Crowds were small but friendly. Lincoln bowed from side to side, occasionally rising to his feet. There were some cheers and hats were waved. A committee of the Common Council fell into the procession. The largest crowds were at the Astor House and surrounding area. The park and adjoining buildings were thick with spectators. Barnum's Museum opposite the Astor House was ornamented with bright flags and banners. Never one to lose an advertising opportunity, Barnum mixed patriotism with showmanship. Outside his museum, he displayed examples of his more popular menagerie of curiosities, including the "man-monkey," "Aztec children" and "Sea Horses." A band played continually. Lincoln arrived at the hotel at about four-thirty. He stood erect, smiling and bowing, though he appeared "very worn and pale." He walked in. A crowd inside rushed forward to greet him. Lincoln talked to aldermen Barry and Cornell and then went to his private apartment. At six, a select group sat down to dinner in room 43 adjoining the reception room. The round table was set for ten. In the center was a handsome bouquet of flowers, on the edge more flowers. The menu was less elaborate than many such, but certainly sufficient, and consisted of soup julienne, boiled salmon, cold dishes, fillet of beef, larded sweet breads, fillet of chicken, Shrewsbury oysters baked on the shell, various vegetables, canvasback duck, stuffed quail, pastries such as charlotte russe, ladyfingers and kisses, and ice cream. Lincoln made a short speech and excused his inability to make a good one "worthy of Clay and Webster." He told his guests that he was waiting for his inauguration as was the custom to make his views known. He stayed a moment longer, then retired.

His next day was a busy one. At 8 A.M., accompanied by General James Watson Webb, duelist and former editor of the *Courier and Enquirer*, and Thurlow Weed, Republican king-maker, Lincoln was quietly spirited out the Vesey Street entrance of Astor House and driven to the home of Moses Grinnell's daughter, where he found about a hundred of the most prosperous merchants waiting to greet him. At 11 A.M., he was at City Hall. There were huge throngs around the building. He was met by Mayor Wood, who had not yet taken his congressional post, and members of the council. A head taller than Wood, Lincoln's eyes did not meet his, though the mayor stared at Lincoln. He greeted the President-elect with a speech in which he expressed his hopes for a restoration of the "fraternal relations between the States." Lincoln quickly replied and expressed gratitude at the welcome. He likened the Union to a ship, and as long as the ship can save the cargo and passengers it should be preserved. So long as the liberties and prosperity of the people can be preserved by the Union, it should not be abandoned. Lincoln received the applause of those who heard him. Wood said nothing in reply. During the day, Bob Lincoln and his mother, a "handsome matronly lady," visited Barnum's showplace. P.T.'s tricks seemingly worked. They signed the guest book under the signatures of "Tommy" and the Prince of Wales. In the evening, Mrs. Lincoln received ladies at the Astor House. Mrs. August Belmont, Mrs. James W. Webb and Mrs. John A. Kennedy were among the crinolined group. She did not accompany her husband that night when he visited the Academy of Music, where he enjoyed a "very excellent" performance of Verdi's new opera, *Un Ballo in Maschera*. Lincoln and his party arrived shortly after the opening bars and he was not recognized until the first-act intermission. Then the audience applauded, Lincoln rose in acknowledgment and "The Star-Spangled Banner" was sung by the performers.

There was an evening reception, an elaborate dinner and midnight serenade. Lincoln left the following day for Baltimore and Washington. He would never return alive to New York. He left a city turned from its traditional attitudes as the metropolis quickly expressed and demonstrated its loyalty to the nation.[2] On Saturday, April 20, eight days after the firing on Fort Sumter, the "Greatest Demonstration the World Ever Saw" took place as the fabled "one half million people" watched or took part in endless parades, speeches and flag waving. Hundreds of trade and benefit societies marched behind flags and bands. People went by in endless waves. Stores, like Lord and Taylor on the corner of Grand and Broadway, A. T. Stewart's at Broadway and Reade, were covered with red, white and blue flags and banners. Illuminations were everywhere, all attesting to the patriotic sentiment and opposition to the "dastardly" attack of "treason and rebellion." The new bronze statue of Washington in Union Square was the center of a mass meeting. Men of all parties assembled, Democrats and Republicans. Leaders of New York were present in solid ranks as the flag fired upon at Fort Sumter was wrapped around the statue. Cheer after cheer was raised for the gallant defenders of the fort, Major Robert Anderson, who stood on the platform together with some officers, and a former Metropolitan who had nailed the Union flag to the mast of the citadel. Mayor Wood announced his support for the mustering of troops to uphold the Constitution and the Union. There was no longer any thought of Tri-insular, a suggestion Wood had made of creating a neutral free city. Even Wood recognized New York City was now part of the state and the nation and would serve. If arms were necessary, the city would be found not shirking, though he appealed to Union men in the South to aid the cause of pacification and to the federal government to be ever ready to extend the "olive branch of peace and conciliation." If this failed Wood

stood behind any measure necessary to protect the Union. Similar sentiments were spoken by many other celebrities. The voice of Union was
clear—or so it seemed.

The bright, hopeful days that followed were filled with more excitement. Raising of regiments was the order of the day, heeding the President's call for volunteers. Tammany early in May formed the Jackson
Guard to "protect the capital of our country." William D. Kennedy, Tammany Grand Sachem, was its colonel. The executive committee of the
guard consisted of some thirty members including Belmont, Purdy, Tilden, Alderman Henry W. Genet, Sweeny (perhaps as a bid toward
Anglicization the last e in the name had been dropped) and Tweed. The
hall was turned into a barrack and drill room. Posters were placed around
the city asking for volunteers. Newspapers were full of announcements of
the raising of National Guard regiments. There were calls for men to join
rifle, Zouave, artillery, sapper, engineer, telegrapher, light and heavy infan-
try companies. At the shortest notice, troops were readied for the field.
Daniel Sickles as acting brigadier general commanded the Excelsior Brigade. Many men from Philadelphia came to New York to enlist. British,
German, Irish volunteers joined a variety of outfits. Money was raised for
the relief fund of the 69th Regiment. Connolly gave $50, Waterbury $25,
Barnard $50, the Irish Emigrant Society $250 and Wood $100, as did John
Kelly. Church services were held by all denominations and prayers were
read on behalf of the Union. The Stars and Stripes was flown over B'nai
Jeshurun Synagogue on Greene Street.

Public praise and support for the troops followed each other in tum-
bling array. If encouragement was needed, it was provided by the tragic
death early in May of Colonel Elmer Elsworth, the first officer lost in the
war. As head of his Zouaves, made up of members from the Fire Department, he had entered the City Hall in Alexandria, Virginia, to take down
a Confederate flag flying from the rooftop. While inside, he was killed by
the caretaker. Elsworth, an attorney, was a well-liked and well-known
officer. His "murder" caused considerable sadness especially to Lincoln, lament and anger. Money was raised to aid his parents and the body was
brought to New York and a fine public funeral was held on May 26.
Among the pallbearers was a large group of Fire Department officials including William Tweed, who had been named one of the Department
commissioners effective as of May 28. Proclamations of sympathy were
given by the council, as well as by public and private organizations. The
death of Elsworth underlined the "treachery" of the South and hardened
the resolve for the national cause. The funeral was the first of many, as
the fallen from the battlefields went in seemingly endless procession to
City Hall, then carried to their graves. Such thoughts, however, were not

in the minds of angry New Yorkers as recruiting continued with greater enthusiasm and cries of revenge.

On May 27, the Tammany regiment, the Jackson Guard of some nine hundred men, was mustered for inspection. Colonel Kennedy could be proud of this hand-picked group. It was as "imposing a body of men that ever left the city." New York was alive with troops. Maine, New Hampshire and Massachusetts regiments bivouacked in the park as they awaited movement to the front. In July, the regiment went to a site known as Camp Tammany in Great Neck, Long Island. They were at a delightful spot—trees, grass and the sparkling waters of Long Island Sound were before their eyes. They had experienced officers. Adjutant Timothy O'Meara had served with the Mexican Army of Juarez, and Captain R. E. A. Hampden, late of the 3rd West Middlesex Militia, England, directed six hours of drill daily. The regiment stayed in Great Neck for ten days and then were sent to the "seat of war" via New York on July 18.

War did not last long for Mr. Kennedy. While in Washington on July 22, he died suddenly of "congestion of the brain." His brother, Superintendent of Police John A. Kennedy, was informed of his illness on Sunday night, July 21. The death of Kennedy plus the news of the disaster at Bull Run plunged the city into gloom. Kennedy was a respected and seasoned political campaigner. Born in Baltimore, Maryland, he never held an elected office, but was an effective street commissioner and had been elected Grand Sachem in place of the absconding Fowler. It was believed that he could have run for mayor in the upcoming election if he wanted the nomination.[3]

With people like Kennedy dead and Sickles and others in the Army there was room to maneuver. There was room for Tweed. War caused a rethinking of ideas and a regrouping of political associations. Tammany labored to erase its identification as an anti-war party, and tried to assume a role as a patriotic organization. There emerged new combinations, one of which became known as "The Aldermanic Ring," seemingly an assortment of dissident pro-war Tammanyites like Tweed, George Barnard, and Henry Genet seeking to wrest control of the hall from regulars like Purdy. The goals, methods and organization of the supposed "Ring" were never very clear, but then little in politics, especially of the Democratic variety, was. Members of "The Ring" met in September at Windust's, a well-known local restaurant and politicians' hangout at 11 Park Row in sight of City Hall. Here Tweed, Dick Connolly, Barnard put together a slate in opposition to Tammany. Tweed headed the ticket as nominee for sheriff in the fall election and Henry Genet was put forward for county clerk. Woodites and Mozart Hallers also gained from Tammany's past. It was thought that Tammany had determined on its slate with "Big Judge"

Michael Connolly for sheriff but expected that "The Ring" was open to bargaining. Woodite Frederick Vultee, Tweed and "Judge" Connolly vied for the nomination. On October 9 at Tammany Hall a series of ballots were taken. Tweed had fifty-eight votes to Connolly's thirty-two and Vultee's twenty-three on the first count. On the third and final ballot, Tweed had seventy-one, Connolly forty-six and Vultee four. The vote at that time was made unanimous for Tweed. Genet gained the county clerk's spot. Other posts went to regular Tammanyites; the split with the party seemed ended, and "The Ring" appeased. Mozart Hallers were also present but did not succeed in getting any attention for their candidate for sheriff, James Lynch. Other parties and factions held their own meetings and fought for position and control of the ticket.

Even Republicans were having problems. Insurgents divided between such groups as Taxpayers Party, St. Nicholas Hotel, Fifth Avenue Hotel, German League, Cooper Institute Reform, and People's Union. What each group generally stood for was self-aggrandizement, reform and lowering of the tax rate. The electioneering was typical of all New York politics —a fragmented nightmare.

Even settlement on an agreed-upon candidate was not necessarily a settlement, as Tweed soon found out. The sheriff's nomination was again opened. Again there were rumors. One report said "The Aldermanic Ring" in order to solidify its gains and further weaken Tammany would have Tweed withdraw in favor of James Lynch, the Woodite who had seen action in the war. There was a cloud over Lynch. This concerned his conduct in battle and, of course, affected his candidacy. The charge was that Lynch, just prior to Bull Run, had ordered his battery to leave the field because he felt his soldiers' families were suffering and his men had enlisted for three months and their time was up, battle or no battle. Pleading by his commanding officer fell on deaf ears and the troops, including Lynch, showed the "white feather" and went home. Lynch's version of the incident was quite different and he was supported in this by Archbishop Hughes and Thomas Meagher. Lynch explained that he left before the battle was "even contemplated," and "after laborious service." Had a fight been imminent he would have stayed, for he was not a coward and he did not belong to a "race of cowards." The affair became a *cause célèbre*, as opponents snickered and continued to vilify him as a deserter under fire.

Tweed in the meantime attempted to quell rumors of his withdrawal by publishing a letter on October 26 that he would not under any circumstances resign from the contest. As the election neared, Lynch was the front runner, while Tweed and Vultee despite the latter's well-publicized campaign were counted out of the race for the "most lucrative of the offices" to be filled in the election. Last-minute efforts were made to drum up support for Tweed. A very short-lived two-issue "newspaper," the New York *Union*, which was given away at street corners, preached the honest, sterling qualities of the "intellectual" Tweed, a man from "Dover Street," a "man of the people, self-made, self-reliant, and self-sustaining, a champion of the working classes and immigrants." The *Union* also backed Oakey Hall and Richard Connolly.

The day before the election held on November 5 placards displaying a list of candidates were placed around town. On Broadway, on the corner of Duane Street, a small forlorn banner read: "For Sheriff, William M. Tweed." Other banners, Mozart Hall, Republican and People's Union were much more prominent. Tammany Hall was quiet and presented a dismal appearance as returns were posted. Factional division, absence of a stated policy openly in favor of the war effort, hurt as much as the lack of popularity of the candidates. Generally the contests were apathetic, except for the vote for sheriff. It was a triumph for Lynch and Mozart Hall. Lynch gained 18,000 votes, Republican Josiah W. Brown 15,000, Tweed a poor third with 9,800 and Vultee 6,300. It was, of course, another loss for Tweed, who was referred to as a "dead officer, having died from cheating." This was in reference to a charge that cohorts had used marked ballots.[4]

Again a disappointing year for Tweed. It certainly began badly. He started bankruptcy proceedings in early February 1861. George G. Barnard granted his discharge on October 3, 1861. Surely news of this didn't aid his fall campaign. Tweed's total debt was $57,150.18, principally as a result of the failure of Tweed and Brother, Chairmakers. Tweed, as required by law, listed his assets on March 27, 1861, as "Three Hats, Two Caps, Two Thick Overcoats, One Thin Overcoat, Three Pair Pants, Six Vests, Two Dress Coats, One Business Coat, Three Pair Boots, Two Pair Shoes, Ten Pair Socks, Thirty Collars, Twelve Linen Shirts, Twelve Cotton Shirts Ten Handkerchiefs." It was a quick turn of fortune caused likely by his tending to politics rather than business. A year earlier, he had been looked upon as a well-to-do businessman.[5]

Still there was something to be gained out of the wreckage. He was quite active as a supervisor and in November asked a committee he established to oversee expenditures on another new county courthouse then building on Chambers Street. It would be something he would long remember. He also became a lawyer, opening an office at 95 Duane Street. It was not necessary then to go to law school; all that was needed was an attorney to say an applicant was of good moral character and had read law for three years. He was also still a fire commissioner and supervisor, but something of a cipher in the political heavens. He would try to change this.[6]

12

Riot

Patriotism and victory were the themes to be played, at least for the moment. At the traditional July 4 celebration, an enormous crowd filled Union Square, which was rapidly replacing City Hall Park as the center of civic life. It was, of course, a good example of the inexorable growth northward of New York. An estimated fifty thousand people crowded around the speaker's platform and adjacent stands. Andrew Johnson of Tennessee and Henry Ward Beecher were among the assembled dignitaries.

Tammany's own festivities were opened by now Grand Sachem Nelson Waterbury, who praised President Lincoln and the war effort. Later in the month, the Democratic State Convention in Albany passed a resolution in "favor of unconditional support of the government in its conduct of the war." Tammany and the Democracy had seemingly laundered its shirt of the red stain of anti-war.

In mid-July, citizens held a mass meeting and parade along Broadway in hopes of raising millions of men and dollars for the "Preservation of our Great Republic." "Little Mac," General George McClellan, was the hero of the day. Speakers vied with each other in pushing patriotism. In August, the city again had something to cheer about when General Michael Corcoran arrived after a triumphant welcome in Philadelphia. Born in Ireland, he headed the 69th Regiment at the First Battle of Bull Run, July 1861, was wounded, taken prisoner and then released. He arrived in New York on August 2 and was given a hero's welcome. The park was full of excited humanity, people straining to glimpse the hero on his way to Union Square, where even larger crowds awaited him. When the convalescing soldier reached the square in the afternoon, he was introduced to a huge throng by Mayor Opdyke, who gave an unnecessary speech asking for support of the war effort. Cries rang through the streets, as newspapers headlined "Erin go Bragh," "Caed Mille Failthe" and "Faugh a Ballagh." It was a day for Ireland.

On August 27, another great outburst was held in the park in honor of Corcoran, the 69th and the Union. The regiment paraded through the city and the park. Recruiting stands were set up. "Are ye's there, me Boys," attributed to Corcoran, were rallying words. Calmly, Corcoran entered the park on a horse. General Sickles and his brigade were present. Albert Cardozo gave a short speech in a voice, he said, "too weak for such a purpose," expressing his certainty for ultimate victory. He stressed the role New York would play in the country's salvation. "The Union," he ended, "shall be preserved as it was, the Constitution as it is." Speeches were also made by many others—Corcoran, Sickles, Opdyke. The crowd frequently interrupted with cheers, such as "Go on, brave boy."[1]

Obviously, approval given to the cause was great and popular. Yet, grumblings were there, faint but present. Some related to the growing army of "shoddy" millionaires, war contractors making money, often illegally and immorally selling defective equipment and clothing, who were visible on the streets or riding through Central Park in opulent carriages. This while an army of the poor, squeezed by inflation and the loss of husbands and sons, grew in number, crowded in basements and hovels. Patriotism glossed over a menacing cloud, but did not dissolve it. The disastrous Battle of Fredericksburg fought in December 1862 made widows of many women and orphans of many children. Lincoln ordered that information of this "Christmas present" be kept from the public until after the New Year, but somehow the news leaked out and there were many sad Christmas dinners. There was talk of a draft and resistance. There was a danger in all of this.

An example of growing unrest could be seen in rising political opposition by Democrats, despite the ringing patriotic sentiments expressed at public meetings. On October 13, a large meeting was held at Cooper Institute. Signs around the hall read, "No prescription for Opinion's Sake" or "Shall Abolition put down the Union or Shall the Union put down Abolition" and "The Constitution As it Is, The Union As it Was, Stand Firm." Rynders, Wood, Henry Genet, Horatio Seymour and General George McClellan stirred the agitated crowd against Republicans for assuming an "undeserved mantle of patriotism" and daring to call leading Democrats traitors, as well as for pursuing unjust policies which led to civil war. A similar evening meeting held in the park on October 28 was illuminated by flares, paper lanterns and torches. Samuel "Sunset" Cox, the "newsboys friend," was the chief speaker. He violently upbraided abolitionists, particularly John Brown and blacks. He asked the noisy crowd, "How would you like to see a black minister from Haiti received in Washington on a par with white ministers?" They responded, "No, never." Signs read, "Our national malady, nigger on the brain" and "Where are you Greeley and your nine-hundred thousand black warriors?" Lincoln's Emancipation Proclamation was denounced, as were illegal arrests and the arbitrary ending of free speech and the press. As war went badly, so did patriotism. Democrats saw an opportunity to translate military defeats into votes, but they would first have to overcome disunity within the party. Splits, especially with Mozart Hall, had been disastrous and needed to be mended. An attempt to reach agreement occurred at an afternoon meeting at Tammany Hall, the "Old Coal Hole," on October 2, Richard B. Connolly and Emanuel Hart on one side and Wood and John Lynch on the other. Though accord was not reached, it was agreed that the general committees of both factions would seek to unite behind a list of candidates for the fall election. On October 9, Peter Sweeny on behalf of a Tammany Committee of Twenty met and agreed to fusion with Wood. Tweed received renomination for supervisor by acclamation.

The Democratic campaign, using the pivot of Union defeat, centered on criticism of the conduct of the war. Seymour, Van Buren, Wood, Purdy, General McClellan were in harmony in condemning blacks, abolitionists, Greeley and Lincoln's "Abolitionist Party." We have had enough of them, shouted angry Democrats, Mozart Hallers and Tammanyites united against government "suppression" of political opposition. Behind banners like "No man shall be arrested" and "Every citizen shall be protected and Abolitionists intimidate the Democracy," committees were formed to make sure of proper election procedures and victory. The union of Democrats proved successful in the November county and state elections. Tweed was re-elected overwhelmingly as supervisor. He had 52,000 votes to 19,000 for Sheridan Shook, the Republican runner-up. As a result of an act passed by the legislature in 1858, this election was for a six-year term. Shook, though defeated, as the losing candidate was appointed to the Board also to serve six years since he had the next highest number of votes. Tweed's victory, though impressive, gained him no more than if he lost. All six congressmen elected from the city were Democrats, as compared to four in the previous Congress. Seymour carried the state. The poor progress of the war, mounting criticism of the Administration, the dismissal of the popular but unsuccessful McClellan and the limiting of civil liberties by Lincoln and a united Democracy were chief reasons for the Democratic resurgence.[2]

The victory was a sweet one, a rebuff to abolitionists, to the keepers of Fort Lafayette, a prison just off the Brooklyn shore used to house captured Confederates and their political sympathizers. The fort was torn down during the construction of the Verrazano Bridge, and the site used as the location of one of the bridge's supports.

Each Union defeat, especially after Fredericksburg, continuous funeral processions, the growing list of casualties, numerous wounded and deserters in city streets, rising prices and finally the momentous but dangerous decision to draft raised increasingly bitter, angry cries of protest. Unrest was in the air, as front lines neared homes. These were times of testing. A. Oakey Hall, the long-time Whig and Republican, began a withdrawal from his former loyalty and in January announced that he would present a lecture to the Democratic Union Association on the "Political Crimes of the Radicals." For Hall, erosion of civil liberties by the Lincoln administration was a chief cause of his discontent. The war caused many things to happen, including the changing of political colors. Nevertheless, a charge of opportunism and turncoatism would always be an albatross around Hall's neck.

On February 10, 1863, John Van Buren was to lecture Young Democrats on the "Rise and Progress of the Democratic Party," but what a shouting crowd heard was an irate denunciation of Lincoln's lack of ability in prosecuting the war, evidenced by his dismissal of General McClellan, whose name was cheered as was that of Fitz-John Porter, removed shortly after "Little Mac." "Prince John" recommended a convention of northern and southern states with an eye to removing the President before his term was over, though he did not think Southerners of the Jefferson Davis stamp would think much of the proposal. He requested a union of Mozart and Tammany Democrats to carry the state by any "decent means" to help restore the Union. Van Buren's speech reflected much of the present thinking of the Democracy. On April 7 at a large meeting at Cooper Union, "Peace Democrats" like now Congressman-elect Fernando Wood and Judge John McCunn opposed national administration policies as "hostile to the restoration of the Union" and "oppressive to the people." The Administration cannot achieve victory and "we declare for peace and conciliation." Further, the right of habeas corpus suspended by Lincoln in 1862 should be restored. At the meeting, McCunn stated that he no longer supported a policy of armed suppression of the South. Wood argued that only special interests of the Washington bureaucrats, railroad magnates and New England war contractors wanted the war and prolonged the unpopular effort at the expense of the poor and national unity. A Democrat should sit in the White House to make things right.

At the same time, a large meeting at the Academy of Music was held to help those starving in Ireland as a result of a famine almost as severe as the one of 1846–47. Food and supplies should be found not only for the Irish, but also for those poor English textile operators starving in Lancastershire because of the want of southern cotton. General McClellan was called forward amid cheers and heard himself referred to as President McClellan. He praised the Irish and their bravery on the battlefield and urged famine relief, as well as national unity. It was supposedly a non-political speech, but it gave McClellan excellent public exposure. General Thomas Francis Meagher, commander of the Irish Brigade, spoke for the cause of Ireland and urged rescue from English oppression. Archbishop Hughes, Judge Daly, Richard O'Gorman and finally even Republican Horace Greeley told of the good work of the meeting. The unity of such a wide spectrum of opinion with the southern cause, while politically acceptable, was a dangerous turn for the peace of the city, as Democrats and even Republicans joined together in common cause. Copperheadism was an active philosophy in New York. Sedition and treason were openly expressed as in few other places in the North. The arrest of Congressman Clement Vallandigham of Ohio because of his anti-war, pro-southern attitude particularly raised cries of protest. For those in the streets, shouts were to indict "sons of b———s," officials of the administration, not the congressman. District Attorney Hall, now an open and ardent Democrat, voiced the same sentiments, but expressed them more politely.

New Yorkers were asked by historian James A. McMaster to organize companies and regiments in the state against Lincoln, whom he accused of treason. Rynders shouted that Lincoln had promised restoration of the Union but delivered the government to war profiteers, "swaggering around Washington with their pockets full of greenbacks." The war should be ended, he continued, as he ominously threatened that a conscription law would never be carried out in New York. The "King in Washington" would be taught a lesson. There were threats of assassination. Wood at one meeting personally urged the crowd to discharge their rights and "strike down the tyrant." The response was great applause and shouts of "we will."

The Tammany organization, now under leadership of Grand Sachem Purdy, joined in support of the peace movement, though more carefully than did Wood. They made their traditional July 4 celebration an event lauding Vallandigham. Tweed was now chairman of the Democratic General Committee, a group which was responsible for carrying out the decisions of the sachems, but was of no importance in making policy itself. The chairmanship was a rotating one probably given to Tweed in order to annoy Richard B. Connolly, who was looking for a job in the city and could have used the appointment to further his ambition.[3]

Several fires occurred in the city on July 4 besides the traditional flares and rockets. A number of buildings were destroyed. New York waited expectantly. The heat was oppressive, the atmosphere heavy. During the first week of July, rumors flew about as to armed resistance to the draft, which was to be instituted during the month, and of plans to seize the arsenal at Thirty-fifth Street. Some eighteen hundred deserters had joined together for battle, ran a prevalent story. These were rumors. Were they true? Governor Seymour met with Mayor Opdyke. General Charles Sandford was called in for consultation. Police Superintendent John Kennedy was alerted, but no plans were drawn. On July 9, one Chauncey C. Burr, an itinerant, delivered an inflammatory speech to citizens of the Twentieth Ward. He counseled resistance to national authority and especially the draft. There was no counterspeech or action. The draft was an expedient but thoughtless bit of legislation, especially in that it allowed the wealthy to pay $300 to be used to buy a substitute. The war became a rich man's war fought "with poor man's blood."

The drawing for the draft was first instituted quietly on Saturday, July 11, at the provost marshal's office at 677 Third Avenue. On Sunday, there were more rumors, plans and plots. On Monday morning, July 13, hell broke loose in New York shortly after the office opened. At the roll of the lottery wheel, an ugly mob seized the equipment and set it afire, then went about destroying the building, and from there went rampaging through the streets in ever growing ferocity and numbers. A screaming crowd "serenaded" Mayor Opdyke at his Fifth Avenue residence, but luckily did no more. Judge Barnard was recognized by another group and given three cheers. He told them that he understood the draft to be unconstitutional, but urged all to go home and respect the law, which would protect "our just and legal rights." They did not follow his advice, but wandered through the streets visiting other homes, including that of General Meagher. Irish laborers, women and children chased blacks whenever found. One unfortunate, pursued by a crowd, turned and fired a pistol at them, wounding or killing a man. Caught near Hudson Street, he was captured and brutally beaten. Stripped of clothes except for a shirt, he was hanged from a tree and his body set afire. Pitiful shrieks and cries came from the tortured black, as "people" danced under the dangling corpse until late at night. A large force of police were dispatched to cut the remains down. Murder, riot, looting, attacks on blacks, police or anyone thought not in sympathy with the frightful mobs, which were often captained by women, some of the worst offenders, were the disorder of the day. Authorities tried to marshal their forces. Governor Seymour and Mayor Opdyke met at City Hall during the second day. Oakey Hall, Charles Cornell and Tweed made their appearance along with several other city officials. Seymour wanted the "disturbances" to be put down, even if surrender was necessary. From the steps of City Hall he asked that peace and quiet be preserved and informed a crowd that the Conscription

Act would be postponed until its legality could be argued in the courts. He pledged further that if the draft continued, the $300 exemption would be paid by the state. Alderman Terence Farley in a near-empty chamber also counseled peace and quiet. Aldermen met again later in the day and voted to raise money to help the poor pay the draft exemption. Archbishop Hughes while condemning the riot could not "recommend coercive conscription." It was thought that he should have used his office to make a stronger denunciation of the rioters.

In the streets there were bullets, bricks and knives. Tweed and Street Commissioner Cornell were quite active and very useful. Because of their "extensive knowledge" of the city, they rendered valuable assistance in carrying out Governor Seymour's orders and furnishing news to authorities in the different wards. They worked hard in gathering information though it was dangerous to do so. Seymour, who had set up headquarters at the St. Nicholas Hotel, was closeted with all manner of advisers as messages were carried in and out. Up to the evening of the third and last night, Tweed, Cornell, McCunn and Sheriff Lynch were constantly at hand informing the governor of developments in the streets. All labored without sleep far into the night. Even Captain Rynders procured muskets from the arsenal for firemen of the Seventh Ward who had organized to protect themselves and citizens. After three days of horror, during which millions of dollars were lost and thousands made casualties, quiet was finally restored, partly by promises of relief, partly by the heat of July, partly by the arrival of troops from Gettysburg to bolster authority in the city, partly by buoyant news of victory at Gettysburg and Vicksburg, partly by work of officials like Seymour and Tweed.

But what now? Opdyke, Seymour, Hughes came in for charges of incompetency and worse. Opdyke particularly was looked on as a fool and coward, whose courage returned only with the end of the riot. A series of trials were started before Recorder John Hoffman in General Sessions ranging from indictments for murder and riot to disorderly conduct. District Attorney Hall appeared for the people. At least a thousand damage suits were filed against the city. The supervisors would be busy with such cases for years, as they were responsible for determining the validity of the claims.[4]

On August 19, conscription was again put into effect and the provost marshal's office at 185 Sixth Avenue became the scene for the drawing of names. The draft proceeded without incident. But the times were different. Victory on the battlefield had its results. The horrors of the riots burned deep, even into hardened souls. There was promise of financial relief for the poor. The city returned to normal without a large segment of its black population, many of whom had fled from the city. Important names were taken from the lottery wheel—Townsend Harris and John Morrissey among them. On August 26, the lottery in the Seventh Ward spun out William M. Tweed, 127 Henry Street. There was a shout of recognition and jokes made about Tweed's new career in the Army.[5] However, like so many other celebrities, Tweed was able either to find a substitute or to argue successfully that his Seventh Ward needed him at home. At forty, he was still liable for duty. While he did not join the Army of the Potomac, he did serve on the Board of Supervisors Exemption Committee, to receive applications for relief of drafted men. All those vital to the city, policemen, firemen, militia, were exempt, as were poor citizens with dependent families, who received $300 to buy a substitute, or if they chose to serve, received the money as a bonus. Three million dollars was raised to meet the next draft in order to buy substitutes. In effect, because of the bonus, no one was really drafted. A draftee could always buy his way out and there were always those who were willing to serve for the money. Orison Blunt and Tweed as a subcommittee were sent to Washington to consult with Secretary of War Edwin Stanton to find out if men procured by the supervisors would be accredited to various congressional districts as part of the next quota from New York County. The subcommittee was greeted with "great courtesies" and after a "full interchange" of views, the Secretary agreed to the requests. The entire committee, Blunt, Tweed, William T. Stewart and Purdy, was able to convey to the Board the commendation of the War Department for its patriotism and determination to "aid and sustain the government in crushing the wicked rebellion and in vindicating the majesty of the law." The committee reported that the County of New York had furnished men and means for the suppression of the rebellion far exceeding its size, and was again ready to show its devotion to the Union against all enemies on either hemisphere. By 1865 over 116,000 men had enlisted and over eighteen million dollars had been expended by the city on the war effort. In January 1866 the city petitioned the federal government for repayment of $800,000 expended by the Union Defense Committee in furnishing the United States with troops, arms and ammunition in 1861 and 1862. The money was "voluntarily tendered at a time when such pecuniary aid was of first importance to the general government." It seems never to have been repaid though the city gave unstintingly at a time of national crisis. The riots, terrible as they were, were in fact a small negative part of a very large positive contribution made by the citizens of New York to the war effort, Tweed not excepted.[6]

Still present, however, was considerable opposition to Lincoln and the "critical condition of the country" requiring "recovery of all political power from the hands of our present rulers." These were given as the reasons by Mozart Hall to work with Tammany in the coming election. Tweed, Purdy and Sweeny were part of the Tammany committee to establish agreement with the Mozart Hall group on candidates for the fall election with the understanding that Tammany and Mozart were to share in a "fair and equal" manner. However, there were problems. Wood did not want to submit to the state party platform, and like his brother Benjamin, editor of the *Daily News*, desired a more pro-southern tone. John McKeon Democrats had their own issue, which was to oppose the granting of monopolistic charters. A charter granted by the council, over Mayor Opdyke's disapproval to the Harlem Railroad Company in April to construct a Broadway line stirred up a good deal of resentment.[7] "Secret sessions held by the aldermen" did little to avert suspicion of deals and influence peddling. McKeon forces, therefore, put forward their own nominations. In some instances, Mozart Hallers had their own nominations for office, for example, Justice John H. McCunn in opposition to Tammany's candidate, Samuel B. Garvin. Tammany and Mozart Hall, however, both agreed on Albert Cardozo, who ran against Justice Henry Hilton, friend of merchant A. T. Stewart, a Republican, for judge in Common Pleas. Generally both factions agreed on the division of the nominations, and as a result Democrats won most of the contests in a low-key election.[8]

Just prior to the elections, one of the memorable events of 1863, other than the terrible riot, was the arrival in September, keeping with the custom of international visitors, of a Russian fleet—five ships under the command of Rear Admiral Lisovski. The effect of their arrival was to help bolster the Union cause. Entertainment of Russian sailors became the highlight of the social season. Fraternity between Russians and Americans was the order of the day. Excursions, toasts, speeches continued endlessly. Captain Boutakopf of the *Culiaba* toasted the Emperor of Russia and the President of the United States. Host General Stewart Van Vliet responded in kind. Then followed toasts to the United States Army and Navy and the City of New York. The Common Council voted the hospitality of the city to Lisovski, Captain Fedorovski of the frigate flagship *Alexander Nevsky* and officers of the four other ships. There was a review at City Hall on October 1 and a tour of the harbor which was crowded with many warships of foreign lands. The veteran English battleship *Nile* attracted considerable attention. Behind her was the H.M.S. *Immortalité*. There were also several French gunboats. The water sparkled as pretty yachts and screeching tugboats were buoyed by the band on the U.S.S. *North Carolina*. Music, sunlight, gentle breezes made the scene a remembered one. New York could be beautiful.

On the evening of October 19, a huge municipal banquet was given the Russian officers. Present were the mayor and members of the city government and foreign consulates. There were speeches, toasts and a spectacular dinner including choices of soup, fish, roasts, turkey, legs of mutton, pork, Cincinnati ham, six cold ornamental dishes including flying swans on pedestals, ten hot side dishes, sweetbreads, fritters of chicken, young pigeons stuffed with champagne sauce, eight cold side dishes, pies of rabbits, pies of fat goose liver Périgord, eleven different vegetables, eight kinds of game, roast larded partridges, mallard duck, saddle of venison, redhead duck and woodcock. Ornamental dessert pieces inclued American, Temple of Liberty, Emperor Alexander II, Equestrian Statue of Washington and the Russian Military Fountain. There were more than a dozen pastries and pies, charlotte russe, American russe, Patience cake, Genois cakes and Bavarian cheese to end the feast.

The festivities ended with a Grand Ball at the Academy of Music on November 5, just after the county elections. At that time, another huge feast described entirely in French, catered by Delmonico, was served. The floor committee was a who's who of New York society—William H. Aspinwall, Hamilton Fish, Thomas Tillotson, James W. Beekman, Theodore Roosevelt, father of the future President, James P. Kernochan. Military bands performed a long musical program which started with Rossini's *William Tell* overture and ran through selections of Verdi, Strauss, Meyerbeer, Flotow, Donizetti and others. Then the ball and dancing commenced, as much as a crowded floor could allow. Détente has an early history.

During the Russian visit another festivity was held on October 22 to honor "Private Miles O'Reilly," pseudonym of Charles G. Halpine of the 42nd Regiment, newly arrived from a southern prison camp. He was a strange quixotic figure, editor of the New York *Citizen* and formerly an editor of the *Times*. Halpine's criticism of the war in a recently published book, a biography of the fictitious O'Reilly, had attracted much attention. Some considered the affair at least the equal of the Japanese and Prince of Wales receptions. Tweed, among many others, was present to honor the hero. It was a Democratic affair which various factions could use for their own benefit. Such wining and dining did much to relieve the monotony of war and dispelled images of death and destruction and helped keep New Yorkers' feet on the ground by raising their spirits.

Tweed was being seen, even if not always at the "right" places. On November 5, the day of the Russian Grand Ball, while members of "society" danced with the Russians, Tweed was present at the dedication of the Hebrew Orphan Asylum at Third Avenue and Seventy-seventh Street. The brownstone building cost about $50,000 to construct and was built with the assistance of the city, which provided half that amount. There were some five hundred people in attendance. For Tweed, attendance at

95

such functions aided him politically. This might have helped him gain a small but growing Jewish vote, though at the cost of losing the bigot vote. Anti-Semitism in New York was quiet, though present, and on the increase with the arrival of more Jewish immigrants. The population of New York was now just under 1 million and Jews constituted perhaps less than 1 per cent of the total. Though small in numbers, an estimated six thousand Jews had considerable influence in various aspects of New York life. Tweed's appearance at this and other minority functions seemed to be part of a conscientious effort on his part to associate with all immigrant groups. Again such support would also cost him the vote and finally the hatred of conservative elements. Even attendance at the Russian affair by politicians could be offset by those angered with any show of favor for "Russian tyranny."[9] For the politician, life had its pluses and minuses. A political calculus was very necessary for survival.

13

Victory and a Funeral

The year 1864 was a presidential one and for Tweed and his party a particularly important one. The major question once more was whether Democrats could continue united or would once again be at each other's throats. Civic issues, particularly in finding ways to curb corruption in office, were increasingly on the political agenda in a return to the "normalcy" of prewar years, a sure sign that the conflict was grinding down. There was no question that "Little Napoleon" McClellan had the hearts and minds of Democrats. A popular officer, in his dismissal by Lincoln he was given the mantle of martyrdom, a "victim" of the voracious wants of "King Lincoln." Tammany jumped on the bandwagon when in late April a decision was announced to send McClellan delegates to the Chicago presidential nominating convention. Tweed, still chairman of the General Committee, was among those dispatched, though as usual he did not take an active role. At the beginning of the year, he had managed to effect a change in the committee membership by enlarging it to 150 and decentralizing the nominating process, thus giving greater power to the ward committees. This democratization, though popular, could be useful in weakening the committee and allowing Tweed some individual leverage. It was an example of Tweed's small but growing influence.[1]

At the Chicago convention, held August 30 and 31, 1864, McClellan was unanimously chosen standard-bearer. The basic platform of the Democrats was a call for immediate cessation of hostilities and the convening of a state convention which through compromise would effect a conciliation. A. Oakey Hall was particularly useful in entertaining crowds with his wit and ability. He urged that the body politic be purged of "Lincoln bite and shoddy humors and no doubt the wound will heal . . ." He ended his talk with a little doggerel:

97

Jeff Davis' cat could eat no fat
Abe's dog could eat no lean
And so between them both
They licked the Union clean.[2]

Harmony within the ranks was not to be. At the state convention held in Albany on September 15, a schism developed. First, Seymour's forces were angered over the party's support for McClellan at Chicago. It was felt that Seymour should have had the New York delegation at least on the first ballot. Then in Albany, Mozart Hall and McKeon delegates asked for seats, but their request as well as the request of a German delegation was denied. At one point Tammany threatened to bolt when it was suggested that city Democrats present a split delegation. Tammany demanded conformity and got it. Tweed was put on the Committee of Electors. Then, despite initial disagreements, Seymour was renominated for governor by acclamation. Tweed and four others were chosen to bring the news of his nomination to the governor. Seymour at first and according to plan told the delegation that his health and personal business matters would prevent his taking the nomination, but at the "hour of the country's peril," he was willing to make the "sacrifice." Members of the convention, when told the story, leaped to their feet with enthusiasm. Acting like a coy Richard III, Seymour was worthy of an Oscar.

While there was seemingly a united support for the McClellan-Seymour ticket, the situation on the local level was as muddled as ever. All factions were active. Tammany, having won at Albany, was in the lead, and further strengthened by the nomination in the city of John Kelly for sheriff. Pushing at Chicago for McClellan, he had been a McKeon partisan, but now was back with Tammany, depriving McKeon of an able supporter. It was not so simple for other positions. Tweed and Cornell favored Henry Genet for county clerk, but they were opposed by Sweeny, Brennan and Boole, "War Democrats," who wanted a more reliable candidate, one not tainted with desertion from the party. When the slate was finally hacked out on October 16, Genet was given the Tammany endorsement, perhaps not so much an indication of the strength of Tweed and Cornell, but the fear of further party disunity. Whether any one group or any one person could be said to lead city politics after seeing the patchwork ticket seems impossible. There were seven parties or factions in the field, a repetition of previous elections. As an example, Tammany endorsed Kelly for sheriff, as did anti-Wood Mozarts, but Wood Mozarts endorsed "Big Judge" Michael Connolly, no relation of Richard B., as did McKeon and German Democrats. Genet was opposed for county clerk by Benjamin P. Fairchild, endorsed by Mozart Hall, McKeon and German

Democrats. Anti-Wood Mozarts ran Charles G. Halpine (Miles O'Reilly). Two Republican organizations and the Citizens Association had their own candidates. Fernando Wood went as a McKeon Democrat for Congress. Thomas J. Barr of Tammany opposed James Brooks, a McKeon and anti-Woodite, Henry Raymond ran as a Twenty-third Street Republican—all for a seat in Congress. And so on in endless confusion.

When the election was over, McClellan had carried the city by 37,000 votes out of 110,000 cast, but he lost in the state, as did Seymour, who was defeated by Reuben E. Fenton. Kelly, Genet, Hall as district attorney, two supervisors (one a Wood-Mozart Haller), three city councilmen, four coroners were elected by Tammany. They were less successful in congressional races, splitting with Republicans four to two. Wood lost, and Henry Raymond won.

A disputed election for Congress occurred in the Eighth District. James Brooks, a Woodite, claimed victory over Republican William E. Dodge, who charged election frauds. Inspectors were called in. Tweed asked that the dispute be held in abeyance until the last day of the charter election to be held in December. He was seconded by Purdy. Tweed was accused of attempted fraud in these delaying tactics. It was resolved to call the canvassers without delay and after some further haggling, the election was given to Brooks, despite Dodge's protests.[3]

Tweed operated more confidently than ever before, as his position became more secure. He had been unanimously elected to the presidency of the Board of Supervisors for the year. In his "inaugural" of January 4, 1864, Tweed had promised to discharge his obligations "impartially and faithfully." He asked for harmony and brought up the issue of avoiding the draft by having "our capitalists" provide enough money to pay bounties for substitutes. He expected that losses caused by the riot would be made up to those who suffered. Finally, Tweed urged economy, and the upholding of law, order and good government. Tweed's concern with bounty funds was real. In February, the fund had been almost exhausted, and the state legislature had refused to allow new loans or extend the city's taxing privilege. Where had this been heard before? Or again?

The crisis was averted when the Broadway Bank agreed to loan the city $400,000, providing the state legislature granted a $2 million loan to the city. This finally occurred at the end of February and on the twenty-fourth, the Volunteer Committee of the Board of Supervisors, which included Tweed, ran an advertisement asking for thirty thousand volunteers who would each receive $777 in state, county and United States bounties. The money was the equivalent of about two years' pay earned by an average workingman. Some "bounty jumpers" re-enlisted several times at different places using different names, amassing a nice sum of money.

Having filled one quota did not fill the next. In June, the Board adopted a resolution asking for an additional $2 million to pay for more volunteers. It might not have wanted to spend this money, but the Board was anxious to show the country that New York was ready to defend the Union. The committee and the Board did their job well; there were few complaints. Perhaps the riots were too much of a reminder that penny pinching could lead to less comfortable results.

Yet the need for soldiers continued into 1865, even though the war was rapidly coming to a close. The Army in January of 1865 asked the city for 21,019 soldiers out of a national quota of 320,000. This was a startling jump over the prior month's quota of 4,433. A group of the Special Committee on Volunteering of the Board of Supervisors was authorized to go to Washington to "ascertain the cause of the sudden and alarming increase," a request made more difficult by the luring of eligible men to adjoining states and communities by recruiters whose booths were found all over the city. The supervisors recommended that such recruitment be ended and the booths closed.

On midnight of January 24, Orison Blunt, chairman of the committee, left for Washington. The next day he met with Provost Marshal James B. Fry, who explained the general need for additional men, but New York was also being punished because other localities had met their quotas earlier than did New York. If New York had not been so late, its quotas would have been substantially reduced, perhaps by about as much as 15,000. Although only Blunt appeared to have gone to Washington, the report of the Special Committee was also signed by Tweed and Purdy, and suggested that the bounty be raised or a draft could not be avoided. Neither proved necessary. The Army did not press its demands as recruitment continued to bring sufficient volunteers.[4]

By March, the war was finally at an end. At news of the imminent surrender of General Robert E. Lee's forces, the city on March 6, 1865, let out a great sigh of relief at a great "National Jubilee and Celebration." Again parades, fireworks, bands and speeches. "Segars" were handed out to thronging multitudes. A huge number of troops started a procession at Fourteenth Street and Broadway, then continued down Broadway to the customhouse, up Park Row to Centre Street, then to Canal, to the Bowery, to Fourth Avenue, to Twenty-third Street, down Twenty-third to Madison Avenue, up Madison and around Madison Square down Fifth Avenue to Union Square. Brigadier General William Hall was grand marshal. He was followed by many officers leading their regiments, including Major General Robert Anderson of Sumter fame and Lieutenant General Winfield Scott, Governor Fenton, members of the state legislature, the mayor and members of the City Council, Board of Aldermen and Board of Supervisors, judges, clergymen, college professors. All paraded. They were followed by still more troops and the city's Fire Department, German, Italian and Irish groups, business and banking firms, insurance and express companies, typographical societies. Sailors carried a full rigged ship and others a model of the *Monitor*. Steinway and Sons had 450 workingmen on parade. There were steam fitters, umbrella makers, hairdressers and tailors. It was a parade of victory, pride and a little bit of free advertising. One sign, for example, read "McAuliffe's Irish Whiskey Cead Mille Faithe. . . . Don't Avoid the Draught."

The crowds, estimated at a million, cheered the names of Lincoln, Grant, Sherman and Farragut and various momentary heroes. They laughed at an elephant dressed in an American flag, horses with hoop skirts and camels in colorful ribbons, all surely part of Barnum's menagerie. There was something for everyone to see in the ten-mile procession. Forgotten were riots, draft, copperheads, attacks on Lincoln. Patriotism is best served by victory.

At news of Lee's actual surrender on April 11, another victory celebration, was held on a smaller scale. Four hundred guns were fired in the park, *Te Deum* was sung at Trinity, speeches were given at the square, produce exchange, customhouse and Chamber of Commerce, as New York joined the nation in the spirit of triumph.[5]

The rejoicing did not last long. On April 15 and 16, New Yorkers read in black-bordered newspapers of the shooting of the President during the night of April 14 and of his death the following morning. The story of the assassination in Ford's Theater, the President's dying hours, the attempted murder of Seward and Stanton were read and reread in disbelief and horror. Shouts of revenge gave way to the slow agonizing awareness of the tragedy that numbed the senses. If the color of the city had been red, white and blue, it was now all black. Mourning and grief were everywhere. "Can it be? Why?" were words expressed in choked emotion. Banners reading "We Mourn Our Loss" were omnipresent as the city paid tribute as if to a father or son. April 15 was Good Friday, which added to the mourning and sense of sacrifice. It was also a time for speechmaking. General James A. Garfield, later to be President, expressed the hope that the country would not become like France and Italy—a nation of assassins. He would have reason for such a wish. Services were held in churches and synagogues. At the Nineteenth Street Synagogue, the Reverend J. J. Lyons led the *Nahan Neshomen*, the prayer for the dead—the first time such a service was held in the United States for a non-Jew. Courts were adjourned, businesses closed. The Board of Aldermen expressed its shock and grief and agreed to take measures for a proper solemnization of the President's death. In a mourning-draped room, the Board of Supervisors noted the horrible crime and shocking calamity of assassination of the "kind-hearted President Lincoln." They expressed sympathy for the President's family and for all Americans and resolved that members of the Board would wear mourning badges for ninety days.

Tweed called the General Committee of Tammany to order, and described the sympathy of Tammany for the loss of Lincoln, "called away by an assassin's hand at the time he appeared the only person who could safely navigate the nation once again upon the path of freedom and once again unite us." Lincoln's "lately manifested" spirit of conciliation, Tweed said, had received the plaudits of even those who had voted against him in the last election. A committee was appointed to draft the necessary resolution to the "illustrious deceased." The hall was to be draped in mourning for thirty days.

A man in the Bowery making "blasphemous" remarks about Lincoln was attacked and knocked down by several men.

New York's depth of sympathy was evident with the arrival on April 24 of the body of the martyred President. It was an incredible funeral. The Clay, Webster and Jackson obsequies were but the prelude. Beginning on April 21, workingmen were busy in City Hall erecting the catafalque on which the body of the President would lie in state. A canopy covered the coffin; black velvet covered the floor; black ribbons hung from the dome. Various organizations were readied to attend the processions. Historian George Bancroft was expected to deliver the major oration at Union Square. The Committee of Arrangements included A. T. Stewart, Moses Grinnell, William E. Dodge and Tweed. William Hitchman headed a special Obsequies Committee of the Common Council. The train carrying Lincoln's body had left Washington on the twenty-first, and had stopped at Baltimore, Harrisburg and Philadelphia before coming to New Jersey. From there, the coffin was slowly carried into New York on the ferry *Jersey City*.

Ships in the Hudson lay quietly, most draped in black muslin. Heads were uncovered. At 11:00 A.M. the *Jersey City* landed at Desbrosses Street, as a German singing society on the vessel sang a funeral ode. General John Dix and some twenty-seven members of an accompanying congressional committee, Mayor Christian Gunther and members of the Common Council were aboard the ferry. On landing, the coffin was placed in a hearse whose sides were of plate glass, the top covered by eight huge plumes of black and white feathers. Six gray horses were covered with black cloth and each had a groom dressed in mourning. All this was supplied by undertaker Peter Relyea. The solemn procession headed by General Dix and the 7th Regiment proceeded down Hudson Street to Canal Street. Mourning cloth draped almost every building. Businesses were shut; the air was still; the crowd silent; drums of various bands were muffled; the only other sound was that of slowly tolling bells. There was no waving, no cheering, no whistling—everything was somber, black caps and capes for the police and gray for the escorting troops. The procession turned down Broadway to the park—the route lined with quiet saddened faces. The crowd in the park was kept behind the fences. The German singing society sang a requiem as the coffin was taken from the hearse, lifted on the shoulders of eight troopers and carried into the black-draped building and put on the catafalque. A line formed at the entrance of the building to wait until the coffin was opened. This was the first time in four years that Lincoln was in the city. But what a different reception and time.

The following day, April 25, at 1 P.M. an elaborate funeral car drawn by sixteen horses drew up before City Hall, a "colored" groom held each horse by the head. The coffin was carried by members of the Veterans Reserve Corps as Claudius S. Grafulla's 7th Regiment Band played a dirge. There were at least seventeen other bands in attendance. Eyes of men and women filled as the procession proceeded to the Hudson River Railroad depot accompanied by veterans of the 42nd, 38th and 14th regiments, West Point cadets, national and state leaders and members of the city government including Tweed and his eldest son, Oakey Hall, Barnard, Hoffman and Cardozo. All the thoroughfares in the line of march and in the immediate vicinity were filled with great crowds, solid masses pushing forward to see the procession and passing hearse. In the rear of the line of mourners were several hundred "freedmen." It took two hours to reach the depot.

There were also ceremonies at Union Square. Bancroft delivered the main address, with the benediction give by Archbishop John McCloskey; Scripture was read by Rabbi S. M. Isaacs. It was, all in all, a day for New Yorkers to remember. The train left the city at 4 P.M. and arrived in Albany at about ten-thirty, stopping for a moment at the many towns along the Hudson. As a final token of appreciation the Common Council directed David Valentine to edit *Lincoln Obsequies*, which was duly published in 1866. The city paid for all expenses—horses, carriages, marshal's badges, saddles, etc. Andrew J. Garvey received $165 for plaster busts of Lincoln and Washington used to decorate the catafalque.[6]

The time of grief passed and only two months later on June 7, New York could show another face as it welcomed General Ulysses S. Grant as the hero of the hour. He was greeted by the 7th Regiment and serenaded by its band that evening after a dinner at the customhouse. At the end of the year on November 18–20, General Grant and his family were again given a brilliant reception by admiring New Yorkers, this time at the Fifth

Avenue Hotel. A. T. Stewart was chairman of this Arrangements Committee, joined once again by Tweed.[7] So grief and glory passed each other in
the city's streets.

There were, of course, other things going on, even in the midst of war
and death. As portent of times to come, the Republican-controlled state
Senate began an investigation of the City Inspector's Office, as well as
other offices. It turned into a general examination of city expenses and
practices, and brought Tweed some unwanted notoriety. The hearings,
which began early in February 1865, first involved Leonard Boole, brother
of Alderman F. I. A. Boole, and others who were charged with allegedly
selling positions to the highest bidder and receiving money for allowing
garbage dumping on the New York shore. Witnesses told of being asked
to raise prices charged to the city for the removal of garbage in a kick-back
arrangement. Still others, however, attested to the honesty of those in
office and the need for money for street cleaning in order to maintain the
health of the inhabitants of the city. Questions as to amounts and regula-
tions of street cleaning made up the bulk of the hearing until the afternoon session of February 24. Then, ex-Judge John W. Edmonds on
behalf of Peter Cooper's Citizens Association, a watchdog organization
formed in 1863, accused the Board of Supervisors of spending $250,000
without authority of law. These charges were not directed against the
Board as such, but to show the city's need for a strong executive with full
power to appoint and remove subordinates. It was at this point Tweed
was called upon to answer the association's allegations. Tweed read a
statement showing that their figures were not correct and that there had
been no attempt by the association to discuss the matter with the supervisors prior to making public charges. But questions remained.

Comptroller Robert Storr produced a statement on the city's finances
in answer to the charges made. It was a long, detailed, itemized statement
of New York's debt, some $43 million. Expenditures by the Street Com-
missioner's Office, of which Tweed was now deputy commissioner, were
scrutinized without result. The furor did little except to show that there
was room for a greater degree of care in the city's finances, and that the
Citizens Association had to continue its watchfulness.

The *Herald* concluded, as in times gone by, that New York City was
"notoriously the worst governed city in Christendom," that bribery, corruption and "rings" ran New York and that there was a need for continued investigations. These Senate hearings for the first time tied Tweed to
scandal. His role as supervisor and deputy street commissioner made him a
natural choice, though this was not necessarily a criticism of personal behavior, but rather of the office. The investigation into street-cleaning contracts continued in a rather lackluster way during the summer. Interest in

rooting out corruption was kept alive by the revelation in August of the loss of several million dollars through forgeries in the United States Paymaster's office. Several army officers were arrested. One of the "ring" leaders was Edward R. Ketchum. For the *Times* the "era of fraud and embezzlement is but commencing." Had it ever stopped? Ketchum, the "Wall Street forger," was sentenced by John Hoffman to four years and six months in the state prison.

In October, the Senate investigation into the street cleaning contract was reopened, but few people attended the hearings. Gadfly John McKeon, "long of visage as though his pocket had been picked of ten thousand dollars," was present. John L. Brown, a street contractor, testified that he had known Peter K. Knapp, a contract clerk; Mayor Gunther; former alderman, now City Inspector F. I. A. Boole; and Comptroller Matthew Brennan and many others, but knew of nothing that was done in awarding contracts which was not "fair and upright." Recorder John Hoffman maintained similarly that he knew of no improper contracts. This testimony was given on October 15 before Governor Fenton. Boole, Brennan and Chamberlain Daniel Devlin through their attorney asked that charges and the investigation be dismissed as "not proved, and originated in party malice." All were cleared legally, but to some moral innocence had not been proven. Certainly, the *Herald* and *Times* were not satisfied. They found a new "ring" managed by Fernando Wood, Thurlow Weed, Street Commissioner Cornell and Supervisor Tweed had been formed. The *Herald* predicted that Wood, Tweed and Cornell would seize control of Tammany and that Wood would gain the mayoralty at the next election. While Wood and his copperhead friends might deny the account, Jake Sharp, of the Broadway Railroad, was willing to swear to every word. It was Wood's revenge for years of rejection by Tammany. Tweed and Cornell, the journal said, were discontented with the party, but they had done "more to injure the organization by their corruptions and their opposition to honest candidates than anybody." The *Herald* reported that Tweed and Cornell were "horribly jealous" of others in Tammany and were willing to work with Weed, even if he was a Republican, and the paper concluded that Tweed held about sixteen city offices and had the "size and weight" to be a chairman of the General Committee, but now wanted to be state senator. Cornell wanted reappointment as street commissioner and perhaps the mayor's office. Tweed was becoming known, at least to the *Herald*.

Whoever supplied the "inside" information for the paper was guilty of at least some exaggeration. That part of the Tweed myth relating to multiple job holding received here one of its first mentions. Yet, there is little to substantiate it. Tweed was at the time deputy street commissioner, receiving $7,500 per year, the same salary as that of the mayor, street commissioner and comptroller. He was also a member of the Board of Supervisors, now being paid $2,000 per year, a member of the seven-man Board of Fire Commissioners and one of the hundreds of commissioners of deeds, both unpaid offices. Where the "about sixteen" positions are derived from is a mystery, even if his son, William Jr., who worked as a recognizance clerk in the district attorney's office at $1,200 per year was added. True, later there were other emoluments. For example at the opening of Morningside Park in 1870, William Jr. received $7,000 as a commissioner and Tweed's father-in-law Joseph Skaden $2,000 as an appraiser, but then the sons, brothers, relatives of a host of officials also benefited from city largesse. It was the way things were and indeed are.[8]

The investigation helped kick off the fall political campaign. The proper atmosphere was created. The scheme "uncovered" by the *Herald* was in time for the upcoming elections.

The testing started at the Albany convention held on September 6. At that time, Peter Cagger and other Democrats met to endorse President Andrew Johnson's policy of reconstruction. The State Central Committee was selected. Cornell and Sweeny were chosen on a compromise slate of opposing factions, representing Tammany. Tweed, one of the Tammany delegation, was made a vice-president of the convention. Schemes flew wildly about. There was a rumor that Wood would back Tweed for the state Senate, but this brought strong opposition from his brother Benjamin, who said he would rather run himself than have the supervisor in office. All expected the short-lived "ring" of Cornell and Tweed would break up.

By October 23, it was reported that Tweed, the "trenchant" chairman of Tammany, would receive the Fourth District nomination to the Senate, despite Ben Wood, and that Cornell had the Fifth District senatorial nomination sewed up. Again, these observations as far as Tweed was concerned proved wrong. Tweed did not receive the nomination for state senator in the Fourth or any other district, probably to satisfy McKeon and Ben Wood.

Democrats did not do well in the county elections. Their internal bickering, the popular support for Republicanism and Lincoln, and charges of corruption did little to aid the cause. There was also no particular issue of importance, and as could be expected, there was a general falling off of the vote. Democrats lost some twenty thousand votes, Republicans four thousand from the 1864 election.

The next order of business was the charter election, in which mayor, corporation counsel, eight aldermen and two school officers were to be elected. There were the usual host of parties and candidates. Tweed's name appeared with a host of others, Purdy, McKeon, Wood, as Democratic candidates for various posts, especially that of mayor. It was suspected that in order to achieve some semblance of party unity, John T. Hoffman and Daniel Devlin would be named for mayor and corporation counsel by Tammany. Hoffman was looked upon as an "unreproachable citizen" without a suspicion of evil.

The *Herald* commented that it made little difference who was mayor, since his hands were so effectively tied by the state that corruption and plunder could continue. There was need for a whole new machinery of government and especially giving some power to an executive. Interestingly, earlier in the year, the *Herald* and others made a provocative proposal to aid the metropolis. That was to return the capital of the state to the city. New York had been the provincial capital and state capital until the 1790s, when slowly state offices left and began business officially in Albany. One who benefited from such a move was Chancellor Robert R. Livingston. It was a matter of convenience for him to hear cases at home in Cleremont, just outside Albany, and in Albany itself, rather than make the journey to the city. New York, which had been the capital not only of the state but of the United States in 1790, had hoped at least that the state capital would be in Gotham, but this was denied. It was not until 1865 that Albany was legally made the state capital, although it was a de facto capital since 1797. The *Herald* argued that its return to New York would serve the interests of the state and city best. It would be geographically and politically an economy, and the problem of defense in the event of a war, a major factor for the original move, was no longer a concern. The Common Council voted to grant to the state any area in the city it wanted from the Battery to Washington Heights. This request was not acted upon by the state legislature. If it had been, many of the city's problems may well have been solved.

Anyway by early December, the slate was completed. Hoffman received the Tammany nomination for mayor. M. O. Roberts ran against him as a Republican and War Democrat as did John Hecker, a flour dealer, who had German as well as Mozart Hall, Citizens Association and anti-"Ring" backing. Tammany did not run anyone for corporation counsel, tacitly agreeing with the Mozart Hall choice. John Hoffman defeated Roberts by 1,300 votes out of 80,000 cast. Hoffman, a descendant of an old New York Dutch family, born in Sing Sing, New York, was about forty-two years of age, almost the same age as Tweed. Graduated from Union College in Schenectady, he studied law, came to the city and became a member of the firm of Woodruff, Leonard and Hoffman. The former recorder had a good record and reputation.[9] He deserved a better fate.

III

Rise to Power

14

"Young Harpies"

The new mayor, young, vigorous and anxious to succeed in his job, found like others before him that there was more needed to govern the city than good intentions. His Honor Mayor John Thompson Hoffman presented his inaugural message to the council after greeting a mob of well-wishers that stormed City Hall. This message, as all previous ones, was a promise of hard work, reform and retrenchment. He asked for a greater "concentration of power and responsibility" in city government in order to end the large number of municipal evils. The address was well received, of course, but there were questions as to whether the city could cure itself, even with the best resolves, or whether finally the state must seize control from "rings," an increasingly popular word, and corrupt politicians. The general feeling was wait and see.

The Board of Supervisors elected Henry Smith, Republican, as president. Tweed, having served two terms, was denied a third. Smith asked for a return of public confidence for the Board and city government. The first order of business concerned Elijah F. Purdy, who died at age seventy during the night of January 8. The "Old War Horse" was honored by the Board for his "distinguished and unwavering integrity" and for his "pure minded and earnest" patriotism. The supervisors draped the chamber in black as a mark of respect to the three-time Board president. Tweed, who was particularly affected, addressed fellow supervisors and advised them that Purdy had expressed the wish shortly before his death that his funeral be directed by the Board and that in his last breath "he spoke in the kindest measure of his associates" and his regrets of leaving their company. Tweed asked for a committee of four to be sent to the family to arrange for the funeral. Tweed, as chairman of the Democratic-Republican General Committee, in a long eulogy, pointed out that Purdy had been a member of the Board since its creation, respected and loved by all for his diligence and honesty. Tweed remarked that he had an enduring relationship with Purdy and felt as if he had lost a father. Having allowed him a useful life, the "Creator saw fit to call him to a happier, holier and better world." It could be that Tweed had mouthed so many platitudes, but more than likely Tweed, a rather disingenuous person, did feel a deep sense of personal loss. If Purdy had lived, would Tweed have become caught up in the kind of events which caused his downfall? Would Purdy have been a steadying, stabilizing influence? Certainly the large gap in Tammany leadership would not have been there for Tweed and others to step into. Funeral services took place at St. Stephen's, Tweed's church, on January 12 and the body conveyed from Purdy's home at 83 Ludlow Street, a short distance from the civil jail. Tweed and a number of other supervisors were pallbearers. From the church, the procession went to City Hall, where Purdy lay in state in the Governor's Room until the following day. Then the body was conveyed to a family vault in White Plains for interment.[1]

Purdy was hardly dead and buried when the supervisors reeled from charges made by Supervisor Smith Ely, Jr., and the Citizens Association against their Committee on the New Court House in regard to gross corruption in that building's construction. Members of the Committee were Tweed, Shook, William T. Stewart and Walter Roche. The courthouse from the time its construction started in 1861 was the center of several investigations. In 1863, Mayor Opdyke vetoed bills for salaries and materials amounting to $94,586.70 on the ground that they had not been properly certified and that the Special Committee did not have the authority to oversee the construction of the building. Opdyke wanted to test an act of 1863 which gave the supervisors the specific right to erect the courthouse. It was his contention that the mayor and a committee appointed by him should have control over such matters. Corporation Counsel John E. Develin in a long opinion sustained the supervisors' position. Now Smith Ely, Jr., who much later was elected mayor, wanted to know about monies received by the superintendent of the courthouse, Cummings H. Tucker, the salary of the architect, John Kellum, whether monies were paid for services not given and whether work was done in good faith, without collusion. There were results. In February, Joseph F. Daly brought suit against the supervisors. The case was heard before Justice Barnard in the Supreme Court. A mandamus was issued to the Board to open their books in regard to the courthouse. Daly argued that only the mayor had power to direct construction.

A history of the courthouse, apart from hysterical rhetoric, has never been undertaken. Yet almost all the financial journals, vouchers, warrants, the supervisors' ledgers have miraculously escaped destruction. Even a cursory glance at these records provides a good deal of information. First, the question opened by Ely Jr. regarding rising costs of construction. The original appropriation by the legislature in 1858 authorized $250,000 to erect the building at the rear of City Hall under direction of the supervisors, the loan to be paid by the county. Construction was started in 1861, and the cornerstone laid on December 26. By 1863, $891,033.50 had been spent, by 1864, $1,422,956.12 and by 1865, $1,748,260.74, including interest, and the end was not in sight. By 1874, the building cost a little over $4 million, with the largest portion, $3.2 million, being spent prior to 1869, when the "Tweed Ring" was supposedly created. Hundreds of firms, large and small, worked on the construction. These supplied cement, brick, marble, lime, lumber, rubbing sand, slate, iron and steel. In 1865, Andrew Garvey received $349.50 for a "model of Capitol" perhaps meaning the molding for the capitol of a column. It took ninety-five days of labor ($332.50), four barrels of plaster ($12) and wax and oil for the molding ($5). Of the large firms, Henry R. McMurray received $33,000 for marble, W. J. and J. S. Peck, $18,000 for brick and lime, John C. Johnson & Co., $2,600 for hardware, Nesbit & Irwin, $10,000 for brick and cement. But the major contractors were J. B. & W. W. Cornell, who earned $118,000 in 1865 for iron work. All the bills, particularly that of the Cornells, were carefully itemized and approved by Cummings H. Tucker. The East Chester Quarry Co. in Tuckahoe, New York, received $32,000 for marble work.

The payroll came to some $280,000 a year, approximately $24,000 per month, less in the winter months. The men were paid every two weeks. Taking an average two-week period, that of June 10 to 24, 1865, for instance, the county employed 203 stonecutters, at $4.00 a day, six "setters" who received between $3.50 to $4.50 a day, a modeler, George Didelot, at $5.00 per day, and a foreman, Michael Gayter, $5.00 per day. There were thirty-three stonecutter laborers at $2.00 a day, plus a foreman, John Simpson, at $3.50, and twenty-five mason laborers at $2.00, one at $2.25 per day, nine blacksmiths at $3.50 to $3.75, and one cartman, $4.00 per day. There were painters at $2.50 and $3.00 per day, four carpenters at $3.00 to $7.00, there were eleven engineers, four gatekeepers at $2.50, three watchmen at $2.50, eight officers, including John B. Corliss ($208.33), R. Wakefield ($104.16), James Gillies ($100), James Watson, county auditor ($37.50), E. A. Woodward, Commissioner of Deeds ($37.50). The last two would be heard from again. Small bills no more than $200 were paid to Keyser & Co. and Ingersoll, Watson & Co.

The total payroll for this two-week period came to $12,290.93 paid to 280 persons. By far the greater percentage of workmen were Irish or of Irish extraction, Sullivan, Riley, O'Shaughnessy, Purcell, Cushing, Burke,

Quinn, Hurley, etc. There were some odd names, Buzzy Battista, Patrick Cohen, but most, including Cohen, surely Cohan, were probably recent immigrants with the courthouse a monument to such labor, a sort of early W.P.A. Interestingly, except for the officers, all signed their names with an "X," not necessarily because they could not write. This may have been done by some clerk just to save time. Think of keeping a long line of impatient laborers waiting while each signed his name to the long payroll. Newspapers also benefited from the construction as they were paid to print certain notices as for loans. All around money was being made and spent.[2] Construction continued; to some it was all worthwhile, but to many it was all useless and expensive and should be ended, and so the eternal war between spenders and savers continued. It surely can never be known if the bills were fair or not. That the bills were all carefully itemized and the work performed would suggest they were honest. No one has specifically ever refuted them. A popular and universal view is, of course, that everyone working for the city at any time, or providing services to the city in some way, cheated through padded bills, services not performed, time taken off. It is as certain as George Washington never told a lie, Abraham Lincoln freed the slaves or all potatoes come from Idaho. But they all made good stories.

After several hearings, during which time no wrongdoing was uncovered, the supervisors dismissed Ely's charges and Barnard dismissed Daly's allegations. But the memory was alive.

Besides the courthouse mandamus, Barnard handed down two other important decisions reflecting concern with corruption. One set aside a grant by the council over the mayor's veto of a twenty-year monopoly for supplying the city with coal gas to one gas company. Barnard issued an injunction against the city, questioning the right of the city to grant contracts for more than one year. In the case of People ex. rel. Richard M. Henry v. Charles G. Cornell, Street Commissioner, he upheld the right of a citizen to inspect public records. Surely the public charges of corruption and malfeasance were at least partly responsible for Barnard's decisions in these two cases. If any "Ring" did exist at this time, it did not include Barnard.[3]

There were other issues besides corruption that caught the eye. The nationalistic Irish Fenian movement also held the spotlight. With a large Irish constituency in the city, all politicians were affected. The direct cause of renewed agitation was heated debate in England over the perennial question and suspension of habeas corpus in Ireland. There were charges by Englishmen John Bright and John Stuart Mill of British misgovernment. In New York, the Fenian flag was hoisted in Union Square and a large meeting was held on March 5 in Jones' Wood despite the protestation of Bishop John McCloskey that the meeting held on Sunday was a "profanation of the Lord's Day," especially as it was the holy season of Lent, and that it would incite the "anger of God no less than the sorrow and indignation of all sincere Christians." Sweeny and Marshall O. Roberts, the defeated but still hopeful Republican, denounced acts of British tyranny and urged an attack on British soil—Canada. At a mass meeting at Tammany Hall, a new circle of the Fenian Brotherhood, itself a secret society, was formed. Frank McCarthy was chairman of a meeting which was addressed by several speakers asking for aid to the "Cause." The movement simmered on the back burner as the main arena was prepared for the fall campaign.[4]

For Richard B. Connolly, long in the political doghouse, thrown out of the General Committee of Tammany, it was the beginning of the long road back. The time was ripe to leave his employment with broker Henry Smythe. As others noisily maneuvered around him, he was able to influence an angry President Andrew Johnson weary of "radical" politicians like Weed to give an important customs post to his relatively unknown but anti-radical employer Smythe. To the chagrin of Tammany, Connolly was very much alive. It was a major coup for him and helped his return to the hustings. Andrew Johnson's visit to New York at the end of August as part of his famous "swing around the circle" underscored his policy against radical Republicans, brought him Democratic support and was a reminder of his appointment power as in the case of Smythe. Connolly waited as Democrats settled on nominations.

At the state convention held in Albany in September, Hall made an impassioned plea for a "Christian gentleman, a young rising statesman of ability" and a "champion of your young men, the champion of the great principles—John T. Hoffman." Amid cheers and applause, Hoffman was nominated unanimously for governor. In his acceptance speech, he promised to support Johnson and help tie the bonds of Union between North and South. Fenians got their due with the nomination of William Gallagher, speaker of the Fenian Congress, as state inspector. Nothing was heard from Tweed, but Sweeny and Cornell were put on the State Nominating Committee.[5]

As the elections neared, the usual jockeying for other positions took place. It was expected that Sickles, with one leg shot off at Gettysburg, would receive a congressional nomination, since neither Tammany nor Mozart Hall would dare oppose him. Tammany supported the renomination of Brennan for comptroller, but "Big Judge" Michael Connolly and Richard B. were there to make a fight of it. The latter Connolly headed a Democratic Union Association meeting held at Cooper Union in denouncing the "Tammany Ring," which, he shouted, fooled Germans by promising falsely that the Recorder's Office would be given to their selection. Irish voters, too, he cried, were not consulted in nominations. Though loyal Democrats in the city and Fenians rallied around Hoffman, the elections were disastrous. "Baron von" Hoffman was looked upon as a "copperhead." He was hurt also by an alleged association of his name with the "Tammany Ring," and especially with Cornell and Tweed. With Tammany, Mozart Hall and McKeon forces active, the mayor could expect defeat. Such prophecies proved entirely correct. While Hoffman carried the city 80,000 to 33,000, he lost the state by 5,000.

Given this defeat, it was expected that Hoffman would move to disassociate himself from "The Ring" if he still entertained hopes for state office. Surely he would have Cornell and Tweed resign as street commissioners, especially as Cornell's term was up at the end of the year and Judge James R. Whiting was appointed by Governor Fenton to investigate Cornell's Street Department, at the request of the Citizens Association—yet another probe. There were results as the press turned its fire on Cornell and to a lesser extent Tweed. While there was little or no evidence, Cornell succumbed and on November 17, Mayor Hoffman received Cornell's resignation. The commissioner said he had answered all questions at a legislative hearing a week before and expected unqualified discharge of any wrongdoing. He accused the governor of bringing in Whiting, a "bitter partisan" and a "rancorous spirit" who spent years as an accuser of public officials. It was an unfair appointment, a political gambit by a political opponent that forced Cornell to resign, not the facts or justice. He would accept an impartial panel, not an "inquisitor" like Whiting.

Cornell's troubles did not end. Councilman Christopher Pullman, Alderman Joseph B. Varnum and Citizens Association members brought a suit against Cornell and the city which was filed in November and continued in December. There were seventeen charges brought against him, mostly for approving improper requisitions and warrants, "for his own or other improper use." Although they were all dropped, the accusations had the desired effect.[6]

Now, Matthew Brennan angrily refused to run for comptroller, probably because the election of Charles Halpine (Miles O'Reilly) in November as register, had played havoc with the Tammany-Mozart Hall association and raised strong doubts about his own re-election, but he was obviously frightened and angered by the treatment of Cornell. In a long letter to businessmen Moses Taylor and William B. Astor, among others, who had recommended that Brennan seek re-election, he wrote that he could take expected criticism from corrupt contractors, jobbers and members of the "Corporation Ring," but what hurt were the unprincipled attacks by the "young lawyers" who managed the Citizens Association, and who in fact while extorting exorbitant fees in handling imaginary complaints were hypocritically snooping, probing, gossiping, destroying reputations. It was their stories that disgusted Brennan most. He had built a home for $11,000, but in the eyes of the association this became a "palatial mansion on the banks of the Hudson," the premise being that Brennan had obviously plundered the city treasury. The association criticized, but never extended a helping hand.

He bitterly concluded "another contest for the office, with the ring of contractors, the ring of the Common Council, the ring of robbers, the ring of reformers and defaulters making common cause with the ring of politicians and all other rings big and little, against me, with the great Albany ring ready to encircle all, present no attractions to me, and an election, in view of the threatened legislation at Albany, no gratification." He was willing to leave cares of office to the "greedy" hands extended for them. Like Cornell, Brennan surrendered to the provocations of the professional reformers, or if of a more cynical mind, to political expediency, and to the "young harpies" of the law anxious to become eagles or vultures. Brennan's angry criticism of the association—even the *Times* questioned the motives of the "one-hundred odd gentlemen" who made up the group—had some impact. If people like Peter Cooper, Smith Ely, Jr., Thomas C. Acton, Jackson S. Schultz—worthwhile members of the Association—were listened to, then something might be accomplished, but most members were in fact "dilettantes" spending their time in dining halls and libraries with little attention to business. Hoffman had his own choice for street commissioner, but persuaded by the party he accepted George McLean, a former cotton broker, a man who "could not be used for any of the corrupt purposes of the Ring."[7]

The comptroller's office was now wide open. A host of bankers and merchants rallied behind Richard B. Connolly, whose shrewdness paid off. A meeting was held at Cooper Union. Connolly's friends were told of the importance of the post and the need to keep it out of radical Republican hands.

Now the *Times* acted, as it always did. If charges, rumors of scandal had destroyed Cornell and frightened Brennan, why not try them on Connolly and Democrats. The old beans were dragged off the shelf and warmed over.

Just prior to the election, the *Times* again went against the supervisors. It rallied against their conduct at the courthouse hearings and their audacity in expending $12,062.25, defending themselves against Ely's charges. It also reported that the Board had its printing done by a "double headed" concern, the New York Printing Company and the Transcript Association, both under "Ring of the Board." The *Times* screamed that the costs to the city were much higher than what would be charged by other printing houses—like the *Times*.

On June 26, Supervisor Tweed presented a resolution that five thousand copies of the report of "The Committee on Charges against the Committee on New Court House" be printed. Ely Jr. was in the negative on a 9 to 1 vote. On July 24, it was resolved by the same margin to give the New York Printing Company the job, which cost $7,718.75. By the same vote, the Transcript Association for printing further reports received $6,398.10. But, by the *Times's* arithmetic this came to $20,000 as a printing bill for publishing the "bogus investigation," and to pile insult to injury it felt that while perhaps ten thousand copies were published, only one hundred were delivered. The paper concluded, the "enormities perpetrated by men in office cannot be paralleled in the annals of human effrontery." It asked the legislature to right these wrongs. Would the *Times* have been so incensed had it received the publishing contract?

It certainly tried hard enough to obtain city contracts for printing. There were long, argumentative letters which passed between editor George Jones and the city in the past, but to Jones's irritation his requests were often denied. There is no anger like the *Times* scorned.

By early December, the political decisions for county office were made. "Greedy" hands reached for the plum, the comptroller's office. Republicans chose Richard Kelly, a long-time police magistrate. Dick Connolly was chosen as expected by Tammany and Mozart Hall, his regeneration well on the way. "Big Judge" Connolly was the McKeon selection for the office. Republicans denounced "Slippery Dick" and a member of the "Ring" faction and "Big Judge" as unqualified for office. In an unexpectedly close contest, Connolly barely got by the opposition, receiving only slightly more than one third of the vote cast.[8]

15

New Tammany Hall

With Cornell and Brennan gone, Tweed followed suit late in December 1866 as he resigned as deputy street commissioner.[1] He did not make any public statement, but he did not have to. His position was made untenable, linked as he was with Cornell. Having achieved such stunning success, the reformers looked for more heads to tumble into the basket. There was a lesson to be learned. While budget expenditures were of interest, what really stirred the imagination and sold newspapers were personalities and any news of corrupt "rings." There was a national mania about rings, Whiskey Rings, Indian Agency Rings, Railroad Rings. Rings were everywhere, of every kind and description—some real, most imaginary—all part of a kaleidoscopic carousel. New York was no exception. The *Herald* in an editorial of March 3 detailed the history and operations of the "famous Tammany Ring." It traced its birth to Democratic victory over the Whigs in 1850–52, to the Jacksonian belief of "to victors belong the spoils" and to "Empire Clubs," which by deception and bribery were able to elect their own tools to the highest office. Aldermen became rotten, then the entire council, and lastly "The Ring" became a combination of working politicians without office. Though people like Cornell and Tweed were not mentioned—in fact, no one was mentioned—they were in mind. The *Herald* charged again without naming names or proof that "The Ring" took 10 to 20 per cent of all claims against the city for themselves, $10 to $25 from each appointed petty official, collected a fixed per cent from every salary within reach, put a few dozen "straw men" upon payrolls and pocketed their wages. Each year, the "harvest" grows, the journal concluded, and "The Ring" now divides $100,000 at a clip.[2] It was a case of Jonah swallowing the whale. Much of this exposé would be repeated for Tweed's benefit in a few years.

The *Times* of March 9, 1867, questioned the efficacy of even legislative action in view of the extensive waste and thievery. There was something basically wrong. George Jones asked whether honest city government could be maintained with a system of universal suffrage, which for city government is an "utter failure." He continued, "The history of New York City proves this . . . all of its government that rests upon suffrage is worse than a failure, it is a nuisance. It is corrupt, inefficient, wasteful and scandalous. The people are overburdened with taxation and there is nothing to show for it. Millions are wasted and nothing is done. The streets are not cleaned; the public health is not cared for; waste and extravagance characterize every department; and although more money is spent than anywhere else in the world for the purpose of government, the government actually procured by it is the worst in the world." Open hostility to mass democracy, voiced by Whigs, was now restated by Republicans. Perhaps the *Times* was in a particularly testy mood because of disclosures before the House Committee on Public Expenditures that Connolly's friend, the newly appointed Republican port collector Henry Smythe, had committed frauds amounting to millions of dollars in the customhouse. Smythe confirmed that his nomination rested upon his agreement that "certain persons" would be "pecuniarily benefited by allotment and concession of revenue monies." He specifically named several firms, two senators and "two friends" of President Grant that "must be taken care of." He was not asked to go into details.[3]

Certainly, the humor of the *Times* and *Herald* was not helped by a July report issued by Comptroller Connolly to the Board of Supervisors on July 1, which concluded that the city had to raise $5 million to pay for various expenses for the current year. He outlined the problem. Of the $24 million raised by taxes for the year, the state received $3.9 million, the county $6.8 million, the city $10.6 million and the remainder went into a general fund to supply deficiencies. Of the additional $5 million requested, $500,000 was intended to cover a deficiency in the state tax of 1865; $500,000 was for the redemption of county bonds issued for repayment of taxes; $485,000 for public construction; $490,000 for redemption for county loans; $300,000 for the new courthouse; and $300,000 for repairing Broadway. Connolly stated that he did not wish to increase taxes on an already overtaxed people, "Wrung as it must be from the hard earnings of the laboring poor," and he urged the supervisors to exercise "utmost vigilance" in every item of expenditure and asked all non-productive city property be sold to reduce the tax burden. Connolly recommended after outlining the extent of the net bonded city debt of $32.7 million as of December 31, 1866, that the new courthouse be speedily completed so that it may be ready for occupancy during the present year and that this "source of financial anxiety and draft upon the resources of the taxpayers of New York be brought to a close." The tax assessment was $2.30 per hundred in 1866 and would be higher in 1867. It went to $2.67. He finished by again stressing the need to curtail vast expenditures and for the supervisors to be most watchful.[4]

Immediately, the Committee on the New Court House, of which Tweed was a member, asked that bills submitted to them be especially scrutinized and audited by the supervisors. Claims submitted included J. B. and W. W. Cornell for $23,810 for iron; Andrew J. Garvey, $9,876 for mason work; John H. Keyser, $1,973 for gas fittings. They would be heard from again. Certainly their bills were on the increase.

One of the acts of the 1867 legislature was the creation of still another "board of audit" consisting of comptroller and four supervisors to look into all unsettled claims against the city and county which had arisen prior to January 1, 1867. Although generally overlooked by the public, the board was created by an amendment tacked onto the tax levy and was given vast power. The same procedure would be followed in 1870. To the *Times* it was a scheme of "The Ring" and one of the "most dangerous and corrupt that could possibly be devised." What number of fraudulent claims would now be allowed, Jones asked. The Supreme Court through a request of the Citizens Association issued an injunction against the board's awarding any claims, particularly one sought by Andrew J. Hackley for $279,000 on a street cleaning contract made in 1861. The city had not paid the bill since it alleged that the city had to clean the streets itself and that the sureties of Hackley now owed the city $2 million, because of his noncompliance with the contract. The injunction, however, was lifted, and the claim finally honored.

On August 27, Hoffman returned a veto message to the Board of Supervisors. It was read on September 3 while Tweed was presiding. Hoffman refused a salary request for the new "board of audit" since he found it an infringement of the comptroller's power of audit. Hoffman also questioned how five men sitting on the board at less than a dozen meetings a year could ask some $24,000 as salary?

Despite the warnings of Connolly concerning the dire financial straits of the city and the rumblings of Hoffman and others, bills from various contractors, not only Garvey and Keyser, but others like Ingersoll, E. V. Houghwaut & Co. and John Kellum, the architect of the courthouse, were submitted and paid. The watchdog Citizens Association objected vehemently. Peter Cooper, the "old man" of the association, traced his own history of the courthouse. Though $150,000 was initially allotted to construction, through 1867, $3,550,000 had already been spent or authorized to be spent. With interest, Cooper found the sum to be $4,161,326. His figures seem exaggerated since supervisors' records show $1.8 million through 1867. He gave specifics. In September 1861, the supervisors contracted for the delivery of the marble from a quarry in Sheffield, Massachusetts. The quarry was to deliver $1,250 worth of marble at first, but by 1867 it had cost $220,000. This, Cooper charged, was $100,000 more than another firm would have asked.

On October 5, 1867, the Briggs Marble Quarry owned by Supervisor John Briggs was sold to the Housatonic Marble Company which would supply more marble to the city, but for $800,000. These statements, intended to show how the city was being defrauded, were not answered, said Cooper. He also charged that Cornell & Co. was supposedly the lowest bidder for iron work, yet many firms could have supplied iron at lower prices but were not told of any bidding. One company said it was told by architect John Kellum that he would tell them when plans and specifications were ready, but he did not do so until after the work was contracted. Further, Cooper alleged that failure to complete the building prior to this time had cost the city $217,509 in rents and repairs to other buildings which had to be used as substitutes. The Brooklyn County Court House was begun at about the same time and was completed several years before at a cost of $549,633. Yet in New York, time and money had been allowed to be squandered. The association demanded a swift completion of the building. They appointed a committee to meet with the supervisors to discuss the problem.[5] Nothing happened. Not yet.

Still another financial problem of minor character, is worth mentioning. Hoffman wrote to City Chamberlain Peter B. Sweeny for an accounting of monies received in his office. Sweeny in a reply dated October 21, 1867, said he had not received a dollar beyond his salary. Sweeny then explained that the half-century-old office had been held by many bankers and merchants and that not one had been asked to make a return of interest on public monies in their care. Such interest was considered an emolument of office, he said. Until a fixed salary was offered, the chamberlain could expect $40,000 to $50,000 per year. From the time of the first chamberlain, Cornelius W. Lawrence in 1832, to Sweeny's predecessor, Daniel Devlin, who held the office from his appointment in 1860 to his death in 1867, such was the method of payment employed and it could, in fact, be looked upon as a legal right long established. Sweeny also stated that his appointment to the office by the mayor had been unsolicited and without "bargain, condition, or encumbrance." Yet given the clamor about the office and its income, Sweeny relinquished the right to interest in favor of a fixed salary of $10,000 per year. It was an act of "public service," of which Sweeny was always proud.[6]

The eyes of the reformers continued to search and pry. They caught Tweed. The first of the satirical articles on the Americus Club located at

Indian Harbor in Greenwich, Connecticut, appeared in August 1867. Details of Tweed's social life began to emerge. The club was founded as "early as July, 1849" as a sort of sporting establishment for "gentlemen of leisure." A small group, the club did not receive attention until the reform drive. Besides political and social personalities, like Thurlow Weed, Matthew Brennan and his brother Owen, members included liveryman George W. Butt, Andrew J. Garvey, City Clerk Joseph Shannon, Terence Farley, Assistant Clerk of the Board of Supervisors Sheridan Shook, Charles Cornell, James Watson, E. A. Woodward, musician Claudius Grafulla, James H. Ingersoll, John H. Keyser, entrepreneur James Fisk, Jr., Jay Gould, George Barnard and Drs. John Carnochan and William Schirmer. The membership was, in general, made up of Tweed's crowd, convivial, generally lower-echelon politicians and middle-class tradesmen, altogether New Yorkers. Sweeny, Hall, Connolly were not members. They moved in different, more sophisticated circles. Admission fees were $250, dues $100 per year. A uniform was required at club meetings. This consisted of "blue cloth, navy pantaloons with a gold cord down the sides, blue sack cloth of navy cut, white cloth vest cut low, and navy cap." On January 5, 1867, Tweed as newly elected president of Americus rented for the club eight acres at Indian Harbor for a period of seven years beginning January 1 at a yearly rate of $1,000 plus taxes.

Tweed had a summer home on Main Street in Greenwich. In 1865, his wife, Mary Jane, had purchased property in Greenwich and in October 1866 was listed as a resident. In October 1867 the property, now two houses on the same forty acres, worth $15,500, was in the name of both Tweeds listed as non-residents. Through the ensuing years they spent some $50,000 in extending their holdings and by 1877 held five houses and sixty acres worth about $60,000. Beginning in 1879 after Tweed's death, Mary Jane began divesting herself of the property, a good deal of it going to James H. Ingersoll in payment of his claims against the Tweed estate. As a bit of gossip, did Mary Jane go to Greenwich to escape her husband? She seems to be alone in 1866. Did she resent the anticipated birth of their last child in 1867, twenty-three years after marriage? Anyway, besides children Tweed was now in real estate, an attorney working for Fisk Jr., Gould and the Erie Railroad. He was beginning to make money. He was particularly proud of his steam yachts, the *Mary Jane Tweed* and *William Tweed*, and he delighted in cruising his friends around islands known as "Tweed," "Little Captain" and "Captain."

Tweed also belonged to other clubs including the Blossom Club, a literary association with Owen W. Brennan as president and Tweed its first vice-president. In 1867, a genial photographer, Ben Gurney, took pictures of all its members in their sumptuous new quarters which housed a five-thousand-volume library gathered by the antiquarian bookseller John Pyne. Whether the books were used or not is not known. Unlike the rather small Americus Club, the Blossom had hundreds of members including all those associated with Americus, but also including Sweeny, Hall, Connolly and Henry Genet.

Tweed was also a member at least a few years later of the American Jockey Club and seems to have joined the more exclusive Manhattan Club, organizations which would have preferred to forget his membership and generally have. On the other hand, Sweeny and Tilden were members of the more prestigious Union Club. Tweed was not. None of "The Ring" made the New York Yacht Club or the Union League Club. Hall was a member of the literary Lotus Club; no one else of "The Ring" was. Club life reached a certain level for Tweed. He never reached into the Establishment. As for the Americus, it became increasingly connected with Tweed, its reputation soaring and declining with his.[7]

Of course, one club that Tweed was intimately concerned with was Tammany. It had come quite a way since its "pig pen" days at Abraham Martling's tavern. On July 4, 1867, the foundation stone for a new hall was laid at 143 East Fourteenth Street between Third and Fourth avenues. In 1928, in another time and era, the building was taken down. The opening ceremonies were typically colorful. At 9 A.M., sachems, braves and various dignitaries assembled and together with friends and relations and led by Grafulla's 7th Regiment Band marched to the site. The architect Thomas R. Jackson designed a three-story structure, 116 feet in front by 122 feet deep. Built of red brick and marble, there were to be three entrances on Fourteenth Street. Inside was a library, 32 feet by 40 feet and a concert room with a 32-foot-high ceiling, 52 feet by 74 feet, containing a stage, gallery and a half-dozen private boxes. About a thousand persons could be seated. It was expected $300,000 would be spent on the building, including a more than life-size statue of a Tammany brave. In the cornerstone was placed United States currency of the year, a history of the society, the address of Gulian Verplanck, photographs of members of Tammany and the *Valentine's Manual* for 1866. Hoffman, as Grand Sachem, in the regalia of the Columbian Order, laid the stone surrounded by sachems Sweeny, Connolly, Bell, Barr, Tweed, Hall, James B. Nicholson and a host of others. The party then proceeded to the flag-bedecked Irving Hall, where the Declaration of Independence was read and the band played "Hail, Columbia." Eighty-year-old Gulian Verplanck, congressman and old-time Federalist-Whig, friend of William C. Bryant and James F. Cooper, was old enough to forget past differences and agreed to deliver the major oration. Verplanck congratulated Tammany for its past accomplishments, for its passing through the dark days of the Civil War and for the new building—a symbol of the growth of New York, so much of which he had witnessed. Letters of congratulations were received from President Andrew Johnson and William Seward. Douglas Taylor, manager of Irving Hall, led invited guests to the refreshment saloon. That erstwhile Republicans could say nothing but good for Democrats came as no surprise for some. For the cynical, plunder was the answer. "Old man [Thurlow] Weed enjoyed many a delightful sugar plum" and the Tammany Ring was willing to "go snacks" with Republicans in jobs and patronage. Though "Tweed and Co. are very anxious to keep their Republican friends from public eyes," the *Times* would not be fooled.[8]

Festivities or no, seasons changed, leaves turned—the fall elections arrived. Assessments of the political situation found a series of permutations and combinations. Mozart Hall held a balance of power and it was thought that the regular ticket of Tammany could muster one fourth of the probable vote. Republicans with patronage in the Police, Fire and Health departments could count on about the same number. Then there were the fringes, McKeon Democrats, Citizens Association and German Democrats. Political victory depended upon a combination. Wheeling and dealing was the name of the game. Many eyes were on the "three little rascals," Hoffman, Sweeny and Tweed.

There were also Connolly and George McLean, now the "protégé" of the reform Citizens Union faction, to be considered. Both were felt to be two of the most cunning and experienced politicians in the Empire City. Connolly's shrewdness, a political writer for the *Herald* stated, was proverbial. He took up Tammany, not vice versa. McLean in an open, jovial way was busy replacing Cornell men in his department with his own. He exerts a "good natured but inflexible veto over Tweed," who was now back as deputy street commissioner. Both men, according to the *Herald*, looked with a "jaundiced eye" on the political firm of Tweed and Sweeny. Tweed, a reporter continued, is "sanguine, active, and exuberant, social, jovial, and shrewd. With all his flesh, he is ever on the alert and almost ubiquitous." Tweed's ability of seeming everybody's friend was able to make even those who disagree go along with him. Sweeny, the reporter went on, is reticent, keeping his own counsel, healing wounds of disappointment. Thus were the major combatants observed prior to the upcoming combat: Connolly and McLean seeking to oust Sweeny and Tweed from power in Tammany. The latter trying to enmesh the former in their individual webs. On the outside, McKeon, Wood, John Fox, Matt Brennan more or less allied with Sweeny, while others like "Big Judge" Michael Connolly, "Long Judge" Nelson Waterbury and Charles Halpine waited for their opportunity, each with an eye for the bigger office. For each nomination, there were several candidates, several factions; struggle for office was a bitter contest. In no way was a single or several single individuals able to dictate nominations, which would come as a result of combat or compromise.

On September 28, delegates met at the Masonic Hall at 114 and 116 East Thirteenth Street, temporary headquarters for Tammany, to select representatives to the State Democratic Convention to be held in Albany in October.[9] Tweed headed the Seventh Ward delegation. This was the second trip of the year to Albany for Tweed, Hall and Cornell. They were there on April 11 at a state caucus to choose delgates to the State Constitutional Convention. The Tammany organization was again able to prevent the seating of factions like the Mozart Hall delegation. Those who were disappointed met separately to chastise the "Tammany Ring."

In the city "Big Judge" Connolly, Waterbury, John D. Crimmins, Halpine and others berated the General Committee and its machinations, which resulted in choosing forty-two delegates, of which thirty-nine were supposedly officeholders. Tilden and Cardozo were among those selected, overcoming initial rejection.[10] The convention first met on June 4, 1867, and ended its work in February 1868. It proposed that the term of senators be extended from two to four years, increased membership of the assembly, conferred suffrage on all regardless of color. The Civil War finally but reluctantly reached New York. Negroes could vote provided they could show payment of taxes above $250, a provision which greatly reduced their political capacity, but following the draft riots, there weren't many Negroes left anyway. When the Fifteenth Amendment was adopted, it was too little and too late. The Court of Appeals was reorganized, providing a chief judge and six associate justices. The tenure of Supreme Court and Appellate judges was increased to fourteen years and the age limit for judges to seventy. The convention disappointed many, though it was a meeting of considerable statesmanship and had debates of meaning and value. But it did not extend the power of the governor or reduce the chances of corruption in the city by emphasizing the responsibility of elected officials. This bothered reformers. In the end only the proposals dealing with the judiciary were ratified by voters.[11] Work of the convention was interrupted by the fall campaign. For Democrats it was the usual noisy mess.

Usually meeting at Windust's, a famed eatery opposite City Hall, the "Lunch Club" political generals, such as Sweeny and Tweed, assembled to map strategy. Alderman James O'Brien, Congressman John Fox, and Alderman Joseph Shannon wanted the Sheriff's nomination. Hoffman backed O'Brien, hoping to obtain his votes for Charles Loew as county clerk, a move which threatened Sweeny. Hoffman was far from being a pliant mayor, and some thought that if Sweeny and Tweed could rid themselves of the "knight with the brown mustache [Hoffman]," they could carry out their schemes and assign Hoffman to oblivion. Deals had to be made, tempers kept from flaring. It was typical New York politics. The Democracy and its factions were busily at work. Hoffman played Loew and the German vote, the "Lunch Club" played O'Brien, Morrissey played Shannon. Tweed supposedly had Hoffman's promise to endeavor to procure for a Tweed man the post of collector of internal revenue, while Shannon was promised Tammany support as the next register. He would eventually become city clerk, publishing the corporation manual for 1868 and 1869. Halpine became register. Wheels were being meshed after a fashion and "Unterrified" Tammanyites found they could vote Cardozo for Supreme Court, James O'Brien for sheriff, Loew for county clerk and Hall for district attorney. Tweed was nominated to run for the state Senate in the Fourth Senatorial District. There were speeches stressing the need for victory and peace with the South. The anti-Negro ploy was waved to rally party disciples. A speaker castigated Republican support of Negro suffrage in the country. The radicals, he said, proposed to put white men in the nation under the will of the black. "Will you sanction it?" he asked his shouting audience. He was answered by shouts of "No! No!"

Republicans had their own internal feuds, the Andrew Johnson versus radicals fight for one. The Negro question, a depression and charges of corruption as in the Smythe affair, as well as other national scandals, had voters tired of Republican rule. The results were disaster for Republicans. Of 112,000 votes cast, 61,000 were Democratic, of which 42,000 went to Tammany. Tweed easily won his contest for state senator by a vote of 16,144 against James E. Kerrigan of Mozart Hall, 5,966, and Andrew Leggett, Republican, 2,175. Tammany candidates, such as Hall, Cardozo and O'Brien, also won rather easily.

Having shown strength in the November election, the next order of business was the election for mayor and city offices. Here the matter was not as simple. Peter Cooper led his forces against Hoffman and "The Ring" citing the city's $24 million budget and demanded reform and strict supervision.

The *Herald* was sure that the "Lunch Club Ring" was startled from dreams of easy success by these charges of corruption. "Toots" Hoffman now had a fight on his hands. The paper held, without evidence, that one month's salary was being collected from every officeholder to fill the campaign debt. Again confusion reigned in the city. The major fight was for the mayoralty, but there were aldermen, school commissioners and trustees and a police justice to elect. For just about every position there were Mozart Hallers, Tammanyites, Democratic Union and Republican candidates. The *Herald* castigated the supervisors' "Ring" and the "large fortunes" made from the courthouse construction. Hoffman was singled out as being directly responsible for "notorious corruption." Supporters of Fernando Wood who met at Cooper Union heard the former mayor tear at the "City Hall Ring" and those who use for their own purposes the "virtuous and honest" Hoffman as "a figure head" to a piratical craft. A "burly" representative of the Street Department had sufficient power to overcome the wishes of all New Yorkers, undoubtedly a reference to Tweed, "because of his influence with Hoffman." With all his merits Hoffman cannot and should not be re-elected, concluded Wood. Only he, Wood, had the experience to be in City Hall.

However, it was not to be. Wood had little support. He maneuvered from political weakness and Hoffman, completing the Tammany sweep, easily won re-election. He received 63,000 votes to Wood's 23,000 and Republican William A. Dunlap's 18,000. It was clear that Tammany, if united and the issues were right, ruled the roost. As for Wood, it was the finish of his political career. The candle sputtered in the wind. For Tweed, it was a good year: deputy street commissioner, a member of the Board of Supervisors, and now state senator. Connolly was comptroller. Sweeny was chamberlain and county treasurer. Cardozo was now Supreme Court Justice, and his third assistant was William Tweed, Jr.[12]

As for Republicans, they had to try harder. There must be a way of destroying the victorious Democrats. They sniffed the air like hound dogs, looking for a scent, a little bit of Tammany Tiger odor.

16

Conventions

It was a happy holiday season as the Americus Club held their annual ball at the Academy of Music on January 3, 1868—admission $5.00 for one gentlemen and two ladies. Tweed was president and fellow supervisor Henry Smith, vice-president of the club. They happily greeted fellow Democrats and Republicans to what was billed the "ball of the season." Grafulla's 7th Regiment Band provided the music, as usual, while Tweed and guests danced through the night.[1]

If things went smoothly at the Academy, they were less so in the Senate. It was a different dance there. Tweed had been elected to a state office, many felt, he did not want. Certainly, his wife preferred Manhattan or Greenwich to her new surroundings. Perhaps Sweeny, Hoffman, McLean, Connolly, rivals in Tammany, convinced him to run, hoping to move an obstacle "upstairs." Once in Albany, power in the city could be divided more easily. Perhaps Tweed was talked into sacrificing himself for party unity or to help marshal party strength in Albany. If Tweed was removed from the city, the city was removed from Tweed. The Senate gave him contact with wider state and national circles, but he was a small fish in a big pond. He needed time to grow and adjust. He did not have that time.

On January 7 at eleven o'clock, Lieutenant Governor Stewart L. Woodford administered the oath of office to the senators, who were reminded by Governor Reuben E. Fenton of the prevailing depression and were asked for "absolute and actual" economy in their transactions and rigid accountability of all public servants. One of the first orders of business for Tweed after being placed on committees of Finance, Charitable and Religious Societies and Internal Affairs of Towns and Counties, was the introduction of a bill incorporating Presbyterian Hospital of the City of New York. It was the beginning of a long series of social legislation that came from his desk. There were numerous bills and petitions for a wide variety of institutions, including those of Mount Sinai Hospital, St. Mary's Church, the orphanage of Shepards Fold of the Episcopal Church, most asking for state aid. He introduced a memorial on behalf of the New-York Historical Society to found a Museum of History, Antiquity and Art in Central Park, the forerunner of the present Metropolitan Museum of Art. There were bills to incorporate the Working Women's Protective Union, to extend Lexington Avenue, to erect a Town Hall in Jamaica. There was a package of out-of-city bills presented, part of the give-and-take of upstate, downstate politics. It was in legislation like this that Tweed moved to meet the needs of an emerging metropolis. His was from the start an active and vital role, an expanding one, one indispensable to New York's well-being, though history has chosen to forget this part of Tweed's career or bury what he accomplished under the muck of scandal.

The Senate reconvened meetings of the Commission on Municipal Affairs which had been investigating New York City street cleaning contracts, an ongoing process since 1865. The bipartisan committee dedicated to cleaning the "Marvel of filth" that was New York met on March 9 in the Metropolitan Hotel, an ornate building on Broadway owned by A. T. Stewart, but then leased and run by Tweed and his son, William. Hoffman was called first, and he testified that all street cleaning contracts were being complied with, though he admitted that most narrow streets were not passable, even if few complaints had been received for non-removal of garbage. James R. Whiting, the current street cleaning contractor, a city office, was doing all he could under difficult circumstances. He agreed though that the contract system for the removal of snow was not adequate. At the end of March, the investigators heard young, sharp-nosed Thomas Jefferson Creamer recommend additional power be given to the Street Cleaning Commission and that contracts be made to have snow removed from the principal streets immediately after it falls. He also thought that all streets should be cleaned at least twice a week, that property owners should keep gutters clean in front of their residence and railroad companies not throw snow from tracks into the streets.[2] So another attempt at defying what appears to be an insoluble problem became history.

Railroads were the order of the day, and not just because of snow. The Trans-Continental Railroad was just about finished. Names like Union Pacific, Central Pacific and crusty Cornelius Vanderbilt's New York Central caught public interest. With the industrialization of the country, railroads took on added significance. They were looked on as a universal panacea, able to solve even the transportation ills of Manhattan. Almost everyone had a suggestion. Elevated lines, an experimental project, had been constructed. The track stood on one-legged supports. Others talked about surface lines, some prescribed tunnel routes.

Among principal railroaders in New York was Vanderbilt, anxious to consolidate the rival Erie track known as the "Scarlet Woman of Wall Street" because her "favors," in this case in the form of watered stock, were sold so often to gullible investors. Even Vanderbilt was tricked into buying stock. James Fisk, Jr., a transplanted Vermonter, and Daniel Drew, a shrewd speculator, controlled the Erie, using all sorts of devices to fleece Vanderbilt and prevent him from capturing the line. It was an incredible affair witnessing several years of skirmishing in courts and in the legislature. It was during his first term in office that Tweed became involved.

During the great railroad war Vanderbilt bought up enough stock, mainly through proxies, to gain control of the company. However, Drew and Fisk simply issued more stock. If this was sustained by the courts, Drew and his allies could destroy the Commodore. Probably Vanderbilt was a better railroad man than Drew, yet his New York Central, composed of the Harlem and Hudson, was generally considered "grasping" and "overbearing," as was Vanderbilt himself.

A suit had been brought by William Belden, a stockholder in the Erie, against Cornelius and William K. Vanderbilt and George G. Barnard, among others, asking an injunction prohibiting the defendants from removing directors of the railroad. Barnard, also a stockholder in the Erie and ally of Vanderbilt, had previously issued an injunction preventing Fisk and Drew from issuing or renewing stock, thus allowing Vanderbilt to gain control. This brought demands for Barnard's impeachment on the grounds that he should have disqualified himself since he was a stockholder in the railroad. Barnard, a thirty-nine-year-old Yale graduate, disregarded his foes. The injunction he issued was, however, set aside by an appellate court. The fight went to the legislature.

What Drew and Fisk wanted was to have that body prohibit Vanderbilt as owner of the Central from controlling Erie no matter how much stock he held. What followed was one of the most interesting episodes in the history of the legislature. It was during the "war" that Fisk became an intimate of Tweed's and it was love at first sight. They are not mentioned together before this time, though Tweed did represent the Erie as an attorney previously. Jim Fisk, Jr., was an improbable character, but so much part of the flamboyant, aggressive "gilded age" that was Victorian America. Like Tweed, he was born poor, though in Brattleboro, Vermont, and became a successful self-made man. Fisk was twelve years Tweed's junior and short and fat. Tweed was tall and fat. They both enjoyed eating of the fruits of the good life. Both were Americus Club members. They became good friends.

It was reported that the Erie combine offered $1,000, $500 down and $500 on delivery for a vote in the legislature. Vanderbilt's rate was thought to be $2,000 to $3,000 a vote. But rumors of a Drew-Vanderbilt compromise quickly drove the price down. Vanderbilt's refusal to buy more votes assured a Fisk-Drew victory. In this big ball field, Tammany and Tweed were just players. They did not seem to be major kingpins. Tweed's role was never quite clear. Later Tweed "confessed" to having been given a share of $150,000, a sum divided equally between Sweeny, editor Hugh Hastings and himself to assure passage of Erie legislation. As with most of Tweed's memories it was vague and shadowy and lacked corroboration. He does not appear to have been really needed, but he became through Fisk a director of the Erie. Within a few weeks an angry assembly passed a bill legalizing the Erie's $10 million issue bringing the stubborn Vanderbilt "up to heel." The Senate including Tweed also went along.[3]

One issue to which Tweed was clearly linked was that involving the excise. Tweed, late in March, moved that instead of considering a bill amending the Metropolitan Excise Law, the Senate should completely repeal it. The motion was lost 14 to 14, the lieutenant governor casting the deciding vote. Tweed, though recognized as the "leader of the Democracy in the legislature," did little to support his own motion. His motives were obvious. If Tweed wanted to be the next governor or even just help the party, why ruin his chances by removing an issue of such great assistance to the Democracy? If the law was repealed, Democrats would lose an issue they could count on to give them votes, especially from Irish and Germans. Republicans were willing to modify the law, but not entirely repeal it. Tweed's tactic ensured the bill's defeat, put onus on Republicans and kept alive the cause, especially necessary in this presidential year when the political pot boiled more actively than usual. It was a clever ruse though a simple and often used one, giving Tweed needed publicity for the coming campaign.[4]

Tweed was among many selected as a delegate to the State Presidential Nominating Convention held in Albany. There he was chosen as a delegate to the National Nominating Convention which was to be held at the brand-new Tammany Hall on July 4. The convention was a festive, exciting time despite the oppressive summer heat. Inside the sweltering hall, proceedings were set in motion. Committees on Credentials, Organization, Resolutions and Platform were established. In Tammany, in the streets outside and in adjacent buildings used as temporary quarters and the nearby Irving House names were mentioned for the presidency. Ex-Governor Horatio Seymour George H. Pendleton of Ohio General Winfield Hancock of Gettysburg fame and Salmon Chase, Lincoln's

Secretary of the Treasury, were the front runners. It was a guessing game. The meeting, called to order at twelve-fifteen, was first addressed by the "mutton-chopped" August Belmont, former representative of Rothschild and now a leading banker in his own right, who welcomed the delegates to the city and state and asked them to remember the accomplishments of the party as opposed to the evils of Republicans. What was needed was a restoration of the "Union Constitution and the Laws" and a defeat of radicals. On Monday, July 6, 1868, Seymour was named permanent presiding officer, a significant decision, and Tweed one of many vice-presidents. The New York delegation divided their loyalty betweed Seymour, Chief Justice Salmon Chase and Sandford Church, former lieutenant governor of New York. On the first roll call Tilden, chairman of New York's delegation, placed Church's name in nomination. As the balloting went on, New York dropped Church and switched to Chase, and then finally the convention, along with New York, decided for the slate of Seymour and Francis Blair. For Seymour, again lured out of retirement, it was perhaps an unwanted nomination, but one accepted given the heated division within the party. Insiders felt that Seymour's nomination came after adherents of Pendleton of Ohio, finding their man's candidacy extremely difficult, sided with Seymour, thus assuming New York support for Pendleton in 1872. It was a bargain that angered many who could not stomach Seymour. Alexander Long of Cincinnati, a Pendleton man, said the alliance was "concocted" at Delmonico's and the Fifth Avenue Hotel between Pendleton people like George W. McCook and Seymour men Tilden, Ben Wood and Peter Sweeny. Tweed was not mentioned. For Tammany, the decision was not particularly a welcome one. Chase could have obtained Wall Street money for the Democracy. Yet, Seymour could be helpful in carrying the state for the Democrats and preserve Tammany's control of the city.

Suddenly in the midst of the activities, fifty-six-year-old Peter Cagger's career came to a sudden end. He had gone for a drive in Central Park on July 7 with John E. Develin. At about Eighty-fourth Street, just off Fifth Avenue, a wheel gave way and both occupants were thrown from the carriage. Cagger's head hit the roadway. Several passers-by in those "good old days" refused to offer assistance. Develin was knocked unconscious and also suffered a broken hand. Cagger died immediately and his body was sent to St. Luke's and then to Albany for burial. The demise of Cagger left Tweed and Tammany little counter in the upstate Democracy.[5] There was a large void in the party; whether Tammanyites could take advantage of it remained to be seen.

Tammany was expected to make a lot of noise for Seymour. Though the hall was the stage, Tammanyites had been very quiet during the proceedings. This was the "big time," and no one of the Democracy made any splash, including Tweed. Perhaps the reason for Tammany's silence was "laziness," but more likely was that playing for marbles in their ball park, the city, was more to their liking and resources.

In the state, the mystery of the nominee for governor was soon solved. Any pretense that Tweed would be a candidate was soon forgotten. Tweed had received a measure of support for the office with the formation of the Seventh Ward William M. Tweed National Democratic Defenders. But it was a joke. If it was an example of Tweed becoming a star in the heavens, it must have had many people laughing. In October, a county convention was held at Tammany Hall to name delegates to be sent to Albany to nominate candidates for state office. With Tweed presiding, the meeting voted solidly for John T. Hoffman for governor. Tweed, Hall and Sweeny were among those chosen for delegates.

The state convention met at the famed Tweedle Hall early in September 1868 and agreed after considerable debate to accept Hoffman as standard-bearer. Brooklyn's Henry C. Murphy wanted the job and his supporters were particularly incensed. They had their chance for revenge when the vote came for lieutenant governor. They were able to defeat the Tammany nomination for that post after a bitter denunciation of the Tammany machine, charging that the Tammany clique cared nothing for the country, or even the Democratic Party, but only sought their own "aggrandizement." Brooklynite Samuel D. Morgan shouted that Tammany had helped Seymour defeat Murphy, the "people's choice" for governor. He railed against the society for its plan to use Seymour to control the country, and went on to storm at the unfinished courthouse, the "thousand schemes of plunder and robbery," and warned the people of the interior to have care in supporting a "corrupt oligarchy." The Tammany delegation, including Tweed, "great of stomach and expert of strategy," were flustered and looked daggers at the speaker. "Well," muttered someone, interrupting the tirade, "we will give you a good Democrat." Morgan replied, "That may well be, but all good Democrats don't live in New York. There are several hundred thousand in other parts of the state." At the conclusion of his speech, Allen C. Beach was selected as the nominee for lieutenant governor. It was a bitter defeat for Tammany, and gave some idea of the hostility felt toward the society by fellow Democrats.

Still the *Times* found Hoffman a good choice for governor. He had a good record and was a "gentleman of culture, suavity and polish." As Grand Sachem of Tammany, he was universally regarded as its ornament, rather than its tool. He had lost the gubernatorial contest two years before, because of the failure of the Democracy's pro-Johnson policy not because of "Ring" connections.[6]

For Tammany, aside from making noise for the national and state candidates, its time was busily engaged in fence mending. On October 22, Tweed called to order a meeting to find nominees for city and county offices. Tweed was nominated for supervisor again, and George G. Barnard for Supreme Court. Tweed was considered a necessity as supervisor, having become in "that chamber a fixture like Elijah Purdy" had been. The *Herald* thought "General Bismarck Sweeny commander-in-chief of the democratic forces" while Machiavelli Tweed was merely his lieutenant. It was how most contemporaries felt about their relationship. Bennett expected that Hoffman would be defeated and hoped Tweed would lose, though all parties for supervisor were probably "equally steeped in corruption." The election went much as most people expected, the *Herald* and *Times* excepted. Seymour and Blair overwhelmed the Republican presidential ticket of Ulysses S. Grant and Schuyler Colfax in the city, but Grant carried the state and the nation easily. The Democratic candidates for gubernatorial office, Hoffman and Beach, won, though Republicans carried the state for national office. Barnard was re-elected to the Supreme Court; it was a little more difficult for Tweed in a three-way race, but still he won.

With Hoffman now governor, the question was who should take his place as mayor. Hoffman's victory exposed Tammany to attack. It left a gaping hole in the defenses. What if Republicans joined with Democratic Unionists? Decision time for Peter "Bismarck" Sweeny. Among the names mentioned for mayor was Street Commissioner George McLean, who supposedly had Tweed's support. If McLean were elected, Tweed could move up from deputy to commissioner. On November 23, the suspense was lifted by "chief minister and master spirit of the party" Peter Sweeny. A. Oakey Hall was nominated for the mayoralty among cheers and as the band on cue played "Hail to the Chief." Hall spoke to a merry audience about the defense of the city's chartered rights and liberties; the fight they were engaged upon was a fight for self-government. Shortly after, the delegates to the convention happily proceeded to the staunchly Democratic Manhattan Club and serenaded the governor-elect. They had added reason to be cheerful. German Democratic Union and Mozart Hall had accepted the decisions. The dreaded schism was averted.

Hall easily defeated his opponent, F. A. Conkling, to serve out Hoffman's term. The election had been quiet and peaceful. Only about half of registered voters took time to cast a ballot. There was general agreement that Hall would make a "popular and efficient Chief Magistrate of the Metropolis." He had broad and progressive views about the city and it was expected that the people would have no regret in choosing him their mayor by such a "decisive and flattering majority." For the *Times*, the question of "The Ring" and the need for reform still loomed large. Hall, even if cultured and personally honest, was only the official representative and agent of "The Ring," a half-dozen men who rule and dictate the officers of the city and who are notoriously "selfish, ignorant and unscrupulous, . . . without culture or experience." They care nothing about the city except to fill their own pockets and the pockets of their followers. The answer, the *Times* still thought, was for the state to administer city affairs.[7]

17

Grand Sachem

With A. Oakey Hall in the mayor's office and John Hoffman in the governor's chair, Tammany, able to mend tears in the political fabric, was in a
seemingly strong position, perhaps the strongest it had been in its long history. Tweed also prospered. One important sign of Tweed's position in the
party came on March 5, 1869, when assembled sachems met to consider
Hoffman's letter of resignation from the office of Grand Sachem. In his
note, dated March 1, he mentioned necessitated absence from the city as
principal reason, but it was probably also something of a Declaration of Independence by "Toots," as he washed his hands of any Tammany stain.
Connolly thanked Hoffman for his services in a post he had held since
Purdy's death. And then came the next step. Tweed was chosen by unanimous vote as his replacement as Grand Sachem of the Tammany Society
or Columbian Order. Emanual Hart and Connolly were sent to notify
Tweed, then in Albany, of his election. For Tweed, this was a big feather
to add to others in his cap. It had been a long, slow climb in the
Democracy, a climb started at the bottom of the ladder. He received this
final honor only after Hoffman's resignation, but it was an indication of
his popularity, as well as recognition of his long years of arduous service.
His winning manner, conciliatory ways, a temper generally under control,
good leadership qualities, a thorough knowledge of parliamentary procedure, his benign use of power were also responsible, so contemporaries felt,
for his nomination. An outgoing, generous man, noted for his charities,
"no one really in need ever turns away from him empty handed." He gave
freely, and without fanfare. Tweed was expected to carry on with dispatch
and capability.

However, exultant as the title was, it did not mean too much. Since
1789 and the days of the first Grand Sachem, William Mooney, there
were twenty-nine such officials, but few are remembered by history. They

were as a group, a rather nondescript bunch, generally accomplishing little. It would be a rare historian indeed who could identify Lorenzo D. Shepard or James Conner. How about Shivers Parker?[1] If it were not for the disclosures, who would remember William M. Tweed? In many ways the nomination was a dead end. Except for Hoffman, very few escaped to pursue public life successfully. Tweed had an opportunity. He was in the state Senate, but combining this and his position in Tammany could be a difficult, if not impossible balancing act. His lines of communication were too long; he was vulnerable to attack. Was he a senator first or a Tammany leader first? It would be hard if not fatal to be both. Tweed overreached himself. It was a fatal decision. He should have followed Hoffman's lead and refused the post, or else resigned his Senate seat. One or the other would have been a wise decision.

Party harmony was new and fragile. New issues were always arising. In the Senate, almost every bill caused or aggravated party division, and Tweed could not wear two hats at one time, though he tried to. Hoffman vetoed a bill authorizing the construction of a railroad across 125th Street, arguing that the franchise belonged to the people and not to individuals. The legislature, he argued, had no more right to give away these grants than to impose a direct tax. Senator Genet moved to override the veto. It was carried 16 to 11. Bradley and Norton voted with him. Tweed did not vote. Here, he tried to be Grand Sachem and senator. Hoffman's veto, as well as his resignation, were the moves of a man determined to carry out the responsibilities of his office as he saw fit. If Tammany sought complete subservience, it was an illusory wish. Hoffman was no tool. The early days of his administration were characterized by a popular anti-monopoly, responsible government stand. It was a marked contrast to the sordid machinations of the Republican Grant administration.

One of the more important bits of legislation that interested Tweed related to the widening of city streets and the development of the "city on a scale worthy of its destiny." To this effect, as a member of the Committee on Municipal Affairs he introduced a bill in the legislature whose result would be the widening of Broadway from Thirty-fourth Street to Fifty-ninth Street. A short time earlier a plan to broaden the famous avenue from Union Square to Fifty-ninth Street ran into strong opposition as another "corrupt scheme" aimed at helping Tammany and contractors. Whether this was true or not is impossible to say, but what is sure is that the chance to enhance that part of Broadway was lost.

The Tweed bill, a good one, was successfully maneuvered through the legislature with the advice of Sweeny, and was approved by Hoffman. The *Herald* screamed in protest at another "Ring Triumph." Hoffman had been exercising vigilance and caution in signing bills. This one was a mistake, argued some. The width of Broadway was sufficient for traffic. Fifth and Sixth avenues took much of the parallel traffic from Union Square to the park. To those who argued that in ten years the upper portion of Broadway would be as crowded as the lower end the *Herald* responded, "This is a fallacy. Why would not William Astor build upon upper Broadway if the avenue was to expand?" Many felt that since Tweed and Sweeny had property in the area, they would benefit from an estimated increase in real estate values by 500 to 600 per cent at an unnecessary cost to the city of $10 million. Whatever the reason, New York had Broadway widened.

Tweed and Sweeny, in fact, gained little from the widening process. In January 1871, the Commissioners of Estimate and Assessment recommended to the Supreme Court a long list of persons to be compensated for resulting damages to their property. Tweed was not included among them, nor was anyone with whom he was associated given an award. Jacob Astor received $25,000 and a number of unknowns received much more. Martin Zabrowski received an award of $225,250, a Charles Johnson $367,535 and a J. Stewart, Jr., $200,000. Though Tweed's properties eventually increased in value, he never received any profits from his real estate investments.

As an outgrowth of the furor, the *Herald* in a last-ditch battle detailed the unwarranted loss of many buildings to be torn down and the unpleasant altering of portions of certain areas, including the destruction of farmhouse landmarks. Support for the project, however, came from Andrew H. Green, the park commissioner, who like Sweeny was interested in developing a system of boulevards like those of Paris. The Paris plan of 1867 gave New Yorkers an opportunity to see how an "ugly" city could be transformed. Similar plans were laid for New York City. These called for a principal avenue, "the Boulevard," to begin at Fifty-ninth Street and Eighth Avenue with a width of 150 feet as an extension of Broadway to run diagonally across to the intersection of Ninth Avenue and Sixty-fifth Street. At the Fifty-ninth Street junction, a large circle, later Columbus Circle, with a radius of 150 feet was then in the process of construction. A "Merchant's Gate" also being built at Fifty-ninth Street and Eighth Avenue at the entrance of the park was especially impressive. Rows of trees were being planted. The gate was to be covered with foliage and was to be one of the most beautiful spots in the city. By the end of the year, the *Herald* rescinded its objection. Common sense and aesthetic values might not have been in the mind of "The Ring," but to the extent the widening scheme was accepted as in the construction of Columbus Circle it proved of infinite value to the city. Tweed is also credited with fostering Riverside Drive and embellishing Central Park. It is unfortunate that "The Ring" was not left alone to continue such work. What would New York look like with a few more boulevards and open spaces in place of the monotonous gridiron imposed on the city by penny-wise, pound-foolish planners?[2]

Tweed also presented another proposal which caused an even greater furor, but was indicative of the leadership position he was assuming in the Senate. This had to do with advancing his program of social insurance; of finding solutions to the problems causing concern to the city's poor since existing private institutions no longer kept pace with the rapid urban growth. While usually derided as simply a vote-getting and personal aggrandizement scheme, it was much more than that.

Tweed had been reappointed to the Committee on Charitable and Religious Societies and in 1869 introduced a bill to have the city pay a portion of annual expenses of parochial schools. Since most such schools were Catholic, these poorly equipped parish schools benefited the most. Republicans smelled a "savor of Popery" and the bill was lost. Tweed then inserted in the tax levy of 1870 a proposal empowering the city to set aside a yearly sum of 20 per cent of the income from excises in 1868 to be distributed to support free schools other than public or charity institutions. Cries against a general "papal conspiracy" were raised from civil libertarians, Republicans and a mélange of anti-Catholics. Tweed retreated though he was able to have a one-year subsidy for 1869–70 approved. In 1870, dozens of parochial schools, mainly Catholic, applied for and received funds. It was the only time in New York's history that Catholic schools received such public grants for instructional purposes. In 1871, the city was prohibited from ever again appropriating money for such purposes.

Undaunted, Tweed pushed for aid for orphanages and homes for the shelterless. In 1868, 68 such institutions received aid. In the Tweed era, that is by 1871, that number had grown to 106. Tweed's program, which included the creation of the famed Manhattan Eye and Ear Hospital, was as necessary for the general welfare of the community as would be the Brooklyn Bridge. But it cost Tweed.[3]

Like the boulevard plan, but to a greater degree, his school and social welfare proposals put Tweed before the public and brought upon him the hatred of Republican anti-city forces as well as an army of waspish bigots. These buzzed about his head and were ready to sting. The days of anti-Catholic, anti-Irish, anti-immigrant riots, the times of street angels and mob violence were not past. They were real and dangerous. But, of course, the school issue had another side. Though the *Times* was probably not so much concerned with the sanctity of public schools as they were with improving Republican political chances and maintaining the status quo, opponents of the Tweed legislation were not all bigots. Many then as now felt that public tax money should not be used for private purposes, that the Constitution guarantees separation of Church and State. The question then as now is thorny and elusive—difficult to solve.

Still Tweed had involved himself even more deeply in city affairs. He was becoming the champion of the immigrant, a leading spokesman for the interests of a vital, expanding New York. There were few other voices than his present. However, Tweed did not speak out on all issues. One of these related to civil rights and the Negro. Many things were changing, some things very slowly. Civil rights was an example of that. During the debate continued from the past year on the ratification of the Fifteenth Amendment, Senator George Beach of Catskill argued against the proposal, as did many New Yorkers, especially those in the city. He remarked that if he had a sixteen-year-old son who was not better qualified to vote than the majority of Negroes, "he would be induced to put him in a lunatic asylum, or if he did not think his wife better qualified he would still be a bachelor." Those wanting to carry out the "grand design" of the Great Emancipator, however, won the day, as the amendment was adopted by a narrow vote. Tweed once again abstained.

Hostility toward the Negro was very deep, especially in the city, and widespread throughout the state. A referendum proposed by the 1867 convention and held during 1869, providing for the lifting of property qualifications as applied to blacks, was defeated soundly. It lost heavily in the city. Henry C. Murphy of Brooklyn, who sat with Tweed in the Senate and who wanted to be governor, was one of the leaders of the anti-Negro forces both in 1867 and 1869.[4] Tweed's abstaining might be considered as a courageous one. It would have been much more popular to curtsy to the bigots, or it could have been a politician's way out of a dilemma. The senator versus the sachem once again.

With the conclusion of the debate on the amendment, the Senate adjourned and Tweed returned to Manhattan.

Independence Day, 1869, was a day to remember. Under the banner of "Civil Liberty, the Glory of Man," Tweed proudly led the festivities. According to custom, the Declaration was read. Then Tweed, dressed in "glittering regalia" and bearing a silver war hatchet, the Tammany Saints symbol, in his hands, led the braves, including his son William Jr., into the Wigwam. Tweed, holding a staff, surmounted by a liberty cap, addressed the assembled "brethren and friends," to remind them of the accomplishments of the Democracy and the principles which allowed mechanics, workingmen, merchants and bankers to be proud of a country second to none. "The Star-Spangled Banner" was played. There was more music and more speeches. A. Oakey Hall blasted President Grant and the Republicans and informed the cheering audience that if the Irish wanted "Alabama cruises" to harry the British lion, they could get them, and if Cuba wanted its freedom from Spain, it would receive American aid for that too. It sounded good on Fourteenth Street.[5]

The wedding of revolution, independence and the immigrant vote was not lost to the audience. Cuba was on everyone's lips. For many years, a Cuban junta, even prior to the war, made up of southern and northern expansionists, sought either annexation by the United States or independence under American protection. Cubans, to escape hostile Spanish rule, came to New York and set up headquarters at 71 Broadway, which was also used to provide drilling rooms. During 1867, 1868 and early 1869 an invasion force of about fifteen hundred, many of them Civil War veterans chosen by Cuban agents in many eastern cities from Boston to New Orleans, was gathered. They received $30 in gold on enlistment and an additional $500 in gold after a year's service. A colonel received $5,000. The men were organized as a regiment of cavalry armed with Spencer carbines. There were two batteries of artillery. War surplus was abundant and cheap. Guns could be bought by almost anyone. The men boarded boats, the *Cool* and the *Chase*, in the East River late in June and headed silently into the Sound. Through the fog they made out Plum Island. Sailing on in the cold damp night they made Gardiners Bay, where two schooners containing munitions and supplies were found, but not the hoped-for steamer, *Catherine Whiting*. The men aboard the vessels were hungry, having had nothing but crackers for two days. A few went to Gardiners Island for water, sea bird eggs and potatoes. There was fear of mutiny. The commanders of the expedition, Señors Alfano and Bassora, suggested sending Cubans to New London for supplies, but the hungry, cold and wet American volunteers objected when news came that the *Whiting* had been seized. All seemed lost. Some three hundred men were left on Gardiners Island while another steamer was prepared. The *Cool* returned to Whitestone Landing near Fort Schuyler in the Bronx and let ashore 150 men. Plans were canceled when the *Cool* was seized by a revenue cutter. All of the expedition, those who did not flee, were rounded up and handed over to the government. For the Cubans, it was a great loss of money and time, as well as support from the United States. General Domingo Golcousis, the alleged commander in chief, and other officers, were placed in the Ludlow Street Jail charged with violation of neutrality laws. All this occurred just prior to July 1. Golcousis refused bail and insisted on a trial to prove his innocence. No trial seemed to have ensued and the affair ended quietly, although there were other such expeditions mounted. Invasion of Cuba seems to be a national pastime.

Hall's support of Cuban and Irish revolutionary causes was further underlined at a Tammany rally called by Tweed in August to rescue an

"[Irish] American citizen languishing in an English prison for an alleged political offense," and also to protest the shooting of American citizens without benefit of trial by Spaniards in Cuba. It was an attack on the Republican Secretary of State Hamilton Fish, who does nothing but sit, and a President who does nothing but junket about various watering places. Hall delivered another blistering chauvinistic speech on rescuing Ireland from "British despotism" and righting Cuban wrongs. "Does not the American Eagle in the Nevada eyrie fly straight to the eyes of the backwoodsman who invades the nest where the young are?" asked Hall. Why do Grant and his secretary allow American citizens to be hounded and butchered? Several American citizens who took part in a previous expedition were executed by Spanish authorities. Hall claimed they should have been protected by American guns. Let the country in coming elections put in officials who would do the job. Democrats O'Gorman and District Attorney Samuel Garvin stressed the Irish cause. Would Warren and Costello, Irish American revolutionaries, be in a British prison if Seymour was President? Would there be a stone left in a Cuban fortress if Seymour was President? England and Spain must be made to feel the anger of the American government and its people. Protection of American citizens was the primary resolve of the cheering crowd. Garvin, his voice rising, urged "we will have Mexico, and we will have Cuba, and we will have all the islands of the sea." It was empty rhetoric, but jingoism of the 1840s and 1850s was still alive at least in the halls of Tammany that August night. Of course, the issue was a political one. One that Democrats hoped would serve in the coming elections and possibly in the election of 1872.[6] Still, as an issue, the Cuban-Irish cause did not go very far. All political capital was made that could be made. There were other more interesting developments closer to home, involving scandal in the Grant administration.

The most notorious scheme centered around a company, the Crédit Mobilier of America, whose president, Oliver Ames, also president of the Union Pacific, and his brother, Oakes Ames, together with others under an agreement with the Union Pacific sublet a contract for the building of the Trans-Continental Railroad at prices less than those received by Union Pacific under government contract to do the same work. The company pocketed the difference. Crédit Mobilier made some $93 million from the scheme. Then the scandal. James Fisk, Jr., brought suit against the Union Pacific for illegally refusing to sell him twenty thousand shares of stock, in addition to the ones he already owned. He wanted a larger slice of the pie. The case came before Judge Barnard in 1868. On July 3, Fisk with David D. Field, as counsel, presented "startling" affidavits to the court which resulted in the granting of an injunction against the company. While debate continued as to whether the case should go to the

United States Supreme Court or remain in the New York Supreme Court, William Tweed, Jr., was appointed receiver. The affidavits brought to light a charge of bribery. The sum of $25,000 had been paid to a United States commissioner to accept a twenty-mile section of faulty track. A very involved and lengthy case followed. In April 1869 with the matter still before Barnard, the books of the Union Pacific were examined. It was revealed that stockholders included Thurlow Weed, George Opdyke, Leonard R. Jerome (the father of Jennie and grandfather of Winston Churchill), Erastus Corning and John A. Dix. As the trial unfolded, so did the most "gigantic swindle ever perpetrated under the shadow of the law." On April 6, Judge Blatchford, in the United States Circuit Court, declared all suits in the state courts null and void. These suits must be heard in the Federal Court, he ruled.

The next day when the case opened before a referee, Field discounted the Blatchford decision and argued that it was mere obiter dictum, just so many words. Barnard declared that he would not recognize Blatchford's decision, accepting the grounds argued by Field. The case was eventually discontinued. No one went to jail. Not having been allowed to join the "club," Fisk exposed the "frauds" of his enemies.[7]

Another excitement, political in nature and like the Crédit Mobilier affair, explained something of public morality of the times. On "Black Friday," September 24, 1869, the speculative gold market crumbled, bringing down thousands of investors as the price of gold plummeted and the "bears" grinned at the fallen fortunes of "bulls." This affair was engineered by "financier" Jay Gould and depended on inside knowledge of Grant's policy on the release of federal reserves, and Gould had the information.[8]

Tweed belonged to these "mauve decades," when business was business, politics was politics and morality belonged in heaven.

Then came the fall election. Who was to run for what? It was Sweeny who was referred to over and over again as the real chief of Tammany, and who made decisions as to all nominations. He was absent during the summer, being on his almost annual trip to Europe and his beloved Paris. Political decisions waited his return. Without his guidance, the Democratic pot boiled over. Tweed was rumored to have wanted a place on the Superior Court, but this nomination, along with others, would have to wait for "Bismarck's" return.

A major obstacle for Tweed was August Belmont. Born in Germany to a Jewish family in 1813, he came to America twenty-four years later. He was now chairman of the Democratic National Executive Committee and a nationally known Democrat, something Tweed was not. But he was vulnerable, especially after the defeat of Seymour. The gnat-like William Tweed Democratic Association of the Seventh Ward met in mid-August to rid the party of the "inefficient, undevoted and unpopular" chairman. They promised further defeat if Belmont continued in office. Hoffman too could lose in 1872. They recommended Belmont retire and Tweed take his place. It was a call to arms for Tammany chiefs returning from summer vacations at Saratoga, Indian Head and Newport. Belmont was now seen as a "pariah" to Tweed, "the chief sachem or rabbi of the Tammany temple." The Irish who predominated in the Seventh Ward were also angered that Belmont, a "moneyed artistocrat, the agent of a throne [Rothschild's] whose loans have propped up tottering thrones in Europe, should be the great executive representative in the council" of national Democrats.

Then came another storm to further shake the brittle foundations of party unity. Jacob Cohen, editor of the German-language paper the *Staats Zeitung* and long active in Tammany, made it known he was after a supervisor's seat. He declared "all Tammany cannot hold him from it," as he announced that he was particularly after Tweed with a "big stick." Tweed was beset by rebellion. District leaders flexed their muscles; the question of wielding power was different from having it. The Jacob Cohen Democratic Association met on August 31, 1869, at Brevoort Hall on Fifty-fourth Street to endorse the election of their man to the Board. Cohen could expect German support. The Independent German Citizens Association of the Seventeenth heard Colonel Simon Levy stress the need for a strong German organization representing the German element of the city. In the Fourteenth Ward at the Independent Democratic Club, a motion was introduced to have German as a regular branch of instruction in public schools. The petition was presented to the Board of Education. The Alexander von Humboldt Memorial Celebration held on the fourteenth of September was organized by the German General Democratic Union and the Deutschland Society, who met at the Scholars Gate in the park to present to the city a statue of Humboldt as a reminder of German influence and accomplishment. On September 1, the Jacob Cohen club met at Botanic Hall, where his candidacy was hailed by German compatriots.

Now the Belmont-Tweed affair returned to raise additional clouds of dust. The Richmond *Whig*, reflecting national Democratic opinion, felt that Tweed could not take Belmont's place, since such an office as chairman of the National Association was in the hands of the members and Tweed was not one of them. Mr. Tweed not "one of 'em," retorted the *Herald* ironically, "shades of Indian Harbor." Then who else was? But in truth Tweed was not known nationally, he was known only in New York to such as the Irish groups, the "bone and sinew" of the Democracy, who siding with Tweed, could not conceive of Belmont's being their national political leader. It "annoyed, disgusted and insulted" them. An "Irish citizen," in a letter to the editor of the *Herald*, refused to "carry the foreign banker a minute longer." Belmont is as "fastidiously aristocratic, as great success in money saving can make small brains: he cannot speak English syntax; he cannot write an able public letter . . . he is not even a citizen of the United States: most of his time is spent in Europe." Belmont was a naturalized citizen, but this seems not to have been acceptable to other naturalized citizens. Irish citizens, the letter writer insisted, have a choice. William M. Tweed because of talent, honesty and popularity deserved the post. If the 1872 campaign is to be won, dump Belmont. Tweed's objection to Belmont was thought to be Belmont's support for Pendleton of Ohio and not Hoffman for the 1872 nominations. Belmont called it "Tweed's Terrible War."

Fortunately for all, Peter Sweeny arrived from Europe in early September aboard the *City of Washington* and order returned. Candidates miraculously resolved themselves after a month of brawling and scrapping. Though the Tweed-Belmont feud continued, it did so for only a short time. Opposition to Tweed mounted, while Belmont remained unaffected. Tweed lost his opportunity to gain national recognition, if that was what he intended. More likely his only aim was to gain a stronger voice in city affairs, and weaken the Cohen movement. The man who came out best was Sweeny, the "great balance of the Tammany organization."

Born in New York in 1827 of Irish parents, Sweeny attended the well-known Dr. Anthon's School and graduated with honor, studied law with James Brady and began his practice with A. J. Willard. He was public administrator in 1853 and elected district attorney in 1858, resigning that year because of health and the necessity of the "genial climate" of the West Indies. Former governor William Marcy recognized him as the most skillful and efficient political organizer in the state. Good friend of Baron Haussmann, the architect in Paris, and Victor Hugo, he was described by the latter as a man of talent and character. It was a tribute to a man of intellect and judgment, to a man who held Tammany together.[9]

In September, Sweeny and other powerful Tammany figures started the first part of their journey to the Syracuse state convention via the steamer *Drew*. It gave him the chance to marshal Tweed. Connolly, Creamer, McLean for the game of politics and poker. Sweeny then met with Hoffman for a few hours in Albany, and went on to Syracuse via railroad, arriving on the evening of September 21, 1869. The main address to the convention was given by Samuel J. Tilden. It was an appeal to bigotry. He criticized the Fifteenth Amendment as taking the control of suffrage from the states and giving it to Congress. Under this amendment, he declared, one half million Chinese could be brought in and allowed to vote with New Yorkers having no say. One half million African slaves could be brought to New York and become voters against the will of the people.

The people of a state, he argued, had the right to determine if Chinese or Negroes or anyone else should have a right to vote or live among them. What if the moon were made of green cheese, what if cabbages were kings? Why not exclude Irish Catholics, Germans, Jews or for that matter all Tildens if that is what the "people" wanted?

During the balloting for state office, Tammany played a neutral game, not wanting to offend state delegates. Tammany's actions or lack of them in the convention were meant to gain strength in western New York, but their acquiescence almost led Tweed and Tammany into a fatal trap. The platform agreed upon at the convention was an indictment of President Grant and the Fifteenth Amendment. Tammany went along with this plank, which was in reality a carefully planned snare laid by Seymour men in a "rule or ruin principle which would have Tammany and Hoffman immolated on the political altar," staking their future on a lost cause. Sweeny shrewdly recognized the gambit and succeeded in pruning resolutions of the amendment to nothing but "glittering generalities." He thus saved Tammany and Hoffman from their "friends." "The Saul of Tammany who towers above all his compeers . . . as the true ruler of fierce Democracy" returned to the city chamberlain's office in the new courthouse with new honors to hear further cases and causes and solve the puzzles of politics.

Tweed returned to put his own house in order, though his standing seemed assured. There was no one to challenge him, this political "fire extinguisher" without whose talent, the *Herald* felt, Tammany would be set ablaze by firebrands. It had said the same thing about Sweeny in the past. The newspaper felt that Tweed as Senator had "acquitted himself with great credit to the party, to the City and State" and was "influential upon all questions affecting the welfare, the honor and interests of the people at large."

On October 27, 1869, a "magnificent" torchlight parade was held for the Tammany slate and Tweed. A colorful procession attended the meeting as various engine companies and their "laddies" paraded. Seventh Warders, a number of red-shirted men, surrounded a ten-horse team wagon bearing a likeness of Tweed now running for re-election as state senator. "Big Six" Engine Company with two hundred men in full uniform ended the Seventh Ward demonstration. Various other wards followed, more engine companies, an American eagle, a troupe of Indians, a rowboat, 1st Artillery Volunteers, drawing a cannon. It was indeed a grand affair. Tweed opened the meeting by telling of his delight at seeing the immense gathering of the "true democracy." What was needed was to wrest control of the national government from those who held it. Hall followed this brief speech with a long, humorous, bitter address. He told the noisy cheering masses to play cricket and tell the "outs" that Democrats will guard the "Wickets" and defeat Grant and radical Republicans. Fernando Wood followed the same line, referring to the Cuban-Irish patriots and their need for support. The parades, speeches, toasts, torches continued well into the night.

Jacob Cohen, running for supervisor on the Independent ticket, hadn't surrendered. At a mass meeting of "workingmen" held at Cooper Union on October 29, John H. Ennis of the Plasterers' Union blistered all political parties and the corruption they spawned. Labor, he said, did not have a voice in their own affairs. Ennis asked for an eight-hour day, an equitable apprenticeship law, and other laws to ensure that "masters should not be like shylocks, working the flesh off the bones of workingmen." A law was also needed so that a lien could be placed against a building where the builder owed more than $25 to workingmen. Cohen stepped forward and announced his pride in receiving the endorsement of the Committee of the Workingmen's Union, and concluded by saying, "workingmen were determined to show that one, two, three men shall not rule New York City." It was not enough to ensure a Cohen victory.

Democrats did well in the election, especially in the city, even if the *Times* railed against Tweed and his friends who had found a "gold mine" which had no equal in California. There were no specifics. Hoffman's promises to root out corruption, the paper charged, were merely feeble mouthings, behind which the city, state and ultimately the nation would be plundered. The alarm bell again rang in the night, but Tweed kept his Board seat until July 1870, when the Board was reorganized.

The struggle had not been easy. Mozart Hall and Democratic Unionists were still active. In many districts maverick leaders, like Jacob Cohen, chartered their own course, independent of Tammany. Various candidates were nominated, and many sought nominations for police and civil justice, which were among the principal contests. J. Walker Fowler, brother of the deceased Chief Sachem Isaac Fowler, wanted the civil judgeship; John Cox, friend of Senator Norton's, wanted the police judgeship in the Seventh District; and so on. Still Tammany candidates got what they wanted. Mozart Hall, Democratic Union and Republicans represented only token opposition. Hall was re-elected to a full term, incredibly receiving 66,000 to 151 for independent Sinclair Tousey, surely the most one-sided victory in mayoralty history. Certainly, a great personal victory for Hall. Cohen and his plasterers, despite their spirited campaign, could try again next year.[10]

Above, a view of Broadway from Barnum's Museum. This scene provides an example of the spaciousness that Tweed envisioned for the length of Broadway. (Courtesy of The New-York Historical Society, New York City)

Below, modeled after a similar structure in London, the Crystal Palace opened in 1853, in a blaze of glory. It was destroyed in a similar but fiery blaze on October 15, 1858. As the first World's Fair held in the United States, it illustrated two points: one, that New York was the cultural and economic center of the country, and second, that few things are permanent in New York. (Courtesy of The New-York Historical Society, New York City)

The photograph above is a view of the "Tweed courthouse" under construction. Begun in 1861, it was completed about ten years later, mainly through the use of Irish labor. The woodcut below is a view, taken around 1871, of the almost completed building. Questions of the cost of the construction were at the heart of the attacks on Tweed and "The Ring." The structure itself is for some a beautiful example of Italianate architecture to be preserved, and for others a sore spot, a monument to graft and corruption which should be destroyed. (Courtesy of The New-York Historical Society, New York City)

SUPREME COURT.

the Matter of the Application of the Mayor, Aldermen and Commonalty of the City of New York, relative to

THE OPENING OF

96th Street

From Fifth Avenue to Harlem River,

N THE CITY OF NEW YORK.

Notice is hereby given, that the costs, charges, and penses incurred by reason of the proceedings in the ove entitled matter, will be taxed by the Clerk of the preme Court, at his Office, in the City Hall of the ty of New York, on **TUESDAY**, the **14th** day of nuary, **1862**, at **10** o'clock, A. M.

SAMUEL JONES,
WILLIAM M. TWEED,
CHARLES BURDETT,

ew York, December 26, 1861.   Commissioners.

A rare poster announcing the opening of Ninety-sixth Street. It is an example of Tweed's long and important service to New York. The commissioners were responsible for adjusting costs which arose during the course of the often involved process of compensating owners whose property became a public thoroughfare. (Author's collection)

Right, sheet music. Grafulla was leader of the 7th Regiment Band, which usually played at Americus Club festivities. The "Solid Men" was probably not a pun on Tweed's size, but a tribute to the staunch qualities of Tweed, who in 1867 became the club's president. (Courtesy of The New-York Historical Society, New York City) *Below*, Tweed's "Mansion," 511 Fifth Avenue, is the four-story Victorian brownstone where his daughter, Mary Amelia, was married. It is at the southeast corner of Fifth and Forty-third Street. On the southwest corner of Forty-third Street is the first Temple Emanu-El, completed in 1868. The House of Mansions, used by Rutgers Female College, in the foreground, is the eleven attached houses between Forty-first and Forty-second streets, opposite what is now the New York Public Library. Notice the horizontal quality, characteristic of Victorian New York. (Courtesy of The New-York Historical Society, New York City)

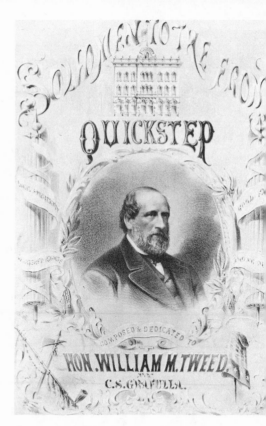

C. C. COOK,
123 MERCER STREET.

Gentlemen should be cautious about visiting here, for the landlady "puts on awful airs," and bars the door against all whom she don't fancy. Here can always be found a plenty of bad gin, and any number of low and vulgar girls, which together with the little pock marked landlady, make the place quite a bedlam.

Mrs Barrett,
125 MERCER STREET.

This is not a house of large size, nor very extensive in its equipments.

Mrs. Soule and Sister,
33 MERCER STREET

This is a tolerably genteel crib, and not much known to the b'hoys. One or two "kept ladies," make their home here; and they do not seem to be very particular as to who visits them.

Emma Laureen,
91 MERCER STREET.

There is something rather "tricky" about this

Right, an early example of "swinging Victorian New York." Seemingly written as a moral guide, it was obviously of prurient interest. Prostitution, brothels and pornography were big businesses, then as now. Reformers were constantly striving to clean the city of such sexual "excesses." In doing so, they also sought to rid themselves of immigrants, liquor and any other contamination of "pure" Protestant America. (Author's collection)
Below, in this 1839 pamphlet, the author, a "Butt-Ender," estimated that the number of known prostitutes in the city was 9,291. This figure represents 6 per cent of the total female population. Price for the night in houses of assignation was $1.00, by the hour, 50¢. The average workingman earned $1.00 per day. (Author's collection)

Anna Robertson,

Very pretty and lisps; she is about seventeen years old, and of splendid figure; she boards in Broom-St. but carries her company to Ann Burt's in Orange st. next door to Walker. Nothing less than a V suits her purpose. She became a prostitute from having a rape committed on her for which the violator of her chastity was sent to prison, but the public exposure she was compelled to make in court, was the occasion of her present prostitution.

Mrs. Barry,

A large, handsome woman, keeps a house at 134 Duane. below Church street. A pretty collection of girls may be found at this house; usually about ten in number.

Ann Eliza Smith,

Seduced on Long Island, by a workman on the farm of her father; is about 21 years old, and slightly marked with the small pox. Lives at the cook cellars, and sleeps at the Arcade in Elizabeth-st.

Mother Smith,

Is the flash woman that keeps two splendid houses in Centre street, No. 18 and the adjoining house, where from eight to ten girls may be found in each establishment, some of them pretty, and others rum customers. Any gentleman can easily get his pockets lightened by calling at this harem.

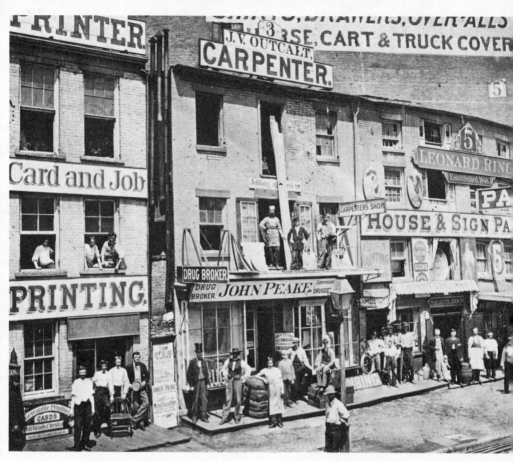

Hudson Street about 1865. John V. Outcalt was at 3 Hudson Street; Leonard Ring, at 5 Hudson Street; and Henry Croker, at 2 Hudson Street. An excellent picture of small tradesmen's cramped and crowded shops—the kind of environment Tweed knew so well. It is a formal photo, but despite this, there is a spontaneity present. Obviously, no one hid behind a barrel and certainly New Yorkers didn't have much use for eyeglasses. (Courtesy of The New-York Historical Society, New York City)

A rare Tweed letterhead reproduced here for the first time. Disappointed in his political career, Tweed returned with new hope and ambition to his father's trade. It didn't work and by 1861, Tweed became bankrupt. If his business had succeeded, how less tragic his story. That he should adjoin Harper Bros., his eternal enemy, is ironic. (Author's collection)

Crowds in Union Square, April 20, 1861, part of a huge patriotic rally in support of the Union. The city remained staunchly behind the federal government throughout the war, supplying men, money and matériel. The use of Union Square, at Fourteenth Street, as a rallying point was indicative of the northward growth of the city. (Courtesy of The New-York Historical Society, New York City)

Past and future are seen in this view overlooking the Distributing Reservoir and Crystal Palace. Forty-second Street in the foreground is largely undeveloped while carriages bring visitors from the lower city into the then countryside. This uptown area received much of Tweed's attention and was important to a changing, growing New York. Expansion was one way the city had of solving its problems. (Courtesy of The New-York Historical Society, New

18

A "New Magna Carta"

For Americans, there was and is nothing wrong with society that reform of existing institutions could not cure. It was all so easy, so simple and so attractive. Certainly, this was true for the Citizens Association and the "Ring of reformers," who were, at least, as organized as any other combination. There was a pressing need to do something. Years of hearings, scandals, charges demanded action. This came at first in the form of a charter revision, a tried if not true answer to accumulated problems. The Democracy did not take issue. Suggestions were many. There were those who thought that the mayor's office should be strengthened, that executive responsibility was the key to honest government. Perhaps the City Council should be abolished or enlarged, in either way destroying the web of secret bureaucracy. There should be some way of limiting the excesses and corruption which appeared to be inherent in the democratic process and behind which thievery flourished. Maybe democracy did not work. Tammany Democrats joined the reform movement—it seemed harmless enough especially as for the first time in twenty-four years they had a majority in the legislature. Republicans liked the possibility of more efficient government and executive responsibility to balance Democratic power. But other Republicans, especially those from upstate, were not willing to restore any power to the city which had been taken away in 1857. They did not trust the city with its own affairs, especially if Democrats were about. In any event, charter reform became a major question before the assembled legislature.

Democrats started the ball rolling when a new charter was presented early in February 1870 by New York's Alexander Frear, long-time member of the Assembly. Under its provisions, the terms of mayor, Board of Aldermen and corporation counsel were extended to four years. All heads of departments were to be named by the mayor and aldermen, and if necessary, removed by the mayor. Half the Board of Aldermen and all assistants would be elected every two years. The council would be expanded. Commissioners, such as Health and Police, would be continued, but their power consolidated and put into the hands of the mayor and aldermen. The Board of Supervisors would be abolished. The "new Magna Carta" had a long way to go as a wave of discontent all but swamped the "parents." Chief opposition came from the "Young Democracy," composed of many factious Democrats. Senators Thomas Jefferson Creamer and Mike Norton spelled out objections which, while seemingly technical, indicated thinly veiled hostility to anything from Tammany. These related to the manner in which departments would be created, and the omission of such commissions as that of Unsafe Buildings and Public Charities and Corrections. They raised questions of motivation in regard to the charter, and they did not want tampering with the existing and "efficient" Park Commission. Another debate arose in regard to the mayor's appointment power, which the rebels argued should not extend to the police commissioners and inspectors of elections—these should be elected by the people. Thus, the Tammany-Albany regency stood by the original draft, the Creamer-Norton Young Democracy stood for revisions found in its "Huckleberry Charter." Debate and behind-the-scene arguments continued through February. Certain changes began to emerge. The Board of Supervisors was to be continued, but the police commissioner would be elected rather than appointed. The Central Park Commission was to be left as is, while the Public School Board was to be elected, one member from each ward.

It was not until March 9, 1870, that a rewritten "senatorial" charter was agreed to after a caucus of senators, Tweed, Norton, Creamer, Bradley and Genet, who had met during the day in Tweed's room at the Delavan House; the angry schism, at least for a time, was seemingly healed. The principal disagreement with the "senatorial" version concerned the Park Commission. Tom C. Fields, a park commissioner, wanted to make sure that the majority of the commission who were Republicans would not control patronage. Assemblyman Timothy Campbell wanted the commission abolished altogether.

Before passage was possible, there was still work to be done and much party discord to be yet overcome. Some of the Young Democracy remained unimpressed. "Sammy" Tilden's soothing voice failed to placate the "rough and ready boys" and the bill was sent back to Frear's Committee on Cities. The quarrel was not really over the "enormities" of the charter, but over the division of the spoils and party leadership. Which appointments were to be made, what parties to be consulted?

There were angry charges by Tweed and others that votes were being bought to defeat the legislation at a cost of $7,000 to $10,000 each. Money was not the only consideration. Dennis Burns of the Second Assembly District voted against the bill for his friends Police Commissioner Matthew Brennan and Supervisor Walter Roche, who feared loss of their positions. Owen Murphy of the Tenth Assembly District sought revenge for past injuries, seemingly a denial of patronage. Abraham E. Hasbrouck and Charles H. Krach of Ulster and James M. Nelson of Rockland voted against the police provisions, in particular, also because they did not want friends of theirs removed from office.

Tweed, Genet, Norton, Creamer and Bradley watched the proceedings in the Assembly with attention, but could do nothing except to level charges of bribery. Then came a break. Republicans badly scared by Hoffman's majority in 1868, and fearful of no charter at all, finally supported the bill after receiving assurances of the passage of a strong registry law. This was not bribery, but expediency.

Angry and hurt, Tweed, "Thunderer" Norton and Creamer worked together for the time being in the Senate. On March 23, Norton appeared before the Committee on Municipal Affairs, whose five members included Tweed and Creamer. He told them that the new charter would do away with the Board of Supervisors, thus providing more executive responsibility, and would also prohibit anyone from holding more than one office, obviously a slap at Tweed, but Tweed accepted it. Norton thought this move and others like it would save the city $2 million per annum. In the evening, Tweed brought the bill to the Senate for consideration.

But there remained ill feelings among some still reluctant anti-Tammany Young Democrats like John Morrissey. What of our bills and future? The rebel Young Democracy were concerned and frightened. Tweed tried a new tack. On the same day, March 23, rumors that Tweed would leave his deputy street commissionership became fact when George McLean received Tweed's letter of resignation. It was the second time he had resigned the post. Though somewhat expected, it caught many off guard. Tweed, who was thought to be the power in the Street Department, left his friends and enemies puzzled. Tweed gave his reasons: he no longer wanted to be a "lacquey," he had been an underling for too many years and wanted out. The bait was swallowed. Young Democrats imagined George McLean had in fact fired Tweed and the "old man" was now politically dead, not to be feared. They thought not only Tweed, but Sweeny and Hall were dead as well. There was now no reason to fear the new charter. But there were those who smelled something in the wind— anyway Norton, McLean and Genet did not have the brains to direct Tammany. They surely would choke before they could digest the tidbit. But Genet eagerly advanced ready to dictate Democratic policy, as he disregarded advice. On the following day, counting on Republican votes, he introduced a strong registry bill. Tweed objected, as part of the act. Whereupon Genet "made his mouth at Tweed" by intimating that he was not surprised at the motives of "that Senator." Creamer, buoyed by the possibility of success, now joined Genet in opposition to Tweed, backing the election bill, which if passed, he felt, would make a new charter unnecessary since intrigues of corrupt politicians would be of no avail. Tweed called a friend to his side; "They've killed me dead, they think. Well, friend, perhaps they have, but I'm Tweed now and I'll be bound if I don't show that I mean to kick the lid off the coffin pretty lively. I'll give them a racket that'll do them good." Tweed and Genet glared at each other and exchanged verbal brickbats on the floor of the Senate. Around City Hall bets were being exchanged. One Tweed admirer put $5,000 to $10,000 on "Big Six" emerging victorious over Genet and Company despite mounting evidence of rebellion in the city.

The revolt within the Democracy reached its height on the evening of March 18. At the Irving House, Young Democrats like Morrissey, English-born George Purser, for some the center of the revolt, Genet, Creamer, Norton, Sheriff James O'Brien, Commissioner McLean and Tom C. Fields organized for a march on Tammany Hall to demand the ouster of Tweed. There were reports that Tammany Hall was ringed with hundreds of policemen to protect the faithful from harm. All this buoyed Young Democrats, but the trap had been set and would be sprung on the merrymakers.

Tammany, with the help of regular Democrats, upset by the specter of disunity, was joined by Republicans who thought the charter and registry law a good thing which could only come to pass if they cooperated with loyal Democrats to cut down the unwary rebels. The unsuspecting and overly optimistic Young Democrats had counted too much on the apparent "weakness" of Tweed. This, plus the inspired efforts of Sweeny, to whom contemporaries tended to give most credit, succeeded in having passed the amended so-called "Tweed" or "Frear" charter. The "Huckleberry Charter" and the revolt were squashed. The Assembly voted for the bill 116 to 5. The Senate soon followed with only two negative votes, 30 to 2, and the perplexed "Angels of Destruction," suddenly and dramatically lost their bid for power. Two to one were good odds. Governor Hoffman signed the legislation on April 5. Historians have universally held in their fairy tales that passage was the result of bribery. Yet at the time there was no such suspicion, except that raised by Tweed with regard to the opposition to the bill. Even though later a desperate confused Tweed "admitted" to his own use of bribery, the buying of votes was really not necessary. The ill-famed but largely mythical "Black Horse Cavalry," which was supposed to be a marshaled legislature selling its votes at the beck and call of Tweed, was in this instance less a "Cavalry" than a band of ill-disciplined skirmishers. It was not bribery that carried the charter, but political maneuvering and expediency. With a vote of 116 to 5 and 30 to 2, was bribery necessary?

It should be pointed out that the charter was supported not only by Tweed and Tammany, but by many of varying political persuasions as a way of benefiting the city. The passage of the charter could not aid Tammany or those seeking to "corrupt" government. To the contrary, its main purpose was to eliminate such abuses. During the debate, various organizations gathered their forces to ensure passage. The Citizens Association, which since its founding had been badgering to secure honest and efficient government, threw its weight behind the measure petitioning the legislature to that effect. The prestigious Union League Club sent a delegation to Albany to urge approval. Horace Greeley, among others, met with Tweed and members of the Senatorial Municipal Affairs Committee on April 3 at the Delavan House, where a rally in support of the charter was held. Greeley, speaking for nearly an hour, without once characteristically twisting his famous red handkerchief, went along with all the provisions. He was assured by Tweed that no changes to the Park Commission were contemplated. Greeley suggested more power be allotted to the mayor in order to fix added responsibility and salaries, but had little more to say. Tilden had reservations, but his statement appeared not to make much of an impression on the committee.

Almost everyone hailed the charter as giving New York City a chance to manage its own affairs and produce effective and efficient government. Even Lord Bryce, the bitter critic of Tammany, called the movement for the charter for the "most part, sound and wise, according to the principle and the most advanced theory of municipal administration." Bribery indeed!

Of course, the *Times* ranted and raved, denouncing the "abominable charter." Manton Marble of the *World* screamed in protest, but could do nothing as Tweed, secure in the Senate, his "good natured face blush[ing] like the rising sun against the white pillar before which he sits while the discussion was progressing," watched his opposition squirm. After Hoffman signed "An act to reorganize the local government of the City of New York" into law, Tweed kept the pen and ink and blotter that Hoffman used. These have long since disappeared. "Jollifications" were held in the rooms of Tweed, Sweeny and Henry Smith. Such moments of pleasure were hard won, but then back to the wars.[1]

During the course of the session, Tweed introduced bills to the benefit of the city of Brooklyn and ultimately as Brooklyn was incorporated into the city of New York, it also benefited. One improved Prospect Park, the other had the effect of preventing the Brooklyn Navy Yard from moving to Connecticut.

It was in keeping with his past performance. Tweed again pushed successfully for more of the kind of urban legislation identified with him. A variety of religious charities, dispensaries and orphanages were incorporated. He introduced a bill to incorporate the Metropolitan Museum of Art, finishing the efforts of past years, and he did the same for the New York Stock Exchange and the Trustees of the Lenox Library, the forerunner of the present New York Public Library. Though his name is never linked with these institutions, Tweed deserves at least a nod for the work he did on their behalf. It was altogether an impressive performance. Tweed's legislative career as a champion of municipal advancement has seldom been matched in the history of the state. It is a contribution that should not be forgotten.

Several further bits of legislation were passed; one on April 12, and others on April 26. Those were not forgotten. This was done without much debate, as they augmented the April 5 charter, yet they were of utmost consequence to Tweed and the city, of much greater consequences than the charter. Under the April 12 laws, a new Board of Supervisors was created consisting of the mayor, recorder and Board of Aldermen. These were to approve all money drawn from the county. All vouchers were to be signed by the mayor, county auditor, comptroller and clerk of the Board of Aldermen. The old Board of Supervisors was now officially abolished as of July 1, 1870. Thus, Tweed lost his seat. More importantly, under the April 26 enactment, the members of a so-called "board of audit"—the term is not in the legislation—consisting of the mayor (Hall), comptroller (Connolly), and the then president of the old Board of Supervisors (Tweed), were under Section Four of the act to audit "all liabilities against the County of New York incurred previous to the passage of this act." The act did not refer to future claims. If theft was in Tweed's mind at the time, it had no future. If a "Ring" existed, it would be of short duration. Still it was a most significant bit of legislation that affected Tweed directly. It was disaster, though at the time no one felt a tinge of foreboding. One of the first changes brought by the charter was the resignation of Sweeny as chamberlain. He was now appointed head of the Parks Commission. This move, it was thought, left him free to attend to national issues, leaving the petty mire of state and city politics. The *Herald* was pleased with Sweeny's record, which set a "high standard of honesty and patriotism." John Bradley, Sweeny's brother-in-law, was expected to succeed him. Tweed became commissioner of public works, a consolidation of the Street Department and Croton Aqueduct Board. George McLean, his former boss, was fired. An army of office seekers followed in the wake of the charter as the government was reorganized. Tweed made many appointments of friends and intimates. A former clerk in the Street Department, William E. King, became deputy commissioner of public works and Charles Cornell water register in the Water Bureau. He retained most of the old employees.[2]

Also, as a result of the new charter, special elections to the City Council were mandated for the third Tuesday in May. Judicial elections would also be held. A nominating convention was held at Tammany on May 9, 1870, in a quiet atmosphere. Grand Sachem Tweed called the meeting to order, and as the triumphant "Boss" spoke of the unanimity of the party, Sweeny glided among the delegates smiling to friend and foe alike. A good ticket, respectable and intelligent, was supplied. The election held May 17 drew a large vote of some 104,000. Democrats won easily, carrying the city by 60,000. They elected and helped elect five judges to the Court of Appeals, four judges of Common Pleas, all fifteen aldermen including George W. Plunkett, a future Tammany boss, and twenty-two assistant aldermen. Tweed later "remembered" he agreed along with Sweeny, Connolly, and Sheriff James O'Brien that Republican candidate for the Court of Appeals Charles V. Folger would be placed on four hundred to five hundred Democratic ballots scattered through the wards, thus assuring election. Jay Gould wanted Folger supported since he was a friend of the Erie. Tweed thought the same was due for Judge Charles Andrews. As usual there was no corroboration. The vote was heavier than expected, and there were no splits in the ticket. There was only Tammany. Even the Young Democracy was unhappily out working for the cause. Jacob Cohen was quiet. Susan B. Anthony did not seek to vote as she had in the past, but two women attempted the impossible, and were arrested.

Much was expected of the new council. Hall, Sweeny, Tweed and Connolly surely would acquit themselves well, their new stewardships giving them an opportunity to redeem themselves and the city.[3]

By September 1870 things had to be made ready for the state convention, this time being held in Rochester. On September 20, a special train carrying Tweed, Sweeny and other Tammanyites arrived in Rochester at 10 P.M. Tweed was serenaded by a crowd and made a brief speech of thanks in return. Young Democrats asked that O'Brien, Morrissey, McLean have admission to the convention, but they were denied. A big loser was Sheriff O'Brien. At one time friendly with Tweed, his "treason" cost him his renomination, though phoenix-like, he received the nomination as police commissioner. At the convention, all was cut and dry. Hoffman and Beach were as expected renominated to run for governor and lieutenant governor respectively. The platform condemned the Grant administration for its failures in Cuba and the Alabama claim suit. Tweed walked around the hall in his usual white cravat and dark suit. He had an air of confidence. Sweeny moved about the arena in quiet efficiency.

As for conditions in the city, it was a different matter. Hall was safe, for his term in office, if not one of distinction, was approved by all. While Young Democrats, however, touted Police Justice Edward Shandley for sheriff, Tammany wanted Matt Brennan. Never say die, Jacob Cohen formed the "New" Tammany Democratic organization. He, too, wanted to be sheriff. Problems with the nomination ended when Shandley in a speech to the Oriental Club on September 27 announced that he had withdrawn from the race. Having fought for the nomination, he found himself "overreached" and acquiesced to fate. He would help Tammany and Democrats in the fall contests.⁴

As part of the campaign, an interesting item was reported. During the hot summer, the city came close to running out of Croton water. An engineer of the Croton Aqueduct Commission told a curious story. The Croton supply was dwindling, but there were certain lakes discovered in Putnam County that could be used to add to the water supply of the city. The land could be purchased, but there was no money in the treasury for that purpose. Tweed, president of Public Works, personally advanced $25,000 and so 50 to 60 million gallons of water were made available daily. Use of personal funds was a credit for Tweed, but was it public concern or selfish desire to make a profit? "Time," the *Herald* said, "would tell."⁵

Tweed during the year successfully introduced legislation to establish public baths in the city, especially needed, given the rudimentary sanitary facilities available to most New Yorkers. When the baths opened at the end of June at the Battery, Tweed was there, but not having a quarter—at least that was his excuse—he did not use the facility.⁶

Tweed, however, had more than a quarter. He had invested in real estate, borrowed and lent money, was on the payroll of the Erie as its counsel, was a practicing attorney, was director or president of such institutions as the New York Mutual Insurance Company, New York Gas Light Company, the Guardian Savings Bank, incorporated by Tweed, Bowling Green Savings Bank, National Broadway Bank, was a director of the 125th Street Railroad Company and Third Avenue Railroad Company, both incorporated in 1870, and had large investments in the stock market. Tweed had money, made money, and all quite legitimately, or as legitimately as any businessman or investor of the time. No one contested this.

If there was a point to be chosen which marked the beginning of the end for Tweed, a good selection would certainly be an event which had little to do with politics. This concerned the marriage of his twenty-one-year-old daughter Mary Amelia to Arthur Ambrose Maginnis, Jr., of New Orleans on May 31, 1870. Very little is known about the couple. What was the attraction for the daughter of a relatively unknown northern politician of mean background for and by a member of a very socially elite and prominent southern family, especially so soon after the war? There also oddly was another Maginnis-Tweed marriage, this of Tweed's daughter Eliza "Lizzie" C. to John Henry, Arthur's brother, on February 3, 1869. A year earlier William Magear Tweed, Jr., married Eliza A. Davis, possibly related to Tweed's old friend from Oswego Henry L. Davis. These events, however, attracted none of the publicity of Mary's marriage. Tweed in 1868 or 1869 was not news. Surely, though, it was at Lizzie's marriage that Mary met Arthur. The Maginnis family, still very socially prominent, has long since preferred to forget these skeletons, relegated to the secret family closet. Other families related to the Tweeds have followed suit in drawing a high fence around themselves and closing the door to all inquiries. Tweed still dishonors the genealogical tree.

For Tweed, these affairs, must have brought considerable satisfaction, though unknown to him they brought the first tremors of disaster. But surely none of this entered his mind as he prepared for Mary's marriage. Toward evening, carriages lined the streets around Trinity Chapel on West Twenty-fifth Street near Broadway. Murmuring crowds watched as the bridal party arrived at 7:30 P.M. and proceeded up the central aisle to the rail where stood the ever present Rev. Dr. Joseph H. Price, rector of St. Stephen's Church. Richard M. Tweed, the bride's brother, came first with Miss Maggie Maginnis, the bridegroom's sister, on his arm, followed by nephew Frank Tweed and Miss Josephine S. Tweed, the bride's sister. Then came Mrs. Mary Jane Tweed, the bridegroom, and finally William Tweed supporting his "lovely daughter." Nephew Alfred Tweed was an usher. At the conclusion of the ceremony, the couple went to 511 Fifth Avenue at the corner of Forty-third Street, Tweed's residence. There they received guests amid flowers brought from their Greenwich, Connecticut, home. The list of those paying respects was large and minutely reported. Present were, William Edelstein, Dr. John Carnochan, Andrew J. Garvey, Thomas Jefferson Creamer, "Sunset" Cox, James Fisk, Jr., Justices Cardozo, Barnard, Bedford and Ingraham, and Coroner Schermer, among many others. Presents filled the rooms and were estimated at $700,000, a figure surely concocted by imaginative reporters. There was a silver ice dish from Mrs. Richard B. Connolly, a silver French bowl from Mr. and Mrs. E. A. Woodward, a clerk in the finance office, two silver cake baskets from George S. Miller, city contractor, pitcher and goblets from Matt Brennan, three soup ladles from Charles G. Cornell, soup tureen and dish from Frederick W. Douglas, Tweed's future son-in-law, a silver ice dish from T. J. Creamer, silver flower holder from James Fisk, Jr., an Etruscan gold necklace and diamond pendant from James H. Ingersoll, chairmaker, coral jet jewelry from Mike Norton, a pearl necklace, brooch and earrings from Richard M. Tweed, a diamond cross pin from Charles Loew, an amethyst breastpin, earrings and sleeve buttons from Mr. and Mrs. Harry Genet, a silver card case from Mr. and Mrs. John H. Maginnis, a set of breastpin armlets, earrings and a solitaire ring surrounded with diamonds from Peter B. Sweeny. Thurlow Weed gave a silver sugar bowl shaped like a beehive, while a silver coffee urn, salver and goblets came from Andrew Garvey, plasterer, an ormolu writing desk from Tiffany and Company, and a silver nut pick came from Jay Gould.

Father and mother Tweed gave two hundred pieces of silver and a $5,000 bankbook. Alfred Tweed presented a mother-of-pearl lace fan. Jennie, George and Charlie, Tweed's children, gave bronze statuettes. It was a day to remember, as a tribute to the married couple as well as to Tweed. Gifts came from acquaintances and friends, from political enemies and political associates. They came from Tweed's circle—the ambitious like Woodward, tradesmen like Miller and Garvey. They would become well known. Missing were the social elite—the Astors, Lenoxes, Belmonts, Goelets, Rhinelanders. Missing also were Republicans Greeley, George T. Strong, Bennet, Cooper, and Democrats Charles P. Daly, Morrissey and Hall. Also not present were national figures and state leaders. Tweed had obviously gone a long way, but many doors remained closed and always would.

The marriage was seized upon by a hungry press that literally drooled over the details, undoubtedly inflated by headline-conscious reporters. Tweed is said to have ordered dinner for five hundred guests from Delmonico's at a cost of $13,000. Questions were asked. How did a public servant having a salary of $7,500 per year acquire the money to pay for such an affair? It was all surely out of proportion to the status of the family. It portended some kind of thievery. Those with sharp noses for these types of things smelled reeking corruption. Now a highly visible figure, Tweed's head was being readied for a platter, and the platter was large and deep.[7]

The *Times* specifically went after Tweed beginning with an editorial of September 4, 1870. Later, a clerk in the Auditor's Bureau, William J. Copland, would testify he informed Sheriff O'Brien of certain enormities in the fall of 1870. O'Brien would say he provided his own suspicions to Jones. Jones obviously had sources of information. The editorial was a criticism of the Rochester convention and cited Tweed as the "engineer" responsible for foisting upon a great city "the most licentious government ever known." Let the public beware! Why Tweed? Why not

Sweeny, Hall or Connolly? Perhaps it was his figure; even in a world of big men and women, the later "Floradora Sextet" of entertainers was also known as "six tons of beef on the hoof." Tweed was big and fat. "Herculean," he was about 5 feet 11 inches and weighed some 280 pounds. He had easily caricatured features, as Thomas Nast soon found out. He was good copy and the much publicized marriage of his daughter whetted public appetite. He was vulnerable and visible, and without Sweeny's guidance not too adept. He was simply a big target, hard to miss, useful as an election gimmick, and Republicans were desperate. Most importantly, by now he was identified as the leading spokesman for the interests of the city and of the immigrant. Moreover, the Grant regime floundered in corruption and the championing of the blacks in the South was costly in New York. Democratic victories in 1868 and 1869 added to despair. The election of May 1870 was a final disgrace. Republicans needed something. Tweed would do very well. And there were the disenchanted—the disgruntled Democrats.

And there were newspapers to sell. There were a lot of sharp knives around town. One, of course, belonged to the *Times*. For George Jones, the denial of city largesse in the form of more advertising money made him a knife wielder par excellence. Surely the offensive launched against Tweed was, at first, a trial balloon, a desperate long shot by those who had little to lose. The gambit worked. Editorials which followed became stronger, nastier and more biting. Tweed was at first the "engineer," then the "Dictator" and finally the "King." The term "Boss" was rarely used then. The theme was the same, almost word for word, in every issue. There was Tweed and Company, Tweed's hirelings and dupes, his "vast fortunes" made from ill deeds. There was the "King" defrauding honest citizens. Only the most corrupt days of Rome and Venice could rival present-day New York. How much longer would honest Democrats and other citizens tolerate the "incumbus" of Tweed and his "minions"? How did Tweed, a chairmaker, manage to put by $10 million in the course of six or seven years, asked the *Times* on September 28, 1870, not by "dishonest means and centralism"? The paper never explained how it arrived at that figure. It really did not know. The next day, he was "King Tweed" holding court with James Fisk, Jr., and ruling like a Mongol despot over overtaxed New Yorkers, who were being driven out of the city by the thousands because they could not afford to live within its boundaries because of rising costs and taxes. This was the "worst-formed, worst-lighted city in the universe," yet the highest-taxed. Tweed led the most degraded and unprincipled local government in the United States. There is nothing beyond their grasping and greedy hands. Where are comptroller's reports, where are accounts of city finances, the *Times* asked. Why Tweed? "We look upon Mr. Tweed," answered the *Times* on September 29 to those who asked, "as the incarnation of all the vice in the City government. It is Tweed who has dictated the nomination of Governor Hoffman. Practically, it is for Mr. Tweed that citizens are invited to vote next November for Governor—for Mr. Tweed, whose colossal fortune has been built up on the earnings of industrious taxpayers. . . ." Even Democrats must now be willing to throw Mr. Tweed and his nominees overboard. Every day, Tweed, "The Ring," "The Erie Ring," corruption. It was an endless campaign of vilification, of charges without proof or evidence. Despite this barrage, Tweed did not reply. It was a mistake—and when he finally did respond it made little impression.[8]

The Tammany convention was held in October as always. The crowded hall was called to attention by Tweed. Norton and Genet asked that delegates from the newly formed Workingmen's Union be admitted. This was affirmed, thus taking some wind out of Jacob Cohen's sails. Tweed then moved to nominate candidates. Resolutions were read from the Albert Cardozo Club which eulogized Hoffman, Tweed and Sweeny. Later that night of October 19, a mass meeting and torchlight procession was held at the junction of East Broadway and Canal Street. The basic effect of the meeting was to voice support for Tweed and nominate Ed Shandley for register. Tweed was at "home again among the friends of childhood" and he aired some of his anger and frustration. Among this assemblage he could talk freely and openly. "Reviled as man has seldom been, traduced as man has seldom been, maligned as man has seldom been, I point proudly to my friends to prove my character and only ask a fair, a bold and a very impartial investigation at an early day of all my official acts," said Tweed, as he looked at his audience. Asked by friends why he had not responded to newspaper attacks, he went on, "No man can answer newspaper attacks and stop with the reply. The proper place, the true place, the only place where men should be adjudged guilty or if not found guilty, acquitted, is before a proper and legal tribunal." He was ready to meet his accusers, but not when they stood behind the "mighty engine of the Press." Only a child would attempt to do this. The only real verdict is before the people and in this he asked for their support when he sought re-election to his Senate seat. It was a decent speech, but it did not answer his critics. It would in a short time prove prophetic, as the "mighty engine," the press, did indeed grind him down.

In the meantime, the usual splitting between Democrats continued. Young Democrats denounced Tweed, Connolly and Company as "blacklegs and ruffians." In preparation for the election, some fifty thousand red-shirted Democrats carrying torches and banners on October 27 paraded around Tammany Hall and adjacent Union Square. Horatio Seymour spoke of Republican corruption, the Canal Board and the rising costs of transportation. Fernando Wood criticized Grant, the "impersonation of pretense and political harlequinancy," and lauded Hoffman, the "incorruptible magistrate." Of these two, asked a contrite Wood, running for Congress, "which would you choose in the coming November for the Presidency?" Hoffman supporters were looking beyond 1870. At one rally, one of the speakers was "Jubilee" James Fisk, Jr., who appeared probably for the first time on the "stump." His short exhortation was a favor to Tweed. He told the cheering crowd that he had never voted the Democratic ticket, but was going to do so now. He would vote the whole Tweed ticket, and while not the orator his friend was, would do his best to aid the cause. So the speeches went, followed by a grand display of tumultuous pyrotechnics.

Republicans basically played on the issue of illegal voting and the corruption of the "Tweed Brigade." Roscoe Conkling raised the "bloody shirt," a reminder of riot and civil war and Democratic opposition to law and order. But charges of corruption were answered by a committee including Moses Taylor, John J. Astor and Marshall O. Roberts, who having examined accounts in the Finance Department found that they were kept in a "correct and faithful" manner. Hall also went on record in defense of Comptroller Connolly, "who had swept away the old abuses of former Chamberlains who kept large bank accounts on which they were paid interest which they pocketed."

On the night before the election, Tweed, Hall, O'Gorman and others met at Cooper Union. Tweed, pleased with the turnout, asked those assembled to vote early and get their friends to do the same. Now was the time for work. The election elicited a good deal of betting. One hundred dollars got eight that Hoffman would win his race for governor by 45,000 votes. The odds were two to one he would win by 50,000. Five hundred dollars would get four hundred that Hall would win for mayor by 20,000. On the day of the election, Hall, Brennan and Barnard assisted at the opening of the Sisters of Charity Metropolitan Bazaar held at the 22nd Regiment Arsenal on Fourteenth Street. Berstein's band supplied the music, as electioneering continued around the clock.

When the results were in, Tammany had gained another victory. Hall was re-elected mayor. Connolly defeated his Republican-Young Democratic opponent for comptroller by some 20,000 votes. Hoffman won by 50,000. It was a show of strength with no charge of manipulation or trickery. Hoffman was ready for the presidency in 1872 or possibly 1876. Tammany was ready too. The waters ahead looked smooth and calm. It was deceptive; there were ripples and the great *Times* wind machine had just begun to grind.[9]

After the election, Jones appealed to Democrats of unimpeachable character, Belmont, Tilden, O'Conor, to reject Tweed, Hoffman and "The Ring." But there were those who had other views. Talk from upstate had Tweed running for governor in 1872. The Binghamton *Democrat* found him a "large, trained progressive," who did not find that the world would be finished in the next century, and who was in favor of enlarged canals and the free use of them, as well as extending state and county aid to railroads. Tweed, the article concluded, "is a common sense man with common sense ideas," who could bring to the governor's seat more practical experience than any predecessor.[10] Tweed in the capital, however, was a frightening specter for some, and the urgency of criticism was evident. He had introduced legislation to provide extensive assistance to private institutions with which large numbers of the city's poor came in direct contact. His "program of official social insurance came at a time when rapid urban growth was placing even greater demand upon these private institutions."[11] There were those who saw nothing good in this.

The *Times* found it difficult to criticize such legislation openly, but castigated Tweed and Sweeny for giving $50,000 of their own money to the poor, money which was probably earned in a single day from an issue of the *Transcript*, a newspaper devoted to publishing official city news. The hyprocrisy of it, said the *Times*, was that Tweed robbed the poor, made them poor by heavy taxes and corruption, and returned a portion to "contemptuously fling a bone to them to stop their mouths."[12] There was no proof to the allegations. The $50,000 could have been $5.00 or $50 or a turkey. Stories were easy to tell and they could undermine public confidence in Tweed and his works.

It was at this time also that the tale of the statue was told. Charles A. Dana, editor of the *Sun*, had an idea. In the December 7, 1870, issue, he published a short announcement that a statue was to be erected in Tweed's honor, and ten cents had been contributed. It was a joke, a satirical joke at Tweed's expense. Tweed did not fall for it, but the gullible did, the *Times* and Tweed historians included. It was to them an example of the arrogance of the man. Silly as it was, it became another part of the myth and another dart in the "Elephant's" hide. The idea, however, was taken up by some "friends." On March 13, 1871, Tweed wrote a letter to Edward Shandley, president of the Tweed Testimonial Association, who seemingly became the head of a committee of citizens who indeed planned to erect the statue. In it he expressed gratification of the "friendly feelings" manifested by the proposal, but "I most emphatically and decidedly object to it." Tweed informed the group he never considered it more than a jest brought forward by a "newspaper in our city, a jocose sensation, for which that journal is famous. Statues are not erected to living men, but to those who have ended their careers and have no interest except to question the partial tributes of friends. . . . I claim to be a live man, and hope (Divine Providence permitting) to survive in all my reign, politically and physically, more years to come." A statue, moreover, would be a public acknowledgment of vanity and Tweed hoped the joke would be ended. Of course, it was not, but a statue of a different kind was being erected and it was not a joke.[13]

IV

Witches' Sabbath

Some of these worthies masquerade as reformers. Their vocation and ministry is to lament the sin of other people. Their stock in trade is rancid, ranting self-righteousness. They are wolves in sheep's clothing. Their real object is office and plunder. When Dr. Johnson defined patriotism as the last refuge of a scoundrel, he was unconscious of the then underdeveloped capabilities and uses of the word reform . . .

SENATOR ROSCOE CONKLING

19

Where There's Smoke

Tweed arrived in the state capital late on January 1, 1871. He met Sweeny, who had arrived a few hours earlier. Both put up in a suite of rooms at the Delavan House. For Tweed, the storms of the winter lingered. A reporter for the *Herald* received an interview with the jovial "Boss," the name now commonly used, amid a small gathering. What of the $50,000 donation to the Seventh Ward poor, the reporter asked. Tweed's smile left his face. "Advertisers making use of it, eh?" he blustered. "That question as you call it, is a subject I would rather not speak about. It has already given me a great deal of trouble. I don't want to talk about it at all. I would rather nothing was published about it." He paused and reflected. "But . . . it is quite impossible to please everyone." He had not expected any notice would be taken of the gift, as it was his practice "since I have been any way comfortable to give a little of what I had to others." Certainly, it could be imagined that the money was used to help obtain votes, but this was not his intended purpose. "I know that a public man's lot is a hard one," sighed Tweed. "He's got to stand abuse and I am not thin-skinned in the least, but when a man [is] abused even when he is doing what no person of good heart can call a bad act, it is almost unbearable." He was particularly concerned with the effect of the adverse publicity upon his family. The reporter took his leave.[1] Tweed went back to the gathering, perhaps reflecting on the nature of politics and man.

But there were more pleasant matters at hand. Returning to New York, he celebrated a belated New Year's Day with a few friends at his Fifth Avenue home. There John McBride Davidson, a safe manufacturer having considerable dealings with the city, Cornelius W. Lawrence, the old-time Whig and former mayor, and others presented Tweed with a huge painting by Gustave Doré, to "adorn the gallery of his mansion." Whether Tweed appreciated the painting by a then popular Victorian artist and illustrator is not known. Anyway, he didn't really have the time. For the next night he was at the Americus ball taking part in a full-dress affair of "beauty and splendor." Members of the newly formed William M. Tweed, Jr., Club were in prominent attendance. Tweed even received two notes from August Belmont requesting Tweed do him the "honor" of dining with him. Tweed did not respond to the first invitation and Belmont hoped he could count on the "pleasure of his company" in the second.[2] Tweed beamed in delight. It was a happy time. There weren't too many left.

Then back to Albany, where there was legislative business at hand. On January 17, he introduced the annual tax levy bill, allowing the city to tax itself so that it could function. A feature designated the mayor, comptroller, commissioner of the Department of Public Works and commissioner of the Park Department as a "board of estimate and apportionment," whose actions must have the concurrence of the majority of the Common Council in approving all bills submitted to the city. Hall felt these were the most "senior" of public officials—himself, Tweed, Connolly and Sweeny. The levies covering 1871 and 1872 were not to exceed 2 per cent of the valuation of real and personal estate. The main thrust of the measure was to provide a greater degree of home rule for New York so that the people of the city could "clear the snow from their sidewalks or dig out a gutter" without being forced to go to the legislature, which had "no more business in interfering in the government of this city than a Comanche Indian." It was an important bill and central to the city's hope of gaining at least a portion of long-sought independence. Tweed stood at the brink of gaining real political power with New York the beneficiary. He and the city would never go much beyond this point. There immediately arose a shout of protest over "Boss" Tweed's new job. It was denounced as an "audacious" scheme, a "magnificent proposition" for the "Ring monopoly" and the "most unblushing 'nigger' of all in the fence." Here was another "ring" to add to "Commercial Rings, Manufacturing Rings, Market Rings, Shop Rings, Rings political, Rings legislative, each ring a harm and injury to the people," so the *Herald* informed its readers. Besides the rhetoric chief opposition, of course, came from members of the Republican-controlled legislature, who under the old tax levy system found it possible to sandwich in a "job" or two as needed with amendments to tax laws. More importantly, a comprehensive system, especially one giving New York a degree of fiscal control, did not suit the opposition. Some Young Democrats and upstate partisans would question anything introduced by Tweed.[3]

While forces maneuvered for the battle over the levy, Tweed attended to business at a very busy session. He was able to have a number of bills passed; many were of special interest to the city. Early in the session Henry Genet introduced a viaduct railway bill which was to bring mass transit to Broadway. There was fierce opposition led by Republican Thurlow Weed and some disenchanted Young Democrats. Tweed had earlier voiced objection to a similar scheme; "as long as I can help it there will never be a surface railroad on Broadway," he reportedly said. Now, pressured by constituents to approve the measure and needing Genet's support for the tax levy, he worked for a successful passage. Known as the New York Railway Co., stock was subscribed by the city. Tweed became an officer in the company, along with Belmont, Hall, Connolly and Sweeny, while Judge Henry Hilton, friend of A. T. Stewart, became its president. Tweed was also a director of the 125th Street and Third Avenue Railroad companies, whose incorporation he also supported.

He also sponsored a number of changes to the city charter.[4] One, requiring permission of three fourths of the Commission of Public Instruction to remove teachers and purchase schoolhouses, was an example of Tweed's interest in education, an interest which helped modernize the system. His concern with the support of parochial institutions led to Senate Bill No. 30, which authorized religious corporations to erect schoolhouses and residences for teachers on church land. The "evils" of the bill were protested by professional Protestants of the Seventeenth Assembly Union League meeting on March 4 where the dangers of aiding Roman Catholics were reported by David B. Mellish. Tweed was a special target. He also sponsored and introduced a bill to incorporate the New York Stock Exchange Association and the American Mortgage and Trust Company. He introduced legislation for widening of Broadway, a pet project, from Seventeenth to Nineteenth streets. Normal College, present-day Hunter College, received permission to erect its buildings after Tweed brought forward the necessary legislation. He also sponsored bills permitting purchase of land to increase the water supply of the city with expenses in the bill to be kept under $5 million per year. A bill to prohibit the use of Chinese or "coolie" labor was also submitted by him. This "alien bill" was defeated in Tweed's own Senate. Tweed did not press for passage and it was probably a way of putting on more pressure for passage of the tax levy, which was the major issue.[5]

This was of vital concern to the city especially now. In 1823, New York consisted of Manhattan Island. By 1870, it had taken its first steps to incorporate surrounding communities. The island had outgrown itself. It had changed from a small mercantile—almost colonial—community to a world metropolis. What fantastic changes occurred! The closed, tight social structure had opened. What blossomed was mass transportation, elevated railroads, the Brooklyn Bridge, then under construction; there was mass education served by public schools, universities, colleges. The newly opened Museum of Art and Museum of Natural History and the Great White Way provided mass culture. There developed mass housing, including the slums and burgeoning skyscrapers. New York was the undisputed center of American banking and insurance. Its newspapers—the *Sun*, *Herald*, *Tribune*, *Times*, *World*—were known everywhere. So much occurred after the Civil War and within the Tweed period. The war provided an impetus. The city needed new ideas, new structures, new assertiveness; it needed money to build and change. It needed leadership and voices in high places. It needed Tweed.

Through the years, and especially since the Civil War, finding revenue to pay for ever expanding vital services became the chief occupation of its politicians and civic leaders. One school of thought led by the *Times* advocated retrenchment—reduced services, lower the debt, lower tax rates. Increases in these rates drive the middle classes and business out. Another, surely held by the majority, saw spending as a necessity, not to fill the coffers of the crooked politicians, but to provide services, welfare, aid for the host of New Yorkers. The rich could talk of ending support for education, but where would the less affluent send their children? These are arguments heard through the years with little variation.

One thing was certain: taxes, generally property taxes, were rising. So too was the debt, and so too was a betterment of life, if increased services were a criterion. In 1860, the funded debt of the city was $20 million, the tax rate per $100 was $1.69. By 1869, the debt was $56 million, the tax rate $2.27. But over the same period population grew from 805,658 to 942,296, assessed valuation $577 million to $964 million, per capita expenditure from $12.14 to $28.14. What also increased was a budget to parks, $105,000 to $250,000; police, $1.4 million to $2.9 million; fire, $167,573 to $907,940 (the department became uniformed and paid in 1865); asylums, etc. $109,661 to $939,219; printing and advertising, $153,000 to $444,000. Most expenditures doubled or tripled. In this decade and in the next decades they would continue to rise; things rarely fell in New York. All this underlined the age-old question—were tax rises necessary?—and the favorite question—wasn't it all corruption? Critics had special reason to be wary. In 1870, with a population of 1 million, the funded debt rose to $67 million and in 1871, $87 million! It was these figures that led to Tweed's demise. But what critics usually omit is that after Tweed the debt continued to rise. In 1874, it was $118 million, in 1880, $123 million, in 1890, $142 million, in 1896, $186 million. Population was then about 2 million. No one person or "ring" was responsible. It was New York, a quality of life, population growth, industrialism, inflation, a host of factors. In 1850 the state paid for the judiciary; in 1869 it was largely a city expense. For critics it was all simple, all suspicious. So, Tweed with all his supposed power had to come hat in hand to the legislature; the city, the greatest in the country if not the world, had to come hat in hand to obtain permission to exist, for permission to tax itself. It was what the legislature and city haters wanted. Republicans stalled—hopefully the session would end without a decision. Angrily, Tweed chided them for refusing to consider necessary bills because of politics, thus wasting time and taxpayers' money, spitefully disregarding that the "great cities of our state" are in need of such legislation.

Republicans defended their right to consider "partisan" measures for what they were. Tweed was helped at the last moment by a decision of Republican Assemblyman Orange S. Winans of Dunkirk to support the bill and other city measures, even though it meant virtual ostracism by fellow Republicans. "Aleck" Frear, taking the "bill by the horns," presented it again in the Assembly. Tom Fields was successful during the last days of the session in having the Assembly adopt a rule making the levy a special order needing assent of the majority instead of two thirds of the members present, as with a regular bill. Republicans Thomas G. Alvord of Syracuse and DeWitt C. Littlejohn of Oswego attempted to block this "revolutionary" action by "heart-rendering" appeals, but they failed. Then there was compromise, as always basically aimed at appeasing Republicans. What was pushed through was an election law providing a separate ballot box for the congressional ticket; a registry law which allowed inspectors to permit a non-registered voter to vote providing his excuse sufficient; a bill which allowed an increase of salaries to justices of Supreme, Superior, Common Pleas and Marine courts; a charter amendment permitting the mayor to appoint members of the Board of Education. Finally the much debated tax levy was passed, but amended so that if state taxes were increased, so would city taxes, with the proviso that no more than $25 million should be spent in either of the two years to which the act applied. No money could be allotted to sectarian schools or religious institutions; a slap at Tweed, though certain founding homes were exempt. One section of the amendments referred to an appropriation of $750,000 for the new courthouse raised by a new and fifth issue of county stock. Claims of ex-Sheriff O'Brien against the city for $300,000 for services rendered were to be audited by the corporation counsel. It was an accommodation granted one of the leaders of the Young Democracy. There would be repercussions.

Thus, the compromise package passed. It again appears obvious that Tweed did not "dictate" to, or control, the legislature. Politics was a complicated, obtuse business requiring a careful and sensitive hand. Tweed was never able to "ram" legislation through; he was not a ringmaster at a circus, but rather one of the performers, an important one perhaps, but still a performer.[6]

The ending of the session surely came as a relief to Tweed. It was so for members of his family. Margaret Tweed, his sister-in-law, visited the senator, his wife Mary Jane and daughter Josephine in Albany. She wrote about a rainy day sewing and reading, listening to a music box, with Aunt Mary singing. Meals were taken in the parlor, and she had her hair arranged every day. Sundays she attended St. Peter's Church and took a ride with Aunt Mary, still she was ready to come home.[7] Tweed could say amen. It had not been easy, but enough had been accomplished. The city had its levy and was at least in partial control of its own affairs. Through Tweed, Sweeny and Tammany, there was enough political muscle to show a degree of independence. Foes saw the results simply as a way of managing more graft. These enemies of "The Ring" were becoming increasingly vocal, more biting; something was in the wind.

That something was the start of a grand jury investigation, begun in November 1870, to uncover evidence of corruption in city government generally, and to examine the activities of "The Ring" specifically. Its foreman was an unsavory Lucius S. Comstock, an attorney by profession, but an often libeling reformer by choice. Discreet inquiries were made of literally hundreds of banks and brokerage houses in the city as to deposits by "Ring" members. For example, Comstock asked the cashier of the Chemical Bank on December 30, 1870, to list their checks which passed through the bank. Cashier T. F. Chamberlain replied that he had cleared four checks for $5,800 each on July 16, 1870, for Tweed, attorney Hugh Smith, Richard B. Connolly and James M. Sweeny. These checks were deposited with the bank by J. C. Thompson, a builder, who Chamberlain had been told was connected with "The Ring." He vaguely remembered some were endorsed by Connolly or banker "Hank" Smith. Manufacturers and Merchants Bank told Comstock of receiving from the Stuyvesant Bank three checks on October 19, 1870, drawn on the Tenth National for $7,000 for members of "The Ring." The banking house of George Opdyke and Co. upon examining their books found that it had sold New York Midland convertible bonds to the following:

July 15, 1870	Alexander Frear	$ 8,143.84
Aug. 4, 1870	William M. Tweed	20,455.48
Aug. 5, 1870	Hugh Smith	16,368.22
Aug. 9, 1870	A. Oakey Hall	4,095.89
Aug. 11, 1870	Richard B. Connolly	4,917.38
Aug. 16, 1870	John J. Bradley	4,102.60
Oct. 14, 1870	Peter B. Sweeny	15,927.12
Dec. 13, 1870	Richard B. Connolly	3,232.22

The cashier did not know the numbers of the checks in payment of the bonds. Samuel J. Tilden, a private citizen, into whose hands all these supposedly "secret" and "inviolate" grand jury letters and replies were illegally given, made his own inquiries. Between December 4, 1869, and June 10, 1870, Tweed had purchased 2,100 Cleveland-Pittsburgh Railroad stocks. A. Oakey Hall, Richard B. Connolly, James Watson, Hugh Smith, James M. Sweeny, also for approximately the same period, received similar shares. All also had shares in the Erie Junction Railway Company. Every financial institution in the city was thus canvassed. What were "Ring" deposits on hand, what were withdrawals? There were sums going in and out of several institutions, but beyond this, it would take months accurately to piece together all the information.[8] There was time and there was fortune.

On January 21, 1871, James Watson, county auditor, riding his sleigh along Harlem Lane, a favorite racing site, where fast trotters like those used by Watson were put through their paces, was run into by another driver, one Charles Clifton. Watson was thrown, his head struck the pavement and he was fatally injured. He died on January 24 of a fractured skull. On March 4, there was an inquest and the coroner's jury decided Watson's death was due to the careless driving of Clifton, and on March 15, the late auditor's expensive tackle, harness and a string of five horses, including the well-known bay "Charlie Green," were auctioned off before a large crowd of politicians, judges and horsemen.[9]

The vacancy created by his death was filled by Stephen C. Lynes, an employee in the auditor's office and a Republican. He was appointed by Mayor Hall. There was access to all manner of city financial records even before Watson's death, but now they were more accessible. If there were matters which "The Ring" wanted to be kept secret, why did the mayor appoint Lynes to a post in the auditor's office? Similar appointments had been made in the Finance Department to members of the opposition party. There was seemingly no attempt to hide any fiscal transaction. It was especially so after Watson died.

What was important about Watson's death was not that secrets became public, but that information about city finances which he was privy to was now lost. It put a greater burden upon Tweed. Watson was a key link in the handling of city funds. He could be useful to Tweed especially with so many strange things going on. Not only were there leaks of grand jury proceedings and evidence, but individuals in Finance were having a ball. One of these, William S. Copland, a clerk in the Auditing Department, and of all things a "friend" of James O'Brien, spent much of his time making notes. He examined, on city time, apparently without permission or authority, hundreds of warrants from 1869 to June 1870 submitted by Andrew Garvey, James Ingersoll, John Keyser and others and then made a multi-page penciled account of his findings. He discovered that during this period these persons and firms received $11 million. He made no effort to evaluate his notes or to check as to the honesty of each warrant. Suspicion was sufficient. He brought his papers to George Jones, editor of the New York *Times*, sometime in the fall of 1870. He also made his findings known to O'Brien. Copland maintained that he received nothing, as a personal advancement, but acted because he was "sore" for being discharged in March 1871 for "political reasons" by Connolly. Copland received through legislative enactment in 1872 $2,500 for his "altruism." What he received from the *Times* is not known. There were others who made similar findings and transcripts—and made money. There was really nothing secret in city finances, and there was a dollar to be made by anyone with a piece of paper and a pencil. So there were a lot of people around making notes—a lot of them claiming credit for "The Ring's" downfall.[10]

As information, much of it unverified, was gathered, knowledge of what was going on in the grand jury room was sent to people like Tilden and George Jones. It gave them added incentive to pursue the "evil" ones. A witch hunt of magnificent proportion was readied as new "facts" of corruption were brought to light.

In evaluating the results of the recent legislative sessions, Jones informed his readers that the city was "practically in the hands of four persons," Mayor Hall, William M. Tweed, Peter B. Sweeny and Richard B. Connolly. While Mayor Hall, who he mistakenly said was the only elected official and the only one the people could reach, was "only a cypher" dictated to by Tweed and Sweeny, he could not shirk his responsibilities. In an editorial written on July 1, the *Times* reminded its readers of swindles by "The Ring." "People cry what an outrage. The Ring too have heard it, and what did they do? Thrusting their hands into their pockets filled with money filched from the people they have defrauded and then had the gall and arrogance to ask, 'Well! what are you going to do about it?'" The *Times* made it appear that this bit of arrogance was said by Tweed— which was not true. It was a great joke on Tweed, repeated as "truth" by innumerable historians. It was Thomas Nast, the Swiss immigrant, cartooning *Harper's Weekly*, which like the *Times* was on a continuous crusade of justice and salvation, who made it up. Francis H. Bellew and Thomas Worth were also anti-Tweed cartoonists employed by *Harper's*, but they were not as successful as Nast. In the issue of June 10, Nast in an ever growing war against Tweed, now his favorite villain, one so easily caricatured, honed after months of developing the proper anti-Tammany, anti-Catholic, anti-Tweed technique, drew a fat monstrous hand having a large thumb pressing down and smashing the city. Adjoining suburbs were prosperous and peaceful, New York was crushed. The caption read "The Boss: What are you going to do about it?" The *Times* repeated the phrase and in the public mind it was Tweed who had made the statement. It was pure editorial propaganda. There is incidentally no evidence to substantiate the often repeated story that Tweed tried to bribe Nast with as much as a million dollars to end his cartooning. A million? Nast could have been bought for the proverbial mess of pottage. He was not the most respected individual. The *Times* did not stop to explain about the grand jury investigation or Nast, or Lynes, or ask Tweed's side of the story, but called for an end to submission and the beginning of a "Council of Political Reform" to represent robbed taxpayers and bring justice to New York.

Investigate all the transactions, Jones demanded—how much has been stolen, how much actually expended? If Justice Barnard or Justice Cardozo refuses to issue necessary orders, appeal to Justice Charles P. Daly or Justice John R. Brady. If this doesn't work, then the "public will by that time be in a mood to resort to other measures to assert their rights." The paper was on to something. It was like a dog with a bone. Every succeeding issue contained similar statements. Swindle and reform were repeated over and over, though there were no specific details.[11] For its own part, Tammany was quiet. It did not respond. It had been through this before.

On July 4, 1871, the usual celebration was held. Grafulla's 7th Regiment Band played again, the Declaration was read and Grand Sachem Tweed made the welcoming address. He greeted a happy crowd as "friends and brethren," and made a "neat little speech" extolling the virtues of the Democracy. He dedicated Tammany to the service of all, to carry on "strict government," to recognize the rights of the electorate and to call persons elected to high office to account for their conduct in office, to wrest government from those who betray public trust. He ignored Jones, Nast and the baying hounds at his heels.[12]

On July 12, it was time for the Protestant Orange Irish to parade, much to the anger of Catholic Irish, and there was more trouble for Tweed. It was expected one thousand Orangemen and three thousand American sympathizers would march in commemoration of the Battle of the Boyne, the eternally remembered defeat of Catholic Irishmen in the late seventeenth century which led to the forming of Protestant Ireland. Hall asked Orange leaders to discontinue their plans. O'Donovan Rossa, who had fought the British in Ireland, asked for toleration. He was hooted and jeered into silence. Police Superintendent John Kelso prohibited the parade. He called a council of police captains. Tweed and Hall were there. They decided to put police and troops into the area. Guns were distributed among both sides—hotheads tempered their steel. Governor

Hoffman arrived in New York early on the eleventh and immediately issued a proclamation ordering police and state militia to protect the marchers and ordered all persons to clear the line of march. Hoffman reasoned, if the threat of a mob can stop orderly citizens in exercising a civic right, where was law and order? Concessions to ruffians as in Kansas helped cause the Civil War. There must be authority beyond that of the mob. The parade went on despite Hall's protestations. All along the line of march down Eighth Avenue, the celebrants were met first with jeers and then with stones and bricks and finally bullets. Police, state and national guardsmen were unable to separate the forces. Hundreds of rioters were killed or wounded; three members of the police died. One supposed taunt greeting the marchers went:

> My name is Kelly, the rake
> and I don't care a damn about any man
> if I had a knife in my fist
> Shure I'd shtick it right into an Orangeman.

Orangemen often replied in kind. Colonel Jim Fisk, Jr., was attacked by a gang as he tried to go to his regiment, knocked about, kicked, his clothing torn. Fisk just made the ferry to New Jersey. He presented a bill to the city.

Those less fortunate, the dead and wounded, were taken to Mount Sinai Hospital, where a number of amputations of legs and arms were performed. Many died of gunshot wounds. Thomas Nast had a field day. Leering, grinning apelike Irishmen were depicted, assaulting the maiden of American liberty. The message of the riot was clear—law and order must prevail. Tammany Hall and their Irish Catholic friends must be shorn of political power. Bloodshed helped intensify the growing storm. Why should a government be maintained that could not control the mob? Who was safe with Tweed and Tammany cohorts in office? Daniel Ullman, champion of Protestant America, drooled over a chance to revive good old-fashioned nativism. He found that goblins in the form of "Romanism—resolved to establish supremacy in the New [World]" were abroad. The time was ripe for the thousands of Democrats filled with "disgust" at the "Supremacy of political Irish Catholics" to be enrolled into the "mysteries" of the P.O.S.A. (Protestant Order of Secret Americans). He went about the business of recruiting for his brand of patriotism.[13] The riots and the attacks upon Tweed brought out the "best" in American society. The stage was now properly prepared, the atmosphere properly charged.

20

Black Headlines

On July 8, the *Times* told of "facts" taken from books in the comptroller's office proving that there were "Gigantic Frauds" in the rental of armories; "thousands of dollars are paid for bare walls and unoccupied rooms," read the headlines. James H. Ingersoll was singled out as a "partner" of Tweed's in the chair business and president of an arms company, "virtually owned by Tweed," the weapons of which "The Ring" was trying to foist on the National Guard. Ingersoll and James Watson were drawing $5,000 a year for an armory that never existed. There was another armory over a stable at the corner of Twenty-sixth Street and Fourth Avenue. The lease for this was carried though the Board of Supervisors by Brooke Postley, late brigadier general of a defunct cavalry brigade. While General Postley was in command, he had two sons of William M. Tweed on his staff and through them became a "skirmisher" for "The Ring." A number of other rentals of armories were given implicating Ernest O. Bernet, a former colonel of the 69th Regiment. None of this was mentioned again. The next day and for many days afterward, the *Times* questioned the honesty and intentions of the New York Railway Co. Tweed, Hall and Manton Marble, who were among its directors, were names not inspiring respect. A "trustworthy" analysis of the financial arrangement of the company raised serious questions about its operations. While there were honest people on its Board, including John J. Astor, still this last "gentleman did not scruple to lend himself to a whitewashing scheme." Even Alexander T. Stewart and William B. Astor did not make the railway project redeemable. It was a fraud exacting 50 to 60 million dollars from the city. Sweeny, Tweed and "Hank" Smith, its vice-president, might benefit from its existence, but no one else would. This charge, like others, was never substantiated by the *Times*. The company continued to transport passengers, and the *Times* continued its name calling.

But a *cordon sanitaire* was being drawn about Tweed. The lines were drawn tighter as the information that George Jones was harboring and doling out slowly was now unleashed in a torrent of huge headlines in large type, the likes of which the *Times* would rarely indulge in again even for war or peace. It was gigantic print and gigantic self-indulgence. The storm had arrived and thunder and lightning lit up the sky. There was howling through the streets, "Proofs of Undoubted Frauds Brought to Light. Warrants Signed by Hall and Connolly Under False Pretenses" was on the front page of the July 22 issue. In ordered columns going back to 1868 were listed payments by the city to Ingersoll, George S. and A. G. Miller, C. D. Bollar and Co., and J. A. Smith for repairs and furnishings to the courthouse, county buildings, offices and armories.

The total given was $2,870,464.06. Carpets for the county courthouses and office buildings came to $565,713.34. The *Times* was sure the "money somehow got back to the Ring." The next day, the twenty-third, the *Times* concluded that even if carpets cost five dollars a yard, the sum would be enough to cover City Hall Park three times over. In all the trials that followed, carpets were never mentioned again. Jones crowed over "Our Proofs of Fraud against the City Government." Through the storm, "Ring" members were silent, though Hall replied that the *Times* was angry because of the city's failure to pay the paper a $13,000 advertising bill and was part of a long-standing feud between Jones and the city. It was the most "remarkable defense ever recorded in judicial annals," retorted Jones. "Let the people judge between us," Jones cackled. The issue is not corporation advertising, "voluntarily" given up by the *Times*, or how the records were obtained, though they are public and gotten in a manner not to be ashamed of, but are the "facts" correct. The paper would not say where, when or how it obtained its information. It never did. The *Times* continued. Andrew Garvey was listed as receiving huge sums for repairs. There was a check for $33,283 drawn on December 28, 1869, to Fillipo Donnarumma, endorsed by one Phillip F. Dummy, and another one to the same person for $33,129.85 three days later endorsed by Fillip Dummen. The *Times* made it appear that these were fictitious names, but there was a Fillipo Donnarumma, an artist, in the city, who was known to the contractors. George S. Miller was the "luckiest carpenter" in the world and Andrew Garvey the "prince of plasterers." On one day, July 2, 1869, Garvey received $45,966.89 for plastering and repairs, for that month he received $153,755.14, "not a bad month's returns for a plasterer." Keyser & Co. were paid $1,231,817.36 for plumbing and gas fittings during past years. How much of these bills were honest, the *Times* never asked. The *Times* had a field day; Tammany hopefully would be destroyed and Democrats supporting Tammany would be defeated. The political gambit was clear. Jones was more concerned with the political consequences of the "frauds" than the whys and wherefores of the "frauds" themselves. How much tar can the brush carry was the theme and how far could it be spread were variations. Jones took delight in printing editorials from around the country praising the *Times* for its "courageous" stand.

Roscoe Conkling, the stalwart Republican who himself would one day find reform to be the "last refuge of a scoundrel," now praised the "sturdy splendid crusade" of the *Times*, which had earned the respect of all honest men. He congratulated editor Louis J. Jennings for the "most brilliant dashing foray seen in the American press within my memory." Conkling expected an overthrow of a venal dynasty. Jennings was an Englishman who had been American correspondent of the London *Times*, but was now on the *Times* editorial staff. A brilliant, temperamental man, Jennings "had an exceptional talent for stirring up the animals." Jones could not have picked a better man for the job. There was one other. This was John Foord, who had also recently joined the editorial staff, who took on most of the work of organizing and analyzing all political and financial evidence. The trio Jones, Foord and Jennings made a real "ring."

They turned waves into mountainous seas, gossip into fact. Day after day more disclosures. Why so much carpentry in a building like the court-house which is made chiefly of bronze and marble? Chairs bought from Ingersoll for an armory would stretch seventeen miles in a straight row. Furniture and cabinet work would furnish three hundred houses on Fifth Avenue from Washington Square to Thirteenth Street. Hall and Con-nolly, having signed the warrants, as required by law, were responsible for the frauds. Then more headlines, "Millions of Dollars Obtained on 'Fraudulent' Warrants." Astounding bills of a "Furniture-Dealer, a car-penter, a plasterer and a plumber. $9,789,482.16 signed away without question. Are the Tammany leaders honest men or thieves?" roared the *Times* on July 29. Again in banner print the "Literal Transcripts from Comptroller Connolly's Books" were made public. What books, and what transcripts, by whom, where, when, the *Times* gave no particulars. Tweed, leader of the old Board of Supervisors, "was privy to every fraudulent transaction concocted in that body." "Hank" Smith was the Tammany Republican. Mayor Hall was equally responsible, being able, if he wished, to save the city $7,750,000 from the $9,800,000 given to Garvey, Inger-soll and Keyser. Garvey received $2,870,464.06, Ingersoll and Co. $5,663,646.33, Keyser & Co. $1,231,817.76 and J. W. Smith the remainder. On the same date, July 29, in large German script, the only time the paper ever printed in a foreign language and obviously to obtain German sup-port, appeared a translation of the charges. "Sind die Führer den Tam-many-Partei ehrliche Männer oder Thieves?" The answer in German, English or Hindustani was obvious. "A Simple Story" appeared on August 3. The city debt on December 31, 1869, was $34,407,047 and on April 30, 1871, $84,541,186, a $50,134,139 increase, while the budget of the United States decreased. It said nothing of the city, its needs, its services, its growth. Jones demanded that "Ring" members be brought to justice. The paper asked who are C. D. Bollar & Co., A. S. Smith, R. S. Hennessy, T. C. Cashman. Where are the carpets, furniture? Who took the money? Justice must be meted out. The paper had presented the evidence, had the trial and found all concerned guilty; any other decision or view meant collusion with "The Ring." Jones castigated the *Tribune* "pulpit" for daring to print "Ring" explanations. It scorned arguments that accounts represented a period of five years, not just one or two, or that work was done on other than the armories and the courthouse. No explanations were acceptable. Results from the exposures were fast in coming. On August 1 a most impressive lot of businessmen, Moses Taylor, Marshall O. Roberts, John J. Astor, August Belmont, J. and W. Seligman, Harper Brothers, George Opdyke, Jay Cooke and dozens of others called for a public meeting at which time steps would be taken to investigate the grave charges. Before the meeting the *Times* printed another exposé. The Harlem Court House at the corner of Fourth Avenue and 129th was built on land owned by Tweed. In 1869, Tweed purchased the "National Hall," a building on the corner of Fourth and 129th Street and adjoining lots for $66,650. Tweed then leased part of the building for a courtroom. What wasn't mentioned was that many connected with the city did the same—the Woods, Goelets, Astors etc. Alfred Tweed, his nephew, was made a clerk of the court. "Six years ago," the *Times* concluded, "neither Tweed, McQuade or Porter [justices in the court] could buy a pair of boots and well spare the money"; now they had extensive property. How else could money be gotten but by theft? Before the Harlem Court House is finished Garvey, Miller, Ingersoll and Keyser should add some 5 or 6 million to the cost.

The drumbeat continued. On August 8, a meeting of the Twelfth and Nineteenth Ward Citizen Association was held in Yorkville. It was an angry affair. Denunciation of "The Ring," Connolly and Hall was severe. Why was the city $200 million in debt? "The Ring" has stolen or caused to be stolen at least $7 million. The *Times* reported noisy interruptions by "rowdies who sought to stifle free speech" by asking questions. One George J. Wilkes rose and suggested that if Hall and Connolly are guilty, and it would seem they signed the vouchers as a bank teller would at the will of the directors, then let them be tried by a jury, not by "buncombe." There were cheers from "Tammanyites" present. Nevertheless, the meeting resolved to ask that Hall resign his office forthwith as head of the corrupt administration. Let William F. Havemeyer be mayor. The *Times* now accused Hall and Connolly of stealing or causing to be stolen between 10 to 12 million dollars between them. How the figures flew. The case is as simple as ever sent a man from the dock to jail. "Will the public stand this forever?" demanded the *Times*. On the same day, that is August 10, "More Light" was shed on Tweed as a "Financier" of a printing establishment and newspaper, the New York *Transcript*, "owned by Tweed and edited—if the term may be employed," by Charles E. Wilbour, who was distantly related to Greeley and received large sums for corporation advertising. Tweed also had his men, no names given, in the Bureau of Elections receiving salaries totaling $24,000. Clerks, no names given, in the various courts received $412,895.76 per year. James M. Sweeny, brother of Peter, was deputy chamberlain. William Tweed, Jr., worked in the district attorney's office. "Ring" men in "Ring" jobs. "Ring" clerks in various city offices received $26,700 per year. James Muldoon, a janitor working in the county clerk's office, received $83.33 per month, cleaning women like Bridget Brennan, working in the Supreme Court, received $54.00. Another janitor in the new courthouse "occupies a large suite of rooms," has all the light and fuel he can use and received $208.23 per month. It is "all very suggestive," concluded the *Times*, and on and on and over and over went the columns, the small, the large, the *Times* used black ink with happy abandon.

It was all a deluge of accusation, a confusion of figures, a confetti-filled extravagance, but little evidence.

Horace Greeley urged calm and moderation, much to the *Times*'s displeasure. Greeley and other newspaper editors defended "corruption" because they printed corporation advertisement, shouted Jones. The *Tribune* receives $50,000 from the city. The *World, Herald, Sun, Star, News, Express, Commercial Advertiser* and *Staats Zeitung* are all in Tammany's favor. Tammany's Republicans like Greeley and others were working for "The Ring." Thus, anyone criticizing the *Times* was on "The Ring's" payroll, or so Jones and Jennings hysterically charged. Jennings was also able to continue an old war against Greeley and Horace's past defense of socialism. Having disposed of criticism, Jones again asked, "What are true Republicans going to do about it? What will the anti-Tammany Democrats do?" It was a call for a lynching.

Democrats were, of course, concerned. Tilden, coming from behind a curtain, now made his move. A bachelor, sitting in his Gramercy Square mansion, he had ambitions, though very little else. One contemporary wrote, "He is vain and ambitious. He hated Tammany because it ignored his claims to political promotion, but he courted and flattered its chiefs." Many felt the same way about "Silk-Stocking Sammy." Tilden would show them to be correct. He had an idea that came quietly, but explosively. He did not share the view of some upstate Democrats that the "recent explosions" would do no harm. The party, he felt, could not defend wrongdoers, "taking its chances on possible defeat now with resurrection hereafter," but Tilden reasoned it would be more prudent to disavow and denounce the wicked and educate our people to a new leadership. By new leadership, Tilden referred to himself. Tilden for years had been friendly with Tweed. When the disclosures first broke, he kept in the background amassing information illegally taken from the grand jury. Certain that the wind was blowing in the right direction, Tilden, basically a second- or third-rate politician, trimmed his sails and went after his erstwhile friend hammer and tong. It was a decision which catapulted him into the governor's seat and almost into the White House. Tilden's motivation was purely political and personal. Tweed could serve as an excellent foil. The *Times* reinforced Tilden's views as it warned that leaders of the party like Seymour and Church could go into another convention as tools of "The Ring," but better join the *Times's* crusade and clean house.[1]

Hall was the only one who fought back. Tweed was silent. The mayor sent an itemized account of expenditures during 1870–71 to the Board of Supervisors. The total spent through June 1871 was just $5,200,000. The *Times* complained that Hall's report was erroneous and did not show whether work had been completed. On August 28, a Joint Special Committee of the Board of Supervisors and Board of Aldermen and Associated Citizens met in the Supervisors' Room in the new courthouse. This committee became known as the Booth Committee after its chairman, sugar dealer William A. Booth. Its job was to investigate charges of larceny and corruption. It employed nine accountants, including Henry F. Taintor, who was paid $432 for thirty-six days beginning September 11 and $600 for twenty-four days in December 1871. Taintor remained on the city payroll for years, at least until 1875, providing evidence and giving testimony and collecting money. The committee also heard from a number of "experts" who evaluated the work done by the contractors and who usually agreed that the city had been overcharged for the work performed. One of these, Orville G. Bennet, received $1,400 for his testimony, which concerned rentals, and the *Evening Post* received $1,377 for publishing the report despite Hall's opposition. Obviously there was money to be made from reform, and it was only the beginning.[2]

Not content to wait for committee reports, on August 30, the *Times* stoked the fires again. The message must be made clearer. In large type, headlines read "The Story of the Accounts," "The Armory Swindle." The cost of courthouse carpets was now put at $350,178.46, but should have been $12,000. What happened to $338,000 for carpets? Why, Jones alleged, were carpets given to furnish Boss Tweed's Metropolitan Hotel? Again an accusation without proof.

Figures flew like confetti at a mad hatters' ball. Now the total for the courthouse came to $13,413,768.39. Results were finally channeled properly and the message clearly understood. There were to be no quiet official meetings. On September 2, the New York City Council of Political Reform, a conglomerate of Protestant churches, appealed to fellow Protestants for contributions to help end "public calamities," and on the fourth, a large Municipal Reform Meeting was held at Cooper Institute. A happy ex-Sheriff O'Brien, Congressman Robert B. Roosevelt and Peter Cooper appeared on the platform to denounce fraud and extravagance in city government. Ex-Judge James Emott asked for a return to reform. "We must repeal this charter; we must compel a complete publication of the accounts . . . We must punish the guilty and recover back the stolen money to the City Treasury." William F. Havemeyer, in conclusion of his remarks, demanded, "What are you going to do about it?" Ex-Governor Edward Solomon of Wisconsin especially went at Hall and Tweed. Yes, let a statue be erected by Tweed, but put on it the words, "Punishment for Official Corruption and the Betrayal of Public Confidence." Speaker after speaker spoke in similar vein. What of the city debt of $139 million? What of the $40–50 million "stolen" from the taxpayers? These were all figures taken from someone's hat. They made little sense, but made a lot of rhetoric. Congressman Roosevelt grieved over the state of the party, and asked as a cure the overthrow of Hall.

A Committee of Seventy was formed to examine allegations and pursue the guilty. Among them were banker Henry G. Stebbins as president, Havemeyer as vice-president, hides dealer Jackson S. Schultz, banker Abraham Kuhn, stationery store owner and gold pen manufacturer John Foley, piano manufacturer Theodore Steinway and Congressman Roosevelt. None knew anything, except what they read in the *Times*.[3] Tilden, silently spinning his web, coyly awaited a specific call to lead the crusade, as he received letters, many from out of town, as far away as London, lauding him as honest, fearless and one who could be expected to take a "knife" and cut corruption out by the roots. Fitzwilliam W. Byrdsall, the old Locofoco maverick of the Jackson era, delighted in the scandal and the embarrassment to his old enemy Tammany. It was like old times to go once again to the barricades to help destroy this worst of all possible "secret societies." Surely, Byrdsall wished to be thirty years younger. It was a Locofoco's dream fulfilled. Belmont gave $500 for the "good fight against rogues and corruption."[4]

A motion was brought on September 7 by an East Side Citizens Association before Justice Barnard and a crowded courtroom for an injunction to restrain the mayor, comptroller and Board of Aldermen from issuing any bonds or paying any monies until order could be restored. Taxpayers had been excessively burdened with debt, and "certain chief officers of the city and county governments, acting principally under covers of the names of other persons, have formed themselves into associations for the effect and design of securing through such combination large sums yearly from the Treasury." Named specifically were Tweed, Connolly, Hall, the New York Transcript Association, New York Printing Company and Manufacturers Stationers Company. Barnard granted a temporary injunction, but stipulated that current expenses of government were not to be interfered with. Hearings on a permanent injunction would take place the following week.

On September 7, another motion came before Justice Barnard. John Foley brought suit as a taxpayer against the Board of Supervisors, Hall, Sweeny, Connolly and Tweed, asking that they be restrained from raising or collecting taxes on real and personal estate. Foley also charged violation of the tax levy and the inordinate increase of the city debt from $50,628,830.80 when Hall became mayor in 1870 to $113,657,258.51 by July 31, 1871. The figures were his. Further objected to was the flagrant manner in which city and county officials carried out their authority, allowing false bills and fradulent claims to be passed. Barnard granted the injunction. If "The Ring" existed and Barnard was a member, he was a weak link. The Foley injunction was greeted by the *Herald* with praise, as a "first step" to sweep away the old rubbish and free municipal government from corruption and the power of Tammany.[5]

By September 10, rumor swept the city that Tweed and Connolly had resigned. A reporter met Connolly, but the nervous, worried comptroller denied his resignation: "It's a ―――― lie." Next to the "Boss." Was he going to retire? No, replied Tweed. "I was born in New York and I mean to stay here too." "You don't seem to be afraid of a violent death . . . I read the *Nation* talks of lynching," said the reporter. Tweed stamped his foot. "Well, if they want me to come, I'll be there. That's all I have to say about it. I'll be there, I'll be there, sir." Tweed continued, "The *Times* has been saying all the time I have no brains. Well, I'll show Jones I have brains," and then vaguely, "You know if a man is with others he must do as they do . . . if he is with others he must take care not to do a rash act. It will hurt them all you know." He added, "If this man Jones would have said the things he has said about me twenty-five years ago, he wouldn't be alive now. But, you see, when a man has a wife and children, he can't do such a thing," and clenching his fists, "I would have killed him." Still, Tweed thought how well to be rid of the whole business. "I'm sick of being dragged into the mud by such scoundrels . . . I'm sick of them. Jones wouldn't have dared to say anything if I had no wife and children."

Tweed was asked about the injunction. "What are you going to do about it?" queried the reporter. It will be handled by the corporation counsel, O'Gorman, perhaps his own counsel. Anyway, it won't stand. "Yes, sir, I'm pretty sure," Tweed replied. It was a furious but disturbed Tweed, a tired and disoriented man whose troubles had only just begun.[6]

On the eleventh of September, the "Great Injunction" brought by the East Side Citizens Association was argued before Judge Barnard again in a densely packed chamber with everyone hanging on to ever ord. Sitting with Barnard was City Judge Gunning S. Bedford, Jr., and Assistant District Attorney William Tweed, Jr. Corporation Counsel O'Gorman began the proceedings with a lengthy rebuttal, producing a complete exhibit of the financial record as well as other evidence. Tweed was represented by a relative unknown, Willard O. Bartlett. Judge Aaron J. Vanderpoel of Brown, Hall & Vanderpoel, Hall's firm, represented the mayor. Connolly had Henry Beach as attorney. Tweed's attorney first addressed the court. He saw the action and the attack on Tweed as purely political, using the judiciary to overturn the vote and voice of the people. The "jumbled Foley" statement and the association report made it impossible to find out what his client was being charged with. The press, as Barnard should well know, uses abuses for argument and reason. What are the charges? Bartlett demanded. O'Gorman, corporation counsel, was next. Similarly, he asked that his clients be allowed to present the case, a presentation denied by the press, who merely sought to goad public opinion. The injunction had the air of a political execution. Beach, Connolly's counsel, opposed delay and wanted immediate action to clear his client. Hall's attorneys likewise wanted to proceed. Barnard spoke up. He wanted to correct an impression that pay to police and laborers was stopped by the injunction. Barnard halted suddenly and announced that in view of the uncomfortable and packed state of the room, the court would move to the adjacent larger Oyer and Terminer room. The crowd stampeded into the new quarters. O'Gorman argued that the plaintiffs had no legal capacity to sue.

Charles E. Wilbour denied that Tweed, Hall or Connolly were stockholders of the Transcript Association or the New York Printing Company. Tweed, had held stock in the Printing Company, but prior to 1870. Archibald McLochlan, president of the Stationers Company, made a similar statement. Bartlett added that the charges against his client, "some frivolous, some grave, are all utterly untrue." On the next day another large crowd filed into the court to hear Tweed's affidavit read. He denied all allegations. He had never alone, or with any subordinate or with any person or persons whatsoever conspired to take any sums from the city treasury; had never connived by himself or with others to grant a printing monopoly to the New York Printing Company; that he had no interest in the New York Transcript Association or the Manufacturers Stationers Company and that he did not combine with others to subvert laws or obtain funds at public expense. James H. Ingersoll was not his agent. None of the claims which he audited or allowed were fraudulent. As a department head he had not allowed any sums over the legal amount, nor was this done in other departments or offices in the city and county.

The injunction case was continued on September 14. O'Gorman asked the court to end the injunction entirely and allow the defendants and the city to function for the good of all. The crowded court heard Bartlett ask if claims submitted by Foley and James O'Brien had been paid, would they have brought suit and made such a fuss. Foley reached for some ice to cool his head, as Bartlett warned Foley that Tweed would bring a perjury suit against him. Tweed, his attorney pointed out, was caught up in a Catilinarian conspiracy to destroy him politically. If the tax levy, or any law, is the heart of the matter, then it should be repealed. It was not necessary to destroy Tweed. After a short exchange with defense attorneys, Barnard announced that the defendants had not really denied the charges of fraudulent claims. Defendants' counsel took exception, but Barnard granted a permanent injunction. The suit was proper. There were, he felt, sufficient irregularities and indiscretions to support his decision. The justice singled out Richard Connolly as the official mainly responsible, though he pointed out that this did not relieve the other officials for their actions. It was a decision greeted with applause in and out of the courtroom. A reporter searched out the "Boss" at Public Works; "a joyous smile lit up the blandness of his face" as they shook hands, "soft plump hands" of the Boss with the reporter's "long digits." "Sit down." Tweed motioned to a leather-covered armchair and removed a newspaper. Do you have anything to say about the present state of affairs, he was asked. Tweed laughed. "No—nothing at all."

> Reporter—The decision of Judge Barnard surprised a great many.
> Tweed (with a smile)—Yes, it did. Surprising things happen every day, but then, you know, public opinion is a great lever.
> Reporter—Your answer in that case was a simple denial.
> Tweed—A general denial. The charges were vague and general. Let them bring specific charges and I shall meet them. I don't intend at my time of life to go fighting windmills.
> Reporter—Sweeny has kept himself in the background all through.
> Tweed—Wise man! Wise man!

Tweed thought the whole affair was a political football to be used in coming elections and the 1872 presidential campaign.

Like Tweed, most New Yorkers were surprised. No one expected Barnard to "go back on his old pals in this way," said one. "Well, anyway," said another, "it proves politicians are all the same—not to be trusted." It was a rainy day, but not many noticed the weather. Surely Connolly will resign, but would Tweed fight and put on his "war paint"?

A *Herald* reporter met Ingersoll at his office. Was he off to Europe? Who was the "and Co." in the firm's name? Ingersoll refused an answer. He had no flight to Europe planned; the rumors were "barefaced lies."

The expected resignation of Connolly did not take place. Friends of Connolly met at the Sixth Ward Hotel at Centre and Duane streets. There various city officials, all "Irishmen" and friends of a "warm hearted Irishman" and "esteemed citizen," agreed at the mass meeting and torchlight procession that followed to support Connolly "though the Heavens fall." Hall and Tweed and Sweeny would not be allowed to have a scapegoat for their misdeeds. There were rumors that Deputy Comptroller Andrew H. Green would ally himself with Connolly against Sweeny and Tweed. Everything was at odds and evens.

Then there were Sunday sermons at places like the Fifth Avenue Presbyterian Church, St. Vincent de Paul and the Broadway Tabernacle where admonitions to fretful parishioners were given. The whole episode was a God-send to ministers. It was finger-snapping stuff. Young men were warned about the dangers of social corruption, old men of the virtue of repentance. Reverend Dr. Thompson of the Tabernacle quoted Isaiah 59:2–4.

> Your iniquities have separated between you and your God, and your sins have hid His face from you that He will not hear. For your hands are defiled with blood and our fingers with iniquity; your lips have spoken lies, your tongue hath muttered perversions; none calleth for justice or any pleadeth for truth.

It was also a day for the spiritualists and the street angels. Everyone looked good when compared to Tweed and the rest.[7] Monday, September 19, was a time for politicians as the Connolly-Green situation took over the front page. Connolly a few days before had closeted with Green to determine procedure. Finally, a decision was reached, "Handy Andy" was to have full power of office, which he assumed on September 16, Connolly remaining only as nominal head. There may have been a tacit agreement arranged by Tilden to "go easy" on Connolly. Hall, angrily, in a letter of September 18 accepted Connolly's "resignation." He would not let Connolly off the hook or surrender to Tilden and the reformers. Hall wanted Democrat General George McClellan as the comptroller, and asked "Little Mac" to accept the appointment. He refused. Connolly refused to resign officially. Connolly argued he could not be made to do so unless by impeachment. All was confusion. Hall argued that Connolly in turning over the duties of office to Green had in fact resigned. Whatever there was of "The Ring," if it ever existed, was apart at the seams as Hall and Connolly exchanged brickbats.[8]

This was, of course, a golden opportunity for "Silk-Stocking" Tilden to gain control of the Democracy. Not only could he put Green in office without the bother of nominations or elections, but he could include Young Democrats and other outspoken enemies of Tammany, thus bringing about a whole new coalition with Tilden at its head. Where could this lead—the governor's chair, the White House? The possibilities were staggering. The two Woods, Morrissey, O'Brien, Roosevelt found themselves along with Tilden staring at a largesse beyond their wildest dreams.

At an anti-Tammany meeting at Apollo Hall on September 18, they determined to "lift New York City from its sleep of corruption." Fernando hopefully relived his "Black Book" days.

"The Ring" had its defenders, but they were few. A letter printed in the Herald of September 20 by "Real Estate" credited the "so-called Ring" with vast improvement in the value of uptown property "upon a scale of magnificence and of great public utility undreamed of by its predecessors." True, expenditures were enormous, but the rise on the value of property still more; progress and prosperity went hand in hand. He warned friends of reform against too restrictive economies.[9]

The "Great Injunction" case reared its head again by the end of the month on September 29. Confusion reigned in the city, especially among city workers, contractors and bondholders. Payments had been stopped in many cases. City finances had ground to a standstill. No one quite knew what was going on. There was great danger in this. Riots, default and the end of services were in the offing. Barnard had to clear the air. The same cast of characters appeared in court. While Justice Barnard held that no monies could be spent beyond that permitted by law and no money spent without the approval of Andrew Green, the comptroller could raise $5 million to pay off and cancel bonds, and various departments could have the necessary money to carry on their functions, thus avoiding what might be dire catastrophe. Irate laborers of the Park Department met several times to ensure that their pay would be continued. Others waited to take more forceful action, if necessary.

Reformers who desired to stop all city payments had lit a bomb, which was at least partly defused by Barnard's last order. Barnard also provided specifically that the New York Transcript Association, the New York Printing Company and the Stationers Company were not to have any claims paid. Early in October, Green was given full control over payments to the various departments. Though a halt was ordered to the Harlem Court House construction, as well as to a new Police Court

House, Justice Ingraham ruled in favor of two contractors, Harrington and
Hoe, who brought a mandamus action against the city demanding that
their contracts be paid. The "Great Injuction" enjoined very little, but
public attention had been focused on "corruption."

Now Tweed was heard from, as his friends rallied at a meeting on
September 21. They cheered the character and career of the senator.
Tweed was there and provided a short speech again to try to answer to the
question that was on everyone's mind. Why hadn't he spoken out against
the charges? Why hadn't he done so in the newspapers? Why the silence?
"It would be useless," he reasoned as before, "for me to attempt to defend
myself by replying to any article that is written about me, for an answer
would bring more articles the next day and the next. I would be kept
busily engaged in writing rejoinders all the time." He preferred waiting to
reply in a court of law. It was an odd speech, a defensive one. It lacked fire
and passion. Perhaps Tweed had seen too much of that already. The next
day, "hard-fisted" admirers of Tweed met in the Seventh Ward at "Tweed
Plaza" on Pike Street to show that the "Boss" was not harmed in the old
Seventh, and to nominate him again for the Senate. Chinese lanterns
lined East Broadway. Pictures of Tweed were prominently displayed. The
Edward J. Shandley Association was brilliantly illuminated, bands played,
fireworks lit the sky, cheers, laughter rose from the crowded streets. It was
an event meant to boost Tweed in the fall election, as well as to thumb
noses at reformers. Tweed's arrival was cheered with enthusiasm. He took
off a little "Scotch Tweed" cap and bowed, happy to be "at home again
amidst the haunts of my childhood and scenes where I had been always
surrounded by friends. I feel I can safely place myself and my record, all I
have performed as a public official before your gaze." Reviled, traduced
and maligned as a man has seldom been, "I point proudly to my record of
the past, which is open to the scan of all, and I want full, open and impartial investigation into all the official acts of my life." As to the universal
question why hadn't he answered his accusers, he again stated that it
would be wasteful of energy while his enemies stand behind "that mighty
engine of popular power—the press." He accepted the nomination and expected an even greater victory than before to answer his detractors.
Speeches followed endorsing the leadership, courage and integrity of a phil-
anthropic citizen, to whom the poor owe a debt of thanks for his contribution and many unsung deeds on their behalf. No one of any note was
on the platform with him, no "Ring" member, no special friend. It would
always be so.[10]

21

"What Are You Going to Do About It?"

These fall days were the last that Tweed would see as a campaigner on the election trail. His days as a politician were numbered and though he did not know it then, surely he must have known that something in his life was over. The rest of his days were to be spent in court, with judges, juries and attorneys. The law and courtrooms would be his new battlefield and the enemy was carefully preparing the onslaught. But first there was to be a test of weapons, a trying out of the arsenal. This would be at the expense of A. Oakey Hall. Any mistakes, any weakness could be rectified for the main event—Tweed.

On October 2, members of the East Side Citizens Committee asked and received an arrest warrant from Police Justice Butler H. Bixby directing Hall to answer the charge of malfeasance in office in that he had willfully and intentionally neglected to investigate or examine into the correctness, justice or legality of a series of warrants presented to him for signature in disregard of Section 4 of the April 26, 1870 Tax Levy Act. Lengthy affidavits went over the old grounds of warrants issued and exorbitant amounts paid by the city. Hall was directed to appear on October 6 at the Yorkville Police Court. It is very important to note here, as it will be again in the case of Tweed, that with all the talk of corruption, theft, looting and stolen millions, Hall was not charged with any of these things. Neither Hall, nor again Tweed, was ever tried for theft, but on a subterfuge, a technicality having nothing to do with what history has charged.

Meanwhile, Tweed, upset with rumors of impending criminal indictment against him, nevertheless attended to business. He quietly attended the Rochester State Democratic Convention and saw to his duties as public works commissioner. A reporter from the *Herald* went to Room 4 at 237 Broadway, the dark, gloomy quarters of the commissioner, where he was affably asked to be seated. Tweed was questioned about Green's position as comptroller-in-fact and the doling out of money to Public Works.

A reporter whose identity is unknown, it was rare at the time for them to sign articles, asked, "What are you going to do about it?" The phrase was now famous, and Tweed was frequently badgered with this baiting phrase. How it must have pleased Nast to see his clever invention so succeed. Tweed replied that he was determined not to let any of his employees suffer. He was certain they would be paid.

An interview took place with the hard-to-find Keyser early in October at the contractor's home at the southwest corner of Seventy-ninth Street and Second Avenue. The reporter was seated in a parlor furnished with Brussels carpets, costly statuary and engravings and upholstery. Soon a man about fifty with gray whiskers and hair, wearing a dressing gown and slippers, appeared. The "apparition" barked, "And so you are one of those newspaper vultures who hound men to their death?" The reporter sensed some sly humor, and replied, "I beg pardon, sir. I may be a vulture who drives men to explain serious charges, but I have no desire to hound you to your death." "Well, what do you want?" said Keyser. "What do you say about the charges?" asked the reporter. Keyser held up an index finger and slowly answered, "Not one word! Not a word, sir." He would reply fully in due time. The reporter asked, "Who was the 'Co.' in Keyser & Co.?" It was not Tweed though that was the rumor. The contractor explained that the "Co.," at first a partner, were employees who received a percentage of the business in lieu of salary. Keyser had failed twice in business, but insisted that he had always paid his debts. His city house cost him $12,000 and was purchased in 1861. His "island" in Norwalk was bought in 1857 for $1,500 and his house, which it was rumored cost one half million dollars, cost $4,000 in addition to $7,000 for improvements and $1,400 for adjoining land. But above everything, all he earned was earned honestly. "I have made no confession, for I know nothing to confess." But he did know something.

On the same day the interview was published there appeared in the *Herald* a statement by Jackson Schultz of the Committee of Seventy relating a confession of Keyser admitting guilt, and promising to return $600,000 to the city. Also appearing on the same day, October 6, was a letter from Keyser denying the rumors that he had burned his books or intended to abscond. In fact, he said he refused to take a vacation ordered by his physician, lest it be interpreted as flight. He had offered his records to the Committee of Seventy. All could see "that every dollar which I have received from the city, I have given full value in labor and materials." In fact, the city really owed him money, some $300,000 in uncollected bills. He had worked for the city since 1864 (it was really quite a bit earlier, at least since 1859) and had provided all sorts of plumbing and heating, and was even now at work repairing sewers. Of the $2 million said to have been paid to him $800,000 he never received. Bills for that amount were forgeries. Keyser here began to point a finger at someone else.

Also, on the same day, October 6, James H. Ingersoll entered Supreme Court represented by his attorneys, William Fullerton, former judge of the Court of Appeals, Francis C. Barlow, a former Civil War general and later Secretary of State of New York, and Elihu Root, four years out of New York University Law School. He would later be Secretary of State under Theodore Roosevelt, but was in the process of erecting a cross he would always bear, having to explain why he involved himself in the defense of "Ring" members. Ingersoll was a cousin of the wife of Alexander Compton, Root's law partner, and it is probably through her efforts that he accepted Ingersoll as a client. Since the issues in the Ingersoll and Tweed cases were similar, Fullerton retained Root as an assistant counsel in the Tweed suits. The group went before Justice Daniel P. Ingraham to answer a suit brought by ex-Mayor Havemeyer. Ingersoll was to have with him all books and vouchers concerning his business for the years 1869 and 1870. Attorneys for Havemeyer were George M. Miller, John A. Stoutenburgh and Albany-born Wheeler Hazard Peckham, brother of a United States Supreme Court justice and son of Rufus W. Peckham, judge of the Court of Appeals. He would become Tweed's prosecutor.[1]

While Ingersoll's trial proceeded, the hook was being baited for other fish—a short-tempered delegation from the Committee of Seventy, Dix, Stebbins and Havemeyer, and Justice Edwards Pierrepont, who had headed the prosecution of John Surratt, one of the conspirators in Lincoln's assassination, visited Governor Hoffman in Albany on the afternoon of October 17. Attorney General Marshall Champlain was present. They asked for a declaration of martial law in the city and talked of stealing loaves of bread from the poor but honest laborers, of frauds, gigantic wickedness, of exposed misdeeds and the fact that still "not a corrupt" or delinquent officer had resigned and not a step had been taken to impeach or remove a single betrayer of official trust. They demanded action, and "even imposition of martial law." Hoffman asked if Justice James Emott, who was in Albany, had been consulted. No, he was too busy, replied the Committee. What of Deputy Comptroller Green, surely he could stop the plunder. "No," Pierrepont replied, he had too "frail a tenure." Hoffman felt that the application of martial law in this instance was beyond his power. He reminded them of current history. President Johnson had removed Secretary of War Stanton, and this was the first ground for impeachment proceedings. He could remove no officer, nor apply martial law; only if the "men in power" in the city caused riot could he act. The governor was sympathetic but it was up to the city to clean its own house.

All was not lost. The committee was handed a note from Champlain to be given to Charles O'Conor, asking the noted and respected attorney, now sixty-seven years old, to prosecute frauds and he would receive help from his office. It was an important memo. It brought the state into the battle. The big guns were rolled to the front line. On October 18, O'Conor agreed to heed the will of the state and "for the sake of justice" prosecute those who committed frauds. He was sure of the guilt of the "Ring" members. Some might be found innocent, though it would be a "very blind man indeed" who held anyone not guilty. O'Conor was quickly joined by others. On the next day a *Times* reporter visited "Sammy" Tilden in order to find out his views. He was told that Tilden was present at various meetings with O'Conor and was directly involved with the investigation. The reporter was told that Tilden especially wanted Wheeler H. Peckham to help in the prosecution, and also that after a look into the city's account with the Broadway Bank, by 1871, it was the National Broadway Bank, he was sure William Tweed and his associates were "decidedly implicated" in the frauds "which have sapped the strength of the city." Further, the evidence long sought after had been found and was enough to "convict" Tweed not only of complicity in the frauds, but of engineering the machinery to enrich "The Ring." Tilden felt triumphant. His months of snooping had brought something. Tweed was visited on the same day by a *Times* reporter at his Public Works office. Tweed was aware of the O'Conor appointment. The reporter told Tweed that he had heard that Tweed was to be the first target. Tweed claimed he hadn't known this; he seemed thoughtful.

Reporter—What are you going to do about it?
Mr. Tweed—I don't know anything about it. What can I do?

For the moment, public attention was focused on Chicago, for beginning on October 8 a catastrophic fire all but destroyed that city. In New York, of course, it was a different kind of fire, but it seemed for many that the heavens were also falling. At the end of the month, the Committee of Seventy, aided by the Booth Committee report, which put the cost of city government for three years at $75 million, agreed to push prosecution against Tweed. Up until this time, no direct action had been taken specifically against him. Any delay, Havemeyer hysterically warned, would be fatal. Tilden moved into high gear. He had agreed to Green's request to inquire into forgeries alleged by Keyser. In fact, he had already done so, and had also examined Woodward's, Ingersoll's, Garvey's and Tweed's accounts. He now had all the answers. Woodward had deposited money in Tweed's account in the Broadway Bank by writing Tweed's name on the deposit slip. He charged that Keyser, Tweed and Woodward were all connected in their deposits and withdrawals. Deposits for Woodward, Garvey, Ingersoll and the New York Printing Company totaled $6,995,309.17. Garvey's, Ingersoll's and Keyser's deposits came to $5,750,458.66. Tilden believed that Garvey and Ingersoll retained only a portion, with $3,182,054.26 going to Woodward. The latter, though a "mere" clerk, was the "general distributing reservoir" of the great mass of "plunder." He deposited $932,858.50 to Tweed's account, and "divided the balance among persons not yet ascertained." This information was gathered on voluminous slips and pieces of paper, covered with additions, subtractions in endless profusion, which are still among Tilden's papers. How anyone could have worked with them is a mystery. For the first time there was something affecting Tweed.

A reporter interviewed O'Conor, who felt Tweed after "one little chapter in a civil suit" could be made to disgorge $3,500,000. "Do you have documentary evidence?" O'Conor was asked. "I think we have," was the reply. He expected the coming suit to influence voters against Tweed in the pending elections. Politics and court suits, one wonders which was first in the minds of Tilden and O'Conor. These were curious times. Figures flew in all directions. There was talk of warrants, vouchers, but little else but talk. While the public pondered these "facts," there were some fish frying.[2]

In the court of Oyer and Terminer, grand jury proceedings against Mayor Hall started on October 19 and finished October 25. The charge was failure to audit bills as provided under Section 4 of the April 1870 act. It provided some really incredible testimony. The hearing began with "Handy Andy" Green as the first witness. He swore he knew nothing. Clerks testified as to procedures with regard to warrants and vouchers in the Auditor's Bureau. William S. Copland, who earlier had been before Justice Bixby, recounted that he had started as an assistant bookkeeper in the bureau in January 1870, on James O'Brien's recommendation. He said that he was discharged in March 1871 for political reasons, that is because he was a friend of O'Brien's, who was then quarreling with Connolly over O'Brien's claim. Copland testified that he and others working in the office noted the enormity of certain bills submitted by Keyser and Ingersoll and he "discovered that there must be something wrong," and because of curiosity began compiling his penciled notes. In November or December 1870, he told O'Brien of the "frauds." He admitted that he would like to see Hall indicted, because he was "sore" about his dismissal by Connolly. Although he was suspicious about certain bills, he really knew of only one bill, a bill for an awning, which was a fraud, so his "common sense" told him, but said nothing about that particular bill to anyone.

Henry G. Stebbins, chairman of the Committee of Seventy, was examined next. When asked if he knew anything to substantiate charges against Hall, Stebbins said he did not, nor did he have information about frauds in general. He had no knowledge at all of Hall's guilt. Yet as head of the committee, he had gone to Albany and seen Hoffman to ask for martial law. Now he admitted he knew nothing of any fraud or corruption. Astounding! Jackson Schultz also only knew what he read in the papers.

Tilden was next. He was asked if he knew anything of Hall's participation in auditing $6,312,000. Tilden answered that he had no evidence on this. He had seen all the warrants signed by the "board of audit"—Tweed, Hall and Connolly—for that sum and felt almost all were fraudulent. All but $112,000 were deposited in three accounts in the Broadway Bank. He did not identify the accounts. Hall had no bank account there and Tilden knew of no connivance of Hall's in any wrongdoing. The next witness, Judge Thomas A. Ledwith, also knew nothing. Nor did James O'Brien, though he suspected Hall received "some emoluments" before he signed the warrants. Finally, George Jones, editor of the *Times* and chief witch hunter, appeared. He, too, knew nothing. A perplexed juror questioned Jones:

> *Juror:* I have read editorials, probably two or three months in your paper, on this question; the paper has not ceased almost daily to brand Mr. Hall as a thief. Can you give us of your own knowledge any information that will help us to come to a conclusion that he has proved himself to be a thief?
>
> *Jones:* There is a difference between me as an individual and the newspaper; the newspaper is an impersonality. I am an individual. I do not propose to answer any question in relation to the paper. I am here as an individual.
>
> *Juror:* Can you furnish names, or evidence or instances?
>
> *Jones:* I see what you are at, you want me to give you the names of persons who gave us information.

Still, the questions continued, though Jones refused to name names.

> *Juror:* Who knew of Hall's corruption or failure to discharge his duty?
>
> *Jones:* There is a flood of evidence. What of checks for furniture that would fill the Court House ten times over, ask Ingersoll or anybody else.
>
> *Juror:* But does Mr. Jones have specific evidence as to Hall's guilt as a thief?

Jones: I stated to you that the *Times* and George Jones were not identical things.

He refused to discuss the workings of the paper and how it arrived at conclusions. He admitted that he had never seen, nor did he know anything specifically wrong with the bills. How could he publish articles calling Hall a thief without evidence? In reply, Jones would only state he was not the *Times*. Who wrote the articles? He didn't know and refused to discuss the matter. It was an amazing performance—evasive, confusing and incredible.

Arthur T. J. Rice was next on the witness stand. He had been in business with Hall for eighteen years and was familiar with Hall's affairs. Rice felt Hall did not have more than $60,000–$70,000 in assets. The cashier of the Tenth National Bank, Robert B. Palmer, said Hall had less than $5,000 in his account, the last time he looked it was between $1,000 and $1,100. The largest amount ever on deposit was $27,000 or $28,000. Rumors that Hall had $250,000 to $300,000 were "absurd nonsense." William A. Booth of the Booth Committee was called. He, too, knew nothing.

Despite Jones, Tilden and all the headlines there simply was no case against Hall. Nothing was shown linking the mayor to anyone in the so-called "Ring." No one knew anything about frauds, though this had not stopped the inquisition. The grand jury, though they found that Hall had been "careless and negligent" in discharge of his duties and not examining vouchers with greater consideration of public interest did not vote an indictment.[3]

O'Conor would not let this defeat stop him. In a letter to O'Gorman of October 21, 1871, he asked what the corporation counsel was doing to prosecute "Ring" suits. In a reply of the same day, O'Gorman gave him a long list of suits brought by the city or county which were awaiting implementation. On October 25, 1871, a preliminary motion to recover the $6 million was filed in Supreme Court against Tweed, Ingersoll, Woodward and Garvey. Affidavits of Tilden, Keyser, Copland and J. H. Masterson, builder of Tammany Hall, were presented. Though nothing seems to have come of this action, it answered for the moment O'Conor's and the Committee of Seventy's demands.[4]

The following day, October 26, as rumors of Tweed's impending arrest swept the city, concrete news was received. Judge Wilton L. Learned sitting in Third District Court in Albany, interestingly not in New York, and probably to make sure a cooperative judge was found, issued an order for Tweed's arrest. An interview quickly followed. Tweed expected that bail would be set. He agreed the charges looked bad, "very bad," but insisted "I have not received a cent of that county money." The action was commenced for political effect, he went on. "I await the issue confident that I can show a clear record. It is strange that a man cannot have borrowed money returned to him without being placed in this position." He appeared worn and tired as he answered questions. Around him were stories of a possible $2 million bail and of a transfer of $4,500,000 in real estate to his son who would provide bail for his father. Tweed worked quietly awaiting his pending arrest. There was excitement around City Hall, as a chilly "Scotch mist" fell. It was a gloomy, dark day.

Deputy Sheriff Justin Jarvis, chief of the Order of Arrest Bureau, was a sought-after man, as reporters crowded around his office. Just before 1 P.M., Wheeler Peckham, now on the O'Conor and Tilden team of self-appointed prosecutors, appeared and talked with the sheriff. He left with "smiles all over his face." He had a summons from Attorney General Champlain and Judge Learned returnable in Supreme Court in the case of *People of the State of New York* vs. *William Tweed, James H. Ingersoll, Elbert A. Woodward and Andrew J. Garvey*. The complaint was the same as the one heard by the Hall grand jury. It charged that $6,312,541.17 was allowed by Hall, Connolly and Tweed in 1871 and that there was no audit or examination of bills. In fact only one meeting of the "board of audit" was held. Basically it alleged that Tweed as a member of the board had signed vouchers without examining the validity of the claims. This was a civil suit brought by the state to recover the money. But added was an allegation of collusion between Watson, Garvey, Ingersoll, Woodward, Tweed and other persons to defraud, with Woodward being the distributing agent. Elaborate schedules were annexed, listing over two hundred warrants paid in 1869–70.

Tweed waited fitfully for Sheriff Brennan and his deputy, Jarvis. He would be glad to have the arrest over and expected to be "triumphantly acquitted." Tweed sang a brave tune, but he should have thought differently. The Hall proceedings would not be repeated for him, if this was what Tweed counted on. Jarvis and Brennan met Tweed at his office and informed him that his bail had been set at an incredible $1 million. Tweed sat with his son William Jr. Clerks gazed in awe at the scene. In the next hour, the sureties arrived: Hugh J. Hastings, editor of the *Commercial Advertiser*, Byran Fairchild, president of the Board of Works, Bernard Kelly, a long-time friend, Terence Farley, a business associate and real estate speculator, and Jay Gould, stockjobber extraordinary. The latter seems not to have provided any bail, but the bond was made. When the long afternoon was over, Tweed emerged. He seemed satisfied, there appeared to be no bitterness on his part. He drove off to catch the four-fifteen to Greenwich.

As Tweed was being served with the arrest order, the final report of the Booth Committee was issued. It listed a series of transcripts copied from the comptroller's books. The committee found that $20,748,664.25 had been stolen from the city and county. Keyser & Co. took $2,801,057.28; Ingersoll, $3,266,163.99; Garvey and others, $3,206,635.62; New York Printing Company, $3,603,309.16; Miller, $1,797,733.52. An investigation of the new courthouse disclosed that from 1861 to 1871 the building of the structure cost $5,734,144.42 and furnishings $2,400,588.77 for a total of $8,134,733.19. With hidden costs and "adjusted" claims the cost would be nearer 11 to 12 million dollars. The committee asked that the criminals be brought to justice. .

Figures, charges, additions, rhetoric rolled in like waves of the oceans. Everyone had different numbers. Tweed was being inundated in the process, but he stood his ground. Slowly the others melted into the background. Keyser, under a "doctor's care," was now in Florida. Woodward, his neighbors in Norwalk, Connecticut, said, was either in Chicago to view the ruins of the recent great fire, or in Europe. Garvey and Ingersoll could not be found to have warrants served upon them. Ingersoll was supposedly in Portland, Maine. Sweeny was a forgotten man, and anyway, he and his brother James had gone to Europe on "doctor's advice." No one really cared. Tweed was the name, and the game. Everyone had taken cover. Tweed remained—a big, fat, sitting target. A *Times* reporter met him on October 28. Tweed was quiet and hesitant. He was asked if he had heard of Ingersoll's flight. He was startled, as if struck with a knife. "How do you know?" he stammered. The reporter replied that he had just come from his office. Garvey was gone too. Tweed was sure that Ingersoll had not run away. He would be back. Tweed remarked that he had wanted to go to New Orleans, to see his daughters, but because of the "hue and cry," decided to stay. He expected, he said, to be re-elected state senator, but refused to say anything about the transfer of his real estate holdings. He was, in fact, busily transferring property to his son. At least he had sense enough to do that. At about the same time, he gave another interview to a *Herald* reporter, to whom he seemed jovial and cheerful. The arrest was only a "bother" for he had to obtain counsel and spend time in consultation. The only real damage was the humiliation of his family; still he expected that the public would support him and he promised to reward their confidence.

There were other proceedings. Jackson S. Schultz, representing Keyser, sued Tweed for labor and services rendered to the "Boss" in the amount of $42,000. Schultz also sued Woodward for $19,000 for similar services. If anyone was to make money from the exposé, it was surely going to be lawyers.[5]

The effect of the scandal on Tammany, the Democratic Party and the political future of Tweed was at first not too ominous. It became so, as the months progressed. Slowly, anti-Tammany Democrats, the remnant of the Young Democrats, O'Brien, Ledwith, Brennan cast about as new life was pumped into almost collapsed arteries. As for Tweed, the contest from the Fourth Senatorial District was the one bright spot in a disastrous year. Though he, Sweeny and Connolly were being edged from party conferences and conventions, and Tilden, now chairman of the Democratic State Central Committee, urged that the "gangrene [be] cut out of the party," Tweed went about his affairs. At the state convention at Rochester, talk flowed freely. How should Tammany and Tweed be treated? Some urged a complete purge, others were inclined to go slow. Everyone talked of vouchers, warrants, the courthouse. On October 7, Tweed appeared as part of the Tammany delegation. Some asked that Tweed and the Tammanyites not be seated. Amid champagne, whiskey and cigars, in small smoke-filled rooms, plots and rumors circulated as freely as drinks. The first day of the convention was a crucial one. The reformers, O'Conor, Benjamin Wood, George McLean, had hoped to have Tammany ejected and themselves recognized. Tammany, however, still supporting Tweed, had something to say. Earlier Tweed had made their position clear. "Go ahead and kick us out if you can get along without us. All right, we want the party to succeed, but if you think you can elect the slate and win without our help, go ahead. We can carry our own in New York County that is all we want." Tweed concluded, "Our county can do without the State, but the State cannot get along without our county." Democrats like "Sammy" Tilden might not like the logic, but it was clear. At the convention, Charles G. Cornell read the Tammany statement of support to the party and then waived Tammany's right to its seat. The ploy won. The audience cheered Tammany, which by retreating gained the necessary victory and was in fact voted in, as the reformers were ousted.

If Tammany gained a victory, it was a small one. There was little representation on committees, for Tweed no specific post. O'Conor was heard on the floor denouncing corruption and the "Municipal Ring," while Tilden after roundly abusing Tammany threatened to resign from the party rather than vote for a Tammany ticket. Rural Democrats also expressed their anger at the Society. In the end, Tweed felt neither victory nor defeat. He expressed confidence in victory in the fall and was satisfied with his treatment in Rochester.

Republicans, of course, could not and did not let the issue slide by. Roscoe Conkling, opening his United States senatorial campaign in Albany on October 11, made a blistering attack on "The Ring." Tweed was in the center arena. Ten years earlier, this Tammany sachem was bankrupt, but was now, except for William Astor, the largest landowner in Manhattan, croaked Conkling. Money spent in the city by three men, Tweed, Hall, Connolly, was greater than that spent by the Forty-first Congress. Gory details and facts were carefully outlined. The city's highways and byways hold sin and crime, offenses are not punished, commerce is driven from its wharves by ravenous officials. Under Republican management, the national debt since 1869 declined by $10.00 per head, while in the city there was an increase of $58.57 per person. Need the voters know more?

Yet, they asked for more. Tweed's friends had gathered on October 19. Tweed addressed the crowd as he sought vindication through the election. "We will win," shouted the cheering audience. Tweed smiled as he accepted the nomination for state senator. "I do so not unmindful of the vilification and unjust abuse that have lately been my portion at the hands of my political opponents." Victory in November would be the answer to his detractors. He also denounced wholesale slanderers at a meeting in the Walton House. He defended his record. Republicans, Democrats, German, Irish were benefited by his work for education, churches and commerce. The Fourth District was "not the most loathful political scab in the United States." It was home for hard-working and patriotic citizens, sensible men who were friends of Tweed.

Excitement in the city was high as the election approached. Meetings and rallies of reformers and Republicans were many. For reformers, the cry was, "What are you going to do about it?" Tweed again was pilloried with words he had never used. The former Irish revolutionary O'Donovan Rossa challenged Tweed, as did reformer Anthony Miller. They expected fraud and asked the mayor to appoint new election inspectors. They sought a mandamus before Judge Barnard in Oyer and Terminer, who refused to grant one since he could find no case for the plaintiffs. He did order that ballot boxes be provided and labeled according to law.

The pulpit was also busy just prior to elections. Rev. James McClancy in St. Joseph's Church reminded parishioners that elected officials were in charge of "your lives, your liberties and your property"; trust none but honest men. Dr. Bellows at All Souls' talked of unscrupulous bloodsuckers. Rev. W. H. Boole at Beekman Hill Methodist, taking a page from Ezekiel, preached "behold a hole in the wall and behold every form of creeping things and abominable beasts and the idols of the house of Israel portrayed upon the wall round about." Tweed was something to sermonize upon.

The election proved to be a Tammany disaster. At City Hall, party workers like Gustave "Gus" Cardozo and Tim Golden sadly looked over the returns. Even Young Democrats Bradley, Genet, Norton, Ledwith were slaughtered. Fifteen assembly seats were lost while Republicans gained 25,000 votes over the previous election. The sudden defeat of so many stalwarts came as a surprise even to vengeful reformers. Only Tweed escaped. He had 19,000 votes to Rossa's 6,700 and Miller's 2,345. It was a personal triumph. His victory, however, was a shallow one—an illusion. Tweed remained, but as a political figure he retained little stature. It only remained to bury him. There were rumors that he would not take his seat, but would flee the country. O'Donovan Rossa was ready to take office. He concluded that there was dishonest voting in the election anyway.

A reporter visited Tweed on November 9. Tweed cheerfully greeted him with, "I didn't sail on the *Russia*." Then, continued the account, those "376 pounds" of politics, muscle, flesh and blood dropped gracefully into a seat and laughed heartily at the idea of a European tour. Tweed would stay. His constituents needed him.[6] So did the reformers. Where would the hunter be without the fox? or the tiger?

Winning the election was really harmful to Tweed, for it served as an added incentive for the hunters. O'Conor talked of plans to continue the prosecution of Tweed. The criminal process which followed waited upon news of the election. Tweed still state senator, having seemingly a semblance of power, was worth more than Tweed a loser. What then would be the point of the hunt? Tweed would have been better served if he had in fact lost. Prosecutors are keenly aware of the political value of their quarry. Politics and law are too often inseparable.

On November 22, 1871, the grand jury of General Sessions was addressed by Judge Bedford, who informed the jurors of their duty to uphold the law regardless of political party. The stupendous frauds against the city treasury demanded justice. Action was called for. The zealot Lucius S. Comstock was continued as foreman of the jury, as more trouble brewed for Tweed. His securities failed to justify their bonds. Tweed's attorneys asked Justice Learned to lower his bail. He refused, but gave him a twenty-day stay to raise the money. And there was more trouble. An outbreak of smallpox killed many. "The Ring" was blamed, since fifty doctors had to be discharged by the Board of Health because of the lack of funds caused by their "thieving operation."

It didn't rain, it poured. Late in November, Connolly finally resigned, his place taken by "Handy Andy" Green, and was shortly after arrested by order of Judge Learned. He was first held at the New York Hotel and then at the Ludlow Street Jail in lieu of $1 million bail. Nephews James M. Connolly and Charles M. Connolly and Henry Hart, a pawnbroker, could raise only $500,000. On November 29, Peckham applied for and received an order to restrain Tweed from disposing of his property. Some felt it was too late. Argument continued in Albany for the reduction of bail for Tweed, who was now represented by John A. Reynolds, a Vermonter, and Edwin W. Stoughton. Tilden and O'Conor represented the state. Reynolds argued that the action for a $6,312,000 judgment was based on questionable information supplied by Tilden; further bail had never been required in a civil suit and was clearly excessive. The people of the state had not been injured and Learned sitting in Albany should not have allowed the suit. Even the people of the city, where the case really belongs, were not injured and the complaint does not so allege. Finally, Tweed was not thinking of leaving town. Tilden followed. He thought that Tweed should not have any trouble raising bail, for he had already been "proved to have $1 million of the public money." As far as Tilden was concerned, Tweed was guilty without a trial and the bail should be continued. Judge Learned after a few days decided that the set sum was correct. Given the size of the theft, it was not large. Although he tried to be free of public clamor, he felt that given the evidence, he could not reduce the penalty. Again it should be remembered that this was a civil, not a criminal, case, and that at present, no bail is given in civil matters. People are not jailed in civil suits even if after a trial a judgment is entered against them and they cannot pay. Certainly, they are not jailed pending trial. Four days later, on December 9, Connolly's bail came on for a hearing. Connolly's collusion with Tweed was pointed out by O'Conor, who also accused him of destroying vouchers to be used as evidence. His bail was reduced to $500,000.

When criminal charges were readied Judge Bedford handed a bench warrant to Matthew Brennan, the portly sheriff, to arrest Tweed. It was December 15. Neither Brennan nor Deputy Jarvis could believe his eyes, but there it was. The pair slowly walked over to the Department of Public Works on Broadway. This was no civil suit—jail was in the offing. They walked up a flight of stairs. "Is Mr. Tweed in?" asked Brennan. "No," replied a desk clerk. "He went uptown." Tweed was located at his son's Metropolitan Hotel. They found the "Boss" seated in his room. "Mr. Tweed," spoke Brennan, "I have a warrant for your arrest on the charge of felony." There were large drops of perspiration on Tweed's forehead, as he asked, "Must I go to prison tonight?" He was permitted to remain in the hotel, but under guard. There were three counts against Tweed. One was that he falsely and fraudulently signed certain warrants, thus acquiring large sums of money for himself. Secondly, that he violated the fourth section of the act of 1870 requiring the auditing of bills; and thirdly, that together with Watson and others he defrauded the taxpayers of the city by specific warrants drawn May 19 through July 17 to Keyser & Co., the warrants Keyser claimed were forged.

The following day, Tweed was driven to Bedford's court in the Tombs on Centre Street. A large and curious crowd heard the "little judge" commit Tweed without bail, but he was permitted to remain at the hotel. Tweed's attorney filed for a writ of habeas corpus. Justice Barnard granted the writ and set bail at $5,000. To a reporter, Tweed appeared to be physically failing. His color paled. Furrows, where there had been none. Rumors of other indictments circulated. They were true, and two days later Woodward and Tweed were indicted in Oyer and Terminer on two counts of grand larceny and two counts of forgery in the third degree. There was still other news. Thomas C. Fields was arrested for having accepted bribes while a member of the state legislature. Tweed's bondsmen were carefully examined. Fairchild, Bernard Kelly, Charles Devlin and young William M. Tweed in place of Terence Farley presented themselves in turn. Tweed Jr. gave a detailed listing of his property. Land at the Circle on Fifty-ninth Street was valued at $300,000, lots on Duane Street at $260,000, and at Sixty-third Street at $600,000. The total value was $1,584,000. This looked good on paper, but the figure was highly inflated. The Circle property bought by Tweed in 1868 cost $200,000 including the assumption of a mortgage of $136,000, which was discharged in 1870. It was given to his son in 1871 and sold for $200,000 in 1873. The Sixty-third Street property was purchased for $91,000 in 1868, deeded to his son in 1871, and sold to Jacob Vanderpoel for $1.00 probably in return for legal services. The Duane Street property cost $260,000 in 1868, and realized $180,000 in 1873. Tweed had speculated heavily in real estate, and as in many other things appeared to have lost quite heavily. Tweed Jr. gave his age as twenty-four, and his occupation as keeper of the Metropolitan Hotel since August. The hotel was owned by A. T. Stewart and operated and rented by Tweed Sr. and then Tweed Jr. and one Abram Garfield. Rent was $12,000 per year. He testified further that he had been a clerk at the New York Printing Company prior to August. The hearing was held over to the beginning of the new year. Tweed remained at the hotel. Connolly, unable to raise his reduced bail, was in the Ludlow Street Jail. No one else of "The Ring," except Hall, was about; all were at places unknown.

The holiday season brought little cheer to the "Boss." At the end of the year, Tweed resigned as commissioner of public works and Sweeny as commissioner of parks. Frederick Law Olmsted, traveler and environmentalist, became head of Public Parks while George M. Van Nort was made commissioner of public works. Tilden and Peckham, aided by Henry F. Taintor who busily still combed comptroller's books and records and Lucius Comstock's grand jury, found the season a busy one. Letters sent by Tilden and Comstock to various New York banks elicited deposit information on all connected to "The Ring." "Where was the money?" The Broadway Bank had such extensive accounts that several weeks would be necessary to present a comprehensive picture. Other banks like the Nassau, Bank of North America, Bull's Head, Metropolitan National, National Trust provided information of deposits of a few dollars to thousands. Tilden was also buoyed by advice from Seymour, Church, Havemeyer, Conkling and Peckham to continue his search. Others told of places to look for the loot. Others wanted jobs to help look. While Tweed waited, the noose was tightened.

In the meantime a financial crisis brought on in large part by the confusion the "exposures" created was affecting the city as hundreds of creditors besieged City Hall to obtain relief from a city close to bankruptcy. A number of banks were in danger of collapse. The Bowling Green Savings Bank, "Hank" Smith, president, and Tweed, director; the Guardian Savings Bank with Tweed as president; the National Bank with McBride Davidson, president, and Tweed, director; and the Yorkville Savings Bank controlled by Henry Genet faced severe difficulties because of the closing of the municipal tap. In addition the city's mishandling of bonds and mortgages, charged a report by D. C. Howell, superintendent of the Banking Department of the state, added to fiscal problems. For many, the world had suddenly been turned topsy-turvy. The Americus Club did not hold its annual ball.[7]

V

The Law

Injustice often arises through chicanery, that is, through an oversubtle and ever fraudulent construction of the law. This it is that gave rise to the now familiar saw, "The more law, the less justice" (*Summum jus, summa injura*).

CICERO, *De Officiis*, Bk. I, Ch. 10, Sec. 33.

22

First, The Justices

How quickly Tweed's world collapsed about him. He seemed unable to conceive of what was happening. If he thought of himself as "Boss," what mockery that title was, what futility. It was a sham title for a sham figure.

Any delusions he may have had were ended when Democrats stripped him of the grand sachemship and threw him out of Tammany to face his enemies and future without the protection of the party he had served for so many years. After a meeting on Saturday, December 30, 1871, Tweed was quickly deposed, without being given a chance to defend himself. As of that moment, Tweed was legally guilty of nothing. He had not had a day in court, he was under the law still innocent. Tammany, however, washed their hands of the stain. Hall, Sweeny and Connolly were also expelled to make sure the smell of corruption was eliminated from the sacred shrine. Augustus Schell, a former port collector, was elected to fill Tweed's place.[1] From this point on, Tweed would have little to do with Tammany or politics. The remaining years of his life were spent defending himself against his accusers. He would no longer campaign in the streets or argue in legislative halls; instead, he would become familiar with the paneled chambers of courtrooms. He would no longer hear the language of politics and public affairs, but the language of law. When the legislature opened its session January 2, amid the usual noise and chatter as old friends or enemies met to exchange amenities, four senators from New York were to be sworn in. When Tweed's name was called, voices stilled as eyes darted to the chair of the ex-"Boss" in the front row. It was empty. From this point, it would always be vacant. In the middle of January, a senatorial commission was sent to New York to gather evidence on the question of the seating or unseating of Tweed. Charges had been leveled against him on opening day citing election frauds. O'Donovan Rossa was convinced he had been robbed. All that was needed was a proper inquiry to set the matter straight.

A *Herald* reporter met Tweed on January 29, 1872. The *Tribune* said you were going to Albany in a day or two. Was that true? asked the reporter. Mr. Greeley knows no more about what I am going to do than he knows about farming, replied Tweed and he continued, "There are not four people that read the *Tribune* in my Senatorial District." The *Tribune* charges that you bribed the Legislature, what of that? Tweed smiled one of his "peculiar" smiles, and wiped his glasses with a white cambric handkerchief and beamed, "What is it Mr. Greeley says about lying? O.K., this is it—You lie you villain, you lie." With all his troubles elsewhere Tweed had little desire to battle against Rossa and the Senate in order to take his seat. He had his hands full with the rising tide of indictments. Legislation was far from his mind.[2]

Tweed's world was made even darker when his close friend "Jubilee" Jim Fisk, Jr., aged thirty-seven, was shot and killed early in January by a former associate, Edward S. Stokes, who had become his successful rival for the affection of "an actress," Helen Josephine Mansfield, known to all as "Josie." Both men were married. Tweed needed friends at this time and Fisk's loss was a particularly sharp and unhappy blow. Stokes served four years in prison.[3] Murder was more tolerable than "fraud."

There seemed to be a ray of hope when Judge Cardozo early in January 1872 accepted his sureties and Tweed temporarily remained out of jail, but Lucius Comstock and his jury continued their search for sin. Peter Sweeny was indicted on the same criminal charges leveled against Tweed, and shortly afterward, though temporarily, returned from Montreal to his home at 104 West Thirty-fourth Street. Harry Genet was indicted on February 3, 1872, on two counts of forgery in the third degree in connection with endorsements on two vouchers. Soon after his attorney, Nelson J. Waterbury, applied for bail before Justice Barnard. On the same day Alderman Thomas C. Fields was indicted for two counts of bribery. Also, on February 3, 1872, employee of Public Works, William Hennesy Cook, was indicted on two counts of forgery in connection with two orders for payment. Bail of $10,000 was posted. None of these except Sweeny had anything to do with Tweed.

Andrew Garvey was indicted on two counts of forgery. Interestingly, he was charged not with submitting fraudulent bills, but with forging the name of Fillipo Donnarumma on two vouchers totaling approximately $66,000—thus defrauding Donnarumma, an artist, of his money. Still another indictment was issued February 3, 1872, and this against James H. Ingersoll. This was for two counts of forgery on two warrants totaling approximately $216,000. Bail was set at $10,000. Tweed, of course, was not left out. Three more indictments were issued against him for forgery and grand larceny.

Indictments continued to be issued like water from a burst dam. The following week on February 10, 1872, Hall, refusing to resign, was punished by being indicted for five misdemeanors, charged in effect with "corruptly" failing to audit five claims, three submitted by Ingersoll and two by Garvey. A "proper" grand jury had been found. On the same day, Connolly was also indicted on the five misdeameanor charges in connection with the same claims submitted by Ingersoll and Garvey. His bail was set at $5,000. Strangely, Ingersoll and Garvey were not charged with submitting fraudulent bills, but Hall and Connolly were indicted for failing to audit these allegedly fraudulent bills. On the same day, still another indictment was issued against Tweed, Sweeny, his brother James M. Sweeny, Hugh Smith and Elbert A. Woodward on the felony of conspiracy, perjury and grand larceny, in connection with payment of several warrants to Keyser. Bail for each defendant was set at $10,000.

Tweed's counsel went before Justice Bedford in February to complain that his client now had five separate indictments in Sessions. The first, handed down on December 15, 1871, was repeated by each succeeding indictment. Total bail set, including the civil suit, was $1,500,000. For the latest indictment of February 10, 1872, for conspiracy, perjury and grand larceny, bail was set at $10,000. The conspiracy charge was also the same as that handed down on December 15. In that voluminous document, Tweed was again charged with approving allegedly fraudulent vouchers. Though Sweeny was named as a co-conspirator in the case, he was not at that time arrested. Tweed suffered other reverses. On January 30, 1872, a new Board of Apportionment and Audit was created. Three men, Andrew Green, comptroller, Frederick Law Olmstead, commissioner of public parks, and George Van Nort, commissioner of public works, constituted the body. As part of the new Board's retrenchment policy, Tweed's claim for rent of $6,750 for premises owned by him on the corner of Fourth Avenue and 129th Street and used as police and civil court was disallowed since Tweed, it was asserted, was indebted to the city greatly in excess of the amount claimed by him. A number of other claims were disallowed including one of Catharine Bradley for rent. The city claimed the property was in fact owned by her husband John J. Bradley, who as a city chamberlain, could not legally contract for such rent. Several years later the claim was paid.[4]

With the indictments, trial quickly followed for Hall. Though not indicted after the hearing before the grand jury in Oyer and Terminer, he now faced trial in General Sessions for the same charges. The scene appropriately was the new county courthouse, Judge Charles P. Daly presiding.

209

Hall was represented by a battery of seven attorneys, including Aaron J. Vanderpoel. Wheeler T. Peckham, Lyman Tremain, former state attorney general, and Henry L. Clinton were prosecutors for the state although not members of the attorney general's office. All received handsome fees. That Daly presided was an example of gross injustice, which would be repeated when Tweed was tried. The dice were loaded from the beginning against the defendants, first Hall, then Tweed. Attorney General Francis C. Barlow wrote a short but astonishing note to Daly on February 21, 1872, a few days before the trial commenced, stating:

> We rely on you to try the Hall case on February 26th, and I hope you will not disappoint us.

In another note, also dated February 21, he repeated his plea:

> Please send word by bearer that we may rely on you for the trial of Hall next Monday. [Gunning S.] Bedford ought not or does not want to try him. With you, we shall have a dignified fair trial that everyone will be satisfied.

Indiana-born Algernon S. Sullivan, assistant district attorney, at the request of District Attorney Samuel Garvin, informed Daly of the trial date and asked him to be in Garvin's office at 10:30 A.M. on the day of the trial, a half hour before the opening of court. Daly, who had taken an active part in denouncing the "Tweed Ring," did not disappoint the prosecution. The obvious duplicity of judge and prosecution as the upholders of law and order was worse than the charges brought against Hall. The impartiality of the court is the cornerstone of American jurisprudence. Here it was openly violated without the slightest hesitation. Barlow also wrote a note to Tilden giving Woodward a deadline of February 3 to turn state's evidence. Woodward did.[5]

The trial began as requested. Four days were spent in selecting a jury. The fifth day, prosecutors recounted the crimes, pointing out the increased city debt and obvious frauds involved. On the sixth day, March 4, Deputy Comptroller Richard A. Storrs was called to the stand to discuss his knowledge of the board of audit. He testified that he had never known the board to meet in a body. Peckham then asked Storrs what he knew of the matter of the stolen vouchers. This was in reference to one of the more interesting and bizarre aspects of the disclosures.

The adventure reportedly began on September 10, 1871, a Sunday. Someone had gone into the comptroller's office in the new courthouse and taken certain vouchers and warrants for 1869 and 1870, those specifically relating to "Ring" frauds. The event had the town buzzing. The doors of the building were locked on Saturday night. Neither the janitor, Edwin

M. Haggerty, nor a watchman, one William Murphy (who is not listed on the city payrolls as working in the courthouse), heard anyone enter during the evening. The next morning Murphy noticed a piece of blotting paper over a glass panel in the auditor's office and saw Haggerty climbing up the stairs carrying a bundle of something. Auditor Stephen C. Lynes returning on Monday morning also noticed that the glass in the door to the bureau had been broken at the lower corner near the doorknob. Lockers were pried open, and thirteen bundles of warrants and vouchers, including the claims of Andrew Garvey, Ingersoll and Keyser, which were in pigeonholes, had been carried away. It was an amateurish job, as if to ensure detection. By September 21, enough evidence had been gathered to have the "thieves" arrested. Charles Baulch, a "part-time watchman" in the new courthouse (and he, too, is not on the payroll), Haggerty and his wife (she was later dropped from the hearings) were arraigned in the Essex Market Court. Tilden, representing the Committee of Seventy, was present. Witnesses, chiefly Mary Conway, a servant in Haggerty's employ, testified she saw Haggerty bring papers into the kitchen and burn them, while Baulch stood watch. Another "man in a gray suit" was present, but he was not further identified by her. A *Times* reporter who went to the scene had examined the charred evidence. There were bits of wooden boards like those used by the county, but "the evidence was not convincing," noted the reporter. On the twenty-second, there was an intensive examination of a "nervous" Haggerty who was "dressed to kill." He continued to deny theft. Lynes and Storrs were called to testify. Lynes was first. He had worked for the city since 1858 and was appointed by Connolly as auditor on May 15, 1871, after Watson's death. He said that the warrants, vouchers and bills "stolen" had been stored in lockers and represented $12 million for the period 1869 through part of 1871. Lynes personally locked the doors of the closets every night. Papers taken were in bundles labeled "Armories and Drill Rooms, Adjusted Claims and County Liabilities." He could not swear that he saw them prior to September 6. Baulch and Haggerty were examined in the Tombs on September 29, before Bedford. The prisoners' counsel John Graham unsuccessfully protested the public hearings, and that his clients were being tried in the press, not in a court of law. He denied any burglary since no outer door was broken. The district attorney rejected these arguments, the court concurred, and the prisoners were committed without bail. Indictments followed on October 30. On November 24, Haggerty and Baulch appeared again before Bedford. The defense alleged that no proof had been introduced. Not so, countered Garvin. Haggerty told Baulch "You did it for me and I did it for another man." The other man or men will also be sent to prison, promised Garvin, if they could be found. At the end of March 1872, the pair appeared be-

fore Justice Cardozo in Oyer and Terminer. There were few persons in the
court, as the public had lost interest. Everyone "knew" what had happened. Tweed and or Connolly had stolen the evidence. It became part of
the legend. Cardozo stated that in the absence of Connolly, who had by
now left the country, he could not try the case, an odd reason, and
directed $5,000 bail for each count for each man. The prisoners were
bailed and discharged. In June 1872, Haggerty, who was replaced in his job
after September 1871, and his family were asked to vacate their rooms in
the courthouse. When they moved, they disappeared into history along
with Baulch. The entire incident was dropped. There were no further
prosecutions, no further discussion.

Yet, what a strange, suspicious affair. First there was the way in which
the "theft" took place. Glass was smashed. Haggerty making sure that the
deed was witnessed, the charred remains all too clearly establish the
"crime." Yet Haggerty and Baulch worked in the building. If they took
the records, couldn't they use a key? Why the "forced" entry? Secondly,
the material "taken" had been listed by Tilden and the state to show "The
Ring's" involvement in "fraud." All but ten warrants seem to have been
destroyed, these ten to be used as evidence to show that claims existed.
One to Keyser of June 10, 1869, warrant 2684, has been found by the author among discarded files. What was not "stolen" were order forms
drawn on the Broadway Bank signed by Hall, Connolly and James B.
Young, supervisor's clerk, covering the same claims as the "stolen"
vouchers. These were put into the comptroller's archives, packed in
bundles, and were in a matter of time forgotten. There is no better place
to lose things than in the city's archives. It was only through accident,
and this only during the course of the writing of this book, that these
particular records were discovered by the author. They had not been seen
or used by anyone since 1871 and had in fact been among the documents
including the Keyser warrant ordered destroyed in the 1960s, although
containing much of the entire financial history of the City of New York.
All was to become shredded. It was really not necessary for Haggerty and
Baulch to "steal" records; leave that to the city bureaucracy.

There appears little point in destroying vouchers and warrants and
leaving the order forms which directed payment for the claims for which
the vouchers were submitted. But still there was something to be gained by
the "theft" besides the supposition that Tweed and "The Ring" would be
branded with the crime and made to look like thieves covering their tracks
or destroying evidence. Why should Tweed or Hall "steal" so clum-
sily, why not simply "lose" the records, including order forms, among the
archives or in some convenient trash bin? Why steal them at all? They

had been published in newspapers and were in court records and the order forms remained. Though the finger of suspicion pointed "obviously" at Tweed and "The Ring," in retrospect it more obviously points at the contractors or the prosecutors; they had most to gain, since the evidence against themselves or Tweed need not be presented in court. The laborious business of shifting through each claim, verifying each item, was avoided. The contractors were protected and the prosecution's job made easier. And there were some odd shenanigans. Charlie Baulch was a handyman employed by the city to do special jobs. For example, in 1865 and in 1866 he was used to move books around the library in City Hall. In 1865 he earned $100 as a sergeant at arms at the July Fourth celebration. In 1868, he was appointed assistant city librarian, but only for the month of August. This brought him $83.33.

He was not on a specific payroll until September 1, 1871, "employed" as "Foreman of Janitors, New County Court House." This terminated September 20, 1871, just after the "theft." He was appointed to this job by the courthouse commissioners including Thomas Coman and Michael Norton, Young Democrats and no friends of Tweed. Charlie was obviously used as usual for a specific task—the great voucher "theft." In July 1872, despite his indictment and trial, he asked for and received sixty-six dollars with the approval of the Board of Audit and Apportionment for services as "Foreman." For this "service," he surely deserved much more. He died soon after without saying anything further. Haggerty was paid for all the month of September, $208.34; his yearly salary was $2,500. His services were terminated after September. There were, of course, important questions to be asked and answered; however, for Tweed to be involved seems pointless. For the public to think he had a hand in the crime was all-important. Again it makes more sense to suggest that it was done on the orders of the Committee of Seventy or better by someone like Wheeler Peckham in order to cast still another suspicion on the "evil Ring." It makes even more sense to suggest that Garvey, Keyser and the rest were involved. What was stolen was not evidence of payment, the canceled checks were not taken, what disappeared were the requests for payment and the attached bills submitted by the contractors. The contractors could now testify to anything. There was no evidence to the contrary. They would be in the clear. In any event, all this might explain why Haggerty and Baulch were released and paid with no questions asked.

Anyway, everyone in the financial offices knew of the records, which were available to be taken out at will. William S. Copland had a free hand with the documents, so had Matthew O'Rourke, "military editor" for one of the city's papers and the man who always claimed the credit for destroying "The Ring." He was appointed county bookkeeper on January

24, 1871, to succeed Stephen Lynes. He too saw the "fraudulent" character of the administration and resigned in May. Before leaving, however, he "fortified himself with some proofs of the frauds." He then went to Jones, who published them. There must have been a regular parade of employees into Jones's office who could know of these vouchers—all the clerks, Sheriff O'Brien, in fact, anyone who had any interest could have copied them and they were in fact copied. It made no sense to destroy them except as it hurt Tweed and so-called "Ring" members.[6]

So, at Hall's trial, the mention of the vouchers was useful, the image potent. It always would be that. Later Tweed told his own story. He remembered that Hall informed him that if the vouchers were not examined by the Booth Committee the prosecution of "The Ring" would end. Tweed then consulted with William H. Cook, who "then took matters into his own hands" and destroyed the evidence. Tweed knew of no other details. Like so much else that Tweed "confessed," there were no specifics and nothing to relate to the known facts. Storrs, under cross-examination, admitted he had no connection of any kind with the "board of audit" and that the vouchers were not in his charge. Lynes again. He explained his duties. Watson would hand him a contractor's bill. He attached two blank voucher certificates, one to be signed by Connolly which stated that the claim had been duly audited under Section 4, Chapter 382, Laws of 1870, and that the county auditor was to draw a warrant for the specific sum, and a second voucher signed by Tweed, Hall and Connolly which stated they had audited the proffered claim. The two vouchers were attached to the bill and all put within the warrant. The order form or check drawn on the Broadway Bank, the institution transacting county business, was also prepared by Lynes, who signed it as county auditor. Connolly and John B. Young, clerk of the Board of Supervisors, also signed. Lynes usually signed all order forms. William M. Tweed's name would be written across the voucher, "I think," said Lynes. The "stolen" vouchers or warrants could not, of course, be produced. There was only one warrant without the vouchers for $41,563.42 dated June 6, 1870, to Garvey, which was shown. Judge Daly allowed this as primary evidence. However, he agreed that the warrant without the vouchers gave no proof that the "board of audit" had affirmed the claim. The court recessed until the next day of trial, March 7. The room was again crowded with an observant, intelligent audience interested in the proceedings. It was not the kind attracted to sensational trials, and given Hall's reputation with the ladies, there were few women present. The trial up to now seemed to be going nowhere. Now a bombshell.

Hall believed, along with everyone else in the courtroom, that Garvey was in Europe. But the "Prince of Plasterers" and "Swiss Traveller" was in fact in the city in a disguise, as arranged by the prosecution, and even in court listening to the proceedings, waiting to be called as a surprise witness—the prosecutor's ace in the hole. The behind-the-scene dealings between Garvey and the state are not clear except that having turned state's evidence, "Michelangelo" Garvey was free from prosecution. Garvey was called about 3 P.M. The room was half empty, most people having left during boring testimony. The court clerk opened the door of the judge's chambers and in walked Andrew Garvey. He went to the witness stand. "Had Garvey risen from the dead and appeared in his grave clothes, he could not have carried greater consternation into the ranks of the defense," Henry Clinton remembered. The court clerk stumbled over the administration of the oath. The defense was "apoplectic." Hall was livid with "rage or fear." Lyman Tremain began direct examination of the witness. Garvey was thinner. He nervously gazed at his work, the plastered ceiling above him, as the court quickly filled. He testified that he had resided since October 1870 at 7 East Forty-seventh Street; and he was forty-three years old, a builder, plasterer and decorator, and had been in business since he was twenty-one. He knew Hall for twenty years and Connolly for ten. He was shown "a fair copy" of the June 6 warrant, numbered 2507, and remembered that he had deposited in the Broadway Bank on that day receipts of several warrants totaling $169,961.26. Burrill objected, the question was of a single warrant; it was sustained. He had received the warrant in the chamber of the Board of Supervisors. He was again shown the document. It was for material and labor in the construction of the new courthouse during December 1869. He had given his bill to Woodward, whom he had known for seven years, and later received the order form and warrant countersigned by Hall, Tweed, Connolly and J. B. Young. A squabble ensued over admissibility. Court then recessed.

The next day, a huge and impatient crowd, different from the earlier ones, clamored to be admitted. This was going to be interesting. The courtroom filled, judge and jury sat. Hall entered with his usual "sang froid" and sat at his usual seat. Edwin W. Stoughton, another of Hall's attorneys, arose to challenge the legality of the indictment against Hall. The charge against his client was that he had failed to audit claims, but he was not liable for their veracity. He committed no moral wrong and he was not "willful" in passing warrants without examination. There was no allegation that the claims were unjust or fraudulent, or that the certificates were given with the intent to defraud the county. Hall and the others —Tweed and Connolly—were accused of signing false certificates, not certificates of false claim. They assumed the claims to be fair and honest, as they were not proven to be unfair or dishonest. Lyman Tremain interrupted, and asked, "If it had been unjustly done, would it be an offense?"

to which Stoughton repeated his position, "There is the very difficulty in this case. If the men knew the claim to be fraudulent, it would be an offense," but without the allegation of fraud and knowledge on their part that it was fraudulent, no offense was committed. Daly ruled that the case would continue since Stoughton's arguments, if accepted, would end the litigation and he wanted the outcome to depend on the evidence. It was obvious why the prosecution wanted Daly. Here was a question of law which was to be decided by the judge presiding, yet he refused to do so. Informer Garvey's testimony thus was crucial. He was asked the critical question—was the claim "a just and honest account"? His answer, "No, sir," stunned the court. Murmurs and whispers stirred the air. Garvey was to "squeal." The truth about "The Ring" was here, at last. In that case, asked the prosecution, how was this particular bill dishonest? There was an objection on the broadness of the question, which was overruled. Garvey, agitated and nervous "as guilty men ought to be," explained that for the plastering, alterations and repairs in the new courthouse, his bill came to $110,900 including work done and in progress up to April 20, 1870. An additional $78,760 was due him for work on armories and drill rooms, plus $75,000 additional for added labor and material and expenses; "outside parties" owed him $126,000 for other expenditures used to "insure" his bills. Part of the $50,000, for example, was cash to Tweed to be used in Albany to "bribe" the legislature. This is the first specific charge of an actual payment to Tweed. Here Garvey was instructed to discuss the specific warrant and not wander. Garvey replied that he gave these particulars in order that the court understand that warrant. The total owed him for all his work was $264,660, plus the $126,000 for "other parties." He added an "anticipated" $5,000 for his "political" expenses in the fall 1870 election, making a grand sum of $395,660. The witness was again warned to confine himself to the specific warrant. Garvey nodded, but paid little attention and the court permitted him to continue. The specific warrant was one of the bills made out to cover the amount due him, but he received only 35 per cent of that bill and all bills.

After a recess, Garvey was asked to spell out details. He gave $50,000 to Tweed, which his brother John Garvey carried to Albany. He did not hand over the money directly. He also testified that he was owed $60,000 for work for Tweed and his friends at Greenwich and Cos Cob, Connecticut. Also, $13,000 was at the order of Woodward for his home in Norwalk, and $3,000 for plastering two houses for Walter Roche on Fifty-ninth Street. These were part of the $126,000, which he was expected to cover in his bills. Garvey remembered giving the June bill and three others to Woodward in April 1870, who glanced at them and brought them to Watson. On June 6, 1870, Woodward "found" Garvey and brought him to a "private corner" of a downstairs courthouse room and Garvey gave Woodward a check for $110,135.13 drawn on the Broadway Bank, before he received the June warrant.

Garvey deposited the money immediately to cover his own check. Garvey admitted he made no affidavit in respect to the validity of his claim. As could be expected, Garvey's story created a sensation. The plasterer was denounced as a "turncoat" and "traitor" by some. Could the testimony of any informer who talked to save his own skin be believed? Others, of course, hailed him as a true prince and honest man driven to clear his conscience. Bradley, who was present in the courtroom, remarked of the $5,000 "political" assessment, "Rather than have said that I would have put a bullet through my head." Politicians had easy answers for others. There was a rumor that a bullet in fact did await Garvey if he talked too much. Garvey's friends felt vindicated. Whatever Garvey had done by way of fraud was done for others and at their behest. There were those who found, however, that Garvey should not be given immunity from arrest and the district attorney should act against him as he had connived in fraud. As for Tweed, a reporter met the harried "Boss" in his office in Duane Street, "Glad to see you, how have you been?" asked Tweed. In a fairly happy mood the ex-"Boss" remarked he thought Hall innocent, that Garvey's evidence would not be of much significance, but that Hall's attorneys were not of the best. He expressed belief in his own innocence and eventual justification.

Hall's trial lasted sixteen days and by March 11, the parties were exhausted. No particular proof was presented against Hall, even with Garvey's testimony. Near the end of the trial, on March 12, 1872, one of the jurors, Matthias Clark, president of an insurance company, died. It gave the state an excuse and a mistrial was declared. Jurors crowded around the mayor congratulating the "Elegant One" and thus ended Hall's second tangle with the law. There would shortly be two others.[7]

Everything was really aimed at preparing the guillotine for Tweed. Hall's case was used as a dry run to test the defenses, to find any weak spots. It was not really Hall who was wanted. It was the "Boss."

Tweed still attempted to act normally, to maintain a degree of authority, a degree of interest. He harbored delusions of the past. Perhaps he still had leverage. In an interview on September 3, Tweed stated that he had no interest in the coming presidential race, but expressed thoughts on it nevertheless. Though originally he leaned toward Greeley running against Grant on a Democrat-Liberal Republican ticket, recent attacks by the *Tribune* on him and his friends had soured his relationship. However, if Greeley treated him more decently, he might help. Tweed thought he still had the loyalty of twenty thousand votes in the city, a loyalty he could sway on behalf of Greeley. Again, the reporter persisted, "Would you support Grant?" "I have not yet decided what I shall do. It depends upon how I am treated, but as yet, I have remained uncommitted." But later he said, "I have always been a Democrat and voted a Democratic ticket, and expect to remain such." Tweed didn't think much of Greeley's chance, or of the present Tammany Hall. The interview was with a desperate man, casting about for straws, seeking aid. How many of the "twenty thousand" could he deliver? And how many if he had endorsed a specific candidate would be lost by that endorsement was not discussed. Tweed was at the edge of the precipice, but he was trying. As for Tammany, John Morrissey, "Honest" John Kelly, Augustus and Richard Schell and Tilden were now the leaders of the party, Tweed a shadow of the distant past. Events moved quickly beyond him.

The fall campaign was rich with intrigues between the Committee of Seventy and Tammany, particularly over endorsing a candidate for mayor. Whatever the decision, certainly Tweed was rarely, if ever, consulted. "Tammany don't amount to anything now," Tweed contemptuously stated in an October 9 interview, "but they are doing all they can against me and my friends." Tweed really didn't count either, except that his name and misdeeds were like a "Bloody Shirt," a reminder of corruption and crime.

Tweed thus took little part in the electioneering and when he did, it was an embarrassing experience, at least as remembered by a contemporary who viewed Tweed's "Herculean figure, flabby face, and eyes that sparkled like a serpent" as he attempted to address a crowd during the 1872 elections. No sooner had he started when someone shouted, "Jail for you, old thief" and threw a cabbage, barely missing Tweed. He tried to smile, "Don't be rude, my friend. If you're in need of a job, I'll see that you get one." Then someone hit Tweed in the chest with a potato. Garbage, stones and sticks followed. Lanterns were broken. In the darkness, Tweed barely escaped to a waiting cab, but the traces were cut and he had to be rescued by a squad of police. The incident, true or not, mattered little. Tweed was politically dead, with only occasional trips to New Canaan or Greenwich, Connecticut, or sometimes a hunting foray to keep his mind off his troubles.[8]

After almost a year of legal maneuvering, Tweed's larceny indictment came before the court of Oyer and Terminer on October 10, 1872, New York-born Justice John Riker Brady presiding. Now fifty-one, Brady, often genial enough, had been on the bench since 1855. He was the brother-in-law of Charles P. Daly. Representing the prosecution were Garvin, Tremain and Clinton, transferring from the Hall case, and as a new addition Peckham. Burrill, two Bartletts, Willard O. and Willard, father and son respectively (Willard was a close friend of Elihu Root's), Fullerton and Vanderpoel, now joined by David Dudley Field, brother of Cyrus W. of Atlantic cable fame, represented the defense. Field, one of the most noted members of the bar, was seemingly angered by the failure of the Committee of Seventy to accept his services free of charge and now agreed to act for Tweed. He had earlier refused a Tweed retainer. The question of a trial date was argued. Tweed's attorneys wanted time to prepare and to inspect grand jury minutes. They asked for the merging of the Sessions indictments with those of Oyer and Terminer, since the February 1872 Sessions indictments covered the same ground as those issued by Oyer and Terminer in December 1871. Moreover, two of the Sessions indictments were part of an earlier indictment in the same court and should be quashed.

The "father of these indictments should be in a pillory," said David Field, Tweed's irate counsel, "for all of his profession to gaze upon, for having purely for political purposes, caused a citizen to be arraigned on many indictments, when he ought only to have been arraigned on one." Field screamed in protest that he had never before realized how manipulative the agents for the state were. Here were the district attorney and the attorney general and assistants twisting the law. He wished all the people were there to see it. Not only were the indictments confusing and in error, but in fact District Attorney Garvin was using them as a political weapon to ensure three more years in office. A gallows had been built for Tweed, but it would be turned into a gallows for the prosecution, pledged Field. He was wrong.

Tom Fields's case was argued on October 18. He had been charged with two counts of bribery in that while a member of the Assembly, he accepted funds to vote for the act of 1870, by which members of the Fire Department could have their claims paid by the comptroller. He denied the allegations and stated that when he had voted for the bill, the section relating to fire claims had not yet been inserted and that the money he received was pursuant to a retainer entered into with his clients prior to his election to the Assembly. Fields was found guilty, although the Court of Appeals reversed and a new trial was ordered. He never stood trial again, having fled to the home of his brother-in-law, the Reverend John P. Hermance, in the parish of St. Andrews, Quebec Province, Quebec. In his absence, since there was question of the legality of the Comstock grand jury of 1872, new indictments covering the same ground were issued against Fields. There was no connection between Fields and Tweed, except both faced the same music, and both were hanged by the same cord.

Criminal proceedings brought against Tweed on felony charges were, as Field assumed, aborted. Another tack was pursued. In October 1872,

Justice Brady, while one case was being readied, issued a bench warrant against Tweed on still other felony and misdemeanor charges. There were now pending a $6 million civil suit, two December 1871 felony indictments, four February 1872 indictments and now two October 1872 indictments. The last October 1872 misdemeanor indictment became known as the "omnibus indictment" and contained 220 counts. Tweed presented himself to the sheriff on October 23. It was on this misdemeanor indictment, and this one only, that Tweed was tried. Brady had concluded after "full and complete consideration" that these October charges were for different offenses than the other indictments. Bail was set at $10,000. Alfred B. Sands and Edward Kenny were bondsmen. Field now wanted the names of witnesses against Tweed placed in the indictments. The district attorney refused, but promised to give him the list of witnesses as they appeared before the grand jury. He never did. Willard Bartlett also wrote Tilden requesting information about irregularities in Sessions grand jury. There was no reply.[9]

Hall was also at this time once again before the court as his retrial began. It was also before Brady in Oyer and Terminer and was a rehash of the earlier trial. Garvey was again wheeled out as chief witness. But this time there were new informers. John McBride Davidson, safemaker and one of the contractors, went to the stand. He told his story. In one instance he remembered a bill for $16,940 was enlarged to $49,000 by Woodward. Stoughton asked how did this relate to Hall. Peckham indignantly rose in response. Surely, Woodward was involved and through him "The Ring" and Hall. The court interrupted and asked that proof be submitted to show that the bill was false and was known to be false. Brady asked for specifics—something the prosecution was short on. When asked how long it had been since his bills had been verified, Davidson replied three or four years. This would be before the existence of the "board of audit." Tremain tried to salvage the damaging admission by saying the board was in existence for three or four months before the bill in question was presented. But the court ruled Davidson's testimony inadmissible. John H. Keyser, one of the contractors and now like Garvey state witness, was heard from. He too had immunity. He was a plumber and worked at his trade for fifteen years, thirteen for the city. A group of vouchers were identified by him. He said angrily that while $900,000 in warrants were cashed in his name, his signature had been forged and he had not received a cent. "The swindlers kept it all." He told also of the padding of warrants by 65 per cent at Watson's suggestion. He admitted, however, that there was a bona fide foundation to the bills and he did not know how many were audited. He knew also of many bills presented for work performed which were never paid. Keyser explained that the city was a poor payer and that he often had to wait years for his money. Given this circumstance, he had borrowed large amounts from Woodward and Watson, whom he repaid when his bills were paid. Thus, the city's inefficiencies were in some degree responsible for the frauds. This explanation would be repeated often. It made some sense. The traditional slowness of the city in paying its accounts then as now far increased cost of goods sold to the city. It is a form of interest. What had this to do with Hall? Keyser could say nothing. Next was Garvey. He linked Tweed and Hall by testifying that Hall at one time asked him if Tweed had any knowledge of the warrants. He knew Tweed for twenty years, and the first payment made to Tweed was in 1867. Percentages paid were first 15, then 20, 30 and finally 65 per cent of the total bill. This testimony was new, more refined than the earlier one. Hall had not asked for any work on his home, but he had signed specific warrants and in 1867 suggested to Garvey's friend Ingersoll that Garvey send him a present. The plasterer sent a piece of silver. After that he presented an enlarged bill to the city. Garvey testified that he did not have an acknowledgment of the gift, but on the fourth day of the trial he almost miraculously produced "a copy" of a note from Hall on the silver. It read:

Dear Garvey,
I accept the Trust. I look less
at the fox and more at the grapes.
                    Yours truly,
                    Oakey Hall.

Beyond this he knew nothing connecting Hall to Woodward, Tweed or any fraud. It was during this testimony that Garvey explained something of his curious movements after the disclosures. He left New York on September 21, 1871, and went to England. He returned to the city via Canada on January 27, 1872. On cross-examination he revealed he had "conversations" with Peckham before and during trial, but would expand no further.

On the sixth day of trial, Stoughton summarized for the defense. He attacked the prosecution's case, pointing out that no proof had been presented to show any conspiracy on Hall's part to plunder the treasury or enrich himself. Hall's meritorious service to the city was well known and had there been a hint in his mind of Tweed's hand in the events, he never would have associated himself in any way with the ex-"Boss." If there was a devil, it was Tweed. The silver incident to Stoughton was like Bardell v. Pickwick in Dickens' *Pickwick Papers* in which the "warming pan, chops and tomato sauce" were made proof of Pickwick's intentions. In any event, a note by Hall was not produced, only an alleged copy. If Tweed and Connolly signed warrants and passed them to Hall, is Hall a criminal? Certainly Hall had no knowledge of any criminal intent. His duties were ministerial, simply to sign his name. Hall, "stainless" of any crime, is to say the least a "social exile," while Garvey, an admitted fraud, is allowed to walk the streets of the city he robbed, protected by the state. "Whatever may be your verdict, my client will be justified in the eyes of all men," Stoughton concluded. Hall shook his hand warmly. Tweed was in court, having been notified to appear in case he was needed. He was not called, however, and he left at the end of the day followed by a large crowd. The next day, Tremain summarized for the prosecution. It was a fiercely withering speech. Hall was used by thieves and plunderers of the city, but because of his political ambition he had maintained a blind eye on what was going on around him. There was proof presented, the case was clear. For example, the silver given to and accepted by the mayor. He had clearly evaded his responsibilities and was guilty of the misdemeanor as charged. Hall had examined Garvey's bills and knew what part was fraudulent. Given the admitted shrewdness and experience of Hall in government, was not this proof of Hall's guilt? It was true, there was nothing "in" for Hall, the mayor did not partake of the fraud, but Hall never did question Garvey. In fact, he helped him in settlement of his supposed debts.

Brady then charged the jury. He asked the members to judge honestly and without prejudice, and not to pay attention to public clamor or the press. Brady explained the terms. To audit is to examine, to adjust, to pass upon. This requires the exercise of judgment and the offense is willful refusal to do so. "Do these elements exist in this case?" asked Brady. Was there any audit of claims submitted by Garvey, Ingersoll or Davidson? The people felt Hall had not audited. The defense maintained that Hall's duty was ministerial. There must be a linking between Hall and Tweed as supervisor and Connolly as comptroller. If there was no willful design, then the defendant was not guilty. The jury retired. Numerous ballots were taken. The vote remained always the same, five for acquittal, seven for conviction. They returned to court and announced, "We cannot agree upon the question of willfulness and intention." The jury was dismissed.

There was still a third Hall trial, which began late in December 1873. It followed the same pattern as the others and differed only in that the presiding Justice Daniels told the jury there was no evidence of conspiracy on hand against Hall. It was during the trial that Allan Pinkerton's National Detective Agency was brought in by Attorney General Barlow, for of all things "shadowing" the jurors and their attending officer. For three days from December 22 to December 24, three operatives, M. H. McN., T.G. and L. B.S[egans]., and Robert A. Pinkerton, brother of Allan and superintendent of the New York office, spent considerable time at the bar and billiards room of the Astor House looking for any irregularities practiced by the jurors. The only irregularity that appeared was the most bizarre, if not dubious use, of the Pinkerton men. What did Barlow think they would find? Tweed or Hall passing money to the jurors? It would not be the only time such undercover agents like the Pinkertons would be used for this and other jobs. This linking of the agency with the prosecution is, to say the least, irregular. Anyway, the jury quickly found Hall innocent. Hall cried while the audience cheered its approval. But for the ex-mayor, his political career was finished. He tried playwriting, became a Roman Catholic and died in 1895, a man haunted by his unheeded protestations of innocence. The most innocent of all his pleas would never be believed.[10] Isn't that all that the *Times* and history really ever wanted?

One fish seemingly got away, but there were others. During the time of Hall's second trial, James H. Ingersoll and John D. Farrington, Jr., were indicted and arrested and also brought before Brady. Elihu Root and ex-Judge Fullerton represented the pair and though they protested that $5,000 was too much bail, it was set. Farrington was indicted for forging a bill of $15,138 for work on the new courthouse. Ingersoll, at the time one of the courthouse commissioners, was charged with securing the bill as part of a conspiracy. Now would they turn state's evidence? The answer was not long in coming.[11]

Even as the "omnibus" case against Tweed was being prepared, arguments over the civil case were also heard in October before Justice George C. Barrett sitting in Albany. He decided the question as to whether the city or state acting for the county had the right to bring suit to recover the "stolen" money by holding that both could bring suit. An appeal was unsuccessfully taken from Barrett's decision. The wheels of justice continued to grind on.

Now the "omnibus" indictment of October 17 against Tweed in Oyer and Terminer inched slowly back into the news. Judge Brady "willing to go to the front without hesitation," presided on November 18, as Algernon S. Sullivan, assistant district attorney, Peckham, representing the attorney general, and Lyman Tremain, as private associate counsel appeared for the prosecution. Tweed entered after Justice Brady was seated and sat behind his counsel, Beach, Field and Bartlett. Tweed's attorneys fired first. They accused Peckham of having an "intense feeling" of enmity against Tweed, a feeling which influenced all his actions. They demanded a complete list of witnesses who went before the grand jury and the minutes of the General Sessions for November 1871 through January 1872 to show that Tweed's indictment was upon wholly inadequate and contradictory testimony. Peckham pressed for a trial date. Brady took time to decide. The next day, he held that the names of witnesses asked for need not be given. Field now demanded that members of the grand jury appear for examination. This, too, was denied. Tweed's counsel wanted more time to examine the "improperly" drawn and "fraudulent" indictment. There was a demand to see existing vouchers. These could be reviewed, said Peckham, in the comptroller's office. Brady granted a one-week delay, enough time to make a motion to quash if this was required. Delay continued beyond a week.

On December 3, the case of the *People* v. *William M. Tweed* was called, but now before Justice Daniel P. Ingraham. On the same day, Peckham informed Tilden that the "deed is done. The man is appointed, and has assumed the office. Better say nothing till we meet and decide to act." "The man" is probably Noah Davis, since he is the one who usually presided at the Tweed trials. It was another example of the prosecution and the judge playing ball together. Crowds were there like vultures about a carcass, wrote a reporter. Tweed's affidavit to quash the indictment, principally on evidence that Peckham had been in the grand jury room, was read. Peckham admitted the point, but stated that he was there on the request of the district attorney and attorney general to prevent the kind of "difficulties" found in the Hall trial. An adjournment was granted at this time to allow those who wanted to attend Horace Greeley's funeral the opportunity to do so. The eccentric old man, who was badly defeated by Grant in the past presidential contest, had died on November 29. His spirit was broken partly because of a scurrilous and unconscionable campaign directed against him by journalists such as Nast. At one point he explained in exasperation, "I wasn't sure I was running for the presidency or the penitentiary." He had become a cartoon figure and the butt of jokes. In his own peculiar way, Greeley sympathized with Tweed. They both had gone through the same mill.

When the hearing continued on December 5, Peckham explained that he had every right to be in the grand jury room to aid the prosecution in any conflict. Field rebutted the next day. He pointed out that Peckham had appeared before the jury after announcing in the papers that Tweed was "the guiltiest man in the country." His prejudice made him unfit to be an adviser to the district attorney. Further, the grand jury is inviolate, yet Peckham forced himself upon it. It was an insensible and dishonest act. Field was probably right, but surely, one of the reasons for Field's anger was that Peckham was a member of the Bar Association's Judiciary Committee when the committee moved to investigate Field's role in the impeachment trial of Barnard which had taken place earlier in the year. There were revelations that Field had "unsavory" connections with the "Erie Ring," and had behaved improperly. In an impassioned and lengthy address to the association, Field denied any wrongdoing and reviewed his part in the Erie and Crédit Mobilier cases. He read letters of support from Murray Hoffman, noted juror, Montgomery Blair, former attorney general of the United States, Amasa J. Parker, ex-governor, and others. Despite Peckham and his sarcasm at the hearing, Field was cleared. The incident surely did little to add to friendship between opposing counsel.

On December 11, Justice Ingraham announced that Peckham was properly in attendance before the grand jury. While it was sometimes irregular for a prosecutor to appear in the jury room, he thought there was precedent for such an occurrence. The motion for dismissal was denied and trial was set for the following Monday, but it did not begin until January 8, 1873. "The man" was not yet ready to begin his job.[12]

It was during the year, while Tweed waited his turn before the bar, that the heavy hand of the law was directed against Justices Cardozo, Barnard and McCunn. Why these three? There are several answers. All were Democrats, all members of Tammany Hall. To members of the Establishment, like George T. Strong, McCunn and Cardozo were foreigners. McCunn, born in Ireland, was to Strong, the WASP diarist, "vulgar and ignorant" an example of the "scum of the popish persuasion," destroying New York. This was in keeping with his belief that the majority of Irishmen were "jackasses." Cardozo, one of the earliest Jewish judges in the city, if not the country, and highly respected, was simply "filth." His elevation to the bench was considered a blemish and blot on the legal escutcheon. To be rid of him and other Jews would be a blessing. As an example, Strong felt that the Columbia Law School, recently founded, had too many "little scrubs (German Jew boys mostly)" and urged that Latin be required for admission, hopefully reducing the unwanted, drawn from "grocery counters on Avenue B to be gentlemen of the Bar." As for Barnard, having a most acceptable ancestry, serving with Strong on a Columbia Law School committee, he was a traitor to his class, because of his association with Tweed—even though at a considerable distance. Strong had a lot of opinions about things. He found the last twenty years' work of the great artist William Sidney Mount "extremely bad." What else since "He had been living at Smithtown all that time, or elsewhere in eastern Long Island, that paradise of loafers, and amusing himself and his friends with his fiddle and pencil sketches." Richard Wagner he thought wrote like an "intoxified pig," Hector Berlioz like a "tipsy chimpanzee." After hearing the *Carnaval Romain*, Strong could "compare it to nothing but the caperings and gibberings of a big baboon, over-excited by a dose of alcoholic stimulus." Strong naturally was elected president of the New York Philharmonic Society.[13]

As for the judges, none of the three were Tweed's intimates. As with

Tweed, until the disclosures, there was very little innuendo or rumor of a conspiracy involving the trio. When the flood came, it came, also as with Tweed, as a sudden cloudburst, inundating all. The judges were as a group and as individuals highly regarded, especially Cardozo, but it did not help them. The first to feel the water lapping around his ankles was Barnard. At the beginning of 1872, a grand jury started an investigation into charges of corruption. Barnard was the major target. He appeared before the jury and gave them a list of those whom he considered his political enemies. He stated that if any evidence of wrong was uncovered, he would resign. He felt the *Times* and *Tribune* had started an unmerited campaign of vilification against him. No indictment was issued, but later, the Judiciary Committee of the Assembly began hearing allegations against Barnard and Cardozo brought by the Committee of Seventy and the newly formed Bar Association. Members of the Judiciary Committee included Samuel Tilden and David B. Hill, later governor. Of nine members, seven were Republicans. Two Democrats were from the city, with Tilden less than sympathetic. There were eight charges and many specifications. Barnard met with members of the committee on March 9, 1872, when he was given a list of specifics. Among them were that Barnard had issued writs of habeas corpus without the knowledge of the district attorney to some fifty persons in cases going back to 1867; that he did conspire with Fisk, Gould and others to "steal" the Albany and Susquehanna Railroad on behalf of the Erie, and "corruptly" to cause the arrest of the officers of the railroad. There were six specifications to this charge. Then was added that he gave a "corrupt" decision in denying a motion for alimony; that he discharged on habeas corpus six men arrested while attempting to register illegally in an election in which Barnard was running for office; and that he exhibited "great fanaticism" against certain litigants. He was also charged with making large and extraordinary allowances in certain cases to lawyers practicing before him; that his conduct on the bench was unbecoming and wanting in dignity; that he used bad language; that he abused respected members of the bar; and that he showed favoritism. It was a compendium of ills—but nothing to do with Tweed or Tammany, although the popular assumption was and is that he had been aiding "The Ring." James L. Coleman, a stockholder of the Erie Railroad, was produced as a witness. He testified that at a meeting in August 1869, Barnard was summoned to "Josie" Mansfield's house to meet Fisk and Gould. Coleman, however, denied that there was any truth in the charges that they were plotting together to obtain the Albany Railroad. Another witness said that Barnard had never once decided in favor of the Erie in any suit brought before him. In fact, he once decided for Vanderbilt, an arch-rival of Fisk and Gould.

Examination was resumed on March 15. Andrew Boardman of the firm of Benedict and Boardman testified that Barnard had a habit of rewarding friends, as example, in one case, Gratz Nathan, Cardozo's nephew, and Terence Farley were given "allowances." Andrews asked Boardman if he had appealed this action. The answer was no. Several persons knowing the Erie struggle were called but said little. Chief of Detectives James Irving, former ex-police commissioner, supported the charge that Barnard allowed four or five illegal voters to be set free, though he admitted they had been arrested without a warrant. Jay Gould was called and questioned on whether he had asked Field to have Barnard be the presiding judge in the Erie case. Gould replied, "No." He knew nothing of Barnard until he read the papers. Gould did remember seeing Barnard once in a opera box with Fisk, but also remembered Grant being with Fisk on another occasion. It was the only time he had seen Barnard and Fisk together. He remembered employing Tilden at a fee of $10,000, but Tilden did nothing and then turned up as counsel for an opposition railroad.

During the investigation, a meeting was held by the New York Bar Association's Committee of Extortions. On March 5, 1872, a long report was read, denouncing excessive overcharges and extortions practiced upon attorneys by the sheriff's, register's, surrogate's and county clerk's offices. There was a demand for a lessening of fees and charges. Perhaps this explains in part the attack on Barnard and the other judges. It was a way of putting fear of the Bar Association into the hearts of such officials, so that fees would be reduced else they might face the kind of inquisition that Barnard was experiencing. It was thus a form of extortion.

The Judiciary Committee next called Superior Court Justice John McCunn to answer for his conduct. The first complaint concerned his handling of the case of *A. B. Clark* v. *A. B. Bininger*. The plaintiff claimed a co-partnership with Bininger, a liquor dealer. The latter said he was the sole owner of stock when the partnership expired. Clark appealed to McCunn for a receiver; a Mr. Hanrahan was appointed. Creditors of Bininger & Co. then filed a petition in bankruptcy. Judge McCunn granted an injunction to stay the bankruptcy proceeding. Some of the creditors disobeyed the injunction and United States marshals seized the store. The receiver threw the marshals out. The United States District Court was asked to grant an order removing the receiver. A question was then raised whether the federal or state court possessed jurisdiction. Judge Samuel Blatchford of the federal bench ruled that the state court had authority, and Justice McCunn was right in ordering a referee. It was this case and McCunn's actions in it that were being questioned. If he was wrong, McCunn said at the end of his testimony he would bear the consequences, but he expected fair treatment. McCunn was given a respite, while Barnard's hearing continued.

Frank P. Blair was now called. He had overheard Barnard say while dining in the Astor House that he "had turned out one group of scoundrels" in reference to a question on an Erie railroad case in which Fisk and Gould were aided by his decision. Justice Ingraham was next and he explained that Barnard was influenced by political consideration in making decisions. Jay Gould followed, and he denied giving any money to Barnard in the Erie case or that Barnard had been used in any way.

The third judge, Albert Cardozo, was now brought forward. The Judiciary Committee, which held most of its hearings in the Fifth Avenue Hotel in the city, considered his case on April 4, 1872. It related to bank accounts. On February 21, Terence Farley withdrew $1,450 from his account, and on February 23 Cardozo deposited a like amount in his account. It seemed ugly. Farley testified he had used $1,400 to pay laborers, and had given $50 to his father. Cardozo's deposit was coincidental. Farley was then asked of the various receiverships to which he was appointed by Cardozo. Farley admitted he was an "intimate" political friend of Cardozo's and had supported him for office. He had received several receiverships, but there were no pecuniary motives attached.

Cardozo was relieved, and McCunn returned. Colonel Burton H. Harrison, who was engaged by the committee to look into McCunn's career, was asked whether or not he was a former private secretary to Jefferson Davis. There was no reply. McCunn attested to his own patriotism and read a portion of a report by a congressional committee which showed that he had helped enlist 1,600 Irishmen in the 37th New York Volunteers without receiving payment for his services. So much for flag waving. There were no sensational or even mild disclosures. It was felt McCunn need not be examined any more and the committee adjourned to attend the funeral of Professor Samuel F. B. Morse, the nativist, but also a talented painter and telegrapher, who died on April 3. However, the committee was not quite through. On April 6, more witnesses were called as the committee asked where McCunn's bank accounts were kept and who gave money to his election campaign. One Henry R. Stevens, a manufacturer of machinery, admitted he gave McCunn some money, but he never had a suit before McCunn.

The professionals in the Bar Association met again on April 9. They read a report admittedly "hastily" prepared and lacking "many specific acts," but which showed that the courts were in a state "not to be endorsed" and that corruption was evident. It concluded that certain judges must be removed. While the committee found no specific evidence of pecuniary corruption, some judges had received "presents" to help favored litigants. "The power to issue injunctions, appoint referees and receivers and make allowances, etc. has enriched favorites," regardless of the damage done to others. Barnard was also accused of siding with Fisk in a Union Pacific case causing a $5 million loss to creditors. He had ordered an insolvent bank pay Fisk, Gould & Co. $400,000, leaving other creditors without a cent. Transactions between Cardozo and Gratz Nathan were "suspicious." There was a grasping for straws. But above all, nowhere was there a connection with Tweed, "The Ring" and the judges. .

The Judiciary Committee then issued its report. It recommended impeachment of all three by the Assembly. Tilden of course seconded the report. David Hill spoke for the report's adoption, but added that though he found the judges guilty of unbecoming conduct and the granting of orders without due consideration, there was no evidence of pecuniary gain. Thomas C. Fields, though under indictment, still sat in the Assembly. He found that the report and the remarks of those in favor of impeachment did not contain facts sufficient to warrant such an act. While there may have been an indiscretion and folly, there was no evidence of corruption. The vote was 33 to 16 for impeachment. All sixteen voting against were Democrats. All members of the Judiciary Committee voted for impeachment. Many Democrats and some Republicans castigated by the *Times* as renegades were not convinced of the validity of the charges. Next the Assembly gathered a Committee of Managers to represent them in the Senate. Tilden was not named a member, although he wished to be. It was a victory of sorts for the trio.

The *Times* was livid. Could a fair trial be had with Tilden and others who fought through thick and thin for impeachment absent? It would be a "mock" trial and "mock" justice. Of course, it could equally be asked, would a fair trial be had if Tilden was part of the procedure?

For Cardozo, the message was clear, and rather than try to outride the swelling tide, and probably as part of an agreement that he would not be disbarred, or be subject to further charges, he agreed to resign. This decision obviously weakened the position of McCunn and Barnard. On May 11, no more than a few days later, William H. Leonard, Governor Hoffman's old law partner, was confirmed by the Senate, replacing Cardozo. Cardozo, a fine jurist, exited into an undeserved obscurity, his career shattered, though he continued quietly to practice law. His son, Benjamin, later became United States Supreme Court justice and supposedly went into law to clear his father's and his family's name of its dishonor. There was no evidence presented that it ever had to be cleared. The bell of tragedy tolled one.

Impeachment proceedings of Barnard and McCunn started before the president, the Senate and judges of the Court of Appeals. Their work began on May 23. Tilden crowed to his cronies of the Bar Association on May 28 that he was sure guilt would be proven; it had already been proven by the Judiciary Committee. McCunn's trial was first. On June 26, a lob was thrown up by McCunn. Under the terms of the law, impeachment needed a recommendation by the governor before the Senate could act, and no recommendation had been made. Further, the Senate could not review acts which allegedly occurred prior to his election to office. McCunn's counsel advised their client to resume his duties and leave the Senate to do as it pleased. If the Senate impeached, the courts would find otherwise. The Senate, regardless of technicalities involved, went about its business. John E. Parsons of the Bar Association addressed the body. It was not that they objected to the power of judges to appoint receivers, but the circumstances which attended it. In the Bininger case the expectant receivers went to McCunn's home at midnight, taking with them two bottles of wine. "Who heard of such a miserable bribe," said Parsons. The result of the midnight "revel" was the appointment of a "miserable fellow" to a receivership of over $300,000. McCunn also received $14,000 for his house "bled" from the Clark-Bininger matter. The corrupt conduct charge relating to this affair was passed 27 to 0. A second charge of conspiring to defraud in another case was passed by a vote of 27 to 0. Charges three through six involving corrupt practices were defeated, but impeachment was voted. A *Herald* reporter found the shaken judge at his home, an unassuming three-story brick structure at 208 West Twenty-eighth Street, and was admitted to McCunn by a "tidy Irish girl." McCunn did not feel well, but he would see him. The interior was modest, perhaps the home of a lawyer on $10,000 per year, the reporter noted. The paintings were of good taste. There were no pictures of Tweed, Connolly and Hoffman, etc. McCunn was in great physical pain, and spoke with difficulty. The reporter asked whether McCunn's dismissal was a blow to Tammany. McCunn brightened, "Tammany Hall, sir, is irretrievably gone. You might as well attempt to galvanize into life the dead carcass of Benedict Arnold." Can you outlive this blow, Judge? asked the reporter. "Outlive it! Yes, sir," McCunn smiled. "They have removed me illegally," but could not take away friends or books. "Mark this," McCunn continued, "I will come out of this as the pebble quit the ocean—brighter and more polished from the friction of the angry waves." He went on to discuss the trial. Rules of evidence were ignored, still, he told his interviewer, he could have gotten clear, he was sure, if he had been willing to pay $50,000. This had been suggested to him by a "party." He expected to carry the impeachment to the Court of Appeals. The interview ended. McCunn's wishes were not to be, but his ordeal was a short one. He died a few days later, probably of a heart attack, and his funeral services were held at St. Peter's Church on Barclay Street on July 8. Among the pall-bearers was Charles O'Conor.

Two down, one to go. The delayed Barnard trial was next. It was held in Saratoga beginning on July 17, 1872. The counsel for the prosecution included Colonel Burton H. Harrison, "a young, sharp featured fighting looking Southerner." Counsel for Barnard asked for a delay, since his client was suffering from the gout. A few days were granted, and on July 25 the court resumed. The prosecution began "Judges can be impeached for bad manners or for violation of the law." The first taken up was bad manners. They went to the "scoundrel" remark made not only in the Astor House, but in open court. This is not impeachable, objected counsel. Judge Martin Grover of the Court of Appeals decided to wait and see how the remark related to expanded evidence before a ruling. As for improper and corrupt conduct, a witness, Adrian Hersig, said he made chairs for the Erie Railroad and saw some in Justice Barnard's chambers, obviously an example of a payoff by the "Erie Ring." Barnard arrived after the trial began. His figure was straight and athletic, a soldier-like carriage, though he limped on a cane. He had "a handsome and dramatic" face. The first day was spent in going over the complicated Erie Railroad case and Barnard's relation to it. The affair was an attempt by Drew and Fisk to hoodwink Vanderbilt by issuing watered stock. Barnard granted an injunction to Vanderbilt ordering the pair to cease and desist. It was at this time that Tweed's, or better, Tweed Jr.'s name was mentioned. Barnard appointed him receiver during the litigation in 1869. There were witnesses who told of Barnard meeting Fisk occasionally. William Beach, another of Barnard's lawyers, insisted that the meeting was no proof of collusion. It was entirely hearsay evidence. The witnesses under cross-examination did not remember Tweed Jr. ever being a receiver. Ever ready Garvey was called and went over familiar ground. He had known Barnard for twenty years, the same time he knew Tweed. He had seen Barnard and Fisk together in Fisk's private opera box. He did fresco work in Barnard's house in 1868 and 1869 and was never paid. Was Garvey ever paid for anything? Barnard, Garvey noted, said to him one day, "I wish some work done on my house and I can have any work done I want; I have seen Mr. Tweed." The work was done and amounted to $1,000. On cross-examination, Garvey, hazy on details, could not quite remember where he saw Barnard. Beach brought defense witnesses. David D. Field did not hear Barnard say anything of rascals and scoundrels, though he was present in court when the supposed incident took place. He never saw Fisk and Barnard together. Thomas C. Durant of the Union Pacific, however, said the rascal remark was made and meant, he felt, to be a bit of blackmail by Barnard to frighten Union Pacific officers. Beach also showed that Tweed and Connolly bitterly argued with Barnard to stay the injunction issued against Drew and Fisk, but still Barnard went ahead. Surely, Beach argued, this was not collusion. Dr. Henry F. Quackenbush explained the chairs. He testified that one day he went with Barnard to Fisk's office. Barnard admired Fisk's chairs. They cost $55 each, but Fisk sold them for $50 to Barnard, who wanted them delivered without the Erie monogram. On August 7, John H. Strahan, one of Tweed's counsel, was called for the defense. He told of Barnard's injunction against the city's further issuance of money and bonds. Barnard fought Tweed's attempt to remove the order. Other judges refused to issue the injunction, but he had the courage to defy "The Ring." James Garvey, Andrew's brother, also told of work in Barnard's house. This was followed by the revelation that Barnard made use of liquor in Jo McBride Davidson's store. Beach countered by calling a parade of witnesses to testify as to Barnard being a model of purity and conscientiousness. By mid-August, the Senate went into secret session.

Barnard was found guilty on twenty-four of thirty-eight articles, some of the guilty counts by split votes. This was also true for some not guilty counts. Most of the guilty articles related to improper conduct, especially in actions involving the Erie Railroad. These included a guilty vote on appointing William Tweed, Jr., a receiver of the Union Pacific and the appointment of receivers to various companies. On the conspiracy charge, the vote was not guilty. As to the chairs and the bribery charge, not guilty. He was found not guilty in using indecent language at a divorce trial or in the "scoundrel" incident. The vote on removal followed and was 33 to 2 in favor.

What the trials did not prove was any specific connection of Barnard with Tweed, except in a nebulous way. At another time, the charges would probably never have been raised, impeachment never contemplated. But these were witch-hunting days. The decisions were a triumph for the Bar Association and reformers. Judges, the *Times* felt, had learned a lesson.[14] Surely, a very severe one, one death, one resignation, two impeachments. Were the verdicts really justified? Strong cackling in his diary was delighted.

> Very good as far as it goes. But downright Bishop Latimer would have gone a step further. There lacks hangum tuum, a Tyburn tippet to take with him—. Latimer is right. Barnard's skeleton neatly hung on wires in a glass case should print a moral and adorn the new court house.[15]

What would Strong have done to Tweed?

Senate investigators were kept quite busy, not only with the justices, but for a good part of the year with bribery charges brought against Senator James Wood, of Geneseo, chairman of the Judiciary Committee. As the Senate committee sat in the St. Nicholas Hotel, someone whispered to Tweed, "This seems to be the era of investigations." "Yes, it seems to," answered the venerable "Boss," moving his eyes to the ceiling, as was his habit. Tweed, Hugh Smith and a number of others were called to the secret session. The charge against Wood was that Tweed and Jay Gould had given him bribe money for his vote. Wood held the money was a loan. During the hearing, Tweed testified that while he tried to influence all senators, especially on the tax levy, and he spoke to Wood and indeed lent him money, he knew of no bribery; anyway, he did not need his vote on the tax levy. Wood in a "moment of weakness" borrowed $15,000 from Tweed in September 1870, the money from Gould was used in a whiskey business. It was, Wood insisted, a legitimate transaction. The committee heard enough to issue a long report finding Wood's "conduct inconsistent with his position as senator." The evidence was not conclusive, and Wood was not impeached. This surely was an era of indictments.[16]

23

Then Tweed

Tweed's trial was renewed in Oyer and Terminer on Tuesday, January 8, 1873, before "The Man" Justice Noah Davis and an excited crowd. Feeling that it had its strongest case on the October 17 misdemeanor charges, the "omnibus" indictment, the prosecution proceeded on these, rather than on any one of the seven felony indictments which had been handed down between 1871 and 1872. None of these were ever pursued.

Apparently the prosecution felt that it could not prove any of the felony charges, that they had no proof of theft, and therefore proceeded on what was really a technicality, that Tweed like Hall had failed to audit. Although, as has been stated before, history has pictured Tweed as a thief and larcenist, this is something for which he was never tried, and consequently could never be found guilty of. If he were guilty of theft, why not try him for theft? Why use a subterfuge?

Justice Davis, now fifty-five years old, was born in New Hampshire and appointed to the New York Supreme Court in 1857. In November 1868 he resigned to seek a seat in Congress as a Republican. After a year, he resigned as congressman to become a United States attorney for the Southern District. He resigned that office upon his election to the New York Supreme Court in December 1872 in time for the Tweed trial. He was back where his career had started. He remarked of himself at one time, "It is my nature to form strong convictions." Tweed would have reason to say "Amen." Davis became Chief Justice of the New York Supreme Court after loyal service and duty.

If Davis had been hand-picked by Peckham and Tilden, and there is evidence he was, it would not have been a novel approach. Nor could they have found a better choice. A Republican, an active reformer, aware of political nuances, he would provide the necessary "proper justice." Surely, they had an especial friend in court in Davis. Tweed's counsel suspected all manner of manipulation was afoot, but knew of no specific deed. Tweed was in fact being led like sheep to slaughter.

Tweed, bright and cheerful, entered into the court with his array of counsel, John Ebenezer Burrill, David Dudley Field, William Fullerton, Willard Bartlett and Elihu Root. His sons, William Jr. and Richard, were present. Peckham and Tremain represented the prosecution.

Wheeler Hazard Peckham, ambitious and anxious, seized an opportunity to direct the Tweed investigation—at a price. Like so many others, he found a chance to expand his career in the cause of political reform. Impatient for his work to commence, he was a true "Tiger."[1] He became president of the New York Bar, district attorney, and received a nomination to the United States Supreme Court from Cleveland. He was not confirmed.

The first order of business was the selection of a jury. There were some hundred names available on the jury list, but of that number, only twenty-eight showed up for examination; the rest were fined $250 each. Tweed's trial or not, jury duty was and still is not the most attractive prospect. The first potential juryman was excused after relating that he had concluded on the basis of newspaper reports that Tweed was guilty of frauds. The first accepted juror who said he was impartial was Louis Arnheim, a clothing dealer. Henry Warren, also in the clothing business, was sworn as well. Having exhausted the list, another panel of one hundred was ordered. From this list John D. Hamlin, auctioneer, John S. Rockwell, a liquor dealer, Henry Hazelton, piano manufacturer, Thomas M. Roche, produce dealer, Denison R. Parker, in the oyster business, Patrick J. Keary, toy dealer, Richard Dawson, liquor dealer, Samuel C. Hine, restaurateur, Henry M. Williams, claim agent, and Solomon Marx, shoemaker, were drawn. The jury was chosen during January 8, 9 and 10, days of considerable disagreement between prosecution and defense. The major difficulty was in finding unprejudiced jurors. George Strong ridiculed a system that required jurors to have no opinion and to have no common sense. He longed as usual for the days of Judge Jeffreys, England's notorious hanging judge.

The hearing of testimony was set for Monday, January 13. Peckham opened the proceedings on the 220-count indictment and for ten hours basically repeated the same charges he had made in the Hall case. Taxes rose from $10 million in 1860 to $20 million in 1870. Under Section 4 of the April 1870 law, a "board of audit" was created to examine all claims pending against the city. Claims were accepted and paid without examination. Connolly, Hall and William M. Tweed had approved between May 5 and September 1, 1870, claims of $6,312,000, which were all "false, fictitious and fraudulent." Now a new twist. Tweed had bills made up, approved them and induced the other members of the "board" to do the same. It was Tweed who was responsible for the whole fraud, but again this was not what he was accused of. Six million dollars were acquired in three and one half months on bills drawn principally by Garvey, Keyser, Ingersoll and G. S. Miller. Of that sum, over $900,000 was deposited in Tweed's account, plus an additional $384,000 on his behalf deposited in the New York Printing Company account. Thus, the "boss thief of the world" forced Garvey and the rest to hand over the "lion's portion" of their earnings including $50,000 to be used to lobby in Albany. Peckham rehashed details about the work done on Tweed's and Woodward's homes in Connecticut. Charges leveled against Tweed were admittedly misdemeanors, Peckham announced, punishable in total by a fine up to $250 and prison up to one year. But the punishment of Tweed was not the purpose of the case. It was to protect in the future the "interests, safety and permanence of society and the community under which we live." Curiously, no attempt was made to question non-county bills amounting to hundreds of thousands of dollars paid by the city to the contractors even through 1871. Bills going back certainly to the sixties were never questioned. It could be inferred that the prosecution was not interested in the contractors, had no evidence of fraud and could "nail" Tweed only on the audit charge.

Field opened for the defense and moved for dismissal. He argued that the now famous Section 4 was illegal. Passage of the tax levy, had to be by a two-thirds vote of each house. Since the bill was not passed by such vote, the act was not in force. Secondly, the appointment by the legislature of the "board of audit" was unconstitutional. Field cited a number of decisions on this subject, including one by Chief Justice Marshall, which held that "no member of the legislature shall receive any civil appointment . . . from the legislature during the time for which he shall be elected." If he was to be tried, let another indictment be found. He could not be chargeable for not having performed or fulfilled an office which he did not legally have. Tremain rebutted Field's technicalities as "frivolous arguments." If the defense was upheld, Tweed could never be indicted for any crime. The public would be without redress. Although the two-thirds vote was not certified, in fact the bill passed both houses by three-quarters vote. As to the second point, Tweed as member of the old Board of Supervisors had these powers continued in the new "board of audit." It was a continuation of an old appointment, not a new power. Tremain cited decisions in favor of this view. A series of discussions followed and Davis overruled Field's motion. He regarded Tweed as an active officer fulfilling his duties, never questioning the constitutionality of his office.

A dense fog covered the city as the trial continued the following day. Deputy Comptroller Richard Storrs was recalled. The day before he had told of seeing various vouchers in his office signed by Hall, Tweed and Connolly. Some shown as evidence were dated after July 1870 when Tweed ceased being a member of the Board of Supervisors and were objected to. Field was overruled. The court held Tweed was a de facto officer. A heated argument ensued, but the court held to its decision. When Storrs was asked about the "stolen" vouchers, the defense objected and stated that there was never any proof of the burglary, nor that Tweed was responsible for the "lost" papers or had ordered them destroyed. The court ruled against these objections.

William S. Copland and Stephen Lynes followed with their recollections. Lynes admitted he knew nothing of the stolen vouchers, and could not link Tweed with them. Judge Davis recalled for the jury Storrs's testimony that Tweed's signature was on the "stolen" or "lost" vouchers and warrants, and such evidence was thus admissible.

The defense attempted to show that the "lost" vouchers were mere "forms." Hall and Connolly were responsible to themselves; Tweed could and did not control them, and since the indictment was no conspiracy, their acts could not be attributed to him.

The next day Garvey and Davidson were brought forward. At the mention of Garvey's name, Tweed "looked like a lion restrained." His rage was clearly visible. Davidson, the safemaker, testified again as to a claim of $16,940 which was raised by a warrant to $49,170.49 out of which he received his claim from Watson. Unlike the second Hall trial Davidson's testimony was not challenged. Davidson said he endorsed the back of the warrant, and was not shown the amount on the face. On cross-examination, Davidson admitted he never saw Tweed, but dealt only with Watson and Woodward. It was Watson who physically prevented him from seeing the front of the warrant. At the time he knew nothing of any fraud.

Garvey now came forward. He moved deliberately and assuredly. When Garvey told of his claims against Woodward and Tweed for personal work, the defense reminded the court of Garvey's involvement and interest. Garvey had been indicted for forgery and his testimony must be carefully weighed, especially as Watson was dead and Woodward driven away by "foundationless indictments." The court nevertheless admitted Garvey's testimony. Tweed, impatient and frowning, glared at the tall, immaculately dressed plasterer. Tweed's arm twitched, he muttered low, inaudible snarls. Garvey later said Tweed's words were "blasphemous." The witness now spoke rapidly and nervously as he did at the Hall trial. He was owed $395,000, mostly for work done for the city. Woodward and Garvey agreed to a settlement. Garvey should make out bills so that 35 per cent would be sufficient to repay him. The bills were first made out in April 1870, and subsequently as required. Seven warrants handed to the witness were identified as being drawn in his favor by "Jimmy" Ingersoll. The defense objected to the name "Jimmy" as connotative of "a burglary tool." They were overruled. Garvey identified warrants totaling $1,177,000, of which he received $395,000. Garvey gave his check for 65 per cent before drawing that amount. The bills had an audit certificate attached on which Tweed's, Connolly's and Hall's names appeared most of the time. He knew that money was deposited by Woodward to Tweed's account at the National Broadway Bank. Garvey made three deposits like that himself. He also told of giving $10,000 to William E. King, deputy commissioner of public works. He amplified earlier statements. Ingersoll came to him and said the "old man" wanted $50,000; $25,000 from Keyser and $25,000 from Miller. He gave a $40,000 check, and included the earlier $10,000 given to King to make up the $50,000 that was taken by his brother to Tweed in Albany. He remembered a receipt of $60,000 to cover Tweed's Greenwich work and being told by Tweed to say to anyone asking that the money was from Watson. "That was a few days before they got me out of the country," about September 13 or 15, 1871. The defense claimed the testimony should be stricken, and Garvey changed his answer to "before I left the country." This part of Garvey's testimony was new. He had not said anything about this in the Hall case. Time had jogged his memory.

The trial continued on January 20, 1873, as the defense started its cross-examination of Garvey. First he testified that he knew nothing about a letter from the attorney general directing that the "plasterer" not be prosecuted on civil suits, but then admitted it had been shown to him briefly by Sheriff Brennan. Yet, the defense asked, how was it possible for the witness to repeat the letter practically word for word? Justice Davis refused to allow the letter as evidence. The defense pressed the point, was Garvey part of an arrangement to give evidence and escape indictment? The witness answered in the negative, and added in emphasis, "I am aware I must tell the truth." Asked whether he knew that in his previous testimony concerning the frauds he had opened himself to criminal prosecution, Garvey answered, "I believe I am slightly culpable," but despite the consequences he was determined to "tell the truth." "O'Conor told me if I told the truth on the stand and they were to be the judges, no harm would come to me."

> Q: What did you mean, then, by saying that you are here to tell the truth regardless of consequences?
> A: I mean I am gone; I am lost, unless I tell the truth I am a lost man.
> There was laughter in the court.
> Q: Who are the judges?
> A: They.

Q: Who?
A: The people.
Q: How can they all hear what you say?
A: I suppose it is Mr. O'Conor.

Garvey then admitted that he had twice visited O'Conor at his home shortly after he returned from England. He used his middle name Jeffreys in registering for the return voyage, and in Europe he was known as Andrew Jeffreys. Again laughter in the courtroom. He and his wife were driven to leave the country. The ticket was obtained for a McDonnell, another assumed name. He returned when informed O'Conor asked him to "tell the truth." He could not remember the dates of his passage too well, but could remember the attorney general's letter detailing his immunity almost line by line, defense counsel repeated. Davis interceded and told the jury "the witness went away to evade proceedings against him." Defense counsel held it was his own "guilty conscience" that made him leave. He left with a large quantity of gold and jewelry received from the sale of his real property. Davis instructed the jury to the fact that Garvey returned and gave evidence "under a promise that he would be exonerated from harm." Defense counsel pressed the concession and then tried to show that the attorney general "selected the guiltiest man of the lot and promised him a pardon, without coming here to get the consent of the court." Davis held he had a right to do so; Tweed's counsel replied that he had no right to appoint a deputy [O'Conor] to make the arrangement. Davis tried to end the debate on this point. Field, despite Davis' frowns, continued to question Garvey's relationship with the prosecutor. When did Garvey go to the grand jury? It was on October 17 and October 22, 1871. He also held about a dozen conversations with Peckham in February 1872.

When did he last call on Peckham? He responded that he was with Peckham for about twenty-five minutes the night before. The question of what they spoke about was objected to by Peckham. The objection was sustained and exception taken. He met Attorney General Barlow once at Barlow's house. Counsel wanted a copy of statements Garvey made. Overruled. Garvey was asked about his financial affairs. He had given his wife a gift in 1870 of jewelry valued at $30,000. He thought he had $275,000 to $500,000 in property. He followed with a confused "rigmarole" when defense counsel sarcastically suggested that a "Philadelphia lawyer be telegraphed to take care of this witness." Davis answered: "Don't bother with Philadelphia lawyers. We have lawyers enough here already."

Garvey returned to the stand on January 21, 1873. What was the "truth" of bills presented for $395,000? It was $240,000. All the items in the bills were true, work had been done, but the falsity was in "running out" the items. He admitted he was not compelled to enter $5,000 of the

$395,000 to cover election expenses. How many times was Tweed's name written across the warrants? Garvey was asked. "I can't say," he replied. He admitted he never examined them. Counsel then produced various bills from 1867, all supposedly signed by Garvey, though some of them he claimed not to have signed. Davis asked, "What is the purpose of the questioning?" Counsel replied, "Garvey swore Mr. Tweed told him to add fifteen percent." Garvey supposedly asked Tweed what that was for, and Mr. Tweed replied, "that's for me, put it on, and I'll take care of your bills." Now we offer here proof "that he swore the bills [in 1867] were true [honest] which he [now] says were false and that in other words he was not only a thief, but a perjurer." There was no such arrangement. Davis impatiently retorted, "The Court cannot sit here until Doomsday to try the issues. You want to go into every case where he made an affidavit and prove there was perjury." The justice refused to permit further questioning along this line. Field went on another tack. He asked Garvey whether he ever saw warrants in the name of Fillipo Donnarumma, or T. C. Cashman or R. J. Hennessey on which Garvey supposedly had endorsed their names and drawn the money. Garvey replied that he did not endorse Donnarumma. He did receive warrants for Cashman. He first thought Cashman an imaginary person, but then admitted a Cornelius Cashman worked for him, and Fillipo Donnarumma, a payee on a warrant, was an ornamental painter on Third Avenue (51 Third Avenue), formerly in Garvey's employ. A harried Garvey now admitted he accepted these warrants in Donnarumma's name after a conversation with Watson. Who endorsed Phillip F. Dummar in place of Donnarumma? Garvey admitted he did. First Garvey refused knowing an R. J. Hennessey, but he did know J. R. Hennessey, and then agreed that he did endorse a $32,695.63 warrant for R. J. Hennessey and deposited the money in his bank. Several bills to T. C. Cashman and J. G. Penchard were signed by Garvey as payee and he deposited the money, although he assured the court he received only a "small proportion" of the deposits. There were prosecution objections. The defense counsel replied that this line of reasoning was to show that Garvey used names of persons he thought would be undetected, slight variations were tried to protect himself, but the endorsements were forgeries, and "instead of this witness being coerced into this system of speculation, as he alleges, in order to obtain the money actually due him, he was engaged independently by these devices for his own benefit."

These admissions are very important in understanding the means by which many frauds might really have taken place. Garvey was never indicted for presenting false bills; he had been indicted for forgery, as for example, endorsing Donnarumma's, Cashman's and Hennessey's names. These forgeries were never linked to Tweed or "The Ring." They were

Garvey's way of defrauding the city, something which he admitted in his testimony. The idea was his, Ingersoll's, Miller's and the other contractors', all of whom were indicted for forgery—none of whom were brought to trial, except for Ingersoll—and in his case because he refused at first to turn state's evidence. Though admitting presenting false bills and these forgeries, Garvey was never punished since he was willing "to tell the truth." It would seem that the "gigantic frauds" were not really planned by "The Ring," but rather were individual frauds carried out by the contractors, partly as a result of the city's delay in paying its bills. This view was a keystone in Tweed's defense. The court, however, struck all of this evidence, saying it was not relevant to the issues before the court.

This is an interesting view—for certainly the reliability of a witness is relevant and if he can be shown to be a thief and a perjurer, his testimony must be considered in that light. Nevertheless, the court struck the entire line of questioning.

Garvey was asked by the defense if he thought it was wrong to be paid money to which he was not entitled. Garvey replied, "I regret to say I didn't think much about it at the time." He admitted that he did not see Tweed actually sign vouchers given to Woodward.

On redirect examination, Garvey related that he had business with many people, many establishments, Jay Cooper, the Olympic Theater, the Church of St. Vincent de Paul and Vassar College among them. In 1867 he was worth $100,000 to $200,000 and before he went to Europe over $500,000. His assets came from real estate and his business with the city and county. The court permitted Peckham to question Garvey on his motives for his departure. He first saw supervisor Walter Roche at the latter's home on Fifty-fifth Street. Doors were closed "mysteriously" after him. He was told by Roche to leave town as his life was in danger. Defense objected and was overruled.

Garvey left the stand and was followed by his brother John, who was asked by Field whether the reason for his brother's return was an interview with city authorities and O'Conor. John Garvey answered, "No, sir." Hadn't he seen Peckham prior to the trial? He answered in the affirmative. Field then related a detail brought out in the Barnard impeachment in which John Garvey said he had not informed his brother about negotiations with city authorities prior to his return. Garvey admitted this, but explained he did not consider Peckham a city authority. He could not remember details of a conversation with Tweed, nor would the court permit questions about a conversation with O'Conor regarding immunity.

John H. Keyser was called the next day. Keyser was shown certain bills. Peckham asked what percentage of the bills were correct. Keyser answered two thirds. The bills were made up in the Board of Supervisors room in the presence of Watson and Woodward. He never attended "board of audit" meetings and never saw anyone including Tweed sign the vouchers. Warrants were given to Watson and Watson paid the money. All of the bills exhibited to Keyser he claimed had forged endorsements. Field asked if 33⅓ per cent added to bills was to cover trouble and delay in collecting them. Keyser agreed that was so. The bench asked a question as to the propriety of such an addition. In reply, Keyser said he did not expect to receive any part of that percentage. Arthur E. Smith, bookkeeper at the Broadway Bank, was next. He kept the Tweed and Woodward accounts. He produced the Tweed ledger and it was admitted over objection. He testified he never personally delivered any passbook to Tweed. He kept records of withdrawals. Woodward, not Tweed, made the transactions, he thought. On May 17, 1870, withdrawals were $333,626.06, balance $41,395.41. July 11 withdrawals $934,343.84, balance $63,922.74. October 17 withdrawals $382,823.52 and balance $16,417.11. He had a record of one deposit. On December 15, 1870, there was a deposit of $60,000. This last evidence, however, was not admitted, as it might prove a felony and be used at a later trial.

"Sammy" Tilden came next. The crowd stirred. Even Tweed seemed relieved that the wearisome testimony would be changed. Tilden produced his accounts, in the compiling of which he was aided by Edward Cooper's bookkeeper and "one of his boys." Field objected. Tilden was not an accountant. He objected to presentation of information volunteered and not called for. Overruled. Tilden was then shown individual warrants dating from May 1870, including one for $28,434.21. Yes, a like sum was deposited to Tweed's account, but the deposit checks themselves were missing. Tilden could not tell if they had been taken from the bank or not. John H. Draper, secretary of the grand jury in November 1871, testified he had not seen the deposit checks of anyone but those of the New York Printing Company. A Mr. Allen of the District Attorney's Office stated the checks could not be found. Tilden was recalled. Garvey had withdrawn $88,316.19 and at the same time that this sum was deposited in Woodward's account on May 31, 1870, Woodward then withdrew $30,996 and Tweed's account showed a similar deposit. Three warrants to Keyser & Co. were exhibited for sums of $31,067.77, $28,093.70 and $16,924.62. Such sums were deposited in Woodward's account. Woodward withdrew $35,031.37 and on the same day the sum appeared in Tweed's account. There were several other similar transactions. On June 6, $64,411.68 went from Woodward to Tweed, on June 10, $66,513.38 was seemingly transferred. On June 13, $16,200 and $39,907.92 went from Woodward to Tweed. Monies went from Garvey and Ingersoll to Woodward's account, and paid from Woodward to Tweed. Tilden was ex-

hausted at the end of his testimony and the hearing was adjourned. Tilden returned to his Gramercy Park home, opposite the one owned by
Field. It was speculated that snowballs would be flying between the two
houses that winter night. Court resumed on January 27, the fifteenth day
of the trial. Tilden took the stand again as figures, checks rattled around
the room; defense counsel seemed too tired or confused to challenge.
Smith could not tell if deposit slips and checks were forged. Peckham
asked Tilden what was the sum total of Tweed's accounts from May 5
to September 1, 1870. He was at first too confused to answer. Tilden was
asked the sum total of deposits at the Broadway Bank. Tilden explained
that he had added deposit tickets, compared them with deposit ledgers,
and the sum was $1,287,453.50. This was different than on his earlier testi-
mony. Burrill could not see how the figures were related to the indictment. But Tilden continued. Total deposits to Woodward's account were
$3,639,618.30. Of this, $3,581,224.26 was from warrants. From June to August, Tilden found on examining the comptroller's books and bank ledgers
that the warrants to Garvey, Ingersoll and Keyser totaled $3,549,329.18.
What proportion of Woodward's account did you find as a percentage of
Garvey's account? asked Peckham. An objection was overruled. Tilden
said it was almost 66 per cent. Whenever a deposit was made by Garvey,
that percentage was withdrawn and put in Woodward's account. Woodward deposited 24 per cent to Tweed's account. Tilden's motives were
questioned on cross-examination.

Tilden admitted he was counsel on the civil suit and gave an affidavit
against Tweed at the time of Tweed's arrest and appeared against Tweed
in the Albany hearings. He also appeared before the grand jury as a witness.

Q: Have you and Mr. Tweed been in violent political antagonisms for
   years past,
A: We haven't generally sympathized very much (laughter in the court),
   but I never had any malice toward him. [Tilden admitted he opposed
   the 1870 charter but was not allied with the Young Democracy]—I
   acted on my own hook—an independent personal hook.

There was a roar in the audience. Davis tried to suppress laughter and
chuckled, "no other man than Sammy Tilden." It was Tilden's tone, ac-
cent and naïve expression that had everyone laughing as much as the
thought of Tilden doing anything independently. With the court quieted,
Field asked how did Tilden get at the bank books. Tilden now became ir-
ritated and complained of being browbeaten. He accused Field of insolent
and indecent conduct. Sparks flew. Tilden after a few moments said he
did so as a "member of the last legislature." He did not have a specific

process, but he did not say that nothing mattered as "long as Tweed was disgraced . . ." On questions relating to books and entries, Tilden again became confused. He needed the aid of Henry F. Taintor in going over the evidence. Field objected to this assistance. There were angry shouts. The air was charged and the court adjourned. It took Tilden off his "personal hook."

The next day, Wednesday, January 28, Tilden was again on the stand. He admitted he did not make a transcript of the books. This was done by his aides, George W. Cuitt and P. H. Rhodes. He thought he checked the Tweed transcript with the ledger and Woodward's account with deposit tickets. The bank officers had said they were Woodward's signatures. There followed questions about Tilden's accounting experience. Tilden again complained of being badgered by counsel. Field asked, "Have you not got up these tables with a view to this prosecution?" Tilden shouted, "No!" Field attempted to show that Tilden tried to push through a bill to prosecute Tweed; but this line of attack was stalled by the impatient judge. Field went at another tack. Didn't Tilden argue the Tweed case as well as the civil suit, in Albany in special term, presenting a brief against reducing the $1 million bail? The witness responded affirmatively. He also agreed to appear before the Sessions grand jury on a subpoena issued when the "jury was out of business," but he had the jury extend its term. With Tilden's testimony, the prosecution's case ended, and the defense began.

The first witness was Edward Gilbert, Garvey's attorney. Burrill asked if he had commenced a suit against Tweed in 1872. Davis asked the reason for the question. Burrill replied—to contradict the evidence of Garvey. Davis refused to permit the testimony. Undersheriff Joel Stevens was to testify as to the good character of Watson. He was excluded. Eugene Durain, a former commissioner of deeds who knew Garvey, wanted to testify that Garvey's bills were verified as true by Garvey. Davis excluded this as collateral evidence. An employee in the Public Works office, Charles T. McClenachan, was called to show how well Tweed did his job. He testified that Tweed signed his name hundreds of times a day on vouchers, warrants, etc. and under these conditions Tweed could not be expected as member on an audit board to get to the bottom of everything. Then why not resign if you can't do the job, asked Davis. Burrill said Tweed had only two months to prepare for his new duties as auditor. Still Davis held there was "no excuse for neglect." Testimony excluded. Evidence that Tweed took no oath as auditor was also excluded. William S. Copland was called by the defense even though he had testified against Hall earlier. He remembered seeing Garvey in the attorney general's office during the Hall trial. George H. Drew testified he knew Garvey and was asked if he

Broadway at Duane Street, facing south toward St. Paul's Chapel in the distance. Taken about 1870. Transportation on the famous boulevard, the center of fashion, was a major concern. The building of an elevated line or viaduct which could solve this problem was prevented by the fear of long interruption of business and traffic. This part of Broadway was still cobblestoned. (Courtesy of The New-York Historical Society, New York City)

ROMISH POLITICS—ANY THING TO BEAT GRANT.

A bigot, panderer to the coarsest tastes and morals of society, Nast depicted the Irish as drunken, brawling, ape-like creatures, Catholic clergymen as alligators, Negroes like simpletons and Tweed like a thieving vulture. Horace Greeley complained after seeing some of Nast's political cartoons of him during 1872's campaign that he didn't know if he was running for the presidency or the penitentiary. Nast has come down in American history as a model political cartoonist. (*Harper's Weekly*, August 17, 1872)

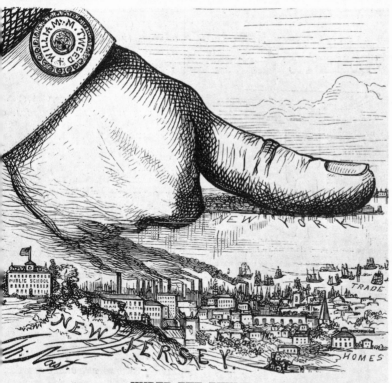

UNDER THE THUMB.

THE BOSS. "Well, what are you going to do about it?"

Above,
"What are you going to do about it?"
fiction by Thomas Nast but accepted
by history as fact.
Tweed never made such a
statement, but it was of no
matter. Nast repeated the phrase in
several other cartoons and reporters
frequently badgered Tweed with this
question after the disclosures.
(*Harper's Weekly*, June 10, 1871)
Right, Tweed photo taken by William
R. Howell of 867-869 Broadway
probably in 1871. Tweed was now
forty-eight. Reproduced here for the
first time. (Author's collection)

Lincoln's funeral procession along Broadway. A remarkable photograph capturing the crowds; the shuffle of a funeral march. Lincoln had visited New York only once just prior to his first inaugural in 1861. It had been a mixed reception. Now the mourning of the nation was as deeply felt in New York as anywhere in the country. (Courtesy of The New-York Historical Society, New York City)

Tammany Hall, headquarters of the Tammany Society. Erected in 1867, it was at 143 East Fourteenth Street. In 1868, at the time of this photograph, it served as the site for the National Democratic Presidential Convention. The decorations were for the event. Marschall & Milhauer, piano dealers, were at 149 East Fourteenth Street. Daniel E. Bryant's Minstrel Show occupied part of the premises. It fit. Entertainment is never far from politics. The building was destroyed in 1928. (Courtesy of The New-York Historical Society, New York City)

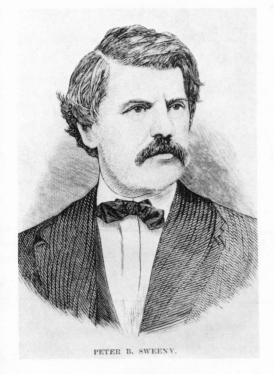

PETER B. SWEENY.

A composite of three members of the so-called Ring. Hall was found not guilty of any wrongdoing, Connolly escaped to France and was not tried. Sweeny, a frequent visitor to Paris, settled out of court with New York City. All protested their innocence, but their promising careers, especially those of Hall and Sweeny, were cut short. (Courtesy of the New York Public Library, New York City)

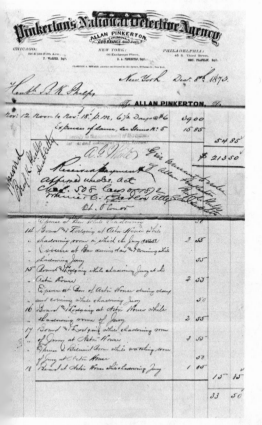

SHERIFF'S OFFICE

OF THE CITY AND COUNTY OF NEW YORK.

December 6th, 1875.

$10,000 Reward.

The above reward will be paid for the apprehension and delivery to the undersigned, or his proper agents, of

WM. M. TWEED,

Who escaped from the Jailor of the City and County of New York, on Saturday, December 4th, 1875. At the time of his escape he was under indictment for Forgery and other crimes, and was under arrest in civil actions in which bail had been fixed by the Court at the amount of Four Million Dollars.

The following is a Description of said WM. M. TWEED:

He is about fifty-five years of age, about five feet eleven inches high, will weigh about two hundred and eighty pounds, very portly, ruddy complexion, has rather large, coarse, prominent features and large prominent nose; rather small blue or grey eyes, grey hair, from originally auburn color; head nearly bald on top from forehead back to crown, and bare part of ruddy color; head projecting toward the crown. His beard may be removed or dyed, and he may wear a wig or be otherwise disguised. His photograph is attached.

WILLIAM C. CONNER,
Sheriff.

Left, unique example of the secretiveness employed by a suspicious prosecutor during the Tweed trial. Pinkertons were used quite often for similar kinds of shadowing; usually this was unknown to the victim and unknown by the public. (Historical Documents Collection, Queens College, New York City)

Right, escape notice distributed by Sheriff William Commer at his own expense, since he was held responsible for Tweed's escape. A similar notice was used to identify positively the escapee in Spain after his capture. (Courtesy of The New-York Historical Society, New York City)

Tweed, alias John Secor, on his arrival in Spain. Compare the tired, frightened old man with the Howell image or the "Solid Men." Tweed was fifty-three. (National Archives, Washington, D.C.)

Alias William Hunt, Tweed's companion in Cuba and in Spain. Was he a Pinkerton agent? A government spy? No one ever questioned him. Instructions from the State Department to Spanish authorities were to release him. (National Archives, Washington, D.C.)

heard Garvey make a certain remark off the stand. "Why this question?" asked Peckham. To show that Garvey said, "I will send Tweed to state prison, if I hang for it," Burrill replied. Davis ruled against admissibility.

January 29 proved to be the last day for presentation of evidence. Again, an audience packed the court. The impressive array of counsel underlined the importance of the proceedings. Tweed and his sons listened quietly and intently to the first summations. Field asked that testimony regarding vouchers, certificates and warrants not relating to the indictment be stricken out. Davis overruled and Field took exception. Fullerton rose to address the jury on behalf of Tweed. He alleged that the prosecution, aided by the attorney general, with the best private counsel in the state and supported by an excited and a tyrannical public press urged on by "unreasonable public opinion," had done all to bring conviction. There was nothing in the "history of litigation to parallel this effort." Before and during the trial, the public had been whipped to frenzy, the jurors intimidated so they could bring in only one verdict. Fullerton attempted to read some newspaper articles on the subject. Davis restrained him. His summations must concern only the evidence. Fullerton shrugged and continued. The whole case arose from the 1870 act, Section 4, and the basic question was one of motives and evidence of deliberate intent. The so-called "board of audit" had a ministerial responsibility in examining bills. If the legislature passed a law that bills presented by O'Conor and the attorney general should be audited and paid by the comptroller on the certificate of the pair, the comptroller would pay the bills—that was as far as his "audit" went. He could have pointed out the board as such was not named. The act provided only that there be three auditors. Moreover, under the charter, a specific auditing bureau was provided. Fullerton went on. The act of 1870 creating the board had a precedent in an act of 1867, when a similar board was created. Then as in 1870 the power of examining and swearing witnesses was not expected. Even if Tweed and the others on the board went to the armories and drill houses and inspected the courthouse, how could they tell if the work was done or was correct? They were not mechanics. They could not summon witnesses; they simply signed the necessary documents. They had ministerial responsibility and relied on Watson, not aware of his infamy and guilt, who as even Garvey stated, was a "man of judgment," and they accepted his word. The board did their duty; there is no evidence to the contrary. Garvey and Keyser never went before them nor need they have. Lastly, there was no evidence that Tweed directly ever shared in the proceeds or prepared false bills. This was done by Watson, Woodward and the contractors. Tweed's time was devoted to being commissioner of public works. Maybe he should not have accepted an additional post, but again, what was his intention or purpose? It was Garvey who made up false bills, who plundered the city, who lied, cheated and had a miserable excuse that he was forced to do so by Watson. He did not go to Tweed, Connolly or Hall to explain his case. He never mentioned his problem to anyone. He did not say that the city owed him money, that it did not pay on time, that he was forced to commit fraud, but rather willingly went to Watson and continued cheating. Watson, Garvey, Woodward, Ingersoll and Keyser worked together. They were the real "Ring." There is no evidence involving the auditors. Garvey broached the matter to Woodward and used Woodward in the scheme. Garvey did not deal with Tweed until 1870. And then it was Garvey who went to Tweed with a bill for $60,000 for work on the Connecticut houses. The endorsement on the bill suggested it was done after he returned from Europe in preparation as a witness. A conspiracy? Why didn't he see Tweed many times, why only Woodward, why not look at Tweed face to face? Tweed was not a friend or confidant of Garvey. Tweed did not make any deposit at the Broadway Bank. He did not know where and when the money was deposited or withdrawn. If money is found deposited today to the credit of one of the jury, even if money had been stolen, no one should conclude the juror knew it. Fullerton saw the case in this way. Garvey, the arch-scoundrel, was in the office with Watson. A warrant was taken apart in Watson's inner office; the certificate of audit was detached to be used again on another bill. Copland, who had exposed the frauds, testified that the certificates were sometimes wanting and first pages having Tweed's name were missing—this would appear on another bill and the conspirators would get the money. Existing vouchers mentioned in the indictment did not have Tweed's signature. "Tweed was as innocent as a child," Fullerton concluded. The conspirators' guilt was apparent by Garvey's flight. Tweed didn't leave. Why did Garvey return? It was to serve as prosecution witness and to be granted immunity. He even used disguise and secrecy after his return. Then he drove nine miles to O'Conor's home. There they decided if he "told the truth," the state would be satisfied. The "truth" were words to convict Tweed. Fullerton continued, "though by the breath of his [Garvey's] nostrils the doors of a prison are to be opened to receive Tweed. He says, I will come and tell all I know if I am only to be spared. Gentlemen, you all despise a thief and a liar, but this man Garvey sinks several degrees below either, as a perjurer and that loathsome thing, a public informer. The prosecution itself, though it loves the treason, hates and despises the traitor, the mean informer, whom that great Irish lawyer Curran, so eloquently denounced." Counsel then proceeded to quote authorities as to the caution with which the uncorroborated evidence of informers and accomplices should be received and ended, "Andrew J. Garvey stood alone here; he was not in any manner whatever corroborated.

Strike the testimony out and there is nothing left on which to predicate any wrong done by this defendant. And it would be a novel thing if it were to be left to this jury, in the nineteenth century, to convict a man, to sacrifice his reputation and his liberty, on the unsupported evidence of an informer."

Peckham then arose. The defense has presented nothing to controvert the facts. There were two questions to decide: did the defendent audit certain accounts and did he use his auditing power corruptly and fraudulently? The board could not delegate such power to Watson. The auditors, including Tweed, never audited any bill. Tweed signed bills not knowing, or at best not caring, if they were fraudulent, and Watson merely fixed his stamp after that was done. Tweed was guilty, not Watson or some underling like Woodward. As for public abuse, "the voice of the people is the voice of God." Field objected to this kind of language, but was overruled. Peckham concluded by saying that Garvey made a "clear showing" in his testimony. He appealed to the jury to say by their verdict "what is the standard that in America is demanded for a man to fill high position as a trusted and honored officer of the public." The next day, Mr. Tremain, his left arm in a sling, like an embattled warrior concluded the prosecution's summation.

Davis then charged the jury, and explained the meaning of the charges. Tweed as a member of the "board" (it should be repeated there was no board, but everyone used the term) had duty to audit liabilities against the city and county. Auditing, he continued, was more than mere signing of a signature. The board was responsible for its examinations and could not place the blame on others. The next question was that of willful neglect, conspiracy and the corrupt use of the auditing power. He reviewed the Davidson testimony. If Davidson charged $16,940 for safes, who altered it to $49,170.49? This money appeared to be given to Woodward, who transferred 24 per cent to Tweed's account. There must be a satisfactory account of the transfer. What would be a reasonable conclusion? Keyser claimed here was a strange mixture of new and old bills added to by 33⅓ per cent, which showed evidence that they were never audited. What would be a reasonable inference as to the auditing of these bills? Davis warmed to his task. Keyser's name on these bills was forged without doubt, and the transfer of money from Keyser to Woodward and Tweed showed a pattern of human "fallibility." Did Tweed answer the allegation of the $60,000 bill of Garvey? Yes, Tweed was not required to testify, but what was a reasonable inference? The case was not only important to the defendant and his family but also it was important to the community. Tweed was a high public officer. Were such officers having high trust to be held accountable for their proper fulfillment? Tweed was a servant of the people charged with seeing that the public was not plundered. Did the defendant fulfill that obligation? Short of asking for a guilty verdict, Davis could not have done more.

The jury began its deliberation. On Friday morning, January 31, 1873, as in the first and second Hall cases, the jury announced it could not reach a verdict. There were a clamor and shouts in the courtroom, as well as a good deal of pushing and shoving. Shouts of congratulation were directed at Tweed. Others muttered oaths. Slowly the room quieted and many left. After the tired jurors were dismissed, Peckham, disappointed, removed a toothpick from his mouth and moved for an immediate retrial. The jury should have found a decision. Perhaps another one will do its work better. Field, like everyone else, was tired and cross, and he found the motion for an immediate trial remarkable. Tweed's civil suit was to be heard in February, and counsel needed time to prepare. Public clamor and pressure should not be allowed to dictate to the court. Let violent, more important crimes be tried, a misdemeanor could wait. Peckham snapped he didn't feel the strain, and was anxious for the new trial—postpone the civil suit.

Tweed went to his Duane Street office. The ex-"Boss" felt all along that he would be acquitted since it was only a political trial. "Anyway, Peckham has got nothing else to do. Nobody ever heard of him till he got started in this reform business . . ." Tweed took a brief vacation, the only one he would have to the end of his life. In April, he went to Boston with his wife and two of his children and heard a performance of *Le Centenaire*. Sometime during the summer, he went to California, but just where and why is not known. Tweed had passed a hurdle. Much worse lay ahead. In looking at the trial, it seems clear the prosecution had a weak case. There was no direct evidence of Tweed's culpability; certainly little evidence of a "Ring," except that of the contractors. Garvey's evidence was especially weak, as Field and Fullerton pointed out. If he was made to fill out fraudulent claims, why not protest? Why not go to the authorities or to the press? Why agree to the swindle? He was not forced to do anything illegal. His seems the weakest link in the prosecution's claim. He seemed guiltier than anyone. What can be done to regain the money in Garvey's pocket, asked the *Herald* as it turned its attention to that subject, forgotten at least for the moment. Some historians have argued that the jury was of "exceptionally low character," that most of its members had little education or intelligence; several were liquor dealers. One was a "bummer" at the docks, and one had been a lobbyist for Tweed in Albany. The sheriff, a Tweed henchman, was accused of refusing to summon decent men. Sheer nonsense. Of course, the only thing wrong with the jury was that they did not arrive at the "correct" verdict.

The jurors generally refused to discuss their deliberations. There were from forty to fifty ballots taken. Thomas Roche, one of the jurors, denied any pressure was present to acquit Tweed and stated that the verdict was the result of honest convictions. The *Herald* reported that eight of the twelve were for acquittal, but that figure was not supported by jurymen. There was a rumor the vote was eleven to two for Tweed. "How was that?" asked a reporter, that makes thirteen jury men. Include the judge, that makes thirteen, said a relaxed Tweed. Clearly, majority voted for acquittal. Henry L. Clinton later wrote nine were for acquittal and of the three for conviction, two would have changed their vote if the last would. Tweed mentioned that he had received word that a juror was in the prosecution's hands, having several United States indictments pending against him. Perhaps this was the man that prevented his vindication and an end to his torment.[2]

Tweed's relief at the decision was short-lived. The flood of indictments, like rain from the sky, continued to inundate him. Fifteen indictments were handed down against him by the grand jury in Oyer and Terminer in February 1873. Six of the indictments were for forgery, seven for misdemeanors and two for felonies. They were issued by the grand jury, whose foreman was now merchant Hugh Auchincloss. An unsuccessful attempt was again made to quash all of these in view of their similarity to the December 1871 General Sessions indictments. Tweed pleaded not guilty on all counts, and like the earlier ones was never tried on any.

A new trial on the "omnibus" indictment was scheduled for early in June 1873, but was apparently adjourned because of the ill health of John Graham, who was now along with William Edelstein added to the staff of Tweed's counsel. And still other indictments continued. On June 16, several supposed members of "The Ring" were named. Michael Norton, ex-alderman Thomas Coman, James H. Ingersoll, John J. Walsh, John D. Welsh, Jr., Joseph B. Young, A. G. Miller and George Seaman Miller were charged with various counts of bribery, conspiracy and false pretenses. Eventually, by March 1, 1882, all of these were marked "Nolle Prosequi," which simply means that they were dropped and never prosecuted. Their purpose, however, was served even without trial. For the more indictments and the more "smoke" the more the public was convinced of "fire" and guilt. Then as now, indictments were too often used for political purposes. To the public, indictment usually means guilt, even if the matter is never brought to trial. The trial is not necessary and is an inconvenience forcing some district attorney to understand what the litigation is about. In this case, the June indictments were basically against the courthouse commissioners. Although having nothing to do with Tweed, they were intended to stir up public opinion against Tweed and were made to seem related to Tweed by the press.[3]

During the summer, preparations for the upcoming retrial were readied. Often when a jury disagrees and the majority of the jurors are for acquittal, further prosecution is ended. But this was Tweed, the stakes were high, and the prosecution, plugging certain loopholes, particularly in regard to jury "selection," went about its business. Then on November 5, 1873, Tweed, looking healthy and rested, together with his counsel appeared before none other than Justice Noah Davis. Peckham and Tremain were there as were Assistant District Attorney Henry C. Allen and attorney Henry L. Clinton, brought over from the Hall trial, who accepted a retainer from the attorney general, on behalf of the prosecution.

As soon as the trial began, there was an explosion in the courtroom. Davis was handed a note by defense counsel. He looked at the paper and flew into a rage and shouted that the contents were full of lies. Davis was charged by Tweed's counsel with being biased against their client, that his opinions would prejudice the impartiality of the jury. Since Davis had ruled adversely on important points in the previous trial, he would now be in a position to review his own decisions, something which was in violation of the spirit of the Constitution. The justice was asked to disqualify himself. The letter was signed by Field, John Graham, Willard Bartlett, Elihu Root, John E. Burrill and William Edelstein. Davis, his face flushed angrily, adjourned the court to discuss the matter with his colleagues. When he returned in the early afternoon, now even more upset than before, he heatedly denied all charges and implications. The statement, he held, was utterly false. He refused further argument on the subject and demanded the case continue, protestation of the defense notwithstanding. He hinted darkly of consequences to the offending attorneys, but still the haggling continued during the next days.

Bartlett asked the court to request, as in the previous trial, that the press not comment on the trial. Davis felt this was proper, but he could do little about it if they did. Then came the matter of selecting a jury. The first potential juror, Robert M. Orrell, a broker, was challenged by Bartlett. He was prejudiced. Davis ruled him competent and refused to hear another word on the subject. "Sit down, sit down," shouted Davis, his face red with anger as he hammered with his gavel. Defense, who were only given five peremptory challenges despite all the counts, now used one of these. A number of potential jurors were excused. Then David Palmer, a wine merchant, was asked by Fullerton whether he had said that those indicted for fraud were guilty. Palmer denied making the remark and the juror was ordered to a seat. He became the foreman. Davis would not permit any witnesses to be called to show Palmer's bias. Adolph Opper, a lace merchant, was the second juror accepted. Samuel Sinn, importer of clothes, became the third. The hearings were then adjourned.

On November 10, Theodore Goldsmith was called. He felt that Tweed was guilty, but he would listen to the evidence. He became the fourth juror, though the defense took an exception. Richard H. McDonnell, a resident of San Francisco doing business in New York, felt someone was guilty of fraud. The defense challenged him for cause, but Davis angrily refused to sustain the challenge and he became juror five. Daniel Webster Lebourveau, a stove dealer, had decided opinions on the case, he said, but would listen to the evidence. The court found him competent, the defense excepted. He became juror six. The seventh was William Schlemmer, a hardware merchant. David Bradley, a long-time resident of the Seventh Ward, had voted the Democratic ticket, but claimed that he did not know Tweed, nor his friends. He was peremptorily challenged by the prosecution. The jury selection continued on November 12. A new jury panel of 50 was objected to by the defense as being chosen from only 2,800 names, instead of from the entire available citizenry. Davis overruled the challenge. David Elihu Field, a jeweler, was called. He had put up a clock for the courthouse and knew Tweed as a customer. He was accepted by the defense, but the court rejected him, as having a "reluctant manner" in answering questions. Assistant District Attorney Allen raised a question about potential juror Elias H. Lubry. First accepted, he was re-examined when he was seen by Pinkerton James Wilkerson talking to a Captain Walsh, who was thought to be a friend of Tweed's. Defense objected to the examination of the juror and of Captain Walsh, who was nevertheless called to testify. He had known Lubry and Tweed for many years and had talked to Lubry about other matters. Davis discharged the juror, suspicious of his friendship with Walsh and Tweed. In the next days, a Mr. Mayo became the eighth juror. Nine became Alfred Schutzer. The tenth juror chosen was Frederick Lewis. He said he was "not perfectly unbiased" and asked to be excused. Davis denied the request. Mr. Simeon Davidson became the eleventh juror and William Sloane the twelfth.

During the course of the jury selection, rumors abounded that there was something wrong with the prospective jurors. The defense heatedly questioned the select jury panel available. But they had no proof of anything specific. There was reason to be suspicious. The Pinkertons were at it again. O'Conor, Attorney General Barlow and Benjamin Phelps were up to old tricks. Beginning with November 5 and ending November 18 four operatives J(ames) E. W(ilkerson), H. C. B(erman) and two from the Hall trial, M. H. McN. and L. B. S(egans) spent their time "shadowing" jurors and prospective jurors, as well as Tweed's brother, Richard.

They were at the barroom at the Astor House and at Cahills at 17 Park Row. As part of their "cover" they purchased cigars and had an occasional game of billiards. What would the operatives do if a juror went into a "house of ill-repute"? Well, it was all for the Agency. As with the Hall case what did they hope to find? Later Henry Clinton revealed the prosecution's manipulation of the panel. Having agreed rather reluctantly to work for the state, Clinton "proceeded at once to investigate the lists of prospective jurors and to superintend investigations of their character, business and associations." The key to conviction, Clinton, was convinced, was in finding a "proper jury." Instead of detectives to search for good jurors, a small army of young lawyers was employed. They made reports as to each prospect—stating his business, his character, integrity, what his neighbors and business associates said about him, together with any other point that was thought to be of importance; also an opinion as to whether he would make a good or bad juror. All the reports were pasted in a large black book. Clinton was thought that "probably no more thorough investigations as to the qualifications of jurors were ever made." Yet so sure were Clinton and the prosecution that Tweed was guilty that in effect they had a blue-ribbon panel and more than friendly judge to be sure of conviction. Such evidence today would have thrown the case against Tweed out of a fifteen-story window. Tweed might suspect, but again he knew nothing. Under such circumstances, Snow White would have been found guilty of loitering with intent to commit prostitution.

During selection, jurors were allowed to return to their homes as usual, "but each was 'shadowed,' that is watched by an officer of the Court." One day, Clinton continued, among those selected was "one who appeared to be an Italian." Clinton took a dislike to the man who had claimed he had never heard of Tweed. He had the juror watched and "before twelve o'clock that night he was traced in communication with Tweed." How in communication, with whom in communication? These are not answered. The next morning when the court convened the juror was dismissed with a scathing rebuke from Davis.

The first day of trial was November 15. It was a rehash of everything brought out in the previous suit. Arthur E. Smith remembered seeing deposit tickets of Tweed, Garvey and Ingersoll in the grand jury room, though these had since disappeared. He again repeated the deposits he found in Tweed's account. He thought he knew of some Tweed deposits in Tweed's own hand, but he was not sure when he made examinations of Tweed's account. Yes, he was now working in the comptroller's office, having been hired after leaving the National Broadway Bank in March 1872. His testimony obviously won him rewards. John L. Everett of the Broadway Bank saw Tilden select deposit slips, but these had also disappeared though usually kept in the bank for years. Tilden then returned. He had been well coached by Peckham who told him the questions he would ask, prior to the trial. He advised Tilden to have the written answers with him. Tilden then testified he had examined Tweed's account in the fall of 1871. The total amount of warrants in question in the indictment were $5,710,913.98. Deposits by Woodward were $3,581,224.26, less than his earlier testimony; checks drawn were for $932,858.50. These appeared as deposits in Tweed's accounts, again different than before. Withdrawals from Woodward's account often were penny by penny the same as deposits in Tweed's account. Tilden had printed schedules which were distributed to the jury. It prevented his embarrassment at the previous trial when he could not remember figures. The defense objected to the procedure and were overruled. Davidson took the stand next. He repeated his previous testimony. Next came John Garvey. He testified that he had seen Tweed several times in September. His brother had been threatened in Tweed's office by a Mr. Cook (possibly William Hennessey) and Walter Roche. He went away to save his life, not because of threatened lawsuits. This testimony was somewhat new, and given interestingly not by Andrew who allegedly received the threats, but by his brother.

Smith was recalled. Some of the deposits were in Tweed's handwriting, he now discovered. Previously, he said he had nothing to do with deposits, just with withdrawals and not by Tweed. Defense thought it strange that slips had disappeared, perhaps the bank was frightened of having accepted forged slips and would be made liable. John Keyser also came forward. He repeated his earlier testimony. After Keyser Peckham announced the prosecution case was closed. The star witness Andrew Garvey was not brought forward. Obviously, the prosecution now felt that his testimony could be as damaging to them as to Tweed. The defense counsel were not prepared for the sudden end of the prosecution's case. Elihu Root moved to dismiss the indictment. He argued that the statute under which Tweed was indicted made his neglect to audit punishable at most by a fine of $250. True he was a member of the "board of audit," but he counted on other city officials, Board of Supervisor auditors, as well as the mayor and comptroller. Bartlett maintained that auditing did not mean meeting, and that one man was not solely responsible for the actions of the entire board. The motion to dismiss was denied by Davis and the trial continued. The defense called Copland. He admitted that he did not see Tweed sign certificates to any vouchers. Copland numbered the warrants. Lynes made entries and would take warrants to Mr. Watson's office, where Keyser and Garvey were frequently present. Keyser said the warrants were forged, yet Copland said he was present when they were made out. Not all the vouchers were returned to pigeonholes. When returned they were loose, with a comptroller's certificate and certificate of audit often missing. There were erasures on warrants. Copland was cross-examined and asked whether he had ever testified that all the certificates on the vouchers were signed by Tweed. Yes, replied Copland, he had said that at the earlier trial but now replied that he presumed that when Lynes drew up a warrant there was a corresponding signed certificate. He denied seeing Tweed's name signed to every Garvey voucher. What he had said to the contrary in an earlier trial was put into the record on Peckham's insistence. Peckham admitted he drew up Copland's affidavit at the first trial, but had never heard Copland say he had not seen all the vouchers. Copland was the last witness.

The next day summations were heard. The defense again went over old ground and argued that the word "audit" was not clear; its meaning cannot be determined. That Watson's and Woodward's word was accepted by Tweed, who also accepted the word of Hall and Connolly. If they did not meet as a board, it was not Tweed's fault. His duties as commissioner of public works prevented very close attention to the auditing. He had no control of the payment of bills, nor was he responsible for any lost vouchers and bills. As for the missing tickets, "they are suppressed to accomplish his damnation. They were lost between the bank and the grand jury room. They were lost in the hands of an officer of the law, or there was collusion between Woodward and someone in the bank." Tweed was known always as an honest and worthy man. There is no proof of his guilt. Garvey was to be the principal witness against him, but he was not brought forward as he might "fall to pieces" under examination. At this point, Davis refused to allow any further reference to Garvey. The deposits by Woodward to Tweed's account rather than by Tweed were evidence of Tweed's disapproval and lack of complicity. If he were guilty, would he be so stupid as to deposit money in his own name? These deposits to Tweed's account were a plan of Woodward's and those within the auditor's office. Garvey and Keyser who admitted to signing warrants face down were part of the real conspiracy. They agreed to name Tweed if the plot was uncovered. Keyser's warrants had not been shown to be forged. Woodward was gone, fled because of twenty indictments. The prosecution dared not call Garvey to swear his bills were manufactured. The Davidson bill was the only bill presented in the trial and that transaction was between John Garvey and Davidson. Tweed was in no way connected to this bill. The jury was asked to look at Tweed with mercy and charity. "Deal with him as you would desire to be dealt with."

Tremain summed up for the prosecution after recess. The size of the fraud had never been seen before. The law had no adequate precedent. The act of 1870 charged Tweed and the other members of the board with a mandate to audit and to act honestly. They could not delegate their power to Watson or Woodward. There is no conspiracy against Tweed. He has $1 million to pay in fees for the best attorneys. For such money, no wonder his counsel finds him to be St. Tweed. Tweed was the "Boss," the board looked to him for direction and orders. He concocted the scheme in the Senate. It was always fraud with forgery. Who had his pocketbook in the Broadway Bank looking for 24 per cent? Tweed must have known that the vast expenditures on the courthouse which were more costly than the Houses of Parliament were illegal. Garvey was not needed to testify as the case was "abundantly" proved without him. The jury need not be burdened by added witnesses. Garvey would "tell the truth," but with a case clearly proved why complicate the proceedings? Tweed was the center of "The Ring" controlling the city, for example his son was assistant district attorney. It was by accident that Tilden uncovered the gigantic frauds and the accounts were thrown open. Copland was right in his first testimony and was "impeached" by his own affidavit. Tweed received his loot, vouchers were destroyed, and yet counsel says Tweed is innocent. Tweed must be found guilty or justice will be defeated. Children must be shown the error of theft, the city's honor must be vindicated.

Now it was Davis' turn again. He charged the jury at night, as two candles were stuck into bottles to bring light into the courtroom. True, the day had ended, everyone was tired, but he would instruct the jury, even if some objected to this procedure. The jury would benefit from his words and his years of law. Davis was in rare form. He pulled out all the stops. He began slowly as the candles flickered, casting moving shadows along the walls. Davis intoned that the rich and powerful who had plundered public money and violated the law have attempted to turn the law through their money and power to protect themselves. Such an immunity if allowed to occur would make government in the United States an "awful procedure." The case is that simple, stated Davis. He referred to the act of 1870 and the auditing provision as he had in the earlier trial. Such power cannot be delegated. There should have been meetings of the "board of audit." There was only one such meeting. If there is a neglect of duty "you are to convict." If accounts were permitted which were not just, he is guilty. He asked the jury to consider the Davidson bill, the $3 million in Woodward's account, the $982,789.52 in Tweed's account, the Keyser accounts for plumbing and roofing, Garvey bills to the courthouse for $43,000 and $46,000 occurring one after the other. Are all these the mistakes of reasonable and honest men? If the jury finds evidence of neglect of duty and abuse of power, the community must be given protection against rapacity, avarice and wickedness of its public officers. At the end he concluded that if Tweed was found guilty on a number of counts, the jury was instructed to state how many. Defense took exceptions to the charge. The jury retired at 9:05 P.M.

It deliberated through the night of November 18, 1873. They asked for ice water, then brandy, which Tweed furnished. The evening passed slowly. At 3 A.M., Davis announced that the court would reconvene at ten in the morning. Day returned and a reporter met Tweed. He was cheerful. "How do you feel?" asked the reporter. "Never felt better in my life," was the reply. He became serious for a moment. "They may convict me, but my exceptions will knock their conviction higher than a kite."

When court reconvened, Tweed, his son Richard, his private secretary, S. Foster Dewey, and his counsel entered the crowded courtroom. The judge entered at 10:05 A.M. followed by the prosecution and the jury. The jury required further instruction on the fourth count. They returned ten minutes later: the courtroom was quiet as every eye gazed at the jury. The verdict was reached. "How say you, is William M. Tweed guilty or not guilty?" asked the clerk, John Sparks. "Guilty." "Of what?" asked the clerk. "Of 204 of 220 counts," replied the foreman. Fullerton demanded the jury be polled, which was done. The defense immediately asked for an adjournment to argue a motion to arrest judgment. It was pointed out that counsel had not slept for eighty hours. "Perhaps to tomorrow," said Davis, "but not to next week." Tweed was removed by Sheriff Brennan in his custody immediately, even though sentence had not yet been rendered. Tweed reeled, his emotions barely under control. He turned white. As he was led away, he regained his composure and smiled weakly. Richard Tweed, his brother, seemed greatly moved. He was described romantically as "an aged white-haired and white bearded man, with the same prominent and marked Jewish features that are noticeable in all the male members of the Tweed family, both young and old." William "General" Tweed, Jr., was described as a "dark visaged person with side whiskers, [who] has the appearance of a good-natured young fellow about town," but now his eyes were red with weeping. Ambrose Maginnis, Tweed's son-in-law, was also crying. Charley Lawrence, a friend, looked appealingly at Davis, "but the face was like the face of a rock set against the storm." A mass of people followed Tweed and Brennan. He was led into a carriage, the door slammed shut. It moved sharply toward Broadway and past Stewart's department store. He was taken to 95 Duane Street, his old law office, to meet some friends and have lunch. Warden Johnson at the Tombs awaited his arrival. But he did not arrive that night. Brennan assured reporters that Tweed was safely in custody.

Jurors were interviewed. Mr. Opper said that from the first all jurors felt Tweed was guilty. He would not say why the long deliberation. He did not find evidence of attempted bribery of the jury by Tweed. Simeon

Davidson said all agreed as to guilt. It was a question of degree. As to the fourth count, the most troublesome, some jurors felt Tweed did not commit willful corruption, but simply gross carelessness. Palmer, the foreman, was somewhat sorry about the verdict. At one point, he thought Tweed was not guilty, having been persuaded by counsel's summation. He had heard nothing of bribery and anyway they were too closely guarded.

The whereabouts of Tweed was on everyone's mind. All that was known was that Tweed was with Brennan. The sheriff refused to say exactly where, but was deciding whether to jail him or just "keep him." Later Tweed was seen with Brennan and his deputies entering his Forty-third Street home. It was reported that in front of his family, his wife and children, Tweed lost his "fictitious courage." Assistant District Attorney Sullivan was angry that Tweed, the ex-"Boss," was free; he should be in the penitentiary.

Tweed and his counsel appeared before Davis on the following day, November 19, early in the morning. The usual crowd filled the courtroom. The rumors were there. He had escaped or he would be sentenced to one hundred years. The content prosecution emerged, Peckham, Tremain and Henry L. Clinton. Next Brennan and Tweed, not the jovial figure, but an "old worn out man, with the mask of guilt on his brow and the furtive glance of the criminal in his eyes." William M. Tweed, Jr., followed. Davis appeared about ten-thirty. Tweed had his head buried in his hands and did not look up to hear the judge. Counsel told Davis of an appeal to the Court of Appeals, and read a Court of Appeals decision which made commissions like the one given to the "board of audit" unconstitutional. Surely Davis would stay the judgment pending appeals. Davis held that such arguments did not relieve Tweed of his responsibility for his acts, and he would not stay the execution of the judgment. He would not leave Tweed free pending appeal.

Then came something from left field. Tremain suggested the justice could sentence Tweed to 204 separate counts, for the "time of mercy had passed." Counsel for the defense were astounded by this remark. Everyone had always assumed that the maximum sentence for a misdemeanor charge was one year. Tweed's counsel John Graham leaped to his feet and angrily turned toward Tremain.

> Mr. Graham: Your motion (Mr. Tremain) is perfectly startling. That we should have been upon a volcano like this, from the time of the commencement of this trial till its close, through the rendition of the verdict, that the Jury should be kept in utter ignorance of the fearful consequences that were to follow upon their action, when I think they must have gained the impression that they were not of the present formidable character, and that this surprise should be broken upon us at this mo-

ment, is, if I may speak for myself, and I know I speak for the balance of my learned associates, a thing without parallel and without precedent.

The Court: The counsel for the prosecution gave you notice, last Monday, that this motion would be made.

Mr. Graham: No, sir; I had not the slightest idea he was serious in it, for the reasons I will now suggest to your Honor. When I read the announcements in the public papers, I merely treated them as matters of news gathered hurriedly by the gentlemen of the press, from parties who were willing to speak where they had no right to speak; who neither knew authoritatively, and I supposed had no right to know authoritatively, the intention of the counsel.

I say, that until the present hour, with the exception of what your Honor has alluded to as transpiring in this Court the other day, as I will show you, I have labored under the impression, and so have my learned associates, that this verdict carried with it but one consequence, and that was the utmost punishment that could be inflicted, the highest penalty pronounced by the statute which is now invoked, or a modification between the infliction of that penalty and the smallest penalty specified by statute. It seems to me, if the Court please, that we should have been admonished at an early stage of this case that something like this was meant, because I apprehend it would have made, although jurors have nothing to do with consequences, a difference in the estimate in which they would have held their own oaths. It is impossible for human nature, constituted as it is, not to modulate its reflections and its actions very much by the consequences that are to flow from them.

Graham in support of his position and to show how the defendants and the jurors had been misled, read from Mr. Peckham's opening to the jury, which went as follows:

"The defendant, in consequence of this, is indicted for a misdemeanor.

"He is indicted for two separate, distinct things, as it were; in a certain sense, under four counts.

"The first three I will simply state to you together, and it is all that I will find it necessary to trouble you with in that respect. *They are counts put in different lights—the single charge of misconduct in his office aside* from any charge of corruption in connection therewith. That is, that the law made it a duty, imposed upon him by statute, that he should audit these bills that had been brought before him; and another statute provides, whenever a duty is imposed upon a public officer, and he wilfully neglects to perform it, *he shall be guilty of a misdemeanor, and shall pay a fine of not more than $250, or suffer imprisonment, not exceeding one year, or it may be not more than an hour or a day.*

"So that all we have to try in the nature of consequence, or in the nature of punishment, or in the nature of the gravity or the enormity of the offence, so far as the statute law fixes it as a crime, the punishment is to be by a fine of not exceeding $250, or imprisonment for one year, in the Court's discretion, or it may be a fine of five dollars and an imprisonment of a single hour.

A little further on Mr. Peckham says: "We are here to try, not a little petty question of misdemeanor, petty in regard to the consequences, petty in regard to the nomenclature of the crime; it is not because your Attorney-General sees it to interfere, whereby he and the District Attorney act together, and other counsel are brought into the case whereby the action of the defendant himself, in retaining a string of counsel who almost occupy the whole bar—the most able and efficient to be found in the city— *simply for the purpose of deciding whether a petty fine is to be imposed, or whether this man is to occupy a seat in the county jail, for a few months or for a year.* It assumes far greater proportions than that. It is a crime that is proportioned to the magnitude of the offence which is actually committed. The interest is in proportion to that, and the fraud is in proportion to that, and the consequences are in proportion to that."

Not only Peckham, the prosecuting attorney, but also Judge Davis had clearly stated that the maximum penalty that could be imposed was one year's imprisonment. Even Davis at the first trial stated:

"All that the Court has ruled upon the subject is just this: *I have held* that where several misdemeanors are charged in the same indictment, and there be a conviction, either on one or all, for the purposes of punishment, *there can be but a single judgment.* That is all. That is as far as the Court has gone.

"The Court could go no further except with great inconsistency. They are at liberty to prove as many of them as they can; and the jury will render their verdict if they find the party guilty, *under this count, and if guilty under others, the verdict will be recorded;* but when the court *pronounces its judgment, it must look at the indictment as an entirety.* That is all I have ruled. But for the purpose of raising the question in the very best possible form for the appellate court, this present objection is made, as I suppose."

Graham pointed out that the jury might have acted differently if they knew that the sentence could be more than one year. Although Graham did not say so directly, it was obvious that the prosecution and Davis had misled and deceived the jury into believing that the maximum sentence that could be imposed was one year. It was an indefensible procedure.

The "learned, able and impartial" judge replied that in the first trial he thought there would be one sentence, one conviction, but he now found each count deserved a separate sentence. In this trial he had said nothing either way, and at any rate even if he had, "we as lawyers know that it could have had no legitimate effect [on the jury] even if expressed." Even though as a lawyer, he knew that it could have "no legitimate effect," what did he know as a human being? Nevertheless, Davis decided to "temper justice with mercy," despite the seriousness of the offense. Tweed was ordered to rise to hear sentence. "William M. Tweed, you stand convicted by a verdict of twelve honest men, a verdict which could not be otherwise without violation of their values." Davis was in his element. It was an angry, scathing sentence. Tweed's guilt was compounded by the honors and trust given him by his fellow men. Tweed's career of plunder began on May 6, 1870, as he planned to enrich himself and his associates. Tweed's share was clearly 24 per cent. The trial was between virtue and crime, honesty and dishonesty. O'Conor and Tilden had worked hard and long to ferret out the story. It was now simply clear. Tweed had championed corruption and a just sentence to meet the misdeeds would follow. On the fourth count, one year in the county jail and a $250 fine. On the fifth, sixth, seventh and eighth counts one year in the county jail plus $250 per count to be served consecutively after the first term. Nine to twelve, one year plus $250; thirteenth to sixteenth, one year and $250; seventeenth to twentieth, one year and $250; and so it went. The total was thirteen years and $12,500 in fines. What would Davis have given Tweed if he were not inclined to be merciful?

Brennan led Tweed to his office. He was gaunt, his eyes bloodshot and sunken. He looked miserable. His brother tried to comfort him. Tweed asked Brennan if he was going to the Ludlow Street Jail. No, offered one of his counsel, it would be the penitentiary. Tweed's face dropped further. At one in the morning, Tweed was in Brennan's office. His sons and son-in-law, Ambrose Maginnis, and S. Foster Dewey were to accompany the ex-"Boss" to the door of the prison. A supper was sent over from Delmonico's as Tweed expressed his anger at Davis, who he thought was "as smart as a steel trap, but he had no business to keep me standing all that time to be lectured at. His duty was to pass sentence and no more." Nevertheless, he took heart for he expected that his stay at the penitentiary would be short. He also expected that Ingersoll would not be convicted. Of Connolly, he said wistfully, "Dick is living in clover on $3,000 a year, and he is the cause of all this trouble and ought to be where I am." Tired and exhausted, he fell asleep on a couch. Early in the morning he was sent to the Tombs, where he occupied cell six.

The prosecution's success with Tweed cheered the legal authorities, as the "judicial guillotine" was prepared for more heads. Ingersoll and John D. Farrington, Jr., his assistant, were brought to trial on November 25 on an earlier indictment for forgery in the third degree, again before Justice Davis. A trial quickly followed. They were accused of forging signatures on bills for courthouse construction. Root and Fullerton represented them, while Peckham appeared for the prosecution. Farrington, who worked for the New York Manufacturing Company, and Ingersoll both denied forging signatures on bills and alleged that goods were delivered to the city honestly. After a one-day trial, the jury deliberated only thirty-five minutes and brought in a verdict of guilty. Ingersoll was given five years and Farrington one year and six months. At the trial, Tweed's name was rarely mentioned, yet obviously his shadow was large and greatly affected the decision. In any event they went to the Tombs, and then to Sing Sing.

Even though Davis was busy with Ingersoll-Farrington matters, he still had time to complete his work on Tweed's lawyers. On November 24, Tweed's counsel had hoped to argue a bill of exceptions for their client, but found themselves before a real "meat-eating Tiger" who now demanded vengeance. Burrill, Root, Fullerton, Graham, W. O. Bartlett, Willard Bartlett, William Edelstein and David Dudley Field, all of whom early in the trial handed Davis that "mysterious paper" questioning his impartiality, were now accused of contempt of court. Field was in Europe and Burrill said he had withdrawn as Tweed's counsel. All had apologized. It was not enough. He denounced their interference with his court, their attempts to deny him the right to charge the jury, their impugning his right to sit on the case. He was going to make an example of them and show the community that courts are not to be intimidated. They tried to plead their own case to no avail. On November 29, saying that no lawyer can for the sake of a client "degrade the tribunal before which he appears," Davis fined Fullerton, Graham, and Willard O. Bartlett $250 each and ordered them committed until the fine was paid. The younger members—Root, Willard Bartlett and Edelstein—were let off with advice that "good faith to a client can never justify or require bad faith to your own conscience." The fines were paid, though muttering about Davis and his handling of the case were still heard around the room.

Davis, who had denounced the note presented by Tweed's attorneys as "clap-trap" and had allowed those in the courtroom to applaud his words without an attempt to preserve the decorum or dignity of the court, had upbraided the attorneys for just such an effrontery. One spectator, an attorney, criticized Davis for the assumption that it was "necessary to humiliate the profession in order to preserve the dignity of the bench." Perhaps the most important criticism by this member of the bar was that Davis had before him an easy and popular task and he yielded to it. The justice played to the crowd, his impartiality absent as he handled the case "dead against the prisoner." In the contempt citation, he seemed to have predetermined the offense and its punishment, all calculated to appease and win approval of a hysterical public. The hope was expressed that such a spectacle for the "dignity of both bench and bar" would never again be witnessed.

On the day of the sentencing, Brennan told the ex-"Boss" he must be sent to the penitentiary, Tweed's face showing dejection and misery, as he was surrounded by his wife, three daughters, his son William Jr., his brother Richard, and William Edelstein. It was a sad scene. About 2 P.M. the family departed. Tweed was helped into his coat. Supported by William Jr., he was led over the famous "Bridge of Sighs" that connected the Tombs with the court, then down the steps to the waiting carriage. He shook hands with Richard and was driven down White Street to Canal Street and then to the foot of Twenty-sixth Street. Members of the penitentiary staff, the commissioner of corrections and his friends went aboard the ferry *Bellevue* with him. At three-fifteen they arrived at Blackwell's Island. A prisoner at the desk looked at the ex-"Boss" and said, "I'm sorry to see you here." Tweed smiled sadly. Warden Joseph L. Liscomb and Keeper McDonald met Tweed. Some female prisoners pointed him out, exclaiming, "Oh, there's Mister Tweed, there he is." William Jr. and his father, pale and speechless, embraced. The devoted son left. Tweed was conducted to the "barber shop." He was seated and his mustache and whiskers were shaved off. His hair was closely cropped. He then took a cold bath. He was weighed and given a rough suit of gray and brown and a "larceny jacket." Finally he was led to a cell. The full measure of justice was being meted out. More was to follow.[4]

Henry Genet, originally indicted in 1872, was indicted again in 1873, and after a trial found guilty. Genet was arrested for stealing lumber to be used in his own house and fraudulently obtaining money on a warrant of $4,802 for iron work at the Ninth District courthouse. He went to trial before Justice Daniels in the Supreme Court on December 16. Peckham was there. James McBride Davidson was the principal prosecution witness. The safe manufacturer claimed a warrant supposedly given to him was false and he had never seen the money or the bill. Ex-mayor Hall was also called. He testified after having been promised he would no longer be prosecuted, but the promise was not kept. He was not sure about seeing the warrant, but as he signed the record, it was his belief the comptroller had approved it. He did not remember Genet coming to him concerning the bill. Nelson Waterbury defended his client by stating the lumber matter had been inquired into by the legislature and Genet was cleared. Genet had been opposed to Tweed and the 1870 charter, had aided Green and other reformers; all the "Ring" investigations failed to connect Genet with a single dollar. As for the warrant, the iron work was provided and the money paid to Davidson. The prosecution sought to refute this. After several days, the summations were given, the jury charged and Genet found guilty much to his surprise. But he took the news coolly. Early on December 22 Genet was in the custody of Deputy Sheriff William H. Shields. He walked calmly passed the "sleeping" officer and left without being detected. There was considerable noise. Brennan posted a reward for $5,000. Police scoured the city, but he was gone. He had fled to Europe. One of his bondsmen forfeited $10,000 and Charles Devlin lost $5,000. Brennan and Shields were fined $250 each and sent to the Ludlow Street Jail for thirty days, but Genet never served time.[5]

For Tweed and his family all was disaster. Pressure within the family built up and exploded. Shame and disgrace hurt everyone. Everyone tried to hide. His nephew Alfred, trying to set up a provision store in Denver, Colorado, and then in Kansas, received the *Herald* regularly and like everyone else read of the "Tammany Hall troubles." Tweed's immediate family went into seclusion in Connecticut, then went to Europe. There were difficulties and growing family resentments. Though some, like Alfred, knew the trials were meant to gain "political capital," it was hard to hear the insults of neighbors, the stares, the behind-the-back whispers. His nephew Frank found it difficult to obtain a job, because his name was "T--d."

Tweed's mother Eliza had died on July 3, 1873, shortly after the first trial. Though relationships between her and William were cool, he felt the loss and he was sad and tearful at her funeral. Her death exposed sensitive nerves. She had left the bulk of her estate of about $25,000 to her daughter Ann Eliza Young. The remainder was divided in thirds, one each to William, Richard and a grandson, Charles T. Rodgers, named as her executor. William in October 1873 assigned a claim of $500 he had against the estate to his sister-in-law Mrs. Richard Tweed, or more affectionately "Aunt Margaret" or "Sister Maggie." Eliza's "household furniture" was sold at an auction at her home on October 13, 1873. Bronzes which had been given by William to his mother were not in the sale. He felt they belonged to him and not his sister, "Mrs. Young." Tweed gave them to "Aunt Margaret." She went to the house and carried them off to Connecticut to the anger of the executor. On October 14, he addressed a curt note to her demanding the return of the statuettes to his residence at 272 Madison Avenue within three days or the "full extent of the law would be applied." William replied two days later. Surely Rodgers knew full well that his mother had said often enough that after her death all presents given to her should be returned to the giver in order "that they might remain in the family." She had repeated this to him shortly before her death. However, if Rodgers still demanded the statues, Tweed agreed to pay double the appraised value to retain them. He asked that his sister-in-law not be bothered further. Two days later on October 18, Rodgers told his story. Tweed, present at the reading of his mother's will, disclaimed anything but some portraits and one or two specified articles. Margaret liked the bronzes and asked George Young if she could have them. He was unwilling and Margaret said nothing more, but made off with them in an "extraordinary manner." Rodgers, however, agreed to let Tweed pay their value so that Margaret could have them. Tweed wrote back expressing his chagrin at the actions of Young and Rodgers. He asked that his claim against the estate be used to pay for the items. Rodgers wrote back noting Tweed's "spite" against him and that Tweed, knowing the claim would take up to ten years to settle, would in the process tie up the estate and its settlement. Those who attended his mother's last illness including the physician would be denied their money. Tweed denied "spite" and thought the treatment of Margaret "ungenerous and unmanly." He also thought that the sale "of my mother's silver" would raise enough money to pay claims without long delay. Rodgers continued to press and as Tweed had not paid for the bronzes, he notified Margaret on November 1 that he was proceeding in law to regain the property. This brought action. The statues were valued at $100. Margaret through Tweed agreed to pay that sum. It was to be taken out of Tweed's $500 claim, and the remaining $400 paid to her so that the matter could end. And it did. All that about $100, but then it was illustrative of bitter family feuding.[6]

During 1873, while Tweed was preoccupied with legal battles and family relationships, hearings were being held concerning his seat in the state Senate to which he had been elected. There were some technical questions. For example, he had never taken his seat; therefore, could he be expelled? Others argued that since his name had been called by the clerk during roll calls, he was in fact a member. In mid-March, a new investigation committee was appointed. They met Tweed in New York at his rooms in the Metropolitan Hotel on March 22. Tweed's counsel maintained that Tweed had abandoned his seat and thus the inquiry was unnecessary. Still the committee decided to press on. An examination of Garvey was proposed. "It will take more than ten years to get Andy Garvey to speak the truth," Tweed suggested. At the next hearing on March 25 in Albany, Tweed protested, pointing out that he had not taken his seat as senator and had never accepted the office. Tweed's counsel offered again to have his client resign. The committee said it was not empowered to accept his resignation and moved the hearing forward. Tilden was called and gave his usual testimony. Had he heard of money used to influence legislators? He remembered meeting with Mayor Hall at Manton Marble's home in which the subject was raised and Hall said Tweed had "favors" due him from certain senators. He could say nothing, however, of the specific influence of money. It was during these hearings than an Erie Railroad investigation was also taking place. It was alleged by O. H. P. Archer, a director of the railroad, that Tweed had been paid $131,000 in March 1871 for his legal services. He did not know if Tweed ever performed any services for this fee, and whether the money was for "legislative" purposes. On April 25, 1871, Tweed was paid $35,000 for legal disbursements by Jay Gould according to testimony. As the committee hearings developed, it was alleged that Tweed had received $1 million between 1869 and 1871 for "extra legal services," but no connection was made to Tweed and bribery of members of the legislature. Surely some of these legal fees were the source of Tweed's income, rather than the money allegedly stolen from the city. It also developed that Tilden too had received legal fees from the Erie Railroad, but he alleged that these were limited to $10,000. While the long-drawn-out investigation raised many questions as to ethics and morality, no specific revelation about Tweed and influence peddling was made. By the end of the year, the committee ended its hearings without formally expelling Tweed, though he never took his seat. It was all very vague, but served further to stir public opinion by innuendo. The hearings surely were helpful in preparing a "proper climate" for the November trial, which was why Tweed probably preferred dropping any manner of defense for his senatorial seat.[7]

24

Prison

Tweed adjusted quickly to prison life. He wrote "Sister Maggie," his sister-in-law and confidante, that he was never in "better health," ate and drank well and had plenty of exercise, walking about one quarter of a mile to and from his meals. He slept soundly and went to bed about 11 P.M., arose at 6:30 A.M., breakfasted at 8 A.M. and had dinner at 7 P.M. The schedule never varied more than half an hour. In pleasant weather, he remained one to two hours at breakfast and dinner, with most of the time spent walking about. His was a rare account of prison routine in New York. Tweed also told of the difficulties with Justice Davis and his lawyers, who he felt were intimidated by Davis, but he was convinced of his "ultimate success." Visitors, outside of counsel, seem to have been only his son William and Maggie.

Despite Tweed's impatience, his lawyers were working. They were before Justice Brady on March 11, 1874, and asked to inspect the entries in the minutes and to conform them "as they actually transpired at the time of the rendition of the said judgment on November 22. It was their position that Davis ordered Tweed be placed in the county jail and not the penitentiary. If this were so, and it was so in the printed record, he should be in the Ludlow Street Jail, where he could have certain amenities, including better food and quarters and more visitors, and enjoy the "liberties of the jail" which permitted inmates to leave the prison on occasion under escort. The court clerk, John Sparks, however, offered an affidavit stating that Justice Davis had advised him orally that he meant Tweed be sent to Blackwell's Island. The motion was lost. It was a defeat that was expected. He could have "no favors from any judge here, but in the Court of Appeals, we will be all right," Tweed wrote Maggie. An appeal was taken a week later to the Supreme Court, General Term. An application was made for a mandamus against Davis to have corrections made of the trial record, concerning rulings that excluded two jurors. The minutes did not contain the defense exceptions. Davis was accused of striking out several other defense exceptions. Peckham argued that the court had a right to determine what were the value of exceptions and these could and should be limited by Davis. The importance of the exceptions was that the appeal would be limited to those matters to which exceptions were taken. The argument in General Term was to be before Justices Brady and Daniels. In a long involved opinion, Judge Brady denied the application, generally accepting Peckham's argument.

Tweed, in the meantime, found himself once again in a storm. The *Herald* ran a story of the "good" life Tweed was enjoying in the penitentiary, thus cheating New Yorkers of their revenge. More importantly, there were rumors that Tweed was planning an escape, possibly aided by prison authorities. A reporter visited Blackwell's Island on April 6. He was shown around the eastern wing of the prison and was informed that Tweed was in a hospital and could not be seen. Warden Liscomb also stated no prisoner could be made to see anyone without his consent. A card sent to Tweed was returned unanswered. Liscomb denied Tweed had any liberties or that his escape was imminent. There was no foundation to any of these "canards." This story was followed by an exposé on the lax conditions in the various institutions run by the commissioners of charities and corrections on Ward's, Randall's and Blackwell's islands. The Tweed story died for the moment, though the public was left with the impression that Tweed was living in high style, none the least hampered by his imprisonment.

There was more trouble for Tweed as the $6 million civil suit against him was continued during the year. His counsel unsuccessfully argued before the Court of Appeals that the county not the state was the corporate body concerned with the suit. A mid-year decision by the Court of Appeals written by Judge Rapallo held that the Board of Supervisors were merely state agents and the right of reparation was vested only in the state.

A little later, O'Conor disclosed his satisfaction with the decision. He said in an interview on September 13 that he had an offer from Tweed and the others to settle the suit for $3 million, but this was not acceptable to "public justice." He never explained this any further. Tilden was now in the midst of a tax evasion case brought against him. O'Conor in a classic understatement commented that Tilden's role in the Tweed case would offset this adverse publicity and would help him in his bid to become governor.

On June 19, Tweed was unexpectedly brought to town to testify in a suit brought by his former secretary, S. Foster Dewey. It was the first time

since the end of the previous year that he was off the island. He came
ashore together with Warden Liscomb. There were few spectators at the
Twenty-sixth Street Pier. Tweed was quickly brought to Dewey's office.
His son William and Charlie Devlin were also there. A huge crowd was
at the new courthouse to see the fabled ex-"Boss." He looked as he always
did. His beard and mustache had grown back. The time-honored white
necktie was there; he smiled and nodded to old friends. Dewey was a
"small nervous man, with light brown hair, delicately razored side
whiskers, a rather full mustache and a thin voice." The case involved a
check for $1,000 given by Dewey to a Mr. Corrigan, secretary of the Sev-
enth Ward William M. Tweed Club. Dewey insisted that repayment was
due him, but Corrigan denied this and testified that he and the president,
a Mr. Shell, asked Tweed for $2,500 for the organization. Tweed replied
that he could afford only $1,000 and asked Dewey to make out a check for
the same. He understood the money was for the club and would be returned to him if the club was successful. Dewey said he, not Tweed, gave
the money. Tweed was called to the stand. He did not know of any such
transaction. He did not have any money to give. The jury again could not
agree. It was eight to four for the defendant. As Tweed left, scores of
friends shook his hand. Tweed's expression was "of almost tearful pleasure." He left via Chambers Street, and by evening was again on Blackwell's Island.

Tweed's ever hopeful counsel continued their efforts. When the prosecution failed to prepare a record of judgment which was necessary before
an appeal could be taken, defense counsel drew up the record and presented it to one of the officers of the court for signature by Justice Davis.
Counsel argued that the original record had been altered by changing the
word "misdemeanor" to "misdemeanors." They made a motion, therefore,
to correct the error, if it was that. This motion was denied. Although
seemingly unimportant, the change from misdemeanor to misdemeanors
was significant in terms of the sentence. If only one misdemeanor, he
could be sentenced only for a maximum of one year, not the thirteen
years' sentence given by Davis.

Preliminary motions having been disposed of, it was not until November 1874 that Tweed's counsel finally moved for his release on a writ
of habeas corpus. They argued that his imprisonment was illegal since the
court which tried him did not have jurisdiction to do so, nor was the jury
which tried him properly impaneled, that the judgment was void since the
court had no jurisdiction, and even if the court had jurisdiction which it
denied, he could not be sentenced to more than one year, and he had already served that one year. A hearing was held on December 2, at which

Field unsuccessfully argued before Justice George C. Barrett, who directed that Tweed remain at Blackwell's. This decision was to be appealed.

Stories soon swept Manhattan that a desperate Tweed, denied his freedom, had in fact escaped. Alarms were sounded at police headquarters as the city was put on alert. A *Herald* reporter visited Warden Liscomb, was told that Tweed had visited the court during the debate on his motion, with the consent of the district attorney, but returned in the afternoon and was safe in his cell. It was another false alarm. But surely in Tweed's mind the notion of escape as an answer to his problems seemed feasible. Many had taken this route.

Field was not discouraged; at least he kept on trying. On December 15, Justice Abraham R. Lawrence returned the motion to Oyer and Terminer without hearing argument. Back before Justice Barrett, Peckham noted it was the same motion covering the same ground as before. Barrett refused to agree to a bill of exceptions. A long and involved debate ensued, but the end was the same. The motion was denied and Tweed remained in jail.

Tweed spent another Christmas behind stone walls. Prisoners had corned beef, vegetables, soup and bread. Tweed had an extra dinner supplied by friends, which was consistent with rules. Officials denied he dined at or was supplied from the warden's table. He was described as cheerful and in excellent health. He was shy of seeing visitors and few were allowed to see him in the hospital where he worked. He refused to see journalists.

Tweed was, of course, far removed from politics. His interests were obviously elsewhere. But for Tilden and his fellow reformers, it was a year of triumph as they triumphantly catapulted over the inert body of the "Boss" into the governor's chair in Albany. Not only did Tilden win big, but the Democrats gained control of the Assembly, as William H. Wickham, a diamond merchant and member of the Committee of Seventy, became mayor of New York City.[1] Ah! Reform!

25

Six Million Dollars

Public interest in Tweed had long since abated. He was now a "myth," a "fabled monster," chained forever to a pillory erected by politicians, sensation-seeking journalists and historians, and of course useful to them. News of Tweed was now on the back pages as New Yorkers turned their attention to other circuses. He was news only on special occasions. Nevertheless, his attorneys, like so many Don Quixotes tilting against windmills, labored on. On January 8, 1875, they argued before Justices Charles Daniels, Charles Donohue and Theodore R. Westbrook, asking for his release on bail pending his appeal. The court took the matter under advisement, but on March 12 denied Tweed's motion for bail, although granting him the right to appeal.[1]

In the meantime, renewed stories of Tweed's life of "fun and games" on Blackwell's Island elicited response in the form of a visit of the grand jury, who met with the commissioners of charities and corrections on January 26 and proceeded to the island, where they were quickly shown to Tweed's cell, a sight "hardly calculated to arouse the envy of a tenement house family." The room was eight by ten, adjoining the hospital. From a window could be seen the ice-choked East River and snow-covered Astoria. Tweed remarked that in the summer there was a better view with ships passing by. Now the dreariness of the winter scene was depressing. Still, "It is a good deal to be able to see the sky, whether clear or cloudy, and the river and the trees, either in winter or in summer," murmured Tweed. "Nobody will deprive you of that small comfort," said a jury man sympathetically. Tweed sat on a cane-bottomed armchair. He had a small table, a bed and a few books. He had on a sack coat of coarse woolen fabric of reddish brown and his trousers were woolen of dark cloth. He wore glasses as he wrote out hospital entries. How was he treated? Well, he was grateful for small favors. He looked well, though he complained of his kidneys. His close-cropped beard was now snow-white. His color was still a "healthy red." He took four hours' exercise a day. The warden found him a model prisoner, faithful and zealous in his duties as an orderly. His old quarters had been even dingier, the atmosphere cold and dreary. It was somewhat better now, but still in stark contrast to stories of the "luxury" of his penitentiary quarters.

Others saw the jury hoodwinked by sham and fraud. Tweed's cell was purposely made to look shabby, and he was seen as busily engaged in work, all to arouse sympathy. It was rumored that when the visitors left, all his "rich appointments" were returned and his cell once again became luxurious quarters. Warden Liscomb was relieved of his duties because of stories that he permitted Tweed to avoid wearing prison garb or that he allowed him to use his house when he should be in his cell, even though he denied all allegations.[2]

For Ingersoll, the new year began as one of promise. In early April, he was seen entering his father's house on East Twenty-first Street, although supposedly in prison. Peckham was close at hand. The story soon broke. Ingersoll had been pardoned. The deal, it was assumed, being that he would turn state's evidence and like Garvey "tell the truth." Farrington was also discharged from Sing Sing. Peckham denied the story. "He had never made a bargain with anyone in his life, and did not propose to begin now." Not a pleasant interview; Peckham spoke angrily, but was lying; Ingersoll and Farrington appeared as free men. Behind Ingersoll and Farrington were Peckham, O'Conor and the Municipal Bureau of Correction, an outgrowth of the Committee of Seventy. Ingersoll's testimony would revive flagging interest in the hunt, and help political ambitions, especially that of Tilden. He became a good friend of "Sammy's."[3]

Meanwhile, Tilden and O'Conor were making preparations in the event that any of Tweed's appeals might be successful. One result of their efforts was the passage of the "Public Remedy Law," which enabled the new attorney general, Daniel Pratt, to bring suit against Tweed and the City of New York to recover "stolen" money. The legislature also ended a long legal hassle by making the state the prosecutor of "Ring" civil suits. Peckham was delighted with the turn of events. Anticipating passage of the new law, on March 18, the attorney general discontinued the prior $6 million civil suit without the knowledge of Tweed and his attorneys. Two days later, the very day the law was passed, a new summons and complaint were prepared along with voluminous affidavits from the same persons who had testified earlier. On March 29, Justice Noah Davis issued an order of arrest directing the sheriff to take Tweed in custody if he were freed from the penitentiary and hold him until $3 million bail was paid. An order was then made on April 6, 1875, directing the sheriff to attach all the property of William Tweed sufficient to satisfy plaintiff's demand for $6,198,957.83. Not only property still owned by Tweed, but property already sold was attached. All of this while Tweed was still in the penitentiary.[4]

Nephew Alfred Tweed in Denver was agitated by the account of the new suit. "They seem determined," he wrote, "to break the old man down. I think he is going through the hardest ordeal now, and it will be, in my opinion, an almost impossible thing to find a jury who will give a verdict in his favor." But, hopefully, Alfred remarked, "It is a long lane that has no turn and let us hope for the best." Later, when Alfred heard the Ingersoll news, he was disappointed as he had not expected that Ingersoll would go too "heavy against Uncle William, but liberty is a dear thing" and with the indictments hanging over him, Ingersoll could be expected to say anything. Still, Alfred hoped for a brighter time.[5]

The new summons and complaint went over old ground. How Watson and Tweed through fraud and deceit unlawfully "conspired and agreed together to procure false and pretended claims." The new action stirred things up. Again, the papers were full of warrants, bills, speeches, the courthouse, its carpets, iron work and plastering and more newspapers were sold. Angels and devils again paraded through the streets. This turn of events meant that even if there were a favorable decision in the Court of Appeals Tweed would still be faced with imprisonment.

As matters relating to the new civil suit continued, Tweed's counsel moved for a bill of particulars on the state's cause of action, but did not receive one. Rather, counsel was advised that all the claims mentioned in the complaint were lost and copies could not be made, except for the ten vouchers, copies of which defendant already had. Tweed's counsel, therefore, moved for an extension of time to answer stating that they could not respond without such particulars. Justice Barrett granted them a twenty-day extension on April 28, 1875. The following day, Peckham submitted a terse affidavit stating, "That it is not intended by the plaintiff to serve any bill of particulars herein." Barrett, apparently intimidated by Peckham, changed his own order of the day before and gave Tweed's counsel only a ten-day extension to interpose an answer. No answer, however, was given as motions continued. In June, Field and Peckham went at each other again. Field demanded copies of the "fraudulent" vouchers. Peckham insisted again these were "lost or destroyed" and only ten vouchers now existed. Field still argued Tweed was entitled to specific accounting of each item of the alleged fraud. There should not be one law for Tweed and another one for everyone else.

While the court deliberated, the long story told by Ingersoll, who was now a free man, was published by the Times on June 3, 1875. The "truth" was now out again. Ingersoll in an affidavit said he was thirty-five and lived at 21 East Seventy-third Street and had an interest in his father's furniture-manufacturing firm, Ingersoll & Watson. The firm was in the "habit of supplying furniture to the city." His father knew Tweed and had in fact learned his trade from Tweed's father. In 1867, Ingersoll learned that public officers were to be given percentages of bills presented. Ingersoll's father, Lorin, refused and would not furnish the city with supplies. "It occurred to me I might profitably do so," said Ingersoll, and in that year he approached Tweed, who told him to speak to Woodward, who advised him he could fix his bills by adding 35 per cent, of which 25 per cent was for Tweed, 10 per cent for Connolly. Ingersoll and Co. was used on the bill head at the suggestion of Tweed. Ingersoll regularly handed bills in, but was never questioned by a city agent or agency about the amounts. He "believed" all other firms doing business with the city made the same arrangement, and also believed through talks with Tweed, Connolly, Watson and Woodward that he had only to do as directed and receive his money. The excess would be used to "manage" the state legislature and Common Council, and provide "rewards" for those in local government. It was "common talk" and he "supposed" it was understood by Tweed, Connolly, Sweeny and others. Watson, from 1867 to the day of his death in January 1871, acted as the funnel for all the warrants. After Watson's death, Connolly agreed to let Ingersoll carry on the auditor's duties. On some warrants, Watson and Tweed allowed Ingersoll to use names of persons he knew, but slightly altered to avoid detection. He opened an account in the Broadway Bank on June 9, 1868. After a while, Watson and Woodward wanted Ingersoll to retain only 45 per cent of the bill because of increased "legislative expenses. Fifty-five per cent would go to public offices. Twenty-five per cent went to Tweed, 20 to Connolly and 10 to Sweeny. Ingersoll agreed. About April 26, 1870, just before the creation of the "board of audit," he was informed by Woodward and Watson that he would now be allowed to keep only 35 per cent. The rest went to Tweed, Connolly and Sweeny, with 10 per cent being divided between Woodward and Watson. Five per cent went to William E. King. On July 1, 1870, he opened an additional account under the name of Ingersoll & Watson at the Tenth National Bank.

Money was distributed mainly through Woodward, who wrapped the money in a parcel and gave it to Watson, who then distributed it in sealed packets. Sometimes Ingersoll carried Sweeny's packet to the chamberlain's office and gave it to his "broker," James M. Sweeny. Most of the 25 per cent given to Tweed went through Woodward, who he was "sure" gave it to Tweed, but he stated sometimes he paid money directly to Tweed. He then went on to say that Connolly received returns on some warrants which were used to pay for the construction of his house.

Tweed told Ingersoll to look over his and Connolly's interest. He personally gave Tweed about $30,000 for furniture for his house and advanced $15,000 in cash.

At one point in the summer of 1870, Tweed "made" him pay $112,500, 15 per cent of the $750,000 legislative appropriation for the courthouse in 1871. In the autumn of 1871 after the Havemeyer suit, Tweed ordered Ingersoll to destroy all his books and to tell Garvey, Miller and others to do likewise. "That's Peter B. Sweeny's advice," said Tweed, Ingersoll reported. He complied and except for a few checks saved by accident, destroyed all his records. Despite the destruction of his records, Ingersoll had a "remarkably clear memory of dozens of warrants in regard to dates and amounts down to the penny."

Henry F. Taintor also filed an affidavit. Although ostensibly employed by the Finance Department from December 1, 1871, through June 5, 1874, he was in fact engaged on behalf of the attorney general and his assistant counselors in ascertaining the facts and searching for evidence. He accused Tweed, Connolly, Sweeny, Watson, Woodward and others of systematically obtaining by fraud monies from the public treasury beginning with May 1867. The "peculations" amounted to millions of dollars. Whatever loopholes there were in the case against Tweed were being carefully plugged—the public read these "truths" avidly. It seemed to bear out what was said about Tweed.

Bad news was tempered by a little good. The Court of Appeals in a long-awaited decision on June 15 ordered Tweed's immediate discharge from the penitentiary. The court held in a unanimous decision that he could not be sentenced to more than one year, since cumulative sentences were illegal. It was beyond the power of the courts to join several distinct offenses in the one indictment.[6] Davis and the attorney general were well prepared for this eventuality. Bench warrants were waiting, as well as series of old indictments including a General Sessions indictment of December 15, 1871, for a felony; three indictments of December 18, 1871, for forgery and grand larceny; an indictment of January 20, 1872, for forgery and grand larceny; on October 17, 1872, Oyer and Terminer's indictment for a felony; four indictments issued on February 20, 1873, for forgery, felony and misdemeanor; and a November 22, 1873, indictment for false pretenses. Again none were tried. On June 15, the day the Court of Appeals announced its decision, another indictment was handed down for conspiracy. This in addition to the civil suit and its attendant $3 million bail. There were walls around Tweed miles high. As soon as Tweed could be released, he would be immediately rearrested. Which bench warrants should be honored? The sheriff was instructed to give precedence to criminal ones.

The news of the Appeals decision was brought to Tweed by a breathless S. Foster Dewey. "We have got it," exclaimed the flushed and excited Dewey, who had traveled all night from Albany. "Well," replied Tweed quite composed, "I expected it, but not so soon." The "best part of it," Tweed thought, was that it was unanimous. O'Conor was livid with rage. The Court of Appeals, he felt, had no knowledge of law and their motives were less than honest. O'Conor's opinions were published in the newspapers. Henry Clinton, although part of the prosecution, observed that any lawyer would have been disbarred for making such statements. Davis was also outraged, but was angry more at O'Conor than the court, feeling that the court's decision was largely based on a precedent set in a case O'Conor had argued, but which O'Conor had not made known to him. The decision made Davis look foolish or worse.

George F. Comstock, former judge of the Court of Appeals, and one of Tweed's attorneys in the appeal to the Court of Appeals, had his own view. He accepted a retainer from Tweed because he believed "the law of the land had been grossly violated in accumulated sentences pronounced upon him." Had Tweed stolen $40 million, Davis' judgment would have been wrong. As far as Comstock could see in the whole record against Tweed, there had not been a single charge or suggestion that Tweed was "guilty of larceny, embezzlement or receiving improperly in any form a single dollar of the public money." There was, and as Davis knew, no record of "criminal prosecution in which distinct offenses have been united, tried and punished under a single indictment . . . It remained for Judge Davis to attempt the introduction into one law of a principle so alarming, so full of real danger to the right of every citizen." As for O'Conor, his anger was misdirected and in error. He should study precedent more carefully before abusing the high tribunal.[7]

After a week, Tweed was transferred from Blackwell's Island on June 22, 1875, at midnight. He spent the night at the home of his nephew Alfred H. Sands, at 136 East Twenty-sixth Street. Together with the sheriff, he arrived at the district attorney's office at 10:30 A.M. As seen by friends, he was greatly changed, but was pronounced in good health by prison physician Dr. Kitchem. His hair was white and his figure bent. His face was ruddy as though by exertion. In the district attorney's office, he sat on a sofa and drank three glasses of ice water in succession. He then appeared in Supreme Court, where he was formally discharged from his unlawful imprisonment. Then the group moved over to Oyer and Terminer. Field, the senior counsel, W. O. Bartlett and Dewey were there, as was Peckham and District Attorney Benjamin Phelps. Tweed now pleaded to the indictments issued during his imprisonment. One accused him of forgery in putting Hall's signature on a warrant of $126,797.52 paid to Garvey for alterations to the aqueduct at 113th Street, and another on a charge of conspiracy with Peter B. Sweeny and Woodward of fraudulently obtaining $59,593.85. Field asked that plea be held over until November as he was too burdened with thirty-four other indictments still pending. Phelps asked for an immediate plea as the statute of limitations would soon run out. Brady fixed bail at $4,000 for the two charges, and set the next hearing to June 29. Bail of $14,000 was asked on fourteen old indictments. The money was raised by his nephew Alfred Sands, and Charles Devlin and the court officer said, "Mr. Tweed, you may go now." At long last, he was free. The party walked into City Hall Park, where they were surrounded by well-wishers, and then drove to Tweed's office on Duane Street. His freedom did not last long as he was rearrested by Deputy Sheriff Mcgonnigle, who had the warrant from Justice Davis holding Tweed in $3 million bail on the $6 million suit. It was a cruel game of cat and mouse. The party, including the sheriff, went to Delmonico's where they ate a "sumptuous dinner" and then drove to the Ludlow Street Jail. Warden William Dunham, Liscomb's replacement, received the prisoner and led him to a "well furnished apartment" on the first floor.

Tweed's "freedom" was short-lived. He had not slept from the moment he left the penitentiary until being placed in Ludlow Street Jail. The next day he was visited by his son Richard and S. Foster Dewey. Keyser walked past the prison, but looked neither right nor left. In the meantime, Justice Donohue granted an order in the civil suit to have the prosecution show cause why the bail should not be reduced, especially as $1 million had already been furnished in the original civil suit. Criminal causes before Brady were also pending. On the civil case, Field found himself not before Judge Donohue, but on Peckham's request, before Chief Justice Davis, who having received his reward, was now sitting in Supreme Court. Field looked at Davis and adjourned the motion to vacate the arrest. It would be hopeless. That was on June 29. The next day, the motion to quash all felony indictments came on to be heard before Brady in Oyer and Terminer. This was on various grounds. Field argued that the December 15, 1871, indictment was void since the grand jury continued beyond its term. Moreover, the "omnibus" indictment having been tried, Tweed could not be tried again. In short, all charges against Tweed as member of the "board of audit" had been tried and punishment inflicted. Brady agreed that all indictments issued prior to October 1872 were superseded by the "omnibus" indictment, but the prosecution was free to pursue Tweed by subsequent indictments.[8]

Having been rebuffed in their motion to vacate the order of arrest,

Field now hoped at least to reduce bail on the civil suit. Field argued before a packed court on July 14, 1875, presided over by Justice Barrett that bail in a civil suit was an assault of the "gravest character" on the civil liberty of the people. The right to bail is unalienable and an integral part of English common law. Its abrogation is a blow to the right of every citizen. Further the country is "full of 'rings,'" Tammany, Canal, whiskey, customhouse, carpetbaggers to name only a few. The thing upon which the action is based is that one member is accountable for all. This is clearly unjust as it is to imprison without a trial even upon affidavits. Why allow Garvey, Ingersoll and Keyser their liberty as they have admitted their guilt? Further, the courthouse was built, they were in it, it was being used, it doesn't exist as thin air, how are its costs, even if excessive to be known? All that can be traced to Tweed is $932,000—that given to his account by Woodward. How is it possible, Field asked, to hold him for a greater sum? Barrett reserved decision.

A day later on July 16, 1875, before Justice Donohue, another aspect of the civil suit was decided. The prosecution was finally ordered to present a bill of particulars to show which warrants were false, fraudulent and fictitious, and the proportion of each that was in excess of the proper amount. This turn of events was a decided victory. Legalists saw the prosecution faced with an impossible task. They would have to produce vouchers allegedly stolen from the comptroller's office. Only ten Keyser vouchers existed, according to the prosecution. If the motion stood, the cases against Connolly and Sweeny would also have to be dropped. For the state their only hope was to have the order vacated. Peckham immediately appealed the order to the Supreme Court General Term. A "prominent lawyer" railed at Donohue, and found him to be an 'honest' judge, but a lifelong Democrat, a member of Tammany Hall, who did not take part in the assault on "The Ring," who seemed to fail to appreciate that "great efforts have been made to throw Tweed upon his back."

While the bill of particulars was being debated, Justice Barrett at the end of July found enough precedent to overrule Field's contention. He refused to reduce bail or vacate the order of arrest. The bail was not the issue in view of the huge $6,158,858.85 with which Tweed is being sued. He was not convinced Tweed could not raise $3 million. Field and Deyo pressed on as Tweed remained in jail.

Arguments on appeal were heard beginning on August 23 before Davis, Brady and Daniels on the bill of particulars, as well as the refusal to reduce bail. Peckham was there as was Field. The arguments were the same as presented before. If the prosecution had to present a bill of particulars, a thief would be freed, since any criminal could destroy the evidence and then be set free. Field answered, yes, vouchers may have been stolen or destroyed, but not by Tweed. Specifications in civil as well as criminal cases is a true "American" precedent. The expected occurred, Davis writing the opinion and Brady concurring; the court reversed Justice Donohue's order and upheld Justice Barrett's decision on the bail issue. In other words, the court upheld the ruling of the $3 million bail, and denied defendant a bill of particulars.[9] In effect, Tweed was denied in the $6 million suit the right to know the basis of the suit against him. Today, a bail of $3 million in a civil suit, or for that matter any bail in a civil suit, is unheard of. Imprisonment for debt has been abolished. It should be remembered that during all these arguments Tweed was in jail in a civil matter. Moreover, today it is inconceivable that a person sued in a civil suit would be denied the particulars of the claim against him. That probably was also true one hundred years ago, but not for Tweed.

Meanwhile, on October 8, a second suit, "the little suit," was filed by Attorney General Platt asking recovery of an additional $1 million "plundered" from the city. This was specifically $933,640.44 taken by six warrants drawn by Ingersoll and Co. from July 13, 1870, to August 21, 1870. Tweed was again arrested, even while sitting in jail. Another $1 million bail was set, making total bail now $4 million.

On October 12, Justice Lawrence granted Field time to answer the $6 million "big suit." The following day, October 13, arguments on when the answer was due were heard. Field, Deyo and Edelstein were there, as was Peckham. Deyo pointed out an appeal on the bill of particulars issue had been taken to the Court of Appeals, and arguments would be heard there on November 9. Nevertheless, Judge Lawrence refused to grant the defendant more time to answer, and Tweed's counsel appeared three days later in Supreme Court to answer the "big suit."[10]

While these proceedings were taking place, the first of the "Ring" settlements took place. During the course of a trial against the estate of James Watson before Justice Murray Hoffman in which Garvey, Miller and Ingersoll were star witnesses, a settlement was reached. Margaret K. Watson, widow and administrator, agreed to pay $590,435.94 to the State of New York. It was felt the widow still had a sizable sum of money, perhaps $1 million. This event made everything much darker for Tweed.[11]

Arguments in the "big suit" continued. Field wanted more time and presented new issues. The money received from the Watson estate should be deducted from any amount recoverable from Tweed. He also asked that property belonging to Garvey and Ingersoll which they acquired in the alleged frauds be deducted. Field and Deyo now asked that the attorney general show how the Watson suit was settled and why Garvey, Ingersoll and Keyser were not prosecuted further and why no attempt was made to recover "stolen" money from them. More bad news. The Court of Appeals on November 16, 1875, unanimously upheld the decisions below. The trial of the $6 million suit was set for the December term, while the "little suit" argument as to bail was heard again on November 26. Additional amended answers were filed on November 27 in the two suits by Tweed's counsel. On November 29, Peckham informed the defense that a special or "struck jury" could be impaneled to hear both cases. This was an unusual procedure, rarely used. But this was Tweed. The county clerk selected forty-eight names, each side could arbitrarily strike twelve names. The twenty-four remaining names were given to the sheriff with directions to summon the group and selection then continued normally. Peckham held this procedure was necessary to balance Tweed's fifteen years as a prominent Tammany Hall politician, and to ensure a "fair and impartial" jury. Field and Deyo argued in favor of their client's right to a jury of his peers and against the struck jury to no avail. None of the proposed panel might be called his peers.[12]

Tweed had been silent during his years of litigation and imprisonment. He had always maintained his innocence and the hope that the law would vindicate him. By the end of 1875 it became obvious even to Tweed that there was no hope. Perhaps the last straw was the Court of Appeals decision which upheld the $3 million bail and determined that he need not be apprised of the particulars of the claim against him. Tweed now took matters in his own hands—whether by his own decision or whether being desperate he was tricked into doing so by others—he committed the greatest of all blunders. He "escaped."

26

"Father's Gone"

There had been many rumors that Tweed, like Connolly, Garvey, Sweeny, Keyser, Woodward and most recently Harry Genet, would also seek to flee the endless entanglement and probable punishment of law. A thief would follow thieves. On the night of December 8, 1874, a "444" signal, a rarely used code of extreme urgency, was received at the Nineteenth Precinct Station House at 220 East Fifty-ninth Street. This message dispatched from the penitentiary on Blackwell's brought a dozen policemen running to the foot of Fifty-second Street at the East River where they crowded into a small boat and were rowed to the island. There, with revolvers ready, they nervously awaited a deadly encounter with Tweed, everyone believing that somewhere the "Boss" lurked in the darkness. Met by a mystified Commissioner William H. Laimbeer of Charities and Corrections, as well as by Warden Joseph L. Liscomb, the police were quickly assured that the danger signal was a mistake and that Tweed, in fact, was soundly asleep in bed. The annoyed officers, together with the commissioner, returned to Manhattan, only to find breathless reinforcements awaiting transportation. The police were on their toes.[1]

Rumors and scares, such as in the preceding incident, were constant reminders of an impending escape. That Tweed had not sought this route before amazed many who came to admire the stubbornness and courage of the "old man."

Still it surely came as a relief when the other shoe was finally dropped and the expected happened. News of the event made the front pages of New York newspapers on December 5, 1875. The *Herald's* headline read "Gone at Last." The "Boss" was news again. The judicial process was long and drawn out and even lurid accounts of "The Ring's" corruptions were, a year after the original disclosures, old hat relegated to small print in in-

side columns. But this was really something to be discussed at the breakfast table or at the office.[2]

The incredible drama, which was to have a profound effect on
Tweed, and last some ten months, began shortly after lunch at the county
jail at 70 Ludlow Street. About 1:30 P.M. on Saturday, December 4, 1875,
Tweed accompanied by Warden William Dunham and Keeper Edward
Hagen entered a waiting carriage for a drive into the country. Such privi-
leges were customarily granted to prisoners in civil prison. In the late
eighteenth and early nineteenth centuries "liberties of the gaol" were allowed debtors. They could walk within a prescribed area, and so visit
friends and relations, carry on business, hopefully enabling them to satisfy
creditors, providing as well healthful exercise. By the mid-nineteenth century, the formal boundaries of "liberties" were ended, but persons in
Ludlow Street were at times allowed, under guard, extended trips about
the city. Tweed, as on this occasion, was infrequently given a supervised
trip. Warden Dunham, questioned shortly after the escape, said he had allowed Tweed out about four times since his arrival on June 22, 1875. Deputy Warden William L. Gardner concurred that prior to the Saturday
drive, Tweed had not left the jail for about a month. Corroborating evidence tended to sustain their estimates. Mr. Erchberg, proprietor of a
lager beer saloon at No. 71 Ludlow Street, just opposite the jail, stated he
had seen Tweed go out three times, once on foot with an escort and arm in
arm with his son William Jr. Mr. and Mrs. John H. Clyde, residing at the
same address in the upper story of the building, mentioned almost daily
visits of William Jr., who would customarily stop his carriage on Ludlow
Street toward the corner of Broome Street and enter the jail. When father
and son emerged, the carriage was brought to the entrance and the party,
including warden and keeper, quickly drove away. Mr. Clyde felt he saw
Tweed leave in this way five times. Mrs. Clyde was positive she observed
Tweed leave four times. A *Times* reporter deduced they had thus seen
Tweed, between them, exit seven times. This in a little more than six
months of incarceration. Mrs. Clyde also said she saw Tweed leave on that
Saturday afternoon about 1 P.M. She noted that his carriage was better
than the usual one, a landau with a folding leather top, and she thought
this was Tweed's private carriage. Unusually, it had proceeded directly to
the prison door. She also remembered that the last time she had seen
Tweed leave was on Thanksgiving Day. A neighbor living opposite the
Tweed residence at 647 Madison Avenue remarked he and his family had
never noticed anything unusual around the home.

On the other hand, artist Joseph H. Johnson, a gossip and member of
Tweed's "Big Six" Fire Company said it was "well known" in the city and
among Tweed's friends that imprisonment in Ludlow Street was "merely

nominal" and that he could be driven about the city whenever he wished. Johnson declined any supporting evidence, but said Tweed made several visits to a lady residing on Fifth Avenue and Thirty-ninth Street. A lady, perhaps the same one, but not further identified, was mentioned as aiding in Tweed's flight, but interviewed she denied any such story. Further, she had not seen him at any time since his arrest. Stories of Tweed and "other women" are not frequent. This is one of the few.

James McGoldrick, a night watchman, employed to oversee a row of new buildings erected on the north side of Sixtieth Street, said he knew Tweed well and had seen him visit his son's house at 447 Madison Avenue every week except when the family was out of town. On Saturday he stated he saw a carriage usually used by Tweed at about five at the corner of Madison and Sixtieth and was surprised that Tweed would visit his son twice in a week. Mr. McGoldrick's account, the only personal recollection of "frequent visits," contradicted the testimony of Wardens Dunham and Gardner, Mr. and Mrs. Clyde and Mr. Erchberg. It is also possible he did not actually see Tweed; he did not see Tweed on Saturday, only a carriage, a carriage not like the one seen by Mrs. Clyde. McGoldrick's account does not seriously differ from other estimates since William Jr. was out of town often during the summer months. Tweed's wife and family only returned to New York on November 1, 1875, after a summer stay at their home in Greenwich, Connecticut. In any event, the "accepted" view that "Warden Dunham and his Keeper took Tweed for a drive every afternoon, stopping on the way back at Tweed's home where Mrs. Tweed would have dinner waiting," and Johnson's view of "nominal" incarceration are not be borne out by any substantial evidence.

Tweed's life in civil jail was not for such circumstances particularly hard. It was certainly better than the penitentiary. He had in part-time attendance Louis "Luke" Grant, the black prison waiter whom he paid a weekly wage. There were eighty-seven rooms in the jail. Tweed occupied one room on the first floor just north of the entrance that had been used as the warden's parlor. It was plainly furnished. Photographs of his family and home in Greenwich hung on the wall. There was a small desk in the corner covered with personal papers and newspapers. The room was "methodically kept," noted a reporter. There was no evidence it was furnished to "Tweed's expensive taste." Warden Dunham occupied a room adjoining Tweed's and Charles L. Lawrence, a silk smuggler, one next to that. Lawrence and Tweed, as was perhaps natural, were close companions. Lawrence was an unusual character. Born Charles Louis Lazarus in England July 4, 1844, he was naturalized in 1854 and changed his name in 1865. He married a daughter of Mordecai Noah's, member of a famous New York Jewish family. Lawrence was a member of the Blossom, Jockey and Americus clubs and, in fact, was secretary in the latter club at the time Tweed was its president. Lawrence was part of a complicated case involving a good deal of diplomatic negotiation between the State Department and the British Foreign Office.[3] The *Times* remarked that on the evening of Tweed's escape, Lawrence entertained several lady friends. Tweed also frequently had visitors—part of the routine in Ludlow Street—mostly his attorneys, a few friends and his eldest son—but seemingly no "lady friends." There is no record that his wife or other children, except his daughter Jennie and occasionally Josephine ever came to visit him. At ten-thirty on that Saturday morning, for example, Tweed was called upon by his counsel David Dudley Field and William Edelstein, who handed Tweed an affidavit to sign. It was notarized by Deputy Warden Gardner. The attorneys left.

After lunch, the quartet, Tweed, his son William Jr., Dunham, and Hagen, left the jail. Dunham related that he was allowed out this time only because of the "delicate state of Mr. Tweed's health." They drove along the Bowery to Fourth Avenue and Tenth Street, then on to Broadway, a short distance down to Fifth Avenue and then up to Fifty-ninth Street, north to Kingsbridge Road across the Harlem River into The Bronx, recently annexed to the city. The return trip was through Southern Boulevard over Harlem Bridge through 126th Street to Sixth Avenue and down to the northern edge of Central Park. There the group spent some fifteen minutes on a knoll chatting quietly and walking about. Tweed, Dunham related, was in excellent spirits. He took an active part in the discussions and frequently laughed heartily. He did not show any nervousness, nor did he lapse into silent reverie as he sometimes did. Returning to the carriage, they proceeded to Sixtieth and Madison. Leaving the carriage at the corner, they walked to 647 Madison Avenue, the Tweed home. The Madison Avenue home was a four-story brownstone, with stoop and basement. Three similar houses adjoined it, all recently completed. Two were empty. To the rear of the houses was a nine-foot-high fence. Beyond that was a fence running along the length of Fourth Avenue between Fifty-ninth and Sixtieth streets. A fenced vacant lot was on the corner of Fifty-ninth and Madison. Across the street were five brownstones, all occupied. The newly established neighborhood had an air of middle-class gentility. These were not Fifth Avenue mansions. The interior of the Tweed house was modeled after the "stereotyped modern pattern"—on the first floor were two parlors with a bay window in the back; on the second, sitting room and sleeping quarters; the third and fourth, bedrooms and closets. There were three or four "colored" servants employed by the Tweeds. One report said there was no back door exit, though policemen were stationed at a rear entrance after the escape. In any event, there were fences barring a rear retreat. The group, talking quietly, entered the house about six-thirty. There they met Tweed's younger son, Richard, and Mr. Frederick Douglas, Tweed's son-in-law. The group entered the front parlor and seating themselves talked for a short while. Soon Tweed arose and said he wished to go upstairs to see his wife, who he said was very sick. He left the room and started up to the second floor. The warden heard his steps. It was the last they saw of Tweed. Dunham waited between five to twenty minutes, depending on the somewhat contradictory account given by the warden, and then asked "young Tweed," probably William Jr., to fetch the "old man." He returned in a few moments remarking placidly, as Dunham related it, "Father's gone." Hagan's version was that in fact, Tweed Jr., on seeing his father missing, excitedly pulled his hair and shouted out, "My God, I'm ruined." Still Tweed Jr. and Mr. Douglas were clearly upset and excited. Hagan said Douglas indeed acted like an insane man. Immediately, a search was made of the premises. Dunham ran across the street and saw the carriage still at the corner with Tweed nowhere in sight. Dunham asked the driver if he had seen anyone leave the house. The reply was negative. The worried warden then ran to the Nineteenth Precinct Station on Fifty-ninth Street between First and Second avenues and arrived about 7 P.M. He left Hagen at the house. An alarm was sounded at the precinct at 7:14 P.M. and the message of the escape went to every station house in New York and Brooklyn, followed shortly by telegrams to police stations throughout the country. City police were alerted and detectives in the central office at 300 Mulberry Street were summoned. They received instructions and were sent to watch all ferries and railroad depots leading from the city. At 8 P.M., Warden Dunham arrived at police headquarters and met with Inspector George W. Dilks (like Tweed, an Odd Fellow), repeating his account of the escape. He also visited Sheriff William C. Connor. At about 10 P.M., Connor called at the precinct to inquire of events and what was being done to find Tweed. He was told of known details and of subsequent searches made of the Tweed house by police. Officers were left on guard. At the same time, the warden, his face covered with sweat, returned to Ludlow Street, pale, gasping for air and unable to speak for fully five minutes. He then gave an interview to a *Times* reporter.

What is generally agreed happened was that Tweed went to his wife's upstairs room, retraced his steps, took a broad-brimmed soft felt hat and long black cloak and left through the front door without anyone seeing him. He left his high hat in the parlor and disappeared into the night. The time was about six-thirty. Whether his son or other family members or anyone else knew of the intended flight was not known. There are questions. Mrs. Clyde noted a new carriage on the day of the escape. Why?

Why take the soft hat and cloak and leave the high hat—was it to fool anyone looking for a man with a high hat? Were the cloak and hat waiting to be taken—as if prepared earlier? Was the escape simply a spur of the moment decision? Dunham and the authorities, as well as the family, certainly seemed taken by surprise. Connor, shaken and distraught, knowing that as the official in charge he could face the loss of his job and worse, stated in his defense that he always felt unsafe with Tweed on his hands. He feared an escape, and very reluctantly had given permission for the infrequent outings of Tweed, including the Saturday one. He resignedly expected to have to search all night through the city for the culprit. He was, a reporter stated, in a somewhat dazed condition during an interview in the station house.

The sheriff had cause for concern. Wheeler Peckham, the people's counsel, legal watchdog and guardian of law and justice, patronizingly declared that Connor was liable to the full amount of Tweed's bail—$4 million. "The law," he majestically offered, "does not take into account any excuses. This is not my interpretation of the law," he continued, "it is the law itself. Any good lawyer will tell you the same." Connor could have surrounded his prisoner with an army, and if he escaped Connor would be still liable according to Peckham, the self-appointed high executioner.

Aaron J. Vanderpoel, now the sheriff's counsel, hesitatingly expressed an opinion that his client was correct in allowing Tweed the liberties of the jail. The matter, however, would be, if necessary, resolved in a court. Connor posted a $10,000 reward for Tweed's return, to be paid gladly and willingly. He began circulating notices of the reward, together with a picture and description of Tweed. The reward was never to be collected.

As police began a search of the city and telegraph wires buzzed the startling news throughout the country, various individuals expressed their views of the escape. Peckham was so relieved at the news that he almost gloated. "Flight," he triumphed, "is always interpreted as a confession of guilt and though I have now a case so strong that it must surely carry conviction with an honest jury, I am glad to have this additional evidence." He could say that again. This was a windfall. His case was proven by the felon's confession of guilt—his escape. Peckham evinced no surprise. He expected such a turn, and attacked the "corrupt officials" who allowed Tweed not only to visit his family whenever he chose, but even to attend theaters in disguise. Such liberties would not be extended by honest officials. The sacrosanct counsel for the people offered no evidence.

Similarly, the *Herald* editorialized on the "nominal" imprisonment of Tweed, his daily excursions, his disguises, that "there was no real attempt to deprive him of liberty." The *Herald* hoped a lesson would be learned and that the defeat of all who follow the fortunes of John Kelly, Tweed's successor at Tammany, and of the "Know-Nothing Lodge" (Tammany Hall) on Fourteenth Street, would result. Shaking the Tweed tree still brought results.

David Dudley Field was disappointed by Tweed's desperate and foolish decision. It was "a great mistake for him." It was more. It was a disaster. Flight with its assumption of guilt as Peckham had reasoned was the final proof necessary. Field, although in the midst of arguing a motion against use of a struck or blue-ribbon jury in the $6 million suit, had now to rethink the entire matter. Field held that the defense was strong and the case could have been won if Tweed had stood his ground. Field placed the major reason for the escape on abuses of the bail system. A bail of $4 million in a civil suit was ridiculously excessive, if not barbarous. Fifty years from now Field prophesied such a demand would be "looked upon as one of the abuses of a past age." Field concluded that it was the very size of the bail that was responsible in great part for Tweed's escape. If bail was more reasonable, it could have been met by his friends and they, not the authorities, would be responsible for his remaining at hand. Tweed, free of jail and among his friends and family, would have far less reason to flee. Field argued that bail, like excessive tariffs or taxes, and the misuse of law lead to evasion of law.

Governor Tilden was immediately informed of the doings in New York. He appeared "greatly incensed" at the "unwelcome" news and ordered that Sheriff Connor be held personally responsible. Questions as to the where, hows and whys of Tweed's escape were on everyone's lips. Was there connivance on the part of public officials? Was he being secreted by his family or friends? Did he flee via a coal scuttle in the basement of his house? Could he have climbed over the back yard fences? Surely, it was argued, he was too fat and too old for that kind of physical activity. It was also rumored that a ship owned by an English firm of Charles T. Russell & Co., Liverpool, the *Lord Clarendon*, was off the coast of Long Island on that Saturday and was used by Tweed to flee the country. Soon further stories were circulated that Tweed was at home or was seen in Brooklyn, New Jersey, Staten Island, California and Canada. Photographs and descriptions brought nothing. Private detectives were equally useless. Tweed had simply vanished. New Yorkers went on to other matters.

Months passed and still not a word. The fox had fled the chase—but not for long. Suddenly, the first hint came from an obscure State Department official in Cuba who told of the arrival of two men in a note to his superiors at "Foggy Bottom."

Dispatch No. 414 from the United States consul general in Cuba, Henry C. Hall, was sent to Assistant Secretary of State John L. Cadwalader from Havana on June 23, 1876. In it were transmitted copies of several letters from Consul A. N. Young at Santiago de Cuba. The first, dated June 14, 1876, reported the suspicious landing on June 9, 1876, near that coastal city of two persons, John Secor and William Hunt. The pair told the consul they had taken passage from St. Augustine, Florida, on the sixth aboard the schooner *Mary* (or *Harry*), and on the night of the eleventh were put ashore ten miles from Santiago de Cuba at Socapa. In the morning, after spending a miserable night on the rocky shore, facing the rugged Sierra Maestra, they hired or were found by a fishing boat, which took them to the city. Secor, who was thought to be over fifty, and Hunt, about twenty-seven, said their trip to Cuba was because of the "old man's health," a story doubted by Young. Surely, they were not insurrectionists but simply persons fleeing justice. He doubted that they had come from Florida.

It is possible that "Secor" sent for Young. He was exhausted, his face "terribly" sunburnt and blistered and perhaps frightened that he and Hunt would be taken for Yankee filibusters trying their hands at "Cuba Libre" and if found by Spanish soldiers summarily shot. In the recent *Virginius* incident a number of Americans had been executed as pirates.

Both had passports issued in Washington on April 3, 1876. Secor, fifty-one, held Passport No. 49060, while Hunt, aged twenty-seven, held Passport No. 49061. The documents were not visaed by the Spanish consulate at St. Augustine. Secor told Young of having to hire the schooner and paying fifty dollars each for the passage. The men were interrogated aboard the Spanish warship *Churruco* but "are being very well treated." They are, thought Young, men of good education and with considerable means—the older one was "large and fleshy." Hall and Young asked the department for further instructions.[4]

On June 29, 1876, Hall wrote Young a "strictly confidential" letter. He was sure that Secor was none other than William M. Tweed of New York. He enclosed a photograph and a description of Tweed:

> about fifty-five years of age, five feet eleven inches tall, about two hundred eighty pounds, very portly, ruddy complexion, has rather large, coarse, prominent features and large prominent nose; rather small blue or gray eyes, gray hair, though originally auburn color; head nearly bald on the top from forehead back to crown and bare part of ruddy color, head projecting toward the crown. His beard may be removed or dyed and he may wear a wig or be otherwise disguised.

This was the description issued by the sheriff's office in New York, a copy of which was in the hands of Hall. Hall certainly reached conclusions quickly. The identification was positive which is somewhat odd given Young's tentative description and the fact there were two men, which was misleading. Young was told to be most secretive, not to talk to anyone, but to investigate carefully and cautiously. If Young was sure of his man telegraph VESSEL ARRIVED SAFELY; if not, STATEMENT FALSE. On July 7, Hall received a telegram, VESSEL ARRIVED SAFELY. The next day, Young wrote to Hall, telling of his surprise about Secor and Tweed. Tweed was much thinner with shorter whiskers than in the photograph. He was also suffering from the heat a "great deal and from a complication of diseases," including dropsy, and if detained by authorities for any length of time, he feared he would most probably die. The pair were put up at the Hotel de Shy run by a Madam Adella, after being released by the Spanish authorities. This at Young's request. Young now felt alarmed about their possible escape if they became suspicious of police surveillance. He wanted further instructions. On June 30, 1876, a day after informing Young, Hall also wrote to Assistant Secretary Cadwalader, confidentially telling of his suspicions about the identity of Tweed and "his son" William Hunt. He also informed General Joaquín Jovallar, newly appointed governor of Cuba, of his suspicions and stressed the necessity of secrecy so that the department could be informed of any movement of the pair. Also, on June 30, the department and Hall received further information as to the passports. These were indeed issued on April 3, 1876, upon requisite affidavit executed before Thomas L. Landon, notary public, New York City and mailed to "John Brown, New Court House, New York City." Hunt would seem to have been born in Philadelphia, and Secor in Columbia County, New York. From this, it would appear that Tweed and Hunt knew each other in New York prior to April 3, and that possibly Tweed and Hunt had appeared before Landon in March. Either Landon did not recognize them, or they used proxies. Surely, Tweed was in the New York area at that time. Who was Hunt? An escaped convict? a friend? a relative? or an agent or spy keeping track of Tweed? One story has him as a coachman long in Tweed's employ. He is a strange figure in an equally strange affair.

Secretary of State Hamilton Fish sent a telegram to Hall on July 11. In it Fish queried "If Secor is Tweed and is still in Cuba ask Captain General Jovallar would he deliver Tweed to United States officials if a ship was sent to Santiago?"

Hall replied that Jovallar had in fact at first indicated agreement to such an arrangement, but wanted time to consider the situation, pledging strict secrecy. Hall suspected that Tweed might escape in a private vessel; this could be permitted—if he was followed by a United States naval vessel. Numerous cables and letters, many in code, followed, as Jovallar awaited instructions from Spain. Jovallar was concerned with a positive identity of Tweed. As Tweed and Hunt paced their rooms, perhaps not knowing of the net being woven about them, Fish was informed by telegram on July 22 of a decision reached in Madrid "to surrender

Secor if identified." On the same day, Hall informed Fish by letter that Jovallar said two witnesses and an authenticated copy of the indictment would suffice for identification. Jovallar wanted to let the press know of this decision, but was persuaded by Hall to wait a few days as any premature publicity might "defeat the course of justice." The best-laid plans of the State Department regarding Cuba now became meaningless. On the evening of July 27, Hall received an urgent telegram from Young, SECOR AND HUNT SAIL THIS EVENING FOR SPAIN. Since the telegram offices in Havana and Santiago were open only from 7 A.M. to 7 P.M., little could be done during the night, and General Jovallar, out of town, could not be reached. It seems Tweed decided to leave on July 22, but had to wait until the twenty-sixth in order to have his passport visaed. An irate Hall on July 28 informed Fish that the *Churruco* at Guantánamo, forty miles from Santiago, had sailed in pursuit of Tweed and Hunt, but he expected little by way of success. Hall was sure there was collusion. He enclosed a note to this effect from Jovallar with the further important information that Tweed was bound for Vigo.[5]

The game had fled, but not too far. On August 1, Hall telegraphed Fish that Secor's vessel was the *Carman*, and that Jovallar had telegraphed Madrid requesting the return of Secor to Cuba if he could not be extradited from Spain. Hall's suspicion of collusion was probably aroused by a letter from Young on July 29, 1876, amplifying what had happened. In this Hall was informed that F. N. Ramsden, the British consul and agent of the British West Indies Cable Company, which ran a link between Havana and Santiago, suspected who Secor really was by perhaps intercepting one of the telegraph messages. Tweed was a "great friend" of J. H. Waydell's of Waydell & Co. of New York and Ramsden had been asked by the company to offer Tweed his services. There was a John H. Waydell cooper's materials at 21 Old Slip. This could have been the firm mentioned. Ramsden was instrumental in having the captain of the port allow Secor and Hunt to go to Spain. In another story it was Young who informed Ramsden of Secor's arrival. Anyway, despite Jovallar's instructions, the pair were allowed to leave. Hall asked, "Now, what can be done?" Fish immediately wrote to the aged Caleb Cushing, American minister in Madrid, a short account of the Tweed arrival and detection in Cuba and subsequent "treachery." Cushing was asked to ascertain secretly and cautiously if Tweed could be returned to Cuba.

On the fourth day of August, Hall wrote to Cadwalader substantially the story he wrote to Fish and given him by Young. He added that he was sure it was one of Waydell's vessels on which Tweed escaped from New York and which landed him in Santiago and that he came recommended by way of Waydell to Mr. Ramsden. Interestingly, the interlude in Florida as told by Secor and Hunt was discounted by Hall. A trip directly from New York was more than likely. So ended the Cuban adventure. Tweed and Hunt were now bound for Spain and still more intrigue.

It was of course an odd second "escape." The State Department, Spanish authorities and many others knew the ship and the destination of Tweed and Hunt. In fact, weren't the whereabouts of Tweed always known? How quickly the information of his landing was received in Cuba. Certainly he did not sail to Spain secretly. He probably did not take passage on the *Carman* as a sailor, but rather as a passenger paying demurrage from July 22 to 26. The outlandish legend of his being recognized from a Nast cartoon by some simple Spaniard is a complete fiction. Why flight to Cuba and Spain? Perhaps friends like Waydell & Co. did have influence in those places, perhaps, since there was no extradition treaty, evasion would be possible. The last, if a hope, was a very slim one indeed. Tweed later said he went to Spain, because his "advisors" said there was no extradition, and "good old sherry" was "very cheap."[6] This is as close as Tweed came to mentioning some outside influence on his decision. He never mentioned his reasons or discussed his escape.

As the *Carman* sailed on its slow tortuous journey, the State Department went into high gear. On August 5, Cushing telegraphed Fish that the Spanish Minister of State, Calderón y Collantes, agreed to work with American authorities and to order the arrest of Tweed at Vigo and then to return him to Cuba, expenses to be paid by the United States. On the seventh, Fish showed the Cushing telegram to President Grant. It was agreed no mention would be made in the Cabinet and only the Secretary of the Navy, George M. Robeson, was to be informed.[7] On the ninth, Cushing in a long note told of the minister's responsiveness and of his not wishing to have Spain become an asylum for thieves and embezzlers. Since there was no treaty of extradition, the return of Tweed would be an act of comity. Cushing intended to give the minister a description of Tweed if he could not find a Nast caricature of Tweed in Madrid. Collantes was told by Cushing of Tweed's appearance, his birth, age, large mouth and most prominent nose—again the sheriff's description. Tweed might have picked up some Spanish but even if disguised as a sailor, could not be taken as such. Shortly before, on August 6, a Nast likeness was delivered to Collantes by Cushing. It was a cartoon in *Harper's* of July 1, 1876. Even if the beard were shaved, everybody would say if they saw the man "that is Tweed," thought Cushing. Fish was also informed of Cushing's interview with the other officers in the Ministry of State, and of their assurances of caution and discretion. Collantes was further reminded of the extradition of one Arguelles, a Cuban embezzler, by William H. Seward, and the debt thus owed by Spain to the United States would be paid by the return of Tweed.

Fish was informed by A. Augustus Adee, chargé d'affaires, of a visit of Mr. Rafael Ferraz, Sub-Secretary of State, on the evening of August 24. Ferraz said that the governor of the province of Pontevedra, Don Victor Novoa Limeses, was to visit Vigo on Tweed's arrival and supervise the proceedings himself. Adee then visited Mr. Barca, Sub-Secretary of the Ministry of Colonial Affairs, who asked for more relative information about the *Carman.* There were, he said, some thirty vessels by that name in the Spanish shipping registry. Was it a steamer or sailing ship? Cushing thought it would be a sailing vessel. Barca expected the voyage to last thirty or forty days. Adee felt that in view of Tweed's career, perhaps the governors of the other Atlantic provinces should be alerted since Tweed might bribe the captain of the *Carman.* Adee also suggested considering that she came from a "dirty" port, and that authorities of the Health Department in various ports be alerted. Barca agreed to the suggestions. On the twenty-fifth, Barca received a message from Adee, underlining the necessity of alerting health authorities. Two days later, Fish was told of the added precautions in a letter from Adee. Collantes on the same date informed Adee of the preparations to be made in regard to Tweed. The trap was set.

Finally, news of Tweed's arrival was flashed by Adee on September 7 to Fish in a ciphered message detailing that the governor of Pontevedra had arrested Tweed and his "nephew" Hunt the moment the *Carman* reached Vigo, which was noon, September 6. Later, a *Times* reporter said that Tweed was found by the governor of the province in his shirt sleeves, barefooted in the midst of scrubbing the deck. This was not reported by Spanish authorities or by Cushing. A photograph taken almost immediately after the arrival in Vigo shows he wore clothes similar to the sort he had on in New York. Were these his work clothes? The next day, Adee telegraphed Fish for further instructions. A reply came immediately. Fish requested the return to Cuba of Tweed and Hunt. Adee wired back on the tenth that they would probably be returned on the twentieth perhaps to be delivered to an American warship. The fish had been netted; the careful attention and detail had paid off, and there would be little fuss. News of the arrest of Tweed and a "cousin," William Hunt, again made the headlines. The event was first reported in the *Herald* immediately after Tweed's arrest. Some at Tammany scoffed. The resourceful "Boss" was above capture. He was most likely still in Manhattan. But, as more details were published, the truth of the episode was evident. James Gordon Bennett inquired of Adee if the *Herald* reporter then in Spain, William J. Knapp, could interview Tweed. Spanish authority was willing, was Fish?

This was on September 11. Washington telegraphed a refusal two days later. However, Knapp pushed the matter further and received permission from Spanish authorities. Minister Cushing also informed Adee that he saw no objection to the interview. However, there was hesitation over proper authorization. Fish put an end to all doubt by informing Cushing of his opposition to any Tweed interview.[8]

It was also on the thirteenth that President Grant became more interested in Tweed. "The *Herald* is very anxious to learn whether it is true that Tweed could be used as a witness against Tilden in a suit to recover monies due the government," wrote the President to Fish. It was in reference to the income tax matter brought against Tilden. Tilden, nominated as Democratic candidate for the presidency in June 1876, was harmed by tax evasion charges. He was fined for delinquency. How often the pot calls the kettle black. Fish refused to allow the interview despite Grant's seeming desire that it be done. This could be explained by fear that any such information could as well embarrass many Republicans. The extradition proceedings were themselves being questioned. Fish thought the best policy was continued secrecy. Grant agreed.[9]

In another lengthy letter from Spain dated September 11, Adee told Fish that Tweed and Hunt were arrested and their baggage sealed and all placed under the guard of a detachment of *carabineros* (customs guards) by the governor, Don Victor Novoa Limeses, who asked that the prisoners be lodged in the fortress at Vigo. This was done. Adee then visited Mr. Magallon, chief of the political section of the Ministry of State, who asked if an American warship was being sent to Spain. Adee then went to M. Duran, chief of the San Ildefonso detachment of the colonial office, to arrange preliminary details. Duran asked that a note be prepared for Collantes as to the precise disposition of the prisoners, especially the one called Hunt. Adee asked that Hunt and Tweed be sent via the first steamer from Santander leaving on the twentieth or Corunna on the twenty-first, whichever Spain decided. The note, quickly written, went to Duran and then to Collantes. Adee returned them to Madrid to find the affair in public print. Tweed was called a child stealer. This was derived from the Nast drawing of July 1 showing two small boy-thieves being chastised by Tweed. It was this cartoon Cushing had sent Collantes. Adee also informed Fish that the two men were still in the calaboose of the lazaretto of San Simon, undergoing seven days of quarantine. Barca was concerned with security and the prying of journalists. Adee now understood that the following would take place. The men were to be removed on the twelfth or thirteenth to a fortress at Vigo and then taken under military authority to Corunna or Santander, probably the former, and placed aboard the mail boat to Havana. Since three guards were to accompany them, Adee would try to see that they were bound for duty in Cuba anyway and so reduce expenses to the United States. Adee also evinced curiosity about Hunt and hoped to be able to examine his baggage. Adee enclosed articles taken from *La Época* on September 9 and 10 and *La Política* September 7 about the celebrated North American criminal and kidnapper, child stealer and thief of $6 million. *La Época* sounded the beginning of rumblings in the Tweed affair in an article correcting the "fact" that Tweed was a kidnapper, and stated "in fact" he was an "ancient" employee of New York City accused of "bribery and malversation" and caught *in flagrante*, confessed his guilt and was sentenced. Still, the government in Washington was not accustomed to ask Spain a favor, and since there was no treaty of extradition, perhaps the request would not be honored. *La Época* of the twenty-second amplified its position on extradition maintaining that any "generous conduct" of Spain should be reciprocated by the United States and a treaty of extradition signed. This view, Adee felt, in his letter to Fish of the September 27, reflected the thinking of the new government of Canoras del Castillo. Adee also told of various other persons suggesting such a treaty before Tweed was released. A Spaniard of "importance" asked Adee why did the United States, the leading exponent of extradition treaties, which had such treaties with many countries, yet have none with Spain? During the reign of King Amadeo, General Daniel Sickles, former Minister of the United States, had in fact drawn up such a treaty —it was never ratified. The question was, why not? *La Época* on October 1, 1876, told its readers of the interest in the Tweed extradition. Democrats and Republicans hypocritically wanted to appear before the public "as inspired by the most elevated ideas of morality and reform." The paper was angered over United States failures to turn over escaped criminals from Spain. Yet, Spain complied in the Tweed case without hesitation because it was a courteous, moral and legitimate thing to do. Such courtesies might not last, and again the paper urged a mutual extradition treaty. Other newspapers also voiced resentment.

El Imparcial of October 2, 1876, told of the unaccustomed speed in surrendering Tweed, due, it felt, to the pressures brought by Governor Tilden and the Republican Grant administration. Such action brought mounting criticism of Spain from the press of Europe. The newspaper also charged the United States with failure to dispatch wanted Spanish criminals. On the fourth, *El Imparcial*, while agreeing on the necessity of surrendering Tweed, felt that in view of the lack of an extradition treaty, the haste in the surrender of Tweed resulted in an inequality, to the "disparagement of our dignity as a nation." The Tweed affair came close to causing a difficult international imbroglio. U.S.-Spanish relationships had never been very good, were recently embittered by the *Virginius* affair and were probably not improved at least in the Spanish press by the Fish, Adee, Collantes negotiations. While a storm brewed over the question of an extradition treaty, Collantes told Adee on the thirteenth of September of the steps being taken to send the pair to Cuba on the mail boat. The Spanish government was probably eager to rid itself of a potentially irritating situation. He raised questions as to what guard the United States could provide, perhaps a contingent of detectives and policemen? Adee thought this could not be done. Various suggestions had been offered by the Spaniards but nothing was yet settled. Adee wanted instructions. On the eighteenth after receiving a note for Fish, Adee telegraphed the Secretary of State of Collantes and asked him to assent to a change of plan. Secor was not to be sent to Cuba. The men would be sent to Corunna strictly guarded. Final orders as to Hunt were to be sent. Meanwhile, Adee, always suspicious of treachery and collusion, told Fish in a letter dated September 18 of having received a note from Mr. Camilo Molins, United States consular agent at Vigo, concerning Tweed and Hunt, in which he asked permission to communicate with the pair, especially the "respectable" Mr. Tweed, as an act of humanity. Angered over such courtesies shown Tweed, Adee answered with a flat no. On the same day, Fish again asked Adee to investigate quickly Spanish intention as to delivering Secor in Spain; as to Hunt, the government knew nothing and "do not desire his detention." In return, Adee informed Fish of formal arrangements concluded that day. Now Tweed was to leave from Vigo but Collantes did not wish to release Hunt unless fully identified for fear of letting the wrong man go. A Nast cartoon was still just that and not really sufficient. Spanish authorities asked no questions as to Secor and agreed to turn Hunt over to American officials.

The frigate U.S.S. *Franklin*, formerly carrying the flag of Civil War hero Admiral John L. Worden, had in the meantime been reached. Adee on the twentieth telegraphed Captain Samuel R. Franklin, the new commander, to change course from Corunna to Vigo. Adee also suggested that private orders be sent Captain Franklin for the disposal of Hunt and his luggage. The *Franklin* left for Vigo from Gibraltar on September 21. Adee then as diplomatically as possible told Collantes of the coming of the warship. The minister happily accepted the plan. Collantes desired that Hunt and Tweed plus their luggage be handed over to Captain Franklin and let him decide what should be done with Hunt. Adee did not push the question of Hunt's release given Collantes' frame of mind. Though hobbled by a rheumatic left knee, which frequently kept him in bed, Adee, however, often visited Collantes and sent a constant flow of messages to the State Department trying to ensure every detail of the transfer. At the end of a fifteen-page dispatch from Adee to Fish, the counsel mentioned having received from Governor Limeses photographs of Tweed and Hunt taken by a local cameraman at Vigo early during the pair's confinement, probably on the day of their arrival. That of Tweed was an "admirable likeness" removing any doubt as to Secor's identity. What a forlorn figure Tweed was —a tired old man. It is the only known photograph of Tweed showing glasses. Adee did not recognize Hunt. Agent Molins informed Adee that the *Franklin* entered Vigo at 8 A.M. September 26, and would sail with Tweed, Hunt being freed, on the twenty-seventh. This information was sent to Fish on the twenty-seventh. The next day Adee informed Fish that Tweed and Hunt were delivered to Captain Franklin at 10 P.M. on the twenty-sixth. Captain Franklin wrote Adee on the twenty-seventh from aboard the *Franklin* that Tweed was "safely lodged on board." Hunt was offered passage to New York, but refusing, was set free. Franklin was now awaiting a change of wind and took time to bury a sailor who died on the evening of the twenty-sixth before proceeding on his voyage to New York.

Tweed was again under arrest. His curious, ill-concerned escape netted him ten months of running from the frying pan to the fire. His flight accomplished nothing except trouble. The return of Tweed stirred the front pages again as the *Times* republished an article from the Baltimore *Sun* by reporter G.E.H.H., not further identified, relating the story of the *Franklin* and Tweed. He had been on the *Franklin* during its Mediterranean cruise. The crew of the *Franklin* on the fourteenth of September said farewell to Admiral Worden, the former commander of the famed *Monitor*, at a port in Italy, and arrived in Gibraltar on the nineteenth on the way to the United States. On the twentieth, Franklin, the new commander, received a telegram from Chargé d'affaires Adee in Madrid and a few hours later from the Under-Secretary of the Navy ordering the *Franklin* to remain at Gibraltar. The next day orders were received to proceed to Vigo and pick up Tweed. They arrived the evening of the twenty-fifth of September, but owing to fog remained out of the harbor until September 26 morning. At 10 P.M. on the twenty-sixth as noted, Tweed was taken on board. "The old Boss looks quite jolly and has brass enough to last him a hundred years," noted G.E.H.H. in his dispatch. Tweed was maintained on the *Franklin*, in keeping with instructions that he be "treated with proper respect and allowed liberty as may be consistent with assured security of his person and will not allow escape or intercourse with the crew." He was given the quarters formerly occupied by Worden, consisting of a large salon and two adjoining staterooms, but portholes were shut, doors barred and a sentry stationed in his room day and night. Officers were detailed to be in constant attendance. On his arrival in New York, he was described as looking very seedy, wearing a soiled linen shirt, without a collar, a black alpaca coat that sagged in the back and sides in a "most unbecoming manner," a dirty brown vest and a pair of checked "trowsers." He carried a small handbag. Aware of his appearance, Tweed tried to brush himself off a little "out of respect to the people I'm going to see." He seemed in good spirits. During the long voyage via St. Thomas, made longer by contrary or light winds, Tweed was, except for a few days of seasickness, a "perfect gentleman"—a man of "true grit." Officers played cards with him. Tweed was "sharp" and "lively" at such games. But having been so ordered no one spoke of his New York affairs. He read a good deal, mostly newspapers, and entertained everyone with stories of New York politics. Unfortunately, no one seemed to have made notes of these reminiscences. What stories he could have told! He ate well but drank not at all. There was a report he had contemplated suicide.[10]

While Tweed was at sea, the State Department was not. Cadwalader informed Fish of suspicions about "unfaithful" counsel Young—he should be investigated immediately. Fish concurred with this and also told Cadwalader of his plans to go to New York to confer with District Attorney Phelps "in re Secor." "We must soon prepare instructions as to the disposition to be made of the 'Elephant.' What do you think of offering him to Tilden," was Fish's eloquent query.[11] Political considerations as to the "Elephant" were apparently uppermost in the minds of President Grant and Fish. Of various courses of action, placing Tweed under Governor Tilden's control seemed best as it would hopefully embarrass Tilden in his presidential race. This was concurred in by Grant in an exchange of letters with Fish. Tilden, Grant felt, could raise questions about the legality of Tweed's extradition, still it would be best to give Tilden the responsibility, and hopefully the embarrassment. However, telegrams from Sheriff Connor and Governor Tilden, and letters from fellow Republicans including Charles S. Fairchild, caused things to be altered. Grant agreed to surrender Tweed to Connor, and careful plans were made as to exactly the way the transfer of the "Elephant" was to be made, as well as details as to disposition of luggage. Chester A. Arthur was to examine Tweed's baggage at customs.[12]

At 11 A.M. November 23, the *Franklin* arrived off Sandy Hook. Sheriff Connor, his vigil at last at an end, United States Attorney Bliss and District Attorney Phelps together with custom and health officials, aboard the gunboat *Catalpa*, met the *Franklin* in the bay. Connor and the others boarded, introduced themselves and Tweed and luggage were surrendered. The sheriff and Bliss went below deck and found Tweed playing solitaire. They stared at each other, not a word was spoken. Tweed was taken aboard the *Catalpa*. Here Tweed was told of Woodward's arrest. Tweed asked Connor for news of recent elections. The gunboat reached the foot of Houston Street, North River, about 4 P.M. His baggage was left aboard the *Franklin* and examined by Phelps and U. S. Attorney George Bliss. Papers and other articles were found of little value, even to Tweed. Tweed was next taken to Ludlow Street escorted by five carriages filled with officials and reporters. Hundreds of people were at the dock, the police having to make a path through the crowd. As the carriage approached the jail, crowds were even larger. Tweed met Warden Watson, the new appointee, and shook hands, "Well, I thought I would come back to you." He was placed in his old quarters. He looked about the same as when he left, thought a *Times* reporter. At about four-thirty, Tweed's brother Richard, his son William Jr. and S. Foster Dewey visited the prisoner and stayed until requested to leave at 10:30 P.M. He was home.[13]

What was the effect of his absence on his appearance? Contrary to the *Times* reporter, Dewey found Tweed greatly changed—"you would hardly recognize him." He was much thinner. He looked tanned but was quite ill, suffering from pleurisy. His family physician, Dr. Shearman, was expected the next day. He was in spirit greatly downcast, apparently crushed and humiliated. "He is like a child," Dewey stated, "nervous and apprehensive of dangers." What were future plans? Would Dudley Field visit? Would Tweed finally expose public men? There was nothing that could be said now.

Questions were also asked as to the flight of Tweed, especially as to the months preceding his arrival in Cuba. The *Times* detailed an unverified account of Tweed's going aboard a schooner *Frank Atwood* on May 29, 1876, from a small boat off New Jersey, Staten Island or Long Island. The daily reported that Tweed after his December 4 escape met with "Red" Dan Talmadge, one "Big Bob" and Philip Knighton, a fruit dealer and a former member of the "Big Six," who gave him refuge.[14] All involved denied this story. On April 3, 1877, *Harper's* published another "romantic" story based on a fictitious Tweed "diary" which was reprinted in the *Times*. According to this story, Tweed was harassed and in despair, especially after the unfounded rumor of the death of Charles O'Conor, who Tweed felt was the only one with whom he could work. He learned from his fellow prisoners of laws of extradition and lack of them with Spain and decided to escape to that country. Another inmate, a noted bank robber named Bliss, told Tweed of friends, part of a well-organized group, with whom he could hide. According to the "diary" Tweed visited his Forty-third Street mansion (he lived on Madison, not Forty-third) and upon leaving the parlor when Warden Dunham went to wash his hands, closed the parlor door and left. He was then taken by the desperadoes to a decaying homestead in New Jersey. There he became John Secor. He clipped his beard, and put on a wig of reddish-yellow hair. He went to

Staten Island and with two companions and a Negro boy sailed to Florida. Here on some sandy surf he met Hunt. They traveled around the Everglades, camped out, fished, hunted, etc. Then to Cuba, through the night on a rock near Santiago, their rescue by a fisherman. On to Spain and recapture. The *Times* labeled the account interesting "but lacking one essential point—truth." Tweed later said that the *Harper's* story was the best—probably meaning the best fiction.[15]

Strangely, and this is so much part of the mystery of the escape and indeed much of Tweed's life, Tweed himself said nothing about the episode and the *Harper's* story was never substantiated.

The flight of Tweed was, of course, as Field felt, a catastrophic blunder. It would not help Tweed unless he was willing to spend the remainder of his life as a fugitive. Despite his despair and discouragement, he was still fighting, his case was still being argued, flight could only help Peckham and the state. For the Democrats and Tilden, it would remove an embarrassment. How much could Tweed tell of intrigues within the party? Republicans were quick to seize an opportunity in recapturing the "old man." The party and the Grant administration was itself in deep trouble, rocked by scandal, and many deeds of official and unofficial corruption. The return of Tweed, especially in an election year, as *La Época* observed, would do much to erase some tarnish from Republican banners of morality and honesty. Grant pressed Secretary Fish to find Tweed; it would pull chestnuts from the fire. However, the return of Tweed came too late to play a role in the election of 1876. What of Hunt, a most intriguing and curious subject? He looks like a villain—a thief and worse. Did he come from Philadelphia as related on his passport? If "found" by Tweed, of what use was he to the "ex-Boss"? A companion? There seems no logic to this. Was Hunt a spy for Fairchild and Peckham? They could not have asked for anything better than the "escape," even if they planned it. Did they? Was he used to inform authorities as to Tweed's whereabouts? Certainly, news of his landing traveled very fast and the State Department's identification also came fast. By turning in the "evidence," did Hunt gain freedom? Money? Was he working for the State Department? Why would he stay with Tweed? Tweed was a known fugitive and wouldn't Hunt endanger himself?

Perhaps the most perplexing thing about Hunt is the State Department's or Peckham's failure to prosecute the man for aiding and abetting an escaped prisoner, or to so much as question him. He had been with Tweed for all those months, through the long sea voyage, the days in a steaming calaboose in Cuba, then time together in the fortress in Vigo; surely something might have been said by Tweed which could be of use in further investigation of the escape or the prosecution. Yet no one interviewed Hunt, no one asked anything of his story. If, as Adee had said, there was conspiracy, why not pursue this? What of Waydell & Co.? Were they in fact part of the adventure? But there were no questions. Perhaps most curious of all was the failure even to question Tweed on any of these subjects. What of Tweed's own refusal to talk of his experience? Was he protecting some close friend or relative? Then there is the secrecy which surrounded the event. The cryptic and coded messages of the State Department. The refusal to allow interviews. What could Tweed and Hunt say? Could Hunt have implicated those who did not want to be identified? Chance, or part of a conspiracy to have him escape, the Tweed adventure was a strange affair, stranger even after examination. Tweed gambled, if that's what it was, and lost. He was back where he started from, but much the loser. Everyone stood to gain by Tweed's escape, everyone but Tweed himself. In a pathetic letter written to Charles O'Conor from the Ludlow Street Jail December 6, 1876, Tweed described himself "an old man, greatly broken in health, cast down in spirit, and can no longer bear my burden." His fight was over; he threw himself on the mercy of the court, O'Conor and public opinion. Further resistance was hopeless. He would admit guilt, give names and give up all property and possessions. He was of all things a penitent prisoner petitioning "unqualified surrender," desiring only release.[16] He could not find the key himself. His petition was rejected and his testimony laughed at. Who would ever believe a thief and escaped criminal, proved so by his own deeds, in anything he would say? No one ever would.

27

Surrender

Even with Tweed gone, the suits followed their course with the inevitability of a Greek tragedy. Field and Peckham were at each other like two bulldogs chewing at the then chief bone of contention, the struck jury. Peckham was retained again as special counsel, when Charles S. Fairchild became attorney general at the beginning of 1876. Fairchild would prove to be an even more vindictive adversary than his predecessor. The struck jury was upheld and by January 19, 1876, twelve men were selected. The foreman was John Taylor Johnston, president of the New Jersey Central Railroad, and the others were all from fashionable neighborhoods.

Peckham, of course, was up to his old tricks. Hand-picked juries and judges who played "footsie" with the prosecution, the bribery of witnesses by way of dropping prosecution and cash payments to witnesses. Writing to Tilden on January 20, Peckham related that he wanted William H. Wiggins, formerly clerk in the comptroller's office, as a witness in the upcoming trial. It was arranged. Wiggins, "poor as a rat," had gone to Washington hoping to obtain an appointment. "He has *now received* an appointment as clerk in the office of Clerk of the House of Representatives," Peckham wrote, but was kept in New York and given a leave of absence from his new post, all through Peckham's efforts. So far, so good. He then informed Tilden, now governor, that "we want to keep [Judge] Westbrook, but he had the Albany circuit at that time [of the trial]. Can you not send a judge to hold that circuit for him as to leave him here—he has become familiar with the matter of struck juries, and we think it of great importance that he should be kept to try both cases—Westbrook is very willing to stay if it can be arranged as to the Albany circuit and the case would otherwise have to go over to the February term." Peckham did not want to try Tweed before Davis, whom he wanted sent to Albany. Probably, he felt that again to use Davis, who was angry at O'Conor anyway, might turn public opinion against the prosecution in that the public might begin to think that only Davis could find against Tweed. Peckham continued, "It is important to have these cases now and finally disposed of. Thus far, we are clear that there is no error and that any verdict we get STICK—but we don't want a new man." The next day, Peckham again wrote to Tilden telling him of various judges who could be available for the Albany job. Of those in the Fourth Circuit, he did not know if there was any way of compelling them to move to the Albany circuit, "but if there be, it would be good to get a little work out of their lazy bones. I am ready to go on with the second suit against Tweed before anyone except Donohue. Before him it would be unsafe in the extreme. True, we might reverse him, but that is not what we want." Later, he wrote, "By an order in the bill of particulars he showed his fidelity to Tweed's principles. It is ridiculous that [he] should be permitted to harass us . . ." It was astounding. The requests, the tone, the unwarranted tampering with the judicial process were and are inconceivable.[1]

By early February 1876, with ten suits scheduled during Tweed's absence, the "big suit" was given preference, though a jury was also drawn in the "little suit." The "big suit" came to trial on February 7 and, of course, before Justice Theodoric R. Westbrook in Supreme Court. Peckham and James C. Carter, Tilden's personal attorney, appeared for the people and Field and Edelstein for the defense, William Tweed, Jr., sat with his father's counsel. There was a vacant chair which should have held the elder Tweed. Field began by defending his own career from the attacks of the *Tribune* which accused him of defending thieves and scoundrels. The *Tribune* should know of thieves and scoundrels since its friends and supporters are of that ilk. "It is a fool bird that soils its own nest," Field retorted. Carter recounted the story of "The Ring," the "board of audit," the plunder and Tweed's 25 per cent. It was old stuff. Keyser repeated his story. George S. Miller told his tale of having received his orders from Woodward and Ingersoll, and being asked by Woodward and Ingersoll to raise his bills 65 per cent. He admitted under cross-examination of fleeing to Cuba in December 1873. He came back the following April after his father made an arrangement to keep him clear of prosecution. He destroyed his books in 1871. He never returned any money because he had none to return. Keyser returned to the stand, and admitted receiving a promise of immunity from Charles O'Conor, witnessed by Havemeyer, Green and Jackson Schultz, that he would be released from any criminal and civil prosecution.

Lynes testified that there were ten or twelve clerks in the auditor's office, but he was the only one to examine or keep regular office books. What of Copland? Wiggins? Taintor? He thought the amounts were extraordinarily large but sent them through for Watson's signature. Garvey was called and the old wine flowed. All his dealings were with Woodward and Ingersoll—the story of receiving 35 per cent of all his bills, the rest going to Woodward. He told of being asked by Woodward to build a house for Connolly and to pad his bills to cover the work. Field asked for checkbooks. Garvey said these were destroyed. Carter intimated this was done on orders of the "gang of thieves with which he [Tweed] was associated." On cross-examination, Garvey admitted he was wrong in being a tool of "The Ring," but he admitted even his 35 per cent was more than he could have charged private individuals for the same work. The next hearing was February 14. Cross-examination continued. The foreman, John T. Johnston, asked that the trial be speeded up as jurors were suffering "great personal inconvenience." The jury would have convicted on the first day. Ingersoll testified over Field's objection to the introduction of testimony from a convicted felon. He told the same story of percentages, fictitious names and packages of money. Tweed never complained of not getting his share. Field asked Ingersoll if it was right to recover $6 million from Tweed and none from Ingersoll. Ingersoll replied he was worth only $50,000; anyway his property had been given to his wife and father-in-law. Let Tweed's friends in the legislature pay back the money. It was Tweed's fault. He related he had several conversations with Tweed in regard to making overcharges and "remembered" giving Tweed his share. Davidson was next. He said he never went before the "board of audit" or Supervisors to verify bills. He received about 33 per cent of his warrants. On cross-examination, he maintained all his bills were honest, but contradictorily he generally overcharged the city. When asked to examine a warrant and identify "false" signatures, he had a difficult time and was confused.

The trial took longer than anticipated. The motions, arguments had delayed what should have been cut-and-dry procedure. It was time for Tilden. The governor, soon to be presidential nominee of the Democratic Party, was constantly informed of matters, and on February 19, Peckham asked Tilden if it was convenient for him to be at the trial on Thursday, February 25. He also asked Tilden to "recall" the conversation he had with Tweed before the Tilden investigation into the Broadway Bank became known. According to Tilden, Tweed had asked what he had found. Peckham reminded Tilden that "You told him as to the deposits to his account of Woodward's checks and asked what he had to say about it. He said to you that it was a loan transaction between them. You said that the difficulty with that claim was that the money went all one way, to which he replied that that was their theory anyway." Peckham wanted to bring this out at Tilden's examination—"I will ask you about it tomorrow." As usual Tilden was being well prepared and coached—for it was Tilden.

Tilden appeared on February 25, as arranged, but before that two witnesses, Arthur E. Smith and a Mr. Porter, formerly with Broadway Bank and released "for spite," admitted being coached by Peckham in their testimony, as well as being paid for it. Tilden never admitted this, but muddled as usual, again read his account of his investigations, and this Field strenuously objected to, but the court allowed the governor to continue. Field objected to introduction in evidence of testimony concerning the New York Printing Company in Tilden's statement since there was no connection with his client. Tweed's name, Field said, was being held up as a "red rag was before a bull" to excite people and to connect him with frauds he never had a hand in.

Tilden was sharply cross-examined by Field regarding two laws passed in 1872 and in 1873, both of which directed $75,000 be raised by the county to pay expenses of the Tweed suits, and which law allowed Tilden to be paid a share of the money. Tilden could not find an answer as to what he received, though he stated he did certify some expenses.

Field attempted to show that Tilden's motive in pressing the investigation against Tweed was political and that he manipulated the Green-Connolly episode for his own ends. He also attempted to show that the civil suit was meant not to recover money, but to gain control of the judiciary. Justice Westbrook excluded this line of reasoning. Field's attempt to see the papers relating to Ingersoll's pardon was also unsuccessful. Tilden refused to discuss the matter.

Witnesses were then called in regard to Tweed's deposits. Tellers of the Tenth National Bank said between May and August 1870 about $500,000 was deposited, but they weren't sure if it was by Tweed. On March 11, the prosecutor's case was closed after Arthur E. Smith testified as to his theory, which was that Tweed received 25 per cent only when Woodward received 65 per cent. Where Woodward received only 40 per cent as in some of Ingersoll's deposits, Tweed received nothing.

Field now began his defense. He traced the history of the courthouse, the various appropriations, that from 1856 to 1870 there was but one case involving a disputed warrant. From 1863 to 1870, $3,150,000 was expended without a dissenting voice. In fact the original discovery of frauds was made by himself, and attorneys George Tichnor Curtis and John K. Porter. "This did not suit those prominent in the reform movement," who seized the issue not to recover money but to "secure offices for themselves and to procure a political success for their party." Violent feeling was unleashed against Tweed as a "prominent politician" who should be gotten out of the way. The Court of Appeals decision in Tweed's favor unleashed a torrent of abuse on the court, which was "designed to break down the only barrier that protects our citizens from mob rule." Tweed did not take money from the treasury. This was done by Garvey, Ingersoll and Woodward. His conviction was not for stealing, but for not auditing. "We do not deny, we never have denied, that in a suit properly brought by proper parties, Mr. Tweed may be and should be compelled to refund any and all sums that he is shown to have improperly taken from the City or County of New York. Does justice require more than that?" Field asked. Don't hold his flight against him. "He was fleeing for his life." There is a common phrase, "Tweed's stolen millions," that is claptrap meant for political purpose. More, one conspirator cannot be held for so many. Tweed should not be charged with any sum that cannot be directly proved as being traced to his hands. And that was nothing. The witnesses Garvey, Ingersoll and the rest were paid informers, the most "infamous wretches to walk the face of the earth," prevaricators, convicts, fugitives from justice, participants fully and voluntarily in fraud, their evidence has proved no conspiracy. The prosecution's release of the alleged wrongdoers and their attempt to pin the whole on Tweed were wrong and unjust. On this impassioned plea, Field read a motion to dismiss. The motion was, of course, denied.

Field then called witnesses for the defense—among them Mrs. Garvey, who testified that she telegraphed her husband to return after an interview with O'Conor, promising freedom from prosecution. Richard O'Gorman testified as to the prominent and unsullied position of Tweed, Connolly and Sweeny and instructions from Hall to bring suit on behalf of the city against the four contractors. George T. Curtis was called. He began to testify as to these impending suits. At that point O'Conor, usually a silent counsel, arose to protest the line of questioning. The state is empowered to bring suit and no one else, and the question is about William M. Tweed and his obtaining money by fraud. Field's witnesses would produce irrelevant testimony to confuse the jury. Field replied and raised the question of supremacy of federal law and the Fifth Amendment, no state shall deprive a citizen of life, liberty or property without due process, the evidence of O'Gorman, Curtis and the others was relevant. Westbrook ruled otherwise. Field's attempts to show the political motivation of the trials was overruled, as well as his attempt to show the money should be recovered from the contractors.

In his summary, Field pointed out that the public and the press clamored for a guilty verdict, but he reminded the jury that every American is entitled to due process. Ever since Tweed's escape, he had carried on Tweed's defense without receiving any fee, but he would not forsake his client. He repeated earlier arguments. The case was essentially political. Tweed was a "God send" for politicians. There was no proved conspiracy between Tweed and Watson or anyone else. Garvey said Tweed told him in 1867 to add 15 per cent to his billls and when he gave money to Tweed one time, it fell on the floor and Tweed told him hereafter to deal with Woodward. Could Garvey be believed; was Tweed now responsible for Woodward's actions? Ingersoll sought Tweed for work. Tweed was not the tempter. Ingersoll begged for a job. Garvey and Ingersoll were the most "infamous wretches as walk with the earth." They were the dirty tools who did the work and then came forward as informers. The jury should insist on corroborating testimony as their evidence by itself is not worth a dollar. Ingersoll was an admitted forger. What was presented was a mass of figures and contradictory evidence. The deposits of money were just that; they proved nothing. That bills were padded proved nothing against Tweed. It was a common though deplorable practice. There were many bills such as those of the New York Printing Company, but not a single dollar of these could be traced to Tweed. Field appealed to the jury for "fair play," that every American boy is taught with his "mother's milk" to disclaim the state's prosecution which was for personal and political purposes and to abhor those who use the law to gain office, an obvious reference to Tilden.

Carter summed up for the prosecution. He repeated the necessity of the state's suit, and of "The Ring's" attempt to save themselves from O'Conor as they sought refuge under the "velvet covered fingers of O'Gorman." Tweed did not meet his responsibility as a member of the board. He engaged clearly in fraud and deceit. On March 8, Westbrook instructed the jury. He first complimented counsel in their handling of their respective cases. Westbrook went over the Garvey and Ingersoll testimony. The jury was asked to consider this testimony with respect to conspiracy on the part of Tweed and his failure to audit. His charge read like a summation for the prosecution. The jury retired for two and a half hours and then brought in a verdict against Tweed. Johnston was surely happy with the speed. A motion for a new trial on insufficient evidence was denied. After eighteen working days, the case was brought to an end. Twenty-one witnesses appeared for the prosecution, fourteen for the defense. The jury agreed on a principal sum of $4,719,940.35, which together with interest from September 1, 1870, to March 1, 1876, became $6,537,117.31. The finding was for about two thirds of the original demand on the part of the state. Field wanted to stay the execution of judgment pending appeal, but Westbrook refused to grant the stay. Elated, O'Conor told reporters that the state would quickly follow up and now seize all of Tweed's property. Peckham was satisfied with the result. The sum of $60,000 was allowed to the plaintiff's counsel, and this figure together with costs made the final judgment of $6,635,652.19. A notice of appeal was filed by the defense on April 15.[2]

Later in the year, the city renewed its own complaint for recovery of $7,900,218.75. It was not pressed, but held in abeyance in case the state's $6 million suit was set aside on appeal. In November another struck jury was readied for the $1 million suit. Appeals by Field and Deyo were heard on October 20 in General Term. Field presented his exceptions. The appeal was rejected by Chief Justice Davis on January 12, 1877, as being "absurd."[3]

In the meantime, Woodward's suit was settled in December. He was to return less than $150,000. O'Conor writing to Tilden on October 16, 1876, informed "Silk-Stocking Sammy" that Woodward, who had recently been returned from Chicago, escorted by detectives, was "willing to pay all he can without actually impoverishing his wife and young children, say about $125,000. He will make full and perfect disclosures of all facts within his knowledge and will testify if needed." O'Conor expected "expediency and public policy would allow for settlement with Woodward," but this should not be done "until the effect of close custody upon Tweed's mind shall have been made apparent." Everyone was being accommodated. Woodward, Watson, Garvey, Ingersoll, Keyser were as good as settled, or in fact settled. Sweeny, who returned from Paris during the year, was given a promise that he would not be indicted on any charge.[4] Only the "Elephant" remained. His thick hide had to be hammered to the wall. O'Conor felt the "screws" had to be applied even tighter. He wanted Tweed to acknowledge his guilt and surrender. His strategy worked. By December 6, 1876, Tweed was certainly back where he started from, but much the loser, tired, worn, defeated.

O'Conor happily received the news of Tweed's "unconditional surrender." In writing to Tilden on December 13, 1876, he urged that the letter be accepted "without material delay," for inaction in such a matter cannot be excused by any reasoning. O'Conor's advice was not accepted, and plans for future prosecution were continued. Even unconditional surrender was not enough. O'Conor severed himself from future Tweed prosecution, but Peckham remained to carry on.[5] The wheels of justice grind exceedingly fine, and in this case they pounded like sledge hammers.

28

An Implacable Foe

Tweed had been in jail continuously, except for the period of his "escape," for three years. Defeated, humbled, harried, he grasped for straws—anything that would give him his freedom and his life. By now, no one connected with the scandal was in jail or threatened with jail. Only Farrington and Ingersoll had served time and then only for a short period. Everything had been settled—everything except the matter of Tweed.

It was at the end of 1876 that John D. Townsend became Tweed's chief counsel. Born in New York in 1835, he entered Columbia College at age thirteen. Before graduating, he left to become a sailor. He was second officer on the famous clipper ship *Flying Cloud* when it made its record-breaking trip from New York to San Francisco in eighty-nine days. He remained in California for a short time, becoming a "forty-niner." His wanderlust fulfilled, he married, attended Harvard Law School, and was then admitted to the New York bar in 1859. He had been retained by Woodward and was successful in obtaining a settlement for him. According to Townsend, Woodward asked Tweed to hire him, and it was Townsend who had Tweed write his letter of surrender to O'Conor. The attorney now embarked on a crusade to free his client from the clutches of the "traitorous minions" of the state, although he, unlike Tweed's other counsel, was convinced of his guilt.[1]

Tweed could no longer afford to retain Field or any other attorney. Field and Deyo were replaced by William Edelstein on August 14, but before this in February Tweed turned to Townsend. He could not raise cash to pay Townsend, but gave him ten promissory notes, each in the sum of one thousand dollars. Half could be cashed only if Tweed were freed.

Tweed was as desperate as he was poor. So too was his son William Jr., who in October brought suit against the city for salary due him, from

October 1, 1871, through March 1872 as assistant district attorney, for $4,166.65. Perhaps not wishing to antagonize authorities, Tweed Jr. had delayed his action. The city defaulted in answering and judgment was entered on December 1.[2] Another indication of Tweed's financial straits was his inability to help sister-in-law Margaret, who had come to depend so much upon her brother-in-law. Whatever money she received was not enough. On December 12, 1876, she wrote that she did not have a dollar with which to pay bills or buy winter coal and would sell her house, but Fairchild, probably Benjamin P., a friend of the family, advised her to wait until spring when prices hopefully would rise. In the meantime, she asked Tweed if he would continue his allowance to her, and she would live within her "small means" hoping to keep from becoming a public expense and sacrificing family pride. She knew all of his trials and dreaded adding to his burden, but had no one to turn to. She asked that the letter be destroyed as it was "strictly confidential. I have not shown it to Richard." The letter was delivered to Tweed in jail, probably by her son Frank. On January 7, 1877, she informed Tweed that due to the uncertain state "of her affairs," she was forced to borrow $150 on her diamond ring, but needed $500 more to pay her bills. Tweed replied the next day. He had delayed writing, hoping to have some good news, but instead, "since my return I have only by the most persevering efforts and sacrifices been enabled to meet my expenses." He continued, "I have not had one dollar to use otherwise." There was nothing, there was no use of an interview. "Painful as it is to me I must say at present, I cannot do anything to help you." But Tweed, optimistic as always, added that he hoped he could shortly be of use. He tried to do something. On January 10, 1877, he wrote to Ingersoll telling him he was "physically and financially" in trouble. He asked him to discontinue suits brought against Margaret and Mrs. Young, his sister, for work done by him on their homes. This was all Tweed could do.

Margaret, left more or less to her own devices, was told by a relative to give up her home on Fifty-ninth Street and to make "heavy sacrifices" and "first to be laid on the altar is Pride." Since she had furniture, and a Miss Lamport had references, why not establish a boardinghouse? Perhaps her daughter Anna could give music lessons. It was all made more difficult as Frank, her son, could not get a situation, "the name of T——d rendered it difficult." Frank really had nothing else to do except carry letters to his uncle.[3]

If there was pride left, it was now swallowed. Tweed would "tell the truth," confess, name names, become an informer if only to walk into the sunlight. All the others, Ingersoll, Keyser, Garvey, had taken the route—it finally dawned on Tweed to do the same before it was too late. Now an "old man" at fifty-four, broken physically and mentally, forsaken by his friends, associates and much of his family, he was ready to make a deal. He was ready after years of silence, perhaps in mistaken loyalty to supposed friends, to make a full "confession" in return for freedom.

Perhaps he never had much to say and really knew very little of what was going on around him; that as Field had maintained so often, the conspiracy between the contractors and city officials did not include Tweed, or if it did, he was only a minor figure. But now, whatever he did know, he would tell. He was willing as well, as desperate as he was, also to tell of things he knew nothing about. He would act the part as written.

But this course of action depended on the naïve assumption that Tweed would be treated as the others. The new attorney general, Charles S. Fairchild, Corporation Counsel William Whitney and his nemesis Peckham had different ideas. The "little" $1 million suit against Tweed and one against the absent Sweeny for $7 million were brought up in January before faithful Judge Westbrook. Struck juries were called for in each case. Peckham promised Sweeny a reduced bail if he would return from Paris. This was then reduced to no bail at all, and the promise was then made that he would not be arrested in either a civil or criminal court. This was accepted by Sweeny, but since he did not have time to appear, Peckham asked for and received an adjournment. April was set down for a hearing in both cases. Peckham saw no difficulty in settling the case against Connolly. He was ready to accept any offer Connolly's attorneys might make.[4]

Townsend now began to write to Peckham asking what would be offered Tweed if he "confessed." Peckham, in reply in a letter of February 27, 1877, asked for a list of persons whom Tweed could implicate, as well as any and all corroborative evidence, and whether Townsend felt such evidence plus Tweed's "confession" was sufficient to obtain a verdict against those implicated. On the basis of this information, the attorney general would decide what to do.[5]

During the following months, both sides maneuvered for best advantage. Each side mistrusted the other. An attorney, Carolyn O'Brien Bryant, was used, according to Townsend, as a spy for Peckham to ingratiate himself with Tweed, gaining information without the attorney general having to make a deal. Bryant vigorously denied this accusation; he would be heard from again.

It was rumored that if Tweed would turn over the rest of his property, said to be worth an unlikely $250,000, and end all appeals, he could walk out of Ludlow Street Jail free. Peckham objected to a settlement for such a "paltry sum." He wanted more money, enough to satisfy the public mind. Tweed had not yet suffered enough for his misdeeds. There should be more. Still through March the rumors persisted that Tweed would be freed.

These rumors were an embarrassment to Corporation Counsel Whitney, as a compromise would impose the responsibility upon him for settling the city suit against Tweed—a burden he did not wish to take. Soon to erect a vast fortune through urban transportation, based at least partly on Tweed's bones and fame gained as a reformer, Whitney need not have worried. In April, any hope for settlement was ended. Attorney General Fairchild felt anything Tweed had to offer was useless and would not aid in the recovery of the people's money. At the same time, he discounted a prevalent story that Peckham had received a $5,000 bribe from Woodward to help in settling Woodward's suit. The motives of Peckham were shining pure, he asserted. As for Tweed, Peckham said no appeal could save him and that he would not leave jail, "except by death or by paying the judgment against him." Peckham declared further that those who sympathized with Tweed were deluded. "He was in excellent health, with more energy than many men of twenty years his junior." Tweed died within the year.[6]

Nevertheless, Townsend tried to sell Tweed as a prosecution witness against Sweeny and others, but the idea was refused. News of the negotiations became public, much to Fairchild's anger. On April 16, Townsend journeyed to Albany to see Fairchild. He carried Tweed's unsigned "confession" and proposal to turn state's evidence.[7] The "statement" or "confession," first published in outline by the Herald and in full by the World on April 17, created only a mild furor. It was Tweed's history of "The Ring" since 1867. Tweed said there was a plot hatched in 1867 between himself, Hall, Sweeny, Connolly, Genet and others to have Tweed elected to the state Senate, Connolly comptroller, and Hall mayor. The next order of business was to obtain a new charter, and for this purpose, Tweed gave Senators William B. Woodin of Auburn and Norris Winslow of Watertown $200,000 to be used among those who could help secure passage of the charter in the legislature. Senators Samuel H. Frost of Richmond, Augustus R. Ellwood of Otsego, William H. Brand of Leonardville, James Wood of Genessee, Isiah Blood of Saratoga, George Morgan of Dutchess, and Messrs. Van Pelten, Williams, Crowley, Merriam and Beaman provided "lobbying services." Tweed, Sweeny, Bradley as chamberlain and Henry Smith as police commissioner devised a method of passing on claims and the division of the spoils. Hall was in full accord, and received 10 per cent of the plunder. Hall's "ministerial" defense was fashioned after the exposure, by Hall himself. Hugh J. Hastings, editor of the Commercial Advertiser, received $20,000 from Tweed to be given to Woodin, but Hastings deposited this to his own account. Recorder John

K. Hackett had all his printing and bookcases in his house paid for by the city. There was money paid to members of the Common Council. Names were given—Aldermen Morgan, Jones and Thomas Coman. He also gave the names of five persons who could verify his story, if promised immunity. E. D. Barber, ex-senator Jarvis and Pierce, Alexander Frear and William E. King. After the original disclosures, Francis N. Bixby and James O'Brien came to him and promised security against further investigation in return for $150,000. They alleged influence with Tilden and Justice Barrett. Tweed said he paid $20,000, as did Connolly. Tweed also claimed he paid money to Judge Charles J. Folger of the Court of Appeals and George H. Purser. He promised to tell the full story if he was released from jail.

These were just starters. The account produced mixed results. Most found it too vague, too concocted, and as the *World* stated, "inspire[d] only contempt in the minds of the reader . . ." It was known that Senator Woodin was Tammany's particular enemy and the "confession" a bald-faced falsehood, to gain revenge. The "confession," the *World* was sure, was bogus, as bogus as was ex-"Boss" Tweed, escaped convict and master thief. Thus, few found merit in the disclosures. No one seemed to want to hear more.

Woodin, Bixby and many of those named screamed out in protest. The charges were utterly without foundation, shouted Woodin indignantly. O'Brien, Folger, Hastings, William D. Murphy, Hackett and others heatedly also denied the allegations. Townsend disavowed the story as being badly mixed up, and wrote a note of apology to Fairchild. Townsend wanted Tweed to talk about Sweeny only, and not everybody else.[8]

Still, it was enough to cause the Senate to begin an investigation into Woodin's conduct, although this investigation had been brewing for some time. The first witness examined was Tweed. This was on April 21. Tweed refused to answer questions. He awaited Peckham's reaction and a promise of release. He would give no evidence in support of the charges, but the Woodin investigation continued. On April 24, George Jones was sworn. Though several editorials published in the *Times* in 1870 intimated that votes had been bought to secure the charter, Jones, as usual, knew nothing, and denied any specific knowledge of such transactions, nor did he know of anyone who had such knowledge. Did Jones know anything, about anything? He was convinced the charter aided Tweed and Sweeny, but his belief was based on circumstantial evidence and the "general evidence" of the people involved. He also admitted that he did not know Tweed, and that he met him only once.

James O'Brien, former sheriff, was next. He knew Tweed, but not intimately. He had last seen Tweed in 1872. O'Brien denied Tweed's allegations in regard to himself and Woodin or the other senators. He told of a visit to him by Fairchild and a discussion of the "confession." Fairchild thought there was nothing to it, but O'Brien was not so sure all of it was useless. There were a number of suits pending, as for example, the Navarro Water Meter case. This suit was brought against the city for nearly $1 million, and Tweed had something to say about this matter, namely that the meters were faulty and the city shouldn't have to pay for them. Tweed's testimony might, therefore, be useful, thought O'Brien. Fairchild was not impressed. When asked if he could accept Tweed's "un-supported statement," O'Brien replied, "Yes sir, I would, because I have obtained inferential corroboration of the truth of nearly all of his asser-tions." "How?" he was asked. By talking with all sorts of people, was O'Brien's reply. He was not asked to elaborate. Andrew J. Garvey was next. He said he rarely took part in politics, but was a member at times of the Tammany General Committee and again admitted giving $50,000 to buy votes in the legislature. William King and Woodward had asked for the money. Miller, Keyser, Archibald Hall and Ingersoll also gave sums up to $50,000, which was brought to Tweed by his brother, John Garvey. The money was "carefully secured" in his waistcoat pocket. It was not a pack-age, as he earlier testified. As he looked toward the ceiling, Garvey sancti-moniously said he thought it was a loan or he would not have had any-thing to do with it. He did not know of a senator receiving a dollar of the money. This was different again from his previous testimony.

Other witnesses followed. Ex-senator George Kennedy was acquainted with Tweed. As far as he knew, Republicans voted for the charter and tax levy since Democrats agreed to vote for the election law. The tax levy was voted along party lines. He had no reason to believe any improper influences were used in the passage of the various acts. Charles S. Fairchild appeared on May 1. The attorney general had been asked to bring the "confession." He did not have the document, but he had seen it. It was unsigned and without any affidavit. Fairchild refused to produce it for the committee's inspection. He had told Townsend not to show it to anyone unless he agreed to its terms. He also denied any knowledge of pol-itics surrounding the charter, except that he knew Tilden was opposed to it. He denied consulting John Kelly about the "confession," although he admitted meeting with Tweed and Townsend. Fairchild told them to sub-mit all their statements and he would see if the public would benefit from allowing Tweed out of jail. He wanted corroborative evidence, something he had not yet been given.

John Morrissey was called next. He told of opposition to the charter, and the organization of the Young Democracy at his house in 1870, shortly after the legislative session met. During the debate on this "Huckleberry Charter," most Young Democrats switched to the Tweed charter, no doubt for "some consideration." He knew, however, of no specific incidents of bribery, though he estimated five hundred city employees and desperadoes went with Tweed to Albany, who were used to sway votes. How, he did not explain. He felt that most Democrats favored the Young Democrats charter, but were "influenced" to vote the other way. Still, he did not know of his own knowledge of any instance where anyone, including Tweed, had used money to gain votes.

Charles M. Clancy, who had held, among other offices, that of superintendent of incumbrances in the Street Department, appointed by Tweed, knew of no money used in defeating the "Huckleberry Charter." He had been with others in Tweed's room at the Delavan. He did not see Woodin in Tweed's room, nor Tweed giving Woodin money. Abraham Van Vechten, a member of the legislature, knew Tweed wanted the Young Democracy defeated, but knew nothing of the use of money to buy votes. Amasa J. Parker, a harbor master in New York and former deputy collector of assessments appointed by Tweed, knew Tweed for twenty-one years, and knew of Tweed's opposition to Young Democrats. He was asked directly if he used money to help Tweed defeat the "Huckleberry Charter," as reported in the printed confession. He was advised by his attorneys not to answer, and he declined to reply. As for other money passing hands in bribery, he knew of nothing. He knew nothing of Tweed giving Woodin money.

Woodin himself took the stand on May 2 and categorically denied any knowledge of bribery, or how or why Republicans voted for the charter. All charges leveled against him, he maintained, were without foundation. A few days later on May 10, the report of the Special Committee wholly and unanimously exonerated Woodin of any wrongdoing. Despite all the witnesses, there was no link of Woodin to Tweed, or Tweed to bribery of any member of the legislature.

The "confession," if it really was by Tweed, was a dud. Still he took full responsibility for its publication. If perhaps floated as a trial balloon, it was a dismal bust. It only weakened Tweed's position.[9] But, authentic or not, there still might be something that Tweed could offer. Peckham felt, as he wrote in a letter to Fairchild on May 3, that Tweed could be useful in the Sweeny case. Fairchild in reply stated that any promises of freedom were made by him in return for documented proof, not on any false "confession." And even in the Sweeny suit, Tweed's testimony was not really needed. Sweeny had made an offer of $100,000 to settle, though Peckham, on advice of Whitney, wanted $500,000. In any event, they really did not need Tweed, though by May 25, in a letter Peckham still insisted that without Tweed they could have less than an even chance against Sweeny. It was on the same day that Whitney informed Fairchild that the city could not win the Navarro Water Meter suit without Tweed's testimony. Personally, Whitney concluded, "I feel very much adverse to seeing Tweed set at liberty. His captivity represents the triumph of justice tangibly and visibly, and it is a healthy spectacle," but "immense" claims to be gained in the water meter suit and Sweeny's cases complicated the picture. The decision, nevertheless, was up to Fairchild.

Fairchild adamantly refused. It was no deal. "His testimony would not justify his release," wrote Fairchild in early June. Tweed would remain in jail, even if his evidence could net the city $1 million. Townsend bitterly spoke of now having the "full confession" made public. He angrily wrote Fairchild that he had reneged on his word since he had promised that if any use was made of Tweed's information, Tweed would be freed. He had heard that the Sweeny case was to be settled but only in "great degree" because of information supplied by Tweed. On the other hand, Tweed-hater John Foley congratulated Fairchild's "noble decision" and "noble act," it's about time the pardoning business was at an end and that "all living in the plundered city see that political honesty is the best policy."[10]

For Townsend, these were frustrating days, but to others the fulfillment of a dream. What irked Townsend even more were not only rumors of a Sweeny settlement, but that Connolly would be allowed to return from England and that Genet was in town, a returned fugitive who was free and was expecting some sort of settlement, but for Tweed nothing. Sweeny, who had returned from France in the spring to attend his trial, had a short examination and on June 6 an agreement was reached between Peckham and Sweeny's counsel. Sweeny agreed to pay $400,000 and it was to end his problems. Tweed was not called to testify. Despite the agreement, Sweeny really did not pay any money. The $400,000 was taken from his brother James M.'s estate. Sweeny came out like a rose and lived for many years in quiet retirement maintaining to the end that he was innocent. Years in France, a few days in New York and he was free. But he paid in a different way. Of all the "Ring" politicians, he was the most able and perhaps, were it not for the scandal, he would have gone quite far. He died in 1911 at Lake Mahopoe, New York. Nothing was collected from Connolly, who died in Marseilles, France, in 1880.[11]

Tweed and Townsend could only gnash their teeth. Their friends expressed hurt and sorrow. Peckham refused to see Townsend, and on June 12 returned the unsigned "confession" with a short note, "After careful consideration, I have come to the conclusion that the testimony which said Tweed could give as shown by said statement, would not justify his release." He also returned the letters of Dr. William Schirmer which indicated that Tweed was in poor health and for medical reasons should be released.

Tweed tried again and wrote a letter to Townsend the following day:

Dear Sir:

I wish you to take the necessary steps to at once enable me to confess judgment to all the cases brought against me by the City, County, or State. My defenses in all these matters have been disclosed by me to the Attorney General personally on several interviews on his personal assurance to me that if I made such full statements I should be released from confinement and as you know also to yourself, and it would be useless now to interpose defense; (even had I the desire to do so) and thus save the City unnecessary and further expenses.

Your obedient servant,
William M. Tweed[12]

Townsend tried something else. In a long statement published on June 21 in the *Times*, Townsend demanded justice for Tweed and for himself. He accused Fairchild of professional discourtesy. If what Tweed had told was a lie, and he had attacked innocent people, Fairchild should have acted to end any suspicion. Why continue a "conspiracy of silence"? Townsend had his own story. He met Tweed in 1873 and advised him to make confession and restitution. His advice was refused and Townsend left. He returned to Tweed after he was "kidnapped" and brought back to New York and induced Tweed to tell all, expecting a "great moral effect" upon the public. He then went to O'Conor and Peckham and offered the "confession." On February 23, Peckham, Fairchild and Townsend visited Tweed. Fairchild wanted a full and complete disclosure. Tweed asked what were the subjects to be covered. Fairchild was vague, but expressed interest in a full statement. The next time Fairchild was heard from was late in March when Carolyn O'Brien Bryant, who was assumed to be Fairchild's "mouthpiece," told of continued interest. Negotiations commenced, and accounted for the delay in the publication of the statement. Fairchild then visited Tweed, carried away checks and papers to be used in the Woodin case. These never were returned. Several telegrams were sent by Bryant to "Luke" Grant, Tweed's servant in Ludlow Street Jail, but now the name used by Tweed as an alias to keep messages from being intercepted, telling him of the "Duke's" (Fairchild's code name) interest. It was agreed to have Tweed furnish testimony in the water meter and O'Brien cases, and transfer all pertinent papers to Fairchild and to appear as a witness whenever requested by Fairchild. This was just prior to April 16, when Townsend left for Albany and Fairchild. Townsend was asked by one of Fairchild's "warm political and social friends" to have Tweed prepare a note as to collusion of two senators and two leading corporations, probably in reference to the Erie and Grand Central railroads. Tweed did so and Townsend brought it to Albany. Tweed also agreed to testify about everything, withholding nothing. Townsend went through the motions of filing for Tweed's release. Tweed had played his part. Further, there was no longer any reason to retain Tweed in jail. The lesson had been taught. Why continue the torture? "Can you find no man to harass and annoy so as to give you occupation?" asked Townsend.

Townsend helped create public sympathy for Tweed, the first in a long time and about the only such feeling ever expressed. Wasn't Fairchild interested in getting to the bottom of the scandal? Was there any agreement on which Fairchild reneged? What were Fairchild's motives? The attorney general had to reply. He disassociated himself from Bryant. He had made no promises. Despite cries against him, he felt that he acted in the best interest of the people. The Sweeny settlement was "fortunate" given promises of immunity to Sweeny and there was no proof of Sweeny's role in the conspiracy. Tweed's case was different in the degree of involvement. Tweed now seized the opportunity created by the criticism of Fairchild to push hard for his release. On June 30, he wrote to Townsend and asked him to seek outside aid in determining whether or not he had paid the penalty for his liberty and whether he had not in fact carried out all his promises. Townsend wrote to Fairchild detailing again Tweed's promises and the agreement reached. He again accused Fairchild of reneging, of swearing falsely, of altering testimony against Sweeny and of allowing settlement against the brother's estate. Sweeny settled with the state because he was told that Tweed had turned state's evidence. Tweed had been used and then abused. He again demanded Tweed's release. Peckham returned all papers given by Townsend. As far as he was concerned the matter was closed.[13]

John Graham, though no longer counsel, was in the middle of a brief storm. It was reported he had asked Tweed to make restitution and "confession" not for anything Tweed had really done, but to abate public fury. In four years, Graham said he had earned $16,000 from Tweed, but it had cost him two years of "dangerous sickness" and a permanent impairment of health. He considered himself always a friend of Tweed and his cause.

Bryant again got into the act. On July 10, he wrote Fairchild his account of the proceedings. It added mystery. He accused Townsend of working for the interests of John Kelly and local politicians as part of a bargain in which Townsend would be named Tammany candidate for attorney general. Tweed's "confession" and attack on Senator Woodin was a result of a "malicious spirit" substituting Woodin for Senator Wood. The December letter to O'Conor from Tweed was drafted by him. Bryant was Tweed's voluntary representative since Tweed had given up on law-yers. Townsend made himself by trickery Tweed's counsel. Bryant had seen the Tweed papers and found them without legal worth and did not make a deal with Tweed, though he asked Fairchild to see Tweed and his evidence. Tweed was so desperate, he would swear to anything, including the attack on Woodin. He accused Tweed of having $1 million in a strong-box in the Delavan House collected from others which was to be used to buy legislative votes, but was in fact pocketed by Tweed. Bryant also in-sisted that Tweed paid large sums to mistresses, first a Miss Garrett, later supplanted by Mrs. McMullen. The "old dotard" not only gave Mrs. McMullen a "magnificent mansion," but also $500,000 in United States bonds. Miss Garrett received $100,000 to conceal "certain admissions" which she kept in a private journal. He claimed that Tweed still had vast holdings, $2 million in railroads, and that Tweed was aided in financial affairs by Daniel Sickles, the one-legged veteran. He also related that, a bank robber had been helped by Tweed to escape the Ludlow Street Jail, and he in turn aided Tweed to flee. He accused Tweed of corrupting and attempting to corrupt judges like Westbrook, and urged continued prose-cution. There was a quick response, but no corroboration. In a letter to the public from the Ludlow Street Jail, Tweed angrily denounced the Bryant statement as entirely false, "full of slanders and falsehoods." He had known Bryant, but never trusted him. He had confidence in O'Conor, "that great able and pure man," and accepted Bryant as an adviser because he thought O'Conor trusted him. Bryant had not seen his "statement," only O'Conor, Peckham, Fairchild and Townsend had. Townsend in New London thought, probably correctly, the Bryant story to be an interesting "romance for Summer reading."[14]

It was time for a last desperate maneuver. A "true confession" was first published in the *Herald* and then carried in several papers. A handwritten copy seems to be dated April 1877. It was old and it was new. It was much like the earlier statement and testimony with some different details. The question for Tweed was, could it work? Would the public and more importantly would "Duke" be willing to accept the "new proof"? It was a long, detailed account divided into various subheadings. Tweed went into the formation of "The Ring." Mayor Hoffman, Con-nolly, Sweeny and Brennan frequently dined together with him in City Hall in the keeper's room. They discussed politics and socialized. When McLean replaced Brennan, the dinners stopped and they met daily as the board of apportionment at Tweed's office. They, especially Tweed, Con-nolly and Sweeny, also met in Albany at the Delavan House. It was de-cided that it was important to raise money to effect necessary legislation. The members of "The Ring" met with Assemblyman A. D. Barber of

Utica in Albany to prepare payments for legislators. Tweed took care of the Senate, Barber the Assembly. At first, Tweed and the rest of "The Ring" provided money and then it came from contractors, and ultimately from the city treasury. The provision for courthouse stock inserted into the tax levy of 1870 cost $112,000 and came from Ingersoll and Garvey and was paid by Barber to the legislators. The money was borrowed by courthouse commissioners from the National Bank and was part of the claim of the bank against the city.

As to the financial arrangements of "The Ring," Hugh Smith was Hall's agent and James Sweeny and Hugh Smith agents for Peter Sweeny. Woodward and Watson were agents for Tweed and Connolly. The final division of money was Sweeny 10 per cent, Hall 5 per cent, Connolly 20 per cent and Tweed 25 per cent, and Woodward and Watson 5 per cent. Contractors kept 35 per cent. Tweed strangely said that Sweeny and Hall did not know of the division. Tweed also detailed corruption on the Board of Supervisors. Walter Roche, John Fox, James Hayes, Andrew J. Blakely, Isaac J. Oliver, Henry Smith and Tweed made up a majority of the Board and a percentage of bills approved was given to them. Tweed also implicated Sheriff O'Brien, J. B. and W. W. Cornell and Co. as participating in fraud. The New York Printing Company had Tweed, Sweeny, Smith, James B. Taylor, Cornelius Carson and Charles E. Wilbour as stockholders. The company was formed to control printing for city departments. Sweeny and Connolly approved bills. Each stockholder received $30,000 to $100,000 during three years.

Tweed listed senators who had received funds for votes on bills like the charter or tax levy, including Thomas J. Creamer, John B. Van Pelten, Abner C. Mattoon, Stephen J. Williams, George Beach, Michael Norton and others—both Republicans and Democrats. It was non-partisan. He had little to do with the Assembly and left it to Barber. He implicated Alex Frear and Barber in the Navarro Water Meter case. "Ring" members obtained 10 per cent of the gross amount of the contract. The money was paid through Frear. Tweed was told the meters were useless, and he had the meters tampered with to show they worked well during tests. Tweed at first called off the deal, but after a meeting at Sweeny's house indicated "it was all right" and approval followed.

Tweed also recounted his dealing with the Erie Railroad. In 1868, he opposed the Erie while in the legislature and in fact favored Vanderbilt's Central Railroad. Gould introduced him to Sweeny, who was appointed the Erie's receiver, for which Sweeny himself and Hugh Smith divided $150,000. After that, all money needed to help the Erie in the legislature was passed through Tweed, Barber or Van Vechten under Tweed's direction. Hundreds of thousands of dollars were expended in this way. In consideration of their service Tweed, Sweeny and Smith were made directors and given percentages in stock. Tweed introduced Fisk to Judge Barnard, who gave assistance.

As to the "stolen vouchers," Hall told Tweed if the vouchers could not be examined, "Ring" prosecution would end. Tweed asked William Hennessey Cook, a member of the Department of Public Works, about the possibility of destroying the vouchers. Connolly assisted in the plan to destroy the records, but Tweed did not know the details since Cook declined to inform him. Tweed blamed the disclosures on the refusal of Connolly to pay O'Brien's fraudulent claim against the city. Sweeny, Connolly and Tweed helped secure among others the election of Charles J. Folger to the Court of Appeals by padding votes in the various wards. Tweed exonerated Hoffman, whose only questionable act was to appoint Henry M. Starkweather, his father-in-law, as collector of assessments.

Confession again brought another flood of denials. Fairchild again felt basically all was untrue. He wanted Tweed to "tell all he knew," this would not do. The *Times* and *Herald* felt the "bogus and unblushing falsehood" was of no legal value and Fairchild was right in not giving Tweed his release. "This great felon has no claim on public sympathy." He is getting no more than he deserves, Bennett editorialized. Yet despite the general denials and disbelief, some found merit. Smith Ely, Jr., now mayor, believed Tweed, but most did not.

The "confession" had some effect. On October 31, Senator William Woodin, insisting on his innocence, resigned so as not to embarrass his Republican constituents or the Republican organization. The Board of Aldermen began their own investigation. As for Tweed, it produced nothing. He remained in jail.[15]

The "confession" was curious. If it were true, why did Tweed wait so long to tell his story? Where was corroborative evidence? Of the many named by him as being implicated, and of all the thousands who must have been aware of what was going on, no one came forward. The voucher incident had no verification. Perhaps most glaring of all was the lack of details, for example, his relationship with the contractors or Woodward or Watson or anyone else for that matter. A letter, a note, a stray message would make things more plausible. Fairchild was probably correct, there was no truth in it. But why would Tweed lie? Again, the *Herald* and Fairchild were probably right. He would gain public sympathy and at the same time raise something of a smoke screen. There were others to be caught; not just Tweed. True or not, it didn't work. Were the years of his long silence due to the fact that he really knew very little? He knew little of "The Ring" and little of the "Black Horse Cavalry," and he could not be used to bring anyone to trial. That he was not an intimate to the "frauds" is a conclusion that can easily be drawn. Tweed had seized a desperate straw. He would accept the role of the terrible "Boss," then as a humble penitent hope for the best. It didn't help. He tried something else.

On November 15, a $1,409,558.28 judgment was entered against Tweed in the $1 million suit after he entered a confession of judgment. In the so-called mayor's suit begun in 1871 the city theoretically recovered $10,851,197.09 and also obtained an additional $1 million for the Tweed-Miller and Tweed-Marriner cases. These also were confessed judgments entered on February 13, 1878. When added to other judgments then on record the grand total came to some $25 million. None were paid. Even if freed in these matters he could be rearrested in a number of other suits.

On February 8, 1878, Tweed appealed for clemency to Augustus Schoonmaker, Jr., who had replaced Fairchild as attorney general on the basis of his poor health and in a spirit of humanity. He offered more testimony, but Schoonmaker refused to bargain. Even if Tweed paid the full amount of the judgments entered against him and turned over all his assets, the attorney general felt he could not release him. He did not want the responsibility of "releasing such a criminal as Tweed."[16]

29

Aldermen Again

It was late in July that Tweed's "confession" also became the concern of the Board of Aldermen. Tweed was back to where his career started. Samuel A. Lewis asked for an investigation of "all the facts and circumstances connected with the Tweed Ring." This was agreed to by the Board, and Lewis and James J. Slaven as chairmen, both Democrats, were joined by Republican Rufus B. Cowing. At last Tweed received some sorely needed attention.

There were disturbing questions being asked about the harsh treatment accorded Tweed as compared to the other "Ring" members. What of the "confession"? Was there any merit to it, was anyone being shielded? Everyone else was holding hearings, why not the aldermen? The committee obtained the necessary summons to have Tweed appear as a witness. He arrived at City Hall on September 3, but due to an attack of "bilious colic" suffered by his attorney, John Townsend, the proceedings were postponed.[1]

Three days later, hearings began before a half-empty chamber. Tweed, seeming in "perfect health," recalled that the first "combination" he knew of was formed in 1859 to control inspectors of election appointed by the Board of Supervisors. One Republican member, Peter P. Voorhis, received $2,500 to absent himself at the Board vote, giving Democrats the majority. The "combination" for that one year included Purdy, Walter Roche, John Briggs, William C. Connor and Tweed. When asked why the control of the inspectors was so important, Tweed replied, "so that Republicans could not cheat us."

Tweed then told of the formation of the "Supervisors' Ring." It followed the same lines as in his published confession. From 1860 onward, members of the Board "combined" to steal from the city treasury. He added Henry Smith, John Fox, James Hayes, Andrew J. Blakely, Isaac J.

Oliver as joining over the years. Supervisors passed on bills and claims without examining them and received payment from either himself or Henry Smith.[2]

Hearings resumed on September 12. Tweed's son-in-law, Ambrose Maginnis, sat next to him. Hugh L. Cole, assistant corporation counsel in charge of the examination, asked Tweed to be more specific as to amounts paid to members of the old Board, as well as to which bills were corruptly paid. Tweed could not answer, nor could he seemingly remember who the members of the Board were without referring to the printed minutes of the Board. His memory was not even clear as to who succeeded Hoffman as mayor. He thought it was Hall, but he was not sure.

When asked again by Cole how the claims were passed, Tweed replied:

> "Pretty nearly every person who had business with the Board of Supervisors, or furnished supplies for County works, had a friend in the Board of Supervisors, and generally he was a member of that Ring, and through that one member they were talked to; the result was their bills were passed, and the percentages were paid sometimes to one man and sometimes to another.
>
> Q. Some one of these men who composed the Ring?
> A. Some one of these six or seven [Supervisors].
> Q. Would the claimant be informed by the Supervisor whom you designate as his friend in the board that he must make his bill larger than it really was?
> A. Make up his bill so that he could afford 15 per cent off or whatever was agreed upon.
> Q. And this 15 per cent, or whatever was agreed upon, was paid to the Ring?
> A. To the party who gave that information.
> Q. Did any of these bills have a basis?
> A. Up to 1870 or 1871 I guess they all had a good basis. I think they all had a good foundation—at least, a large portion of them were proper bills.
> Q. Some bills were bona fide?
> A. Bona fide and for a large amount—very near their face.
> Q. And the plan was to add 15 or more per cent to the face of a good bill, to be divided among the members of the Ring?
> A. Added to the amount—either to the quantity or the price.

Tweed was then shown documents of the Board of the Supervisors for 1868, and he immediately identified a series of bills as being probably fraudulent. Although at first arrangements were made with all six members, it "finally mostly drifted into my hands." With respect to the new courthouse, Tweed testified that the bills were bona fide, except for the

15 per cent, and were passed on by Cummings H. Tucker, superintendent of the courthouse construction. The 15 per cent was divided as usual among six Democratic supervisors—2.5 per cent each.

Tweed denied that any money was received from those appointed to fill city posts. Then came questions about O'Brien's claims for $300,000. Tweed said Senator Francis Bixby representing O'Brien induced him to buy one half of O'Brien's claim for $150,000 by telling him that Connolly was buying the other half. In addition, if he bought the claim, he was promised by Bixby that Tilden would "let up on him." Tweed went along with the promise and purchased one half the claim, both conditions of which were not fulfilled. Tweed sighed: It is not the only time I have been fooled; this is only one of many times I have been deceived. He testified further that Section 4 of the tax levy which created the "board of audit" was drawn, he believed, by Hall. The charter was made especially important because of the Young Democratic revolt. It was passed after money was used to bribe the legislators. The money was advanced by the contractors Garvey, Ingersoll, Keyser, Watson and others, as well as Hall, Sweeny, Connolly, Smith and himself. Garvey's brother came to Albany with $100,000. He thought the Erie through Gould or Fisk supplied money which was handed in by Sweeny.

To ensure passage, Republican support was sought and received after five Republican senators, Norris Winslow, William B. Woodin, Theodore L. Minier, George Bowen and James Wood, received $40,000 each. Democrats too received money and other favors. In testimony given a few days later, he named three other senators, William M. Graham, William H. Brand and A. V. Harpending. A. D. Barbour, a deputy collector of assessments, was used to distribute the bribes, which amounted to about $600,000. The charter passed in the Senate with every Republican except one voting for it and every Democrat except Genet.

Next, Cole questioned Tweed on the scheme to rob the city. Tweed testified that he, Hall and Connolly agreed to a plan to repay those who had spent money to bribe the legislature by having contractors receive only 50 per cent of their claims. It was agreed, as Tweed proposed, that Woodward and Watson would prepare the bills and Connolly would pay them. The 50 per cent was to be deducted and handed back to Woodward or Watson, who would distribute it as follows: 10 per cent of it to Connolly, 10 per cent to James Sweeny for Peter B., 10 per cent to Hugh Smith for Hall, 10 per cent to Tweed and 5 each to Woodward and Watson. Shortly after, Connolly objected to his cut. He wanted more, as his risks were greater. Tweed said he ran the same risks. Then he suggested that the contractors receive only one third and the rest be divided. Connolly now got 20 per cent, Tweed 25, Sweeny 10 per cent, Hall

5 per cent, and Watson and Woodward 5 per cent each. Tweed remembered that Hall complained of the slowness of payment to him. At the end of the day's testimony, Senator Bixby smiled, and said surely no one could give serious thought to anything Tweed would have to say. In his previous testimony before the state Senate, Tweed had said he paid no one. The only thing true about Tweed, snorted Bixby, was the fact that he was a convicted thief used by John Kelly "to strike down every Democrat and every Republican whom John Kelly feared in the ensuing election."[3]

Tweed continued on September 18. His memory was still not clear on many points. He fumbled about for notes, could not remember names. On the other hand, he seemed at times very clear and sure of his answers. Still it was interesting. As the proceedings began, Alderman Cowing shouted about punishing wrongdoers, Republicans and Democrats, anyone guilty of a "breach of trust ought to be shot." The meaning of the hearings, replied Corporation Counsel Cole, in agreement was to find the truth "no matter whether it strikes Tammany Hall, anti-Tammany Republicans and Democrats." Politics and patronage were taken up first on this day. Tweed disclosed that Connolly had paid one of O'Brien's early claims in the amount of $75,000 to "stop his [O'Brien's] tongue," but Tweed denied any wrongdoing on the part of the then present Tammany Hall or its members. He did say he heard Sweeny was paid $60,000 for his confirmation as chamberlain and thought Sweeny's friends paid, but did not know to whom. He knew of no money being used to secure such nominations as Connolly's or McLean's. John Morrissey had suggested the above question and several others in an article in the *Sun*. Tweed did not know of anyone in Tammany who was involved in securing Vanderbilt's New York Central bill. He knew John Kelly was a clerk to Watson's friend, but while he presented Kelly's bills to the Board of Supervisors, there was no "sharing" of such bills. Kelly was not a member of "Ring," as you call it, insisted Tweed. But Tweed angrily denounced John Morrissey, now high in the Democracy. "The public should know who he is. At a court of Oyer and Terminer in the city of Troy in the December term of 1848, this man was indicted for assault with intent to kill. In the April term of 1849, he was indicted for burglary, and convicted and sentenced to jail for sixty days." Tweed continued to read Morrissey's record. He was indicted for burglary, assault, breaking of peace. He had been a professional prizefighter, gambler, "proprietor of the worst places in the City of New York." He was an organizer of repeaters, ran gambling houses, the friend of the lowest element of the city. "It is hardly fair," Tweed concluded, "that respectable papers should copy his criticism upon me as an inducement to public belief and faith." Cowing replied he was very sorry that the witnesses had read such a statement. If he had known its contents, it would have been prevented. The committee was not organized to provoke personal discussions. Tweed angrily and excitedly shouted his reply, "Must I sit here and be abused by every public thief? I am tied hand and foot. I am confined in jail and have no means of communication to the press as this man [Morrissey] has . . . I am not to be crushed out because I am unfortunate and oppressed." However, the matter was dropped as questions now shifted to the Brooklyn Bridge, then under construction. Tweed said he was at one time a trustee with 420 shares of stock. He thought that in 1868 or 1869 Henry Cruse Murphy, then president of the New York Bridge Company, said he desired the Common Council to give bonds of $1.5 million for its construction. Tweed thought he had no influence in the council, but would try. A member of the Board of Aldermen thought such a bill could be passed for $55,000 or $65,000 and Tweed was told by Murphy to conclude the negotiations. It was done. Murphy found he was $10,000 short of the required sum. Tweed, Sweeny and Hugh Smith agreed to raise that amount if they became trustees. The money was paid by Tweed to Thomas Coman. Tweed gave his shares to his son, who sold it to Charles Devlin. As a stockholder and member of the Executive Committee, Tweed would receive a percentage of contracts and wages paid to laborers. It was an implied understanding. Other members of the Bridge Company, including Superintendent William C. Kingsley, received percentages of monies expended, including 15 per cent of the cost of construction of the foundation of the bridge tower, plus expenses. These expenses included payments to the members of the Brooklyn Common Council. Tweed thought that Kingsley had an interest in a stone and marble quarry and a sawmill in Brooklyn which supplied the Bridge Company. Tweed knew that he could not place in competition a stone quarry in which he was interested. Kingsley and Murphy heatedly denied all allegations and the matter was dropped.[4]

Next were questions about elections. "Did The Ring control elections?" Tweed was asked. "It did, absolutely," he replied. The key was the counters. These were employed by Tammany Hall. He did not admit to directing anyone to make changes in tallies, but did say he requested such changes at times. When asked to name names, Tweed replied his records had been destroyed and he remembered no one in particular. He had no reason to hide anything; he just couldn't remember.

But he recalled the election of 1868. On the night of the election, Hoffman came to the Metropolitan Hotel. Sweeny, Hall, Connolly, McLean and Tweed were there. Was the election fair? Tweed replied, "I don't think there was ever a fair and honest election in the City of New York." In that year a "great many persons were naturalized." He thought the inspectors of elections rigged the final vote. The vote in the city was important to offset the vote in the state. It was also important the state not know the result in the city, so "one thing we did was to take possession of the wires, and it was determined to have the Bible telegraphed from beginning to end over the wires, so as to keep them employed. Not only was the electoral vote in the city made up, but he thought that of St. Lawrence County was also.

The aldermen were also interested in other matters. What of the "board of audit," did it meet? Tweed replied, "We never met." What of the May 5, 1870, meeting when a resolution of the new board required all bills prior to April 26, 1870, be collected by the county auditor? It was signed by Hall, Tweed and Connolly, after the disclosure by the *Times* at the request of Hall. "It would be a great deal of use to us if a prosecution was commenced against us in the Ring . . ." Tweed remembered Hall saying. This was, he thought, in July or August of 1871.[5]

Tweed again returned to the stand on the twenty-first of September. Tweed was director of the Erie Railroad about 1868 or 1869. What was the story? Hugh Hastings introduced Gould and Fisk to Tweed. They wanted an injunction against Vanderbilt and Drew. Could Tweed get Barnard or some other judge to do it? Tweed at first declined, but Sweeny and Connolly persuaded him. If he would do this, he would become director and be able to make money. He consented if in return he received ten shares as well as a directorship. Tweed then went to Barnard. Barnard agreed out of friendship. "At that time," Tweed said, "I was the best friend Barnard ever had in the world, he owed his position entirely to me, and I risked my life to nominate him." He did not explain the statement. It was the only favor ever granted to Tweed by any of the accused judges.

What of the New York Printing Company? Tweed explained that it was an offshoot of the Transcript Association. One of the stockholders sold his interest to him, and another sold his interest to James B. Taylor. Together they managed the company and Sweeny came in through his brother James M. The Printing Company was formed to sell stationery to the city. Stationery was sold to the city, and the bills were certified by the Board of Supervisors. Tweed thought the bills were in excess by about 25 per cent. The members of the firm each received one fifth of the profits. Tweed's capital investment was $10,000. Each stockholder received $50,000 to $60,000 a year.

On armories—Tweed was asked if there were illegal practices in the granting of leases. He answered that all were illegal. A list of examples of rooms and buildings leased improperly was given. By improper it was meant that the leasees paid money to supervisors to obtain the leases.

Woodward and Ingersoll could give all the necessary information, Tweed thought.

Tweed was then referred to evidence he gave at the Senate hearings of 1872 when he stated that he knew of no influence being brought to bear on Republican senators. He admitted that at that time he lied, as he did when he stated that A. D. Barbour was not used in providing influence and when he said he knew of no payments to members of the legislature in the passage of any bill. Barbour shortly after admitted that Tweed might have paid him $112,500 but it was not for the purpose of bribing the legislature, but for a business venture.

Tweed halted and said that he was giving this testimony under compulsion and duress since the aldermen through the Supreme Court could compel him to answer, for if he did not he might be fined or face solitary confinement. Perhaps this was to show he was saying things against his will.

He repeated that the testimony concerning Woodin, to whom he had "kind feelings," was the truth. In a somewhat contradictory statement, he now said he never paid Woodin personally, though he heard others had. The Americus Club was merely a social club, nothing else.[6]

Tweed and his "revelations" continued on September 29. First to be discussed that day were the Navarro Water Meters. He met Jose F. Navarro in the winter of 1870, although he surely meant 1869. In August of 1870, as commissioner of public works, he signed a contract with Navarro for ten thousand meters at $70 apiece. Tweed did not remember the real cost. When asked what official had an interest in the Navarro claim against the city Tweed was about to answer, but Townsend stopped him. Tweed was then asked of a sewer pipe contract with William Nelson, Jr. The claim against the city was for $54,550.60. Tweed said in approving the contract to purchase the pipe, he received 10 per cent of the profits. He also felt that stationery bills of William C. Rogers and Edward Jones were not "bona fide." He thought Sweeny received "presents" from the stationery firm. He also thought that the claim of the Tenth National Bank for $250,000 against the city was based on money loaned by Ingersoll and approved by the courthouse commissioners, and that these loans were not bona fide.

Tweed then admitted to having a small private payroll. Police Commissioner Abraham Disbecker was paid $50 per month for "pretending to do work of some kind." Edgar K. Apgar, Assistant Secretary of State, was paid for "spouting" (making speeches) in Albany. What of the "Black Horse Cavalry"? They were twenty persons in the lower house, Democrats and Republicans, who could be purchased. But he knew of no names, they voted together. They were organized at the beginning of each session. The people's representatives could be bought up as a "general thing." The press, including the Albany *Argus* and the Albany *Evening Journal,* were "subsidized." Articles were paid for at the rate of $500, $1,000 or $5,000 apiece. Republican editors had come to him promising support on certain issues if he paid for it. Even certain members of the Citizens Association were also taken care of. Nathaniel Sands was given a tax commissionership at $10,000 a year. Richard M. Henry became a dock commissioner and Joseph F. Daly a judge. He had, however, no personal knowledge of the association and its members.

After this testimony, there were more irate replies. The *Evening Journal* retorted that it did not know if its earlier editors were guilty of what Tweed had charged. Attorney General Fairchild denied ever having been told anything about subsidizing the *Argus* or *Evening Journal,* or of hearing any mention about Edgar K. Apgar. Tweed admitted this to be true, but said that it was a subject he was willing to expand on, if asked. Tweed offered several checks and two letters as evidence of his charges. The *Argus* angrily denied in an editorial that it had ever received any money from Tweed, but he produced state printing contracts given to the newspapers between 1868 through 1873, for approximately $750,000, which were in return for favors to Tweed and the Democrats. The *Argus* concluded the squabble by denouncing Tweed as an "infamous old liar."

Democratic Alderman Lewis objected to Republican Cowing's question as to whether any present members of city government might be involved with "The Ring," since he explained that it was not a function of the hearing. Still Tweed answered in the negative, but Cowing drew applause with his statement that the object of his questions was to "pull down" from power those members of the present Tammany Hall General Committee who were associated with "The Ring." Lewis denounced Cowing and his attempts to attack innocent Democrats or to infer that Republicans were completely guiltless.[7]

The hearing resumed on October 11, as Tweed related that he had burned his papers on the advice of counsel, but could not remember which counsel. He still retained a list of personal loans, but he felt that their publication would injure innocent persons. A list of fees, donations, loans and investments was published but without explanation of individual items. When asked who in the Tammany Hall General Committee was associated with the frauds, he replied that he did not know. He knew that $65,000 had been paid to the Board of Aldermen to confirm Peter Sweeny as chamberlain, but he did not know which aldermen received the money. The Republican Cowing asked, "Can you tell us, Mr. Tweed, the amount the city suffered from all the frauds on the Treasury during all the time you were in power?" To which Tweed replied, "I never figured it up." He could not even approximate a figure. Cowing continued:

Q. Besides the large ring composed of yourself, Hall, Sweeny and Connolly, were there sundry little rings or wheels within wheels, moving in the city when you were in office?
A. I have so stated.
Q. Who operated these rings?
A. Watson, Woodward, Ingersoll. I don't remember any others, but if you mention any names and I can recollect then I will give you the information.

Tweed repeated that he could not remember without papers and documents. When asked about Garvey, he replied that he did not know whether he worked in private homes at city expense, but that he had paid Garvey "large sums of money" for work he did for him. "Did Ingersoll furnish provisions to members of The Ring?" Again, Tweed replied in the negative, but "he may have given me a dinner once in a while or an apple," but nothing else. The hearings adjourned with notice that other witnesses would be called.[8]

On October 17, however, Tweed again was on the stand. Townsend placed in evidence Tweed's statement as to his real estate and personal holdings. Limited by lack of records, Tweed testified that to the best of his knowledge, in 1871 he was worth $2.5 million in real and personal property, and "at no time in my life was I worth more than that amount to $3 million." Arrested in the fall of 1871 with bail set at $1 million he transferred all his real estate to his son Richard M. on the advice of counsel with the exception of a few pieces among which were the Putnam and Greene County properties, which as he stated to the attorney general could be transferred to the city. One hundred twelve lots in Long Island City, given to his nephew Alfred Tweed, could also be made available to New York. The property had been transferred to his son so that his son could justify himself as a bondsman for $2 million. However, the $2 million in real estate had fallen to $700,000, which was all that could be realized by sale. Much of his money was used to furnish the Metropolitan Hotel and he lost it all. He had speculated in stocks of the Erie and others and was often the loser. "I have recklessly parted with a good deal of money." He was willing to submit to the closest kind of financial scrutiny by the attorney general or anyone else. He was not now the owner of any money or property of any kind whatsoever from which $5,000 could be realized. Any statement that he had secreted money abroad or at home "is utterly untrue." He was again willing to give "every particle of property" and to place himself at the disposal of all proper officials "to enable them to undo through me, as far as possible, the wrong that I have committed." Tweed submitted an itemized account of his former property and disposition.

Cowing then resumed his partisan examination. He asked Tweed, having the present Tammany list before him, if any members were connected with Tammany at the time Tweed was in power. Aldermen Lewis and Slaven objected, "This is not a political investigation, but an investigation to find out who were connected with the Ring frauds." Tweed was directed not to answer the question. Tweed replied that Tammany Hall and Republican legislators gave him all his power. He had named Republicans, but "not half of them." Cowing dropped this line, unwanted fish could have been brought in. Cowing returned to Tammany Hall. Tweed answered, "Tammany Hall took its power from us ["The Ring"], we did not get any power from them." To the end, Tweed was a loyal Tammanyite.

He was then questioned about individual transactions. He paid $17,500 to Garvey for "frescoing" his Fifth Avenue house after Garvey commenced a suit. His son's partner, Abram B. Garfield, in the Metropolitan Hotel, was paid $20,000 to cancel the partnership. The sum of $550,000 was paid in rent and furnishings over a two-year period. He lost over $600,000 on the deal. He had hired the hotel from A. T. Stewart for $90,000 to $95,000 a year and given it as a present to his son. In 1871 and 1872 $112,000 was paid to Ingersoll in return for loans advanced, even though Ingersoll still had a suit in Connecticut pending for that sum. The sum of $30,000 was given to Jackson S. Schultz as a settlement of a claim Keyser & Co. had against him for $40,000. Also, $60,000 was spent in procuring his escape from Ludlow Street, including his expenses in Cuba and Spain. Then the following exchange took place:

Q. Money paid to officials?
A. Money paid to parties; no money paid to officials.
Q. Who do you mean by "parties"?
A. Parties that aided me in making my escape and furnished me with a vessel.
Q. Were any of these officials of the City and County of New York?
A. No, sir.
. . .
Q. What was done?
A. I don't think I could tell, and if I could, I don't think it would be proper for me to tell. I tried to get away, and did get away and if I had not been kidnapped, I would be away still.
Q. How could you escape from Ludlow Street Jail by means of paying money, unless some of that money was paid to some officials?

A. That is a question I can't answer. I did not go from the jail. I left from my own house . . .
Q. How much did you pay to get your escape from the City of New York?
A. I can't separate it because I don't know how it was paid.
Q. Did you pay it yourself?
A. Most of it.

Townsend arose and said Tweed was embarrassed by these questions. Tweed would say the article in *Harper's Weekly* concerning his escape was perfectly correct and this matter had nothing to do with the frauds. It was a quick way out. Unfortunately, the questioning was not pursued but obviously, he was covering for somebody. His answers indicated the escape was planned for him and not by him. Tweed being used as a pawn, once again fooled.

Cowing went back to his expenses. From November 1871 through 1876, his legal expenses, including printing, stenographers, detectives, traveling expenses, in addition to counsel fees, were $42,000.

Tweed returned to the stand on October 20. He denied receiving any funds in connection with the construction of the capitol in Albany. John Bridgeford, one of the capitol commissioners, was implicated by Tweed in wrongdoing. Incensed, Bridgeford immediately denied all allegations. He never had control of the capitol commissions. There was no agreement between anyone and Tweed as to percentages.

The hearings concerning the capitol ended with all the parties, including William C. Kingsley, who was also a capitol commissioner, shouting that each should be in jail. It was one of the few instances of Tweed receiving corroborative testimony, but again the matter was dropped. On October 24, it was the turn of Henry F. Taintor who was brought forward. Proud of his role as investigator, he retold an old story. He announced that he had been engaged for the last six years in gathering evidence of fraud caused by "The Ring." The foundation of his work was certain vouchers and warrants left in the comptroller's office. It was Tilden in December 1871 who informed him of wrongdoing. This was different from his earlier account. He first examined the Board of Supervisors accounts. In 1868, under the Adjusted Claims Act, 55 per cent of most bills, he testified, went to corrupt officials and 45 to the claimant. This was true to January 1869. In July 1869, the officials received 60 per cent. In November, 65. Tweed got 25 per cent of the original claim, and "multiplying his check by four gave me the amount of the original bill." He did not give figures on Connolly or Sweeny, but felt Peter Sweeny received a portion of the "stealings," not just his brother James. How much real claim was against fraud on the bills? No more than 15 per cent, argued Taintor. He estimated the entire fraud for January 1, 1868, through July 1, 1871, to be

$30 million. If other items were looked into as street openings and the date went back to 1867, the figure could be 45 to 50 million. The actual amount of money recovered by the city by October 1877 was $464,138.18. On the courthouse, Taintor estimated a swindle of from 8 to 13 million, but he could not be sure. It was an estimate based on the valuation of "skilled builders" as to what the building should have cost.[9]

Taintor returned on December 24. He testified with respect to his fees, and it was quite an interesting session. He was first hired by Green on December 1, 1871, at $25 a day to assist Tilden. He received $600 for working from December 2 to 31 exclusive of holidays. He realized the "great responsibility resting upon him," though the pay was inadequate for the great amount of work required. O'Conor "loaned" him $2,500. His services in the Watson case earned him $80,000, less $12,000 paid to an employee. Taintor's statement was an elaborate justification of his work. He had found that $5,814,562.60 was fraudulently paid by the city between May 6 and August 16, 1870, of which Tweed's 25 per cent was $1,403,022.27. He also had "complete proof" as to Tweed's participation in $10 million more of fraudulent county payments. In Woodward's case, he could only trace a small amount to Woodward, and received but $2,000 for his services in that matter. Totaling the settlements made as well as sums still due came to approximately $26 million, most of which the city, he felt, should be able to collect. He would expect to retain 7 per cent for services rendered. He felt his fee was justified since the recoveries were "almost certainly on evidence submitted by me." If Tweed could be made to disgorge more, he would receive more in fees. Bounty and Tweed hunting had its rewards, economic as well as political.[10]

Garvey took the stand on November 21. Tweed was present under guard and few people were in the audience as Garvey repeated earlier testimony. Ingersoll appeared the following day and retold his familiar story. He told of approaching Tweed and Woodward with an offer to supply the city with furniture and to pay over 35 per cent commission on the face of the bills. Cowing then asked if Ingersoll intended to return money to the city. "That is not a fair question," Ingersoll replied. Then he said he could not answer the question. At one time, he was worth $600,000 to $700,000, but had lost $300,000 in a manufacturing company and $60,000 in a defunct life insurance company. Keyser joined the chorus on the twenty-sixth. He was a difficult witness. He claimed illness. He thought Tweed had paid $30,000 owed him, but there was still another debt. He was not sure how much the others returned. He said he was not guilty of illegal practices except to add 33⅓ per cent to his bills, a big except. He was compelled to do this to get his money. He was now going through bankruptcy hearings, and he did not consider he owed the city anything. Woodward appeared on November 27. He was forty-one, a "farmer," living at South Norwalk, Connecticut, and first became aware of illegal practices in 1869 when he was directed, as assistant clerk to the supervisors, by Watson to receive certain percentages to be paid to Tweed and others. Under the "Supervisors' Ring," 15 per cent was a customary return. In that year, Watson told tradesmen that Woodward would handle the percentage arrangement; 65 per cent of the face value, of which Tweed got 25 and Woodward between 2.5 and 5 per cent. The amount deposited by him in the Broadway Bank was $3,581,254.36. Woodward admitted he received 2.5 per cent of that sum. He thought his share was the "honest part of the bills." There was laughter in the court, especially when he maintained his money was "fairly earned." Woodward's chief duties were looking after Tweed's interest. He thought Tweed's percentage was fair, not those of Connolly, Sweeny or Hall. Why Tweed and not the rest? "Because," Woodward answered, "there was a Republican legislature to be bought, and I understand that Mr. Tweed had to put up almost all of the money. Therefore, I consider it right he should reimburse himself out of the city." He refused to answer questions as to his own worth. He had already settled with the city. He paid $105,000 plus $50,000. When he was asked why the city only received $100,000 of the $105,000, he replied that though his attorney paid over the entire $105,000, "Peckham charged me $5,000 for conducting the case." Peckham, of course, was not Woodward's attorney, but was employed by the city, and seemingly took $5,000 without apparently any authorization. Cowing asked him if he thought 65 per cent added to bills was wrong. He answered, "I think so now, but I did not think anything about the subject at that time. The city is different from a private individual; if a person does work for it, he may not get paid in months, or years—perhaps not at all." This line of reasoning occurred rather often; perhaps the scandal, as has been suggested, was a result at least in part of the city's inefficiency in paying bills. He was asked whether he was right in acting as he did, to which Woodward responded to the amusement of the audience, "I think every man in the room would do the same. I don't know that I ever saw an honest politician in my life, and I have met all stripes." Watson and Woodward speculated in the stock market, sharing profit and loss. He felt he was lucky and made about $200,000 to $300,000 in the market. When he left the city employ, he was worth about $500,000. George S. Miller was next. He also was forty-one and lived at 115 East Fifty-ninth. He was not sure when percentages were mentioned to him, though he had been working for the city since 1864 or 1865. Ingersoll told him 65 per cent would have to be added to his bills, and how it was to be divided. He never heard Hall mentioned, and he destroyed his books in the fall of 1871 at the request of Ingersoll, at which time he stopped working for the city. He was worth $50,000 or $60,000.

Miller was followed by former attorney general Francis Barlow and former comptroller "Handy Andy" Green. They had little to say. Sweeny was excused from testifying because of his agreement with Fairchild and Peckham protecting him from all "molestation and interference."[11]

On January 4, 1878, the committee issued its findings. They reviewed the months of hearings, the 750 pages of printed testimony. The evidence "distinctly" showed that officials and representatives of all political parties combined to bring about frauds, and that the robberies would have been impossible but for the "base consideration of the worst men in every political household." The committee did not understand why the people's counsel for the state and city having evidence of wrongdoing by direct confession should not have prosecuted or made the individuals disgorge stolen money. The report protested that "Ring" men were granted immunity. Woodward, Ingersoll, Oakey Hall, Keyser and others should have been prevented from their "enjoyment of the stolen thousands." The committee pointed out that "The Ring" could not have operated without "corrupt procurement of special legislation at Albany relating to our city affairs." Two railroads and powerful corporations were involved in the "degrading traffic," and the legislature no less than the city government seemed to have been "a den of thieves, and even the ermine of the judges was polluted by the wild craze for ill-gotten wealth." This unprincipled participation by persons high in office in the spoils of "The Ring," explains why the thieves had so long escaped exposure and punishment. As to the Sweeny settlement, it ended in a "very curious and somewhat incomprehensible way." Why allow Peter Sweeny his wealth and liberty, why did Peckham allow discontinuance? In the committee's judgment, "Peter B. Sweeny had not only been a member of The Ring and a participant in all the Ring frauds, but that he had been perhaps the most despicable and dangerous, the best educated and most cunning of the entire gang." The committee also did not understand the settlement of the other suits, as O'Brien's and Navarro's. Why settlement in these cases? Certainly, money could also have been obtained from Keyser, and surely the city could have successfully with the evidence available been able to defend itself in these suits. It should not allow those involved to go free. It should prosecute to recover its losses.

Finally, as to Tweed, the aldermen could not understand why everyone in "The Ring" was free except Tweed; why everyone had been allowed to settle except Tweed, even though Tweed had been "by far the most valuable witness," and could be of help in future litigation. The report concluded:

Whereas William M. Tweed has already been punished with much greater severity than any other member of The Ring and with distinction is not in accord with the spirit of our institutions; and whereas, neither moral effect is obtained by the longer detention of William M. Tweed under civil process in a debtors' jail, nor advantage gained by the City in the prospect of money recovery from his longer detention there; and whereas, William M. Tweed has offered to surrender whatever property he is possessed of to the City and to appear as a witness wherever and whenever he may be considered useful, and has proved his good faith by making a full confession of his crimes and of his associates therein, and has thereby humbled himself to the greatest possible extent; now, therefore, Resolved, That, in the opinion of this board, who are the popular representatives of the people of this City, greater benefit can be gained for the City by the discharge of William M. Tweed from imprisonment than by his longer detention. Resolved. That the board recommend the Attorney General and the Counsel for the Corporation of this City to release the said William M. Tweed from imprisonment after securing for the City such property as he may now be possessed of, and after taking such means to secure his testimony as they, or either of them, deem necessary.

The vote by the aldermen was thirteen yeas, seven nays. Cowing and Lewis opposed Tweed's release. Slaven voted with the majority.

Despite the air of inter-political squabbling, the committee did not split along political lines. The suggestion that at the heart of "The Ring" was the failure to allow the city control over its own affairs, thus having to buy a "corrupt" Albany legislature, has substance. In this light, the percentages and the padding take on a different meaning. A major cause was not the city, but Albany.

It was not "The Ring" which created the ball game, it was the nature of political accommodation, city and state. If there was ever an argument for home rule, it was the alleged "Tweed Ring."

The basic question was, however, the veracity of Tweed's story. Here no one came forward. His testimony is open to a good deal of conjecture if not suspicion. First, as always, he provided no corroborative evidence. There are no witnesses, no one to support his allegations. His books, letters, memoranda, checks, deposit slips and such were sadly missing, his memory faulty and unsure, his "statement" merely a desperate attempt to "tell the truth." Surely he believed that like Garvey, Ingersoll and Keyser by turning informer he would gain his freedom. He would testify as to anything, implicate anyone, except those immediately close to him, to make himself a valuable tool for the prosecution. How much was true? How much false? Probably no one will ever know.

Everyone agreed that the bills submitted by the contractors were padded. There seems little doubt that millions were in fact taken from the city treasury, but how, how much and by whom? To what extent was Tweed guilty, to what extent did he direct the operations? If he was involved, at least the aldermen felt he was no more guilty than anyone else and possibly a good deal less.

As suggested by many others during the last years, the aldermen looked beyond Tweed. They saw Sweeny, the contractors, Hall, Connolly, Woodward and Watson as chief culprits. There was little to suggest that Tweed directed that bills be padded or that he received a percentage or who should receive what percentage. A kickback arrangement existed prior to Tweed, during Tweed's time and surely after Tweed. Tweed's testimony, his confession, his lack of facts and figures, his altogether pitiful figure suggest he was indeed a paper tiger, a bench warmer, watching the pros at work.

With the issuance of the Aldermanic report, sentiment began to swing in a greater degree in favor of freeing Tweed. Everyone in the "The Ring" was free, everyone was allowed to settle, why pick on Tweed? Much of the onus for his persecution fell on Fairchild's shoulders. There were rumors he was after Tweed to make sure the "old man" would do no further harm by being used to give information against the "higher-ups." It was perhaps Fairchild's persecution of Tweed that denied him a chance to be renominated as attorney general. John Kelly, who had risen by now to a powerful figure in the Democracy principally because Tweed was destroyed and Kelly had been part of the reform movement, was "disenchanted" by the way the state had been "dishonored" by Fairchild's treatment of Tweed, reneging as he did on his commitment to free Tweed if he used his statement. Kelly, now comptroller, wanted the next attorney general, Augustus Schoonmaker, Jr., to fulfill his promise. In a letter of March 21, 1878, he reminded Schoonmaker that Fairchild had promised that he would free Tweed if Tweed made full confession and surrendered his property. "As a citizen," Kelly went on, "I feel that the State is being dishonored by the breach of faith. As a public officer, I urge his discharge because I believe his further detention in a debtor's prison is neither beneficial to the State as an example of evil doers, nor in any sense serviceable to the city." Tweed, Kelly asserted, could give valuable evidence in pending suits, but perhaps because of this was obviously being singled out to uneven punishment. Schoonmaker responded positively, indicating he would discharge Tweed at the end of the legislative session. This assurance came in the latter part of March.[12] It would do Tweed little good.

30

Final Escape

Death came slowly and painfully. Tweed had in the past been generally free of illness, but years of trial and the debilitating effects of his disastrous escape had weakened him. Age, too, appeared to have taken its toll. He frequently complained of his kidneys and of shortness of breath. Mentally, he was exhausted. Hard years after the disclosures helped create feelings of ill-health. Failure in court made him despondent and his lack of money was embarrassing. Visits from his family humiliated him.

Life in jail was tolerable, but drab. Newspapers reported that upon rising he usually read the Bible, had breakfast, read the papers and wrote letters, read the Bible again after dinner and before going to bed at night. Although he meditated about religious subjects, he also swore a great deal, an "old habit." Still, to readers the fallen idol appeared contrite and humble. Justice triumphant. It sold copy, but was it Tweed? Despite his new-found "religion," Tweed did not call upon a clergyman, even in his last illness.

He occupied his time in his two rooms attending to his flowers, which gave him great satisfaction. Pots of them bloomed upon window sills. Tweed also had a piano, and elastic bands with rings attached to a casement if he cared to exercise. Whether he used either piano or rings is not known. Monotony of prison existence and disappointment over his failure to obtain freedom weighed heavily upon him. He began to think more and more of the death of his father from an apparent heart attack and how this disease would cause his own end. Remembrance of the death of his mother Eliza seemed also to have affected him a good deal. A certain morbidity about his impending demise crept increasingly into his thoughts.

S. Foster Dewey, his long-time counsel and secretary, felt that Tweed had wished for death ever since his return from Spain and that he would

337

have committed suicide except that it would be a cowardly act, a fearful way to end a "terrible wicked life." It would also be an additional disgrace to his children and family. He often said, according to Dewey, that he wished he would go to sleep one evening and never wake up. He was ill in Cuba, ill aboard the *Franklin* and ill on his return, though despite this attended to daily affairs. He was well enough on March 26, 1878, to testify in a suit Charles G. Waterbury had brought against the city. It was the last time he was out of jail. By April 3, his fifty-fifth birthday, Tweed had developed a cold, perhaps from prison dampness, which became steadily worse. Dr. John M. Carnochan was called in. He found Tweed had bronchitis and cystitis, inflammation of the bladder. It was an unhappy and sad day. Few people called on him, few friends, no one from his family. Charles Devlin, a daily visitor, and William Edelstein were there. They had dinner with him, and he sadly recalled that the year before friends crowded in to congratulate him. Townsend had sent a large bouquet of flowers. There were none this year. By April 5, Tweed was confined to his bed and was attended by Dr. Carnochan, who had replaced Dr. Schirmer, Tweed's regular physician, and a number of other doctors who had prescribed for their patient during the last months; he remained through most of the long night hours. There was immediate apprehension that he would not live long. Tweed was soon visited by his son-in-law and daughter, Mr. and Mrs. Frederick Douglas, the only members of his family in New York. Tweed's wife and two sons, William and Richard, were in Europe. His young sons Charlie and George were at school in Connecticut. His family perhaps might have remained by him during the last year, but he was unhappy when they came by, reminders of happier times past, and bitter reminders of the present. Tweed would become especially annoyed at a disagreeable mention of him in the papers, thinking it would further hurt their feelings. Better they were away. He used to write them once a week prior to his illness, but had ceased writing altogether and had not heard from them for a long time.

By the seventh, Dr. Carnochan noted acute pericarditis, a heart condition, had developed. Tweed's condition worsened, and on the ninth Dr. Carnochan detected effusion into the pericardium. On the evening of the tenth, Dr. Carnochan said Tweed was suffering from a "complication of diseases including acute pneumonia, cystitis, inflammation of the membranes of the liver and his old disease of the kidneys. His pulse was now irregular. His legs were also very much swollen." Tweed steadily declined. During the night of the eleventh, Thursday evening, Tweed seemed better, but Dr. Carnochan noted a worsening of his heart condition and gave him anodyne to induce sleep. Tweed slept for an hour. At midnight, he awoke and complained of an acute pain about the heart. In the darkened

338

prison room, Tweed lay fitfully, hardly aware of street noises drifting through the window. At his side was the black male nurse and prison waiter Lewis "Luke" Grant. Grant was now about thirty years old and was a body servant to various well-known men. He had been employed by Frank R. Sherwood, who had been arrested in 1871 for fraudulent Wall Street operations and when bailed took Luke with him to Europe. Luke later returned to his position as servant to Tweed at the Ludlow Street Jail. Tweed hired Luke to attend his needs at a fixed sum per week. Grant would read letters sent to him by a sweetheart. Tweed enjoyed dictating Luke's replies. Tweed was fond of his aide and wanted his attention full time and this was allowed during the last days. About 3 A.M., April 12, Luke entered the sick man's room and whispered, "Boss, are you asleep?" Tweed, lying on his side, eyes closed, answered, "No, I am not asleep. Here, give me your hand. My heart pains me." Luke lifted the old man's head to his chest and rubbed the region about Tweed's heart. The dying man breathed easier. Tweed tried to sleep, but couldn't, moaning, asked variously for barley water, plain water or beef tea. Tweed was given a gallon of water daily to aid his bladder. Some thought this undermined Tweed's condition. He was in great pain now. Tweed cried out, "Oh, what shall I do! Give me something; give me anything so I can get some sleep, I can't stand this pain." Luke then administered a sleeping potion prescribed by Dr. Carnochan—it brought no relief. Tweed remained in agony, again saying, "Give me something to ease my pain; I am going to die anyway." At about 7 A.M., Tweed felt easier and slept for an hour. When he awoke, he again complained of great pain. Dr. Carnochan arrived at 8 A.M. and found his pulse very feeble and irregular. Tweed's friends were sent for. His good friend Charlie Devlin arrived and was shocked at Tweed's appearance. His daughter Josephine Douglas and her husband Frederick also entered. She went for some ice cream and delicacies which Tweed had wanted. Devlin asked Tweed if he wanted to make any last will, did he want a lawyer? Tweed replied, "No, I have nothing left to settle excepting to settle with my God." Edelstein and S. Foster Dewey entered the room. Soon they were joined by Deputy Warden Bernard Fitzsimmons, his wife and daughter. Tweed was breathing with great difficulty at about eleven-thirty, and turning to Dr. Carnochan he murmured, "I have tried to do some good, I am not afraid to die." Dr. Carnochan wrote other words down and read them to the group. "I believe the guardian angels will protect me," reported the doctor. A few minutes later Tweed murmured to Edelstein, "I hope they will be satisfied now they have got me." He fell into a stupor. At 12 noon as a bell in the nearby Essex Market Tower rang the hour, Tweed died. He gasped faintly, the nails on his hands became black. Tweed was lying on his left side, his face turned toward the middle of the room and his head resting upon the palm of his left hand, between it and the pillow. Frederick Douglas took Tweed's hand in his, said haltingly, "Father, can't you speak to me?" There was only silence. The men began to weep. Luke fled in a paroxysm of grief. Josephine entered with ice cream and cakes. They fell from her hand.

Word was quickly sent to Sheriff Connor. Soon the corridors of the jail were filled with journalists and friends of the dead man. Others besieged the front door of the jail, seeking admittance. John Townsend reached the jail about one-thirty and was present at the inquest. He reported that Tweed had told Edelstein, "Tilden and Fairchild—I guess they've killed me at last," and "I have tried to do the best I could latterly, but they wouldn't let me."

A few days later, Dewey said Tweed's last words were, as he could recall them, "I have tried to right some wrongs. I have been forebearing with those who do not deserve it; I forgive all those who have ever done wrong to me, and I want all those who have ever been harmed by me to forgive me." Dewey stated that Tweed said nothing of "guardian angels." Anyone who knew him wouldn't suppose he could talk that way, Dewey asserted. He was probably right.

Coroner Henry Woltman arrived at the jail at about 1 P.M. and began the inquest. An autopsy was not performed. A coroner's jury was sworn in; his old and good friend and his son Charlie's godfather, Charles G. Cornell; William W. Cook, clerk; Solomon Johns; A. M. Ensign; Francis J. Hawkes, a policeman; and finally Tweed's friend, George W. Butt, the liveryman. Dr. Carnochan was the first witness. He testified that he had known Tweed for ten years, at times under his professional care. He was first called to Tweed on April 3 and found him suffering from acute cystitis as well as bronchitis. In a day or two, the cystitis was relieved but double pneumonia developed. On Sunday, the seventh, acute pericarditis and attendant pain plus heart and pulse irregularity set in. The physician chronicled the increased heart pain, the lowering pulse rate. He attributed death to "pericarditis, with effusion and heart clot, complicated with bronchitis, pneumonia and chronic infection of the kidneys." Deputy Warden Fitzsimmons testified that for the past six months Tweed had been under the care of Dr. Carnochan. Deputy Coroner Joseph Cushman found death due to the causes outlined by Dr. Carnochan. This was concurred in by the jury. At the conclusion of the inquest, the body was given to the undertaker, Andrew J. Case of 397 Grand Street. It was taken to the home of Tweed's son-in-law, Frederick Douglas, at 63 East Seventy-seventh Street. Tweed's effects, books, papers and pictures of his Greenwich farm and other such happy scenes, were packed in trunks and carted away. An hour after the body was removed, nothing remained of the occupant of the room. The funeral was scheduled for Wednesday, April 17, 1878, allowing for the arrival from New Orleans of his two daughters, Mary and Lizzie Maginnis. In awaiting the funeral, Tweed's body, which Mr. Case said weighed over three hundred pounds—unbelievable considering his illness—was packed in ice in the back parlor of the Douglas residence. The Episcopal service would be private, conducted by the ever present Reverend Dr. Price. Burial was to be at Greenwood Cemetery.

While Tweed's body lay in the icebox, New Yorkers discussed the latest news and held their own inquest and service. Stories about the "Boss" circulated quickly. Hundreds of people gathered at City Hall. Did Tweed, in fact, really pass away? A police telegraph was put into operation in the basement of City Hall. Many were surprised when the news was confirmed. He hadn't looked bad at the recent aldermanic investigation. Some others thought they had detected a slight lameness and difficulty in climbing City Hall steps, but he had joked with his keepers William Quincy and Deputy Sheriff Mcgonnigle and was in good, crackling humor. Could he die so quickly? Generally the discussions tended to be sympathetic. "De mortuis nil nisi bonum." In some cases, criticism of ex-attorney general Fairchild was bitter. An unnamed judge expressed an opinion that Tweed should have been released following his testimony to Fairchild. Residents of the Seventh Ward remembered Tweed kindly, with pleasant memories of Tweed's past. Those close to him gave varying opinions. Charles Devlin told of last meetings and of the bitterness and disappointment Tweed had with Fairchild. Tweed's failure to obtain a release even after turning state's evidence "finally broke him down." Devlin had visited Corporation Counsel William C. Whitney to obtain relief for Tweed, telling him Tweed could not live much longer in prison, but as usual, nothing was done. Foster Dewey had a like view. The confession broke the old man's heart, Dewey said angrily. He did not want to do it, but the years in jail were too much for him. Despite Fairchild's denial, a deal was in fact agreed to. For people like Dewey and Devlin, Tweed died of a broken heart caused directly by Fairchild and the state.

Mayor Smith Ely also blamed Tweed's death on the confinement in jail. Tweed had an active bustling nature, not given to reading and reflection. For such a man jail hastened death. Ely found Tweed a common, illiterate man, but with great character, able to sway multitudes. Asked if Tweed was like Robin Hood, taking from the rich and giving to the poor, Ely replied, "By no means and whoever robs the people in general robs each other individually." All the people of New York through higher taxes were victims of Tweed. Corporation Counsel Whitney expected that all suits amounting to some $22 million against Tweed would end and no monies would be recovered. While sympathetic to Tweed's lonely death, away from family in a prison cell, it was retribution. "A moral should adorn a sad tale," mused Whitney sanctimoniously, "for a man who had done so much to corrupt the City of New York, it was not befitting that his end should be among the surroundings that attend the deathbeds of the honest and virtuous, else the premium would be transferred from the good to the bad, and the very foundations of society could be uprooted." William Quincy, the undersheriff who was in personal charge of Tweed after his return from Vigo, told of Tweed's last illness, his depression regarding the illusive promises of freedom, and his horror and pain of having to climb steps on occasions of his visits to court. Sheriff Reilly told of sympathy expressed for Tweed. Tweed had a "great many friends among the poor and friendless people of the city, and they regret his death," thought Reilly. Many were sympathetic because of the ill-treatment he received, while others felt he was not a wholly bad man. Comptroller John Kelly, reluctant to speak, nevertheless was sorry to hear of his death—he had hoped to have freed Tweed before long. The *Herald* editorialized that his wife, to whom he was indulgent, though not faithful, and his children, who thought him a kind and even good father, could accept this merciful dispensation. Still Tweed should have been set free to meditate further on a life of crime. His sudden death relieves the public authorities from embarrassing questions. Tweed had abettors as guilty as he, but he was the chief culprit and should be punished; "his death in a prison will operate as an impressive warning."

Tweed's death was also seized upon for the Sunday sermon. It was a golden opportunity. What could be better? Rev. Dr. Talmage preached at Brooklyn Tabernacle about the "Safeguards of Young Men," and pointed out that the "wreck of Friday at Ludlow Street Jail" illustrated on "what a desolate coast a sprung craft may crash and part." Tweed and James Fisk were the "greatest miscreants of the century," he gleefully shouted to his flock. What are "Safeguards," they are love of honor, industrious habits, high ideal of life and respect for the Sabbath. At the Methodist Church in Williamsburg, Rev. J. J. Waite used Luke 16:2—"Give an account of thy stewardship; for thou mayest be no longer steward." Tweed's career served to illustrate the parable. He reigned as a king, stealing millions, raising confederates from scum to prominent patrons—yet he died in prison almost alone. His career shows "honesty and integrity are the cause of true friendship." At the Lee Avenue Baptist Church, Williamsburg, J. Hyatt Smith took as his text Galatians 6:7—whatever a man soweth he shall reap. Rev. W. C. Steel in the Methodist Tabernacle stressed the evil of Tweed's atheism. His downfall, said Reverend Steel, proved honesty was the best policy, and that punishment overtakes the evildoer. Tweed and Fisk poisoned the minds of youth. Their fate is a lesson to youth.

As the funeral arrangements proceeded, more interviews and opinions were given. Dewey expanding on an earlier view said Tweed was worth but $2,500 at the time of his death. Tweed had been very prodigal in his expenditures and never understood the value of money. His wife, running the estate in Greenwich, an estate held by her for twenty years, might manage there if she lived frugally. William Jr. and Richard could support themselves if they lived economically—there was no money for the younger sons. At their weddings, the two daughters received $25,000 and $50,000 each, nothing since. Tweed left many things at the time of his death; he however did not leave money.

As reminiscences, opinions were being voiced about the dead chieftain, funeral arrangements were completed. Numerous friends called on the Tweeds to view the body and give condolences. Devlin hoped the body could be embalmed so his wife and absent children might view it before burial.

There were dark, gray clouds on Wednesday, April 17, 1878, as the day began. Large numbers of people started congregating around the Douglas house, perhaps five thousand in number. A reporter noted they were generally of the poorer classes, come from all parts of the city to express feelings of gratitude. They were not curiosity seekers "but were respectful and decent in their behavior." Six policemen were at hand. These were more than enough to preserve order. All the curtains in the house were drawn, no one was allowed in who was not expressly invited. Between the two parlors lay Tweed's coffin. It was of oak covered with black broadcloth, paneled with black silk and velvet and decorated with oxidized silver handles. The coffin was 6 feet 6 inches long, 22 inches wide and 18 inches deep; open on the top, there was a large silver plate beneath the opening, "William M. Tweed died April 12, 1878, aged fifty-five years." In the cushioned coffin lay Tweed in a black broadcloth suit, immaculate linen shirt and his favorite white necktie. His right hand was on his breast, the left along his side. His face seemed a little worn from suffering, the skin was like marble, hair and whiskers were snow-white. On the coffin were floral wreathes; one read "Our Father." Two baskets of flowers were from the married daughters, and were the only flowers in the room. Among the first to arrive was Charles Devlin, followed by a number of dignitaries, close friends and companions, Sheridan Shook, Coroner Woltman, Deputy Coroner Cochran, ex-harbor master Thomas, John D. Townsend, ex-alderman Thomas McSpedon, ex-alderman Samuel Adams, exwarden Liscomb of the penitentiary, Undersheriff William H. Quincy, expolice superintendent James J. Kelso, John D. Newman, Wiskinkie of

Tammany, Justice Timothy J. Campbell, ex-commissioner Owen W. Brennan, ex-street commissioner Charles C. Cornell, William Edelstein, ex-state senator John Blair, S. Foster Dewey, ex-alderman Bernard Kelley, George H. Butt, George Mountjoy of Philadelphia, ex-alderman Jack J. Reilly, Luke Grant, Emile Botzger, ex-messenger in the Department of Public Works, Mr. Fitzsimmons and daughter, among others. They were for the most part of Tweed's immediate circle. Missing were his opponents, Jones of the *Times*, Nast, Fairchild, Whitney, Peckham, the leaders of the Committee of Seventy, Tilden or any member of the reforming autocracy. Tweed seemed to have forgiven his enemies, did they forgive him? And they owed him so much. Peckham years of salary, Tilden his governorship. None of the elusive "Ring" were present. Neither Sweeny, Hall, Connolly nor any of the contractors arrived to say farewell. Whatever personal bonds existed, if they ever did exist, were not sufficient to overcome shame, guilt or inconvenience which might attend witnessing the ceremony. It had not taken too much to destroy whatever there was of "The Ring." What remained could not raise even a weak sentimental gesture. Missing also were the Democratic politicians; not only Tilden but the local vote getters, Smith Ely, Mike Norton and the up and coming Richard Croker were conspicuous by their absence. No politician of any rank was there to give condolences to the family or to tend a token of respect to the "Boss," even if just for old times' sake.

There were a lot of "ex's," has-beens, formers with little to lose in that dim silent room. They were like Tweed of a long time ago. To be associated with Tweed even in death was too much of a stigma for the living. Of the immediate family gathered in the hushed rooms were his four daughters—Jennie; Josephine and her husband Frederick Douglas; Eliza and her husband John Henry Maginnis of New Orleans; and Mary Amelia, whose husband Arthur Maginnis remained home. Also present were his brother Richard with his wife and daughter, and his father-in-law Joseph C. Skaden. The two younger sons, Charlie and George, were in boarding school and not informed of their father's death. His wife and two eldest sons were still in Europe. Shortly after 10 A.M., Rev. Dr. Price, the old family friend, now pastor of the Episcopal church at Hempstead, Long Island, went to the upper landing of the first floor and in full robes delivered the service. There was no sermon. Those inside took their last look at the deceased and the doors of the home opened to the waiting crowd, who filed past the coffin for nearly an hour. They were for the most part workingmen with rough attire and lined faces, women carrying market baskets. Several "colored" men appeared at intervals. All faces had a sober look mingled with regret and respect. At 11 A.M. even as more people stood to enter the house, the doors were closed. The relatives took their last look, the daughters cried in their grief. The coffin lid was screwed on, twelve pallbearers, Cornell, Kelly, Blair, Butt, Devlin, David Miller, Dewey, Edelstein, Thomas Adams, Charles H. Hall, John Scott and Alexander Brandon, wearing sashes of black and white muslin lined the entrance to the home. As the coffin was carried out and placed into the hearse, a hush fell over the crowd. The pallbearers went two apiece into six carriages, Dr. Price went into another and the family in three others. Eight other carriages, making eighteen in all, followed the hearse as the funeral cortege headed by two mounted policemen went down Madison Avenue to Forty-seventh Street, then to Fifth Avenue, down Fifth Avenue to Fourteenth Street, down Broadway past City Hall to State Street and then to the Hamilton ferry. Mayor Ely refused to allow flags to be put at half-mast.

The early morning clouds which threatened rain dissipated and warm bright sunshine met the cortege at the ferry landing. On Long Island, all moved quickly to Greenwood. It was a rural but fashionable cemetery opened in 1842. William Kent, the Harpers, Roosevelts, Cortelyous and Livingstons were some names on the many elaborate monuments. The Tweeds had lot 6477, section 55. It was purchased in October 1852 by William and his brother Richard. Spring made the cemetery glisten, birds chirped from the trees, flowers and buds bloomed. At the entrance, members of the Masonic Palestine Lodge F.&A.M. and Amity Chapter, Royal Arch Masons, in full regalia stood waiting. The procession proceeded to the family lot, a spot offering a beautiful view of the bay and New York City in the distance. A monument into which were cut the names William M. and Richard Tweed stood within a fenced enclosure. Inside was a heap of clay and a newly dug gravesite. The ground had been covered with many magnolias and other flowers. Nearly fifteen hundred persons were at hand. Fully one third, noted *Times* reporters, were women. They were mostly poor. The coffin was placed on crossbars over the grave. Reverend Price read a final service. This was followed by Masonic ritual, while family and friends and possibly even some enemies watched the coffin being lowered into the ground. The grave was quickly filled and the mourners quietly left, the daughters again being nearly overcome by grief. Tweed was buried alongside his mother.

While Richard Tweed, his wife and daughter were at the funeral, thieves attempted a robbery of his home at 339 West Fifty-seventh Street. Some items were taken, but they were frightened off before they could thoroughly accomplish their task. The death of Tweed and the "morality" of his life were wasted, at least in that instance.[1]

There remained some small additions and subtractions, mostly the latter, as the Tweed family drifted into obscurity. In 1868, Josephine and Jennie S. had taken out an endowment policy on Tweed with the Knickerbocker Life Insurance Company for $10,000. The policy was to run for ten years and to be paid April 1, 1878. If he died before that date, they could receive the entire sum at the time of death. The daughters paid up the premiums for eight years amounting to $1,180 and defaulted. In March 1878, they asked the company to give them a new policy for $8,000 in proportion to the premiums paid. The firm refused, citing a clause in the agreement prohibiting the insured from going abroad without permission. This clearly Tweed did do at the time of his escape and the daughters were not entitled to any premium; the issue went to court, where Aaron J. Vanderpoel presented the appropriate clause, and defense counsel William Edelstein and Robert Sowell replied that eight premiums were paid prior to Tweed's escape, and a clause in the policy stipulated issuance of a new policy after the payment of three premiums. The Tweeds lost the suit. In March 1879, the Tweed homestead in Greenwich, Connecticut, was sold by Josephine Douglas, under a power of attorney executed by Mrs. Mary Jane Tweed in Paris in May 1878. Purchaser was Joseph Millbank, "a wealthy gentleman in New York City." The price was reported to be $75,000, but it was believed the amount was a good deal smaller.[2] Tweed never did so well in real estate.

Epilogue

And so Tweed passed into history to become the fabled legend. It was an undeserved fate. Except for Tweed's own very questionable "confession," there was really no evidence of a "Tweed Ring," no direct evidence of Tweed's thievery, no evidence, excepting the testimony of the informer contractors, of "wholesale" plunder by Tweed. What preceded is a story of political profiteering at the expense of Tweed, of vaulting personal ambitions fed on Tweed's carcass, of a conspiracy of self-justification of the corruption of law by the upholders of that law, of a venal irresponsible press and a citizenry delighting in the exorcism of witchery. If Tweed was involved then all those about him were equally guilty. He was never tried for theft. The only criminal trial that was held was for a misdemeanor of failing to audit, and this trial was held before a hand-picked judge and jury at a time when Tweed-hunting was at its height.

Probably the "truth" about Tweed, "The Ring" and the "stolen" millions will never be known. Is it possible to measure the difference between graft and profit? If Keyser charged so much for plastering, perhaps another could do the work for less, but would it be the same work, could it be done on time? How do you compare the cost of one carpet with that of another? Price is only one consideration. At one point, a decision has to be reached on any contract, no matter who is selected; there will always be someone who could have done it cheaper. Surely there were overcharges, but by how much? The throwing about of figures, 10, 30, 50, 200 million, is of no help. Is it possible to decide at what point profit becomes graft? It is difficult to answer these questions or work out an almost insoluble puzzle. In the end, the easiest solution is of course to blame Tweed, rather than examine financial records, vouchers, warrants. These were allowed to lie dormant silently collecting the dust of a century, in the end hopefully to disappear. How much easier to nail the "Elephant" to a wall or listen to the romanticism of history and the excesses of rhetoric created by Godkin, Bryce, Wingate, Lynch and so many others.

Tweed emerges as anything but a master thief. It was the contractors who willingly padded bills, never calling attention to any undue pressure upon them to do so; it was those lower-echelon agents in the city, espe-

347

cially Woodward and Watson, who were in direct liaison with the contractors, not Tweed. And lastly blame should be placed on the city and state. The former because it did not regulate expenditures properly and failed to pay its bills on time, a point brought up time and again by the contractors, and the latter because it interfered in city business; the city's welfare was subverted by state political interests. The Tweed story, or better the contractors' story, is about as good a reason for New York City home rule as can be offered.

Where did the legendary millions go? None of the contractors, with the possible exception of Garvey, had sizable sums of money, and even he wasn't to be compared to the "robber barons" like Morgan or Whitney or Rockefeller. These could sneeze out in a moment what purported to be the total Tweed plunder. What of Hall, Connolly, Sweeny, Hoffman? There is nothing to show they received any princely sums. No one connected with the so-called "Ring" set up a dynasty or retired to luxurious seclusion. Certainly not Tweed. If money was stolen, it held a Pharaoh's curse. Those who touched it did not enjoy it. So many died suddenly, so many died in dishonor and loneliness. None suffered as much as did William Magear Tweed and the City of New York.

Tweed spent some twenty years in public service. In the Fire Department, as alderman, member of the Board of Supervisors and Board of Education, member of Congress, state senator, commissioner of public works —it was a long list and resulted in a great deal of public good. He was instrumental in modernizing governmental and educational institutions, in developing needed reforms in public welfare programs, in incorporating schools, hospitals, establishing public baths, in preserving a site in Central Park for the Metropolitan Museum of Art, in widening Broadway, extending Prospect Park and removing fences from around public parks, establishing Riverside Park and Drive, annexing the Bronx as a forerunner of the incorporation of Greater New York, in building the Brooklyn Bridge, in founding the Lenox Library. He was of considerable service during the Civil War. Tweed moved the city forward in so many ways and could have been, if he had not been destroyed, a progressive force in shaping the interests and destiny of a great city and its people.

Tweed's concepts about urbanization and accommodation while not philosophically formalized were years beyond their time. Twenty or thirty years later such programs were adopted by reformers and urban planners. Tweed was a pioneer spokesman for an emerging New York, one of the few that spoke for its interests, one of the very few that could have had his voice heard in Albany. Tweed grew with the city, his death was a tragedy for the future metropolis.

His life in the end was wasted, not so much by what he did, but by what was done to him, his work and the city being relegated to the garbage heap, both branded by the same indelible iron. He became a club with which to beat New York, really the ultimate goal of the blessed reformers.

It is time to seek a re-evaluation of Tweed and his time. If Tweed was not so bad, neither was the city. Old legends die hard, old ideas have deep roots, but hopefully some of the old legends will die and the deep roots wither away.

What was learned from the episode? Practically nothing. Politics, politicians, jurists and venal journalists certainly continued to ply their trade, spurred by their success, as in the past, with hardly a glance or hesitation, comforted in the downfall of the "Boss." The devil had been killed; would anyone bother to look at the judges or ask anyone else to do the Lord's work? Every once in a while, a bill is introduced in the Massachusetts legislature to have the Salem witches exonerated and declared non-witches. Some are. It might be time to have the New York state legislature and history provide a similar service for Tweed. Surely, there are other devils around to take his place. And a statue for Tweed? Yes, it would be his city alive and well.

Notes

1. Isaac N. P. Stokes, *Iconography of Manhattan Island* (New York, 1928), VI, 592; *Manual of the Corporation of the City of New York*, 1849, pp. 331–33; 1857, p. 494; 1858, p. 524; 1864, p. 619 (hereafter referred to as *Valentine's Manual*); Mary L. Booth, *History of the City of New York* (New York, 1860), pp. 384–85; Walter Barrett, *The Old Merchants of New York City* (New York, 1885), V, 140–47; Rufus Rockwell Wilson, *New York: Old and New* (Philadelphia, 1902), II, 45–46; Kenneth H. Dunshee, *As You Pass By* (New York, 1952), pp. 162–64; Frederick L. Collins, *Consolidated Gas Company of New York* (New York, 1934), pp. 29, 55–57; New York City Tax Rolls, 1816–40, Historical Documents Collection, Paul Klapper Library, Queens College of the City University of New York (hereafter referred to as H.D.C.). For residences and business addresses throughout the book, see Longworth's, Doggett's and Trow's *New York City Directory* for the appropriate year.
2. For genealogical material, see Baptisms and Marriages (1809–1900) and Burials (1829–91), manuscript volumes, at the St. Stephen's Church, New York City; Holy Bible, presented to William M. Tweed, Jr., by his father and mother on May 28, 1868, Museum of the City of New York, containing a valuable record of family births and deaths; Richard M. Tweed Family Papers, containing genealogical material mainly on the family of Richard M. Tweed, William's brother, at the home of Mrs. Richard Tweed, Borger, Texas (hereafter referred to as Tweed Family Papers); Tweed tombstones, Greenwood Cemetery, Brooklyn, New York, Sec. 55, Plot 64-47; Barrett, op. cit., V, 144. For Tweed's religious views, see Marshall Spatz, "New York City Public Schools and the Emergence of Bureaucracy, 1868–1917," doctoral dissertation, City University of New York, pp. 35–61.
3. New York *Times*, Dec. 2, 1858.

353

4. Robert G. Albion, *The Rise of the Port of New York, 1815–1860* (New York, 1939), pp. 117, 177.
5. The first reference found by the author to "M" as being Marcy is in the New York *Herald* of February 1873. At the time of Tweed's death, the *Herald* mentioned that a gold watch given to Tweed while he was foreman of the "Big Six" was inscribed to William Marcy Tweed, but the watch has disappeared. A speaking trumpet also given to Tweed at the time is inscribed William M. Tweed. Fire Museum, The Home Insurance Company, 59 Maiden Lane, New York City.
6. Tweed Bible, Museum of the City of New York.
7. William M. Tweed to Henry L. Davis, Oct. 24, 1846, March 13, 1847, William M. Tweed Misc. Mss., New-York Historical Society Library (hereafter referred to as N.Y.H.S.L.).
8. Richard Tweed, Jr., to Margaret Tweed, July 17, 1846, Aug. 1, 1848, Richard M. Tweed Family Papers.
9. William M. Tweed to Henry L. Davis, Oct. 1, 1846, Oct. 24, 1846, Nov. 14, 1846, March 13, 1847, Tweed Misc. Mss.; *Journal of the Proceedings of the Convention . . . Right Worthy Lodge of I.O.O.F. of the State of New York* (New York, 1846), pp. 3, 11, 23, 193, 768; Semi-Annual Report National Lodge No. 30, 1875, manuscript, for Tweed's suspension. Library of the I.O.O.F., New York City.
10. This information was received in a telephone call from the Masonic librarian in New York, who would not confirm anything in writing.
11. William M. Tweed to Henry L. Davis, Oct. 24, 1846, Tweed Misc. Mss.
12. Tweed to Davis, Oct. 1, 1846, ibid.
13. *Times*, Dec. 26, 1869; April 13, 1878. For accounts of the Fire Department, see Dunshee, op. cit.; George W. Sheldon, *The Story of the Volunteer Fire Department of the City of New York* (New York, 1882); Lowell Limpus, *History of the New York Fire Department* (New York, 1940); A[ugustine] E. Costello, *Our Firemen* (New York, 1887).

   Joseph Johnson's stories about the formation of Americus are repeated by Sheldon, but are not substantiated by historical evidence.
14. *Board of Aldermen of New York City Proceedings*, 1846, XXXI, 575; 1850, XXXIX, 687, 690 (hereafter referred to as *Proceedings*); *Board of Aldermen of New York City Documents*, 1850, pp. 919–57, 1009–68. See also *Herald*, Sept. 6, 1850.

2. FRESHMAN POLITICIAN

1. For election returns for this and subsequent years, see *Valentine's Manual*, *Times* and *Herald* for the respective year. The results of the elections were usually printed a day or two after the voting. For evaluation of the City Council, see *Times*, Feb. 12, 1852.
2. Ibid., Oct. 3, 4, 11, 14, 22 and 28, 1851.
3. Ibid., Oct. 23, 1851.

4. See particularly report of the meeting of the "Unterrified." *Herald*, Oct. 23, 1851.
5. Allan Nevins and Milton H. Thomas, eds., *The Diary of George Templeton Strong* (New York, 1952), II, 75 (hereafter referred to as *Strong Diary*).
6. *Times*, Dec. 8, 10, 12, 16, 17 and 18, 1851; *Report of the Special Committee Appointed by the Common Council of the City of New York— Reception of Governor Louis Kossuth* (New York, 1852), pp. 278–79.
7. For bills paid by the city in connection with the reception, see New York City Comptroller's Vouchers, 1852, H.D.C. (hereafter referred to as Vouchers); *Times*, Dec. 23, 1852.

3. THE CALDRON

1. *Proceedings*, 1852, XLV, 3; *Times*, Jan. 6, 1852.
2. *Times*, March 8 and 26, May 19, 23 and 27, June 10 and 16, Aug. 21, 1852.
3. Bayrd Still, *Mirror for Gotham* (New York, 1956), pp. 126, 128.
4. *Times*, March 26, June 5, 16 and 18, 1852.
5. Ibid., June 8, 1852. On Aug. 11, 1852, the *Times* in an editorial entitled "The Blues—How to Cure Them" suggested less excitement and getting to bed two hours earlier.
6. Ibid., July 28, 1852. This fresh-air campaign was part of a growing movement to create a park in the city. See issues of May 21 and Oct. 21, 1852. Somewhat allied to this was a short-lived Free Farm Movement headed by the old-time radical John Commerford. Ibid., May 28, 1852.
7. Ibid., June 18, 1852.
8. Ibid., Feb. 12 and 21, March 10 and 11, May 8, 11 and 12, July 15, 1852.
9. *Proceedings*, 1852, XLV, XLVI, *passim*.
10. *Times*, May 6, 1852.
11. *Proceedings*, 1852, XLVIII, 642–43; Stokes, op. cit., V, 1844; New York *Tribune*, Dec. 31, 1852; *Times*, Nov. 16 and 18, Dec. 30 and 31, 1852.
12. *Times*, March 10 and 23, April 1 and 4, July 3, Dec. 31, 1852. For reports of cases before Tweed, see issues of Feb. 14, 19 and 21, Dec. 21, 1852.
13. *Proceedings*, 1852, XLV, 150, 155, *passim*.
14. *Strong Diary*, II, 65.
15. *Times*, March 17, 18 and 25, April 4, Nov. 16, 1852.
16. Ibid., June 11, 1852; *Proceedings*, 1852, XLVI, 519–20.
17. *Times*, July 3, 7 and 19, Oct. 25 and 29, Nov. 14, 16 and 17, 1852; *Proceedings*, 1852, XLVI, 694; XLVII, 15.
18. *Times*, March 10 and 11, Aug. 25, Sept. 23 and 28, 1852.
19. *Herald*, June 10, Aug. 21, Sept. 3 and 21, Oct. 4, 9, 12, 19 and 31, Nov. 1 and 15, 1852. The *Herald* on the latter date indicated in a very laudatory editorial that Tweed had spent twelve years in the New York City

public schools, but did not say which ones. The *Dictionary of the United States Congress* (Philadelphia, 1859), p. 484, edited by Charles Lanman, also indicates that he had a public school education.

4. "ABYSS OF BARBARISM"

1. *Times*, June 18 and 28, July 14 and 16, 1853; *Strong Diary*, II, 127, 129, 131; Benjamin Silliman and C. R. Goodrich, eds., *The World of Science, Art, and Industry Illustrated from Examples in the New-York Exhibition* (New York, 1854).
2. Among other nuisances on the mind of the *Times* was snowballing by "young scapegraces," who made a walk in the street or a trip on a sleigh impossible without a ruined hat or a blackened eye. The paper sarcastically suggested outlawing sleighs or setting aside a week or even a summer to allow boys to throw stones, not over 4 inches in diameter. Another annoyance was a more serious kind, the adulteration of milk with water, chalks and even plaster of Paris. It estimated that eight thousand children per year died, one half of whom were less than one year old, to a great extent because of this problem. *Times*, Jan. 5, 15 and 22, March 28 and 29, April 5, June 3, 21, 23, 24 and 29, Sept. 21 and 23, 1853.
3. *Times*, May 4, 21 and 24, 1853. Late in February, an indictment was handed down against ten aldermen including Oscar Sturtevant for alleged malfeasance in office. David D. Field was the defense attorney. They were found guilty, and Sturtevant was sentenced to prison for fifteen days and fined $250. The case was appealed to the Court of Appeals, which early in 1854 upheld the lower court. *Times*, Jan. 6, 1854.
4. *Ibid.*, June 6 and 26, 1853. Meetings were held earlier in the year. Peter Cooper also stressed poor city financing, especially of contracts. It questioned the sale of Fort Gansevoort, worth $300,000, for $150,000. *Times*, Jan. 13 and 14, March 7, April 1, 1853.
5. *Ibid.*, Sept. 9 and 22, 1853; *Proceedings*, 1853, XLIX, *passim*. It was a busy year for Tweed. He had also asked that the chief of police keep a record of donations to policemen. This was voted down. More importantly, as a member of the Committee on Repairs and Supplies, he helped produce a report concerning a new courthouse on Chambers Street. It was not the "Tweed Court House," but the site was almost the same. *Proceedings*, 1853, L, 297, 321.
6. *Times*, Feb. 28 and Dec. 16, 1853. Others mentioned as shareholders were Peter B. Sweeney, nephew of Alderman Thomas J. Barr, and John L. O'Sullivan, chargé to Portugal. The Broadway Railroad injunction case was also argued at the beginning of the year. Tweed was on the Law Committee of the Board which gathered evidence on Justice Campbell's injunction, which was upheld by the Court of Appeals. *Times*, Jan. 17, Feb. 2 and 7, 1853, Jan. 6, 1854.

7. Ibid., May 6, June 18, 1853; John A. Krout, *The Origins of Prohibition* (New York, 1925).
8. *Times,* May 5, Sept. 2, 5 and 10, Oct. 4, 1853.
9. Ibid., July 6 and 23, Sept. 23, 24 and 30, Dec. 15 and 21, 1853. For tributes to Thomas F. Meagher and John Mitchell, Irish patriots who fit so well into the patriotic messianism of the day, see *Times,* May 21 and 26, Dec. 20, 1853.

5. A TERM IN CONGRESS

1. *Congressional Globe,* 33rd Cong. 1st Session, Dec. 1853–Sept. 1854 (Washington, 1854), pp. 2, 4, 17–19, 34, *passim;* 2nd Session, Jan. 1855–Sept. 1855 (Washington, 1855), pp. 367, 1032, *passim.* Tweed was not active at the start of his incumbency. One of his first acts as congressman, though, was the introduction of a private bill in favor of a William Brown, a "colored" veteran of the War of 1812, for an increase in pension. Tweed's attendance was rather good, but in July 1854 he was absent several days "suffering from indisposition." Fellow Congressman "Mike" Walsh said it was no excuse for his absence. *Globe,* 1st Session, pp. 1872–73.

6. KNOW-NOTHINGS

1. Heywood Broun and Margaret Leech, *Anthony Comstock, Roundsman of the Lord* (New York, 1927); *Times,* Feb. 16, March 9, 1854. No one has ever done a serious study of Madame Restell, but there are a number of exposés, e.g. see Bishop Huntington, *Restell's Secret Life* (Philadelphia, 1897); John H. Warren, *Thirty Years Battle with Crime* (New York, 1874). There is a good deal of primary source material in the records of the Criminal Courts, housed at H.D.C.
2. *Times,* April 5, June 23, 1854. For various problems of the city, e.g. conditions of its streets, see issues of Jan. 19, March 11 and Oct. 12, 1854; for crime and prison conditions which foster more crime and are corrupting to the prisoner, see Oct. 28 and Nov. 21, 1854; on paupers, see Dec. 22 and 27, 1854.
3. Ibid., Jan. 6 and Nov. 1, 1854.
4. Ibid., Oct. 21 and 26, 1854.
5. Ibid., Sept. 1, 4, 8 and 11, Oct. 6, 7, 10, 14, 22 and 26, Nov. 2, 1854.
6. Ibid., June 12, Sept. 4, 6 and 16, 1854.
7. Terry Coleman, *Going to America* (New York, 1972), pp. 161–64; Franklin B. Hough, ed., *Census of the State of New York for 1855* (Albany, 1857), pp. xl, xliii, 110, 111, 118; *Valentine's Manual,* 1854, p. 343;

1855, pp. 300–2, 336; 1869, pp. 136–37; Ira Rosenwaike, *Population History of New York City* (Syracuse, 1972), pp. 33–35.
8. *Times*, April 13, 1878.

7. A SMALL VICTORY

1. *Times*, Jan. 2 and 4, April 5, 1855.
2. Ibid., Jan. 3 and 12, Feb. 16, March 13, April 9, Aug. 2, 1855.
3. Ibid., Jan. 20, May 23 and 28, Sept. 20, 1855. The *Herald*'s view with regard to the spread of pornography and "lewdness" in the city was not nearly as one-sided as that of the *Times*. It questioned the virtuousness of supposedly pure rural communities. In a police raid on a local bookseller in 1857, it was found that his chief customers were New Englanders with Boston at the center. "The chief demand for obscene books and nasty newspapers is in the small manufacturing towns in New England and it is in these towns that the brothels of the metropolis are chiefly recruited." The *Herald* concluded that prostitutes were drawn mostly from rural communities in New England and Europe, that native New Yorkers are rarely found in brothels, and the "vice and immorality of the city is drawn from the country." *Herald*, Sept. 17, 1857.
4. *Times*, March 12, 14, 15 and 19, May 16 and 17, 1855; *Herald*, Nov. 27 and 28, Dec. 2 and 3, 1855.
5. *Times* and *Herald*, Sept. 4, 8, 24, 25, Oct. 6, 9, 21 and 26, 1855.
6. *Herald*, Feb. 20, March 14 and Dec. 22, 1855. At New York University, he was still Abraham and received the poetry prize in 1850 from the Eucleian and Philomathean Society. Printed card in author's possession. For a standard biography of Hall, see Croswell Bowen, *The Elegant Oakey* (New York, 1956).
7. *Herald*, May 18, 1855. For a very laudatory editorial on the six-thousand-member Jewish community, see the *Times*, March 24, 1854.
8. *Times*, April 8, 12, 17, 19, 21, and 28, May 2, 5, 10, 12 and 22, July 3, 1855; *Herald*, Aug. 27, Oct. 26, 1855.
9. For general survey of elections, see Jerome Mushkat, *Tammany, The Evolution of a Political Machine, 1789–1865* (Syracuse 1971), pp. 286–93; *Herald*, Nov. 6 and 12, 1856.

8. PANIC

1. *Herald*, Jan. 7 and 31, 1857, A[ugustine] E. Costello, *Our Police Protectors* (New York, 1885), pp. 137–40; *Valentine's Manual*, 1858, pp. 113–26.
2. *Strong Diary*, II, 342–45; Costello, *Our Police Protectors*, pp. 141–42; *Herald and Times*, April 9, 24, 29 and 30, May 22, 23 and 26, June 3, 5,

10, 11, 12, 17, 18 and 25, July 3 and 4, 1857; Herbert Asbury, *The Gangs of New York* (New York, 1929), pp. 107–10.

3. *Herald* and *Times*, July 6, 7 and 15, Aug. 19, 1857; *Strong Diary*, II, 346–50; Joel T. Headley, *Pen and Pencil Sketches of the Great Riots* (New York, 1882), pp. 129–35; Asbury, op. cit., pp. 112–17.

4. *Herald*, Feb. 1, 2, 5, 8 and 15, May 10 and 12, Aug. 5, 1857; *Times*, May 8, Sept. 11, Nov. 20, 1857. For the Burdell case, see Henry L. Clinton, *Celebrated Trials* (New York, 1897), pp. 1–279; *Strong Diary*, II, 316–17, 320–24, 333–34, 352.

5. *Herald* and *Times*, Sept. 2, Oct. 20, Nov. 3 and 7, 1857; *Strong Diary*, II, 361–70.

6. *Valentine's Manual*, 1858, pp. 77–82; Mushkat, op. cit., pp. 308–11; *Herald*, Feb. 7, April 19, June 8 and 10, July 2 and 24, Sept. 5, 10 and 17, Oct. 18 and 30, Nov. 4, 6, 12, 13, 21 and 24, Dec. 1, 2, 5 and 18, 1857. The *Herald*'s coverage of local political news was far better for this period than that of the *Times*.

9. THE BIBLE

1. *Herald* and *Times*, Jan. 13, Feb. 2, 10 and 26, April 17 and 20, May 4, 6, 7 and 8, July 10, Oct. 10, 1858.

2. *Times*, Dec. 2, 1858.

3. Ibid., Oct. 22, 1858. The *Times* on Dec. 3, 1858, ran an interesting account of the amusements of the people of the city. A "strong-minded" reporter told of seeing *Our American Cousin* at Laura Keene's Theatre, eating "bretzel" at the German "Volks Garten" and visiting the "dancing dens" on the East River "adopted" by the "lower classes of Irish and negroes."

4. Ibid., Nov. 15, 16 and 18, 1858.

5. Ibid., Jan. 1, 5, 8 and 20, Feb. 24, April 9, Nov. 9, 1858. There are few printed records of the minutes of the Board of Supervisors for the period. For the 1850s and 1860s, newspapers like the *Times* and the *Daily Transcript* are the best and often only source of these minutes. For a listing of available minutes, see Stokes, op. cit., VI, 201.

6. *Times*, Jan. 13 and 16, Nov. 15 and 22, Dec. 2, 5, 9, 10 and 11, 1858.

7. Spatz, op. cit., pp. 35–61; John W. Pratt, "Boss Tweed's Public Welfare Program," *The New-York Historical Society Quarterly*, 1961, XLV, 398–403.

8. *Herald* and *Times*, March 5, April 18, May 6, Sept. 16 and 17, Oct. 14, 20 and 26, Nov. 1, 3, 4, 8, 11, 16, 17, 27 and 29, Dec. 1, 2, 8, 9, 11 and 31, 1858.

9. *Times*, Nov. 23, 1858.

10. THE VISITORS

1. Membership List, Society of Tammany or Columbian Order, 1834–1880, New York State Library. Tweed's son, William M. Jr., became a member on December 9, 1867. Tilden was a member since 1853.
2. *Herald*, July 3, Oct. 28 and Nov. 9, 1859. Bennett followed this by a similar article on pauperism and crime among the "Colored Population." April 1, 1860.
3. *Times*, Jan. 4, 1860.
4. Vouchers, 1860; *Herald*, June 9, 17, 29 and 30, Oct. 12, 1860.
5. Stokes, op. cit., V, 1885; VI, 467; *Strong Diary*, III, 42–52. The diarist gives an excellent account of the "week of excitement beyond any event in my time . . . ," though he has nothing to say about Lincoln's visit. See also *Times* and *Herald* for appropriate dates.
6. *Herald*, April 22, May 23, July 3 and 6, Sept. 18, Oct. 29, Dec. 16, 1860.
7. *Proceedings*, 1860, LXXIX, 564; Barrett, op. cit., V, 140–47.

11. LINCOLN'S NEW YORK

1. At an Anti-Coercion Mass Meeting held on January 15, 1861, Isaiah Rynders and others including old-time Locofoco Fitzwilliam Byrdsall voiced sentiments for "our Southern brethren now engaged in the holy cause of American liberty . . ." *Herald*, Jan. 16, 1861. These voices were generally stilled after Fort Sumter, but would reappear.
2. *Times*, Jan. 29, Feb. 20 and 21, 1861. Strong saw Lincoln for a moment and it seemed to him he had a "keen, clear, honest face, not so ugly as his portraits . . ." *Strong Diary*, III, 101, 146, 147.
3. *Herald*, April 21 and 24, May 7, 10, 12, 15, 16, 19, 26 and 27, June 6, July 23, Sept. 17, 1861; *Strong Diary*, III, 129–34; *Proceedings*, 1861, LXXXII, 465. Tweed was on the executive committee of the Jackson Guard along with August Belmont, Elijah Purdy and Samuel J. Tilden.
4. *Times* and *Herald*, Sept. 17, 22 and 30, Oct. 1, 4, 5, 11, 13, 15, 17, 20 and 27, Nov. 2, 3, 4, 6, 7 and 10, Dec. 1 and 2, 1861. New York *Union*, Nov. 31 and 2, 1861 (the date on the former issue is obviously incorrect since November only has 30 days. It is also marked v. 1, no. 1 and since Nov. 2 is v. 1, no. 2, the correct date is Nov. 1). The paper promised to have fifty thousand copies printed daily until election time, but only these two copies are known to exist and are in the author's possession.
5. Insolvency Assignments, 1861; Barrett, op. cit., V, 145–47.
6. He is listed as an attorney after May 1, 1861, in *Trow's Directory*. Who sponsored him is not known since applications for admission to practice for this period cannot be located. They are available for 1800–46 and from 1870–1920 at the H.D.C.

12. RIOT

1. *Times* and *Herald*, July 6, 10 and 16, Aug. 20, 22, 23 and 28, 1862.
2. Ibid., Oct. 11, 14 and 29, Nov. 4, 5, 6, 18, 19, 23, 28, 29 and 30, Dec. 3, 1862. Mushkat in his book on Tammany cites 1862 as a critical year in Tweed's rise to power. He refers to pulling wires behind the scenes in uniting party factions, as well as his hiring of professional toughs to maintain order election night. P. 337. Even if this were so, Tweed was still not a dominant force within the party.
3. *Times* and *Herald*, Jan. 20, Feb. 11, April 2, 8 and 28, May 19 and 20, June 4, July 4, 1863. For pro-war rallies, see ibid., March 7 and 8, April 21, 1863.
4. Ibid., July 6, 11, 14, 15 and 16, Aug. 4 and 5, 1863; Riot Claims Against the City of New York, Vouchers; Adrian Cook, *Armies in the Street* (Lexington, 1974). Cook's book is by far the best account of the riots published to date.
5. *Herald*, Aug. 20, 21, 27 and 29, 1863.
6. Ibid., Aug. 27 and 29, Sept. 8 and 27, Nov. 11, 1863; Warrant 2622, 1869, Vouchers.
7. An injunction was issued against the city to prevent construction of the line. It halted a long-dreamed-about scheme. *Herald*, April 22 and 24, 1863.
8. Ibid., Sept. 6, 8, 10, 11, Oct. 1, 4, 6, 7, 15 and 29, Nov. 1, 3, 5, 22 and 23, 1863.
9. Ibid., Oct. 1, 2 and 20, Nov. 6, 1863; *Strong Diary*, III, 361, 368, 369.

13. VICTORY AND A FUNERAL

1. It is Mushkat's view that Tweed, not Purdy, was running the party and "modernizing the machine to meet new conditions," especially by providing a "response to the popular will." P. 355.
2. *Herald*, Sept. 1, 1864.
3. Ibid., Sept. 1, 15, 16, 17 and 18, Oct. 2, 16, Nov. 5, 9, 10, 23, 24 and 30, Dec. 11, 1864.
4. Ibid., Jan. 5, Feb. 4 and 24, March 2, June 15, 1864; Jan. 26 and 28, July 1, 1865.
5. *Herald* and *Times*, March 4, 5 and 7, April 11, 1865.
6. Ibid., April 15, 16, 17, 22, 25 and 26, 1865; *Strong Diary*, III, 585–88; Vouchers, 1865.
7. *Herald*, June 8, 1865. For summary of New York contribution to the war effort, see issue of July 1, 1865.
8. Ibid., Feb. 23 and 24, July 21, Aug. 11 and 27, Oct. 6, 12 and 14, Dec. 31, 1865.

9. Ibid., Sept. 7 and 8, Oct. 2, 14, 18 and 23, Nov. 7, 12, 19 and 27, Dec. 3 and 5, 1865; Notice on Moving Capital to New York City, *Herald*, Feb. 26, 1865; Adrian Hoffman Joline, "John Thompson Hoffman," *New York Genealogical and Biographical Record*, 1911, XLII, 111–28.

14. "YOUNG HARPIES"

1. *Times* and *Herald*, Jan. 2, 10, 11, 12 and 13, March 1 and 7, 1866.
2. Ibid., March 1 and 7, July 12, Nov. 2, 1866; Ledger A, 1862–64, County Treasury, January 1859–May 7, 1874, Supervisors of the County of New York, H.D.C.; Journal, County Treasury, January 1859–April 1868, Supervisors of the County of New York, H.D.C.; *New York Laws*, 1862, chap. 167, p. 335; 1864, chap. 242, p. 497; *Report of the Special Committee on New County Court House . . . Doc. 6, Board of Supervisors* (New York, 1863).
3. The gas and lamp contract involved Councilman Christopher Pullman. *Herald*, Nov. 2, 1866. The Henry decision came the same day. Barnard's conduct on the bench did not come in for any criticism. In fact, the *Herald* lauded these "fearless" and "unflinching decisions," especially since they were made by a Democratic judge, which would help in putting down the "Corporation Ring," Nov. 3, 1866.
4. Ibid., March 4 and 12, 1866.
5. Ibid., May 16 and 17, Aug. 30, Sept. 2, 3 and 4, 1866. Tweed was put on a reception committee for a mass meeting in support of Johnson along with Hall, Sturtevant, Barnard and some twenty others. The Johnson rally was a non-partisan affair bringing together such moderate Republicans as Henry Raymond of the *Times*, with such Democratic "villains" like Isaiah Rynders. *Herald* and *Times*, Sept. 13 and 16, 1866.
6. *Herald*, Nov. 3, Dec. 28, 1866. For political activity see issues of Oct. 6, 23, 28 and 31, Nov. 3, 4 and 7, 1866. For Cornell's letter of resignation, see issue of Nov. 18, 1866.
7. Ibid., Nov. 11, 17 and 19, Dec. 19, 1866.
8. Ibid., Dec. 2, 1866; *Times*, Dec. 2, 5 and 10, 1866. For later correspondence concerning *Times* claims against the city for advertising contracts, see Richard B. Connolly to George Jones, July 14, 1868, George E. Jones Papers, New York Public Library; Jones to Connolly, July 16, 1868, George E. Jones Papers, H.D.C.

15. NEW TAMMANY HALL

1. *Times*, Jan. 1, 1867.
2. *Herald*, March 3, 1868.
3. *Times*, March 4 and 9, 1867.
4. *Herald* and *Times*, July 2, 1868.

5. Ibid., Aug. 3 and 4. Sept. 4, 12, 14 and 24, Oct. 10, 20 and 24, 1867; Peter Cooper to Richard B. Connolly, Sept. 21, 1868, Peter Cooper Manuscripts, H.D.C.

6. *Herald*, Oct. 24, 1867; Peter B. Sweeny, *On the "Ring Frauds" and Other Public Questions* . . . (New York, 1894), pp. 46–49. In this privately printed pamphlet of Sweeny's interviews and other papers, Sweeny discusses issues contemporary to the publication date. He had little to say about "The Ring," except to proclaim his innocence of any wrongdoing. He also exonerates Hoffman and Hall, but says nothing of Tweed and Connolly.

7. Francis G. Fairchild, *The Clubs of New York* (New York, 1873), pp. 165, 200, 202–14, 250–51; Henry Watterson, *History of the Manhattan Club* (New York, 1915). Watterson makes reference to Sweeny, Hoffman, McLean and George Purser, all of whom had been members, but does not refer to Tweed except in connection with "The Ring." For Tweed property in Greenwich, see Grand List October 1, 1866–78, assessor's office, Village Hall, Greenwich, Connecticut; see also Mortgages, Warranties, Administration Deeds, Libers 31, 33, 35, 36, 38, 39, 43, 45 *passim*, Village Hall, Greenwich, Connecticut.

8. *Herald* and *Times*, July 5, Aug. 21, 1867.

9. *Herald*, Aug. 14 and 20, Sept. 10, 27, 28 and 29, 1867.

10. Ibid., April 11, 12, 13, 17, 21, 23, 24, and 28, 1867.

11. Ibid., June 7, Aug. 26, 1867; DeAlva S. Alexander, *A Political History of the State of New York* (New York, 1909), III, 184–85; Alden Chester, *Legal and Judicial History of New York* (New York, 1911), II, 167-213.

12. *Herald*, Oct. 6, 20 and 24, Nov. 1, 6, 7, 10, 23, 24 and 30, Dec. 4, 1867; Supreme Court Payroll, Vouchers, 1868. Standard sources such as Alexander and Myers attributed the Democratic victory at least partly to thousands of immigrants who had been illegally naturalized, an "indication of the enormous frauds that had been practiced by Boss Tweed and his gang." Alexander, III, p. 188. As a source, Alexander cites Gustavus Myers, *History of Tammany Hall*. In this book, Myers mentions that in 1865 the city had 77,475 naturalized voters. He then on goes to give the opinion that voters were "daily made larger by the connivance of corrupt judges with the frauds of politicians." From there, he goes to "Boss" Tweed, who centralized power in one hand. Myers gives no citations or evidence to buttress his statements, but he himself later is used as authority. So history is written. Charges of naturalization frauds were common whenever Democrats won, but proof of such charges were rare.

16. CONVENTIONS

1. *Herald*, Jan. 9 and 10, Feb. 11, 1868. Bills for goods and services rendered to the club by C. Bollar and others are in the Tweed Misc. Mss., N.Y.H.S.L. For later description of the club, see *Herald* issues of Aug. 29,

1869, Sept. 12, 1870, July 7, 1872. Alexander said the admission fees were raised to $1,000. III, 244.

2. *Herald*, March 10, 1868; Senate Document 62, Feb. 25, 1868, Tweed Misc. Mss., New York Public Library; *Journal of the Senate of the State of New York. 91st Session*. Albany, 1868, *passim*, Jack D. Douglas, "Boss Tweed's Revenge," *Wall Street Journal*, June 30, 1976. In this article the author explains Tweed's "corruptions" as a way of alleviating social ills and further a social program by creating a cohesive political center.

3. *Herald*, March 11, 16, 19, 24 and 28, April 22, 1868; W. A. Swanberg, *Jim Fisk: The Career of an Improbable Rascal* (New York, 1959), pp. 23–121; William W. Fowler, *Ten Years in Wall Street* (Hartford, 1870), pp. 494–511, Tweed Statement, Tweed Misc. Mss., N.Y.H.S.L.

4. *Herald*, April 1 and 2, 1868.

5. Ibid., Feb. 5, March 11, 12 and 29, July 2, 4, 5, 6, 8, 9 and 10, Sept. 1, 1868. Alexander in his very anti-Tweed political history cites the *Tribune* of March 5, 1868, which depicts Tweed as "fat, oily and dripping with public wealth," although Tweed is hardly mentioned at the convention. III, 196–205. Stewart Mitchell, *Horatio Seymour of New York* (Cambridge, 1938), pp. 411–42.

   Sweeny said that Tilden felt slighted at the convention when Tammany decided on Sandford Church as its nominee for the presidency, and never forgave Hoffman's nomination for governor. Yet Sweeny said he held no grudges against Tilden, nor did he question his motives during the "Ring" investigations, but he implied that Tilden did have personal motives for his actions. Sweeny, op. cit., pp. 58–59.

6. *Times* and *Herald*, Sept. 1, 3, 4 and 6, 1868. Alexander accepted the *Tribune*'s view of Hoffman as a man "kept by Tammany Hall." III, 205, citing the issue of Nov. 5, 1868.

7. *Times* and *Herald*, Oct. 6, 13 and 23, Nov. 1, 4, 8 and 24, Dec. 2, 1868. Sweeny later asserted with regard to the Hall nomination that Oswald Ottendorfer, editor of the *Staats Zeitung*, was his choice for the mayoralty nomination, but that the editor declined the offer citing poor health as his reason. Sweeny felt that if he had accepted "what a difference it would have made to the City of New York, and in the fate of many men." This was presented by Sweeny as an example of his innocence. Pp. 51–58 of his pamphlet.

17. GRAND SACHEM

1. *Herald*, March 7, 1869; Minutes of the Tammany Society, 1863–74, New York State Library, Albany; Membership List of the Tammany Society or Columbian Order, 1830–80, New York State Library; Membership List of the Tammany Society, 1829–1924, Kilroe Collection, Butler Library, Columbia University, New York City (this gives the number of Grand

Sachems at thirty-four, rather than twenty-nine); E. Vale Blake, *History of the Tammany Society* (New York, 1901), p. 185.

Tweed was formally installed on April 19, 1869.

2. *Herald*, March 20 and 26, April 10, 15 and 24, May 25, Aug. 17, 1869; March 17, 1870; Jan. 20, Feb. 16 and March 29, 1871. Further provisions for the widening were passed in 1871.

In 1903, at a symposium on "Our City: Its Past and Its Future," held by the Nineteenth Century Club, a speaker Charles R. Lamb suggested that the city owed a debt of gratitude to the memory of Tweed because of his far-seeing policy and imagination in providing parks and the Riverside Drive. He ended by saying "Whatever Tweed and his associates had stolen had been more than made up by the great improvements he had projected and the profits the city made from those improvements. Give me imagination and dishonesty, rather than rectitude coupled with stupidity." It was one of the rare tributes paid to Tweed. Newspaper clipping, in Tweed Family Manuscripts. For another tribute, see Walter L. Hawley, "What New York Owes to Tweed," *Munsey's Magazine*, 1907, XXXVI, 616–20. For a list of Tweed's real estate holdings, see *Herald*, April 15, 1875, and Conveyance Libers in Register's Office, New York City.

3. John W. Pratt, "Boss Tweed's Public Welfare Program," *The New-York Historical Society Quarterly*, 1961, XLV, 400–7; *Journal of the Senate of The State of New York, 92nd Session*. Albany, 1869, *passim*.

4. *Herald*, April 1, 1869; Alexander, op. cit., III, 187–88.

5. *Herald*, July 6, 1869.

6. Ibid., July 1, Aug. 3, 1869.

7. Ibid., April 1, 3, 4–9 and 15, 1869.

8. Ibid., Sept. 25, 1869; Swanberg, op. cit., pp. 134–55; Fowler, op. cit., pp. 512–30. Tweed gave Fisk a check for $100,000 on May 31, 1869. This may have been for stock or possibly the return of a loan, but there is no way of knowing. The check is with the Tweed Manuscripts in N.Y.H.S.L. along with several other checks, but there is no indication as to its use. Certainly, it was a sign of Tweed's growing financial success.

9. *Herald*, July 18 and 25, Aug. 3, 22 and 29, Sept. 1, 2, 4, 5 and 18, 1869; Irving Katz, *August Belmont* (New York, 1968), pp. 189–90.

10. *Herald and Times*, Sept. 22, 23, 25 and 26, Oct. 14, 15, 17, 20, 24, 28 and 30, Nov. 1 and 8, Dec. 1, 5 and 8, 1869; Alexander, op. cit., III, 226–28.

Tweed had a chance during the fall campaign to relax when Hoffman added him to a long list of "distinguished New Yorkers" as a delegate to the Southern Commerical Convention meeting in Louisville, Kentucky, on October 12. If Tweed did in fact go, he could count on Horace Greeley, William Cullen Bryant and Horatio Seymour as company. *Herald*, Sept. 7, 1869.

18. A "NEW MAGNA CARTA"

1. Alexander, op. cit., III, p. 243; *Herald*, Jan. 10, 14, 16 and 23, Feb. 4–6, 26 and 28, March 10–12, 24–27, 29 and 31, April 4–7, 10, 13 and 16, 1870; *Laws of New York*, 1870, chaps. 137, 190, 382 and 383; *Valentine's Manual*, 1870, pp. 29–60.

   The *Tribune*, commenting on the Young Democrats' futile battle, rhymed:

   > "If I am so quickly done for
   > I wonder why I begun for." (March 12, 1870.)

2. *Times*, March 17, 1870; *Tribune*, April 2, 1870; *Herald*, April 12, 1870. *Journal of the Senate of the State of New York*, 93rd Session (Albany, 1870), *passim*.
3. *Herald*, April 4, May 7, 10, 12, 13 and 18, 1870.
4. Ibid., May 28, Sept. 4, 11, 21, 22, 25, 27 and 29, Oct. 2, 1870.
5. Ibid., Sept. 29, 1870, and May 23, 1871.
6. Ibid., July 1, 1870.
7. *Times*, June 1, 1870; *Herald*, June 1 and 2, 1870; Lately Thomas, *Delmonico's, A Century of Splendor* (Boston, 1967), p. 125. Early in 1870, Tweed resided at 41 West Thirty-sixth Street and he appears to have moved to the Fifth Avenue address for his daughter's wedding. The family remained there until 1874, when they moved to 339 West Fifty-seventh Street. In 1875, there is a listing for a William Tweed at 23 East Fifty-sixth Street. For residences, see *Trow's Directory* for the appropriate year.
8. *Times*, Sept. 4, 21, 24, 28 and 29, 1870. Other newspapers, especially the *Tribune* and *World*, also barked up the same tree. See especially, the issues of the *Tribune* dated Sept. 30 and Oct. 19, 1870. For information from Copland, see his Statement, Sept. 9, 1872, Vouchers, 1872.
9. *Herald*, Oct. 9, 11, 13, 14, 20, 23, 26, 28 and 29, Nov. 1, 3, 4, 7–10, 1870.
10. Ibid., Nov. 17, 1870.
11. Pratt, op. cit., p. 399.
12. New York *Democrat*, Jan. 5 and 13, 1871. The Christmas season, always a time for giving, saw the publication of a number of incidents linking Tweed to relief for the poor. On December 27, a notice in the *Tribune* read that the Tweed Poor Association of the Seventh Ward would begin operations in a few days. Seemingly, Tweed provided three thousand tons of coal and $6,000 for flour. Sheriff O'Brien also provided three thousand tons of coal. *Times*, Dec. 10 and 29, 1870.
13. *Times*, Dec. 29 and 31, 1870; *Herald*, March 14, 1871. The New York *Evening Post* wanted the statue to serve as a warning "to our children to avoid his bad example." March 11, 1871. See also George H. Moore to

Christian L. Delavan, April 3, 1876, Tweed Misc. Mss., N.Y.H.S.L.; Candace Stone, *Dana and the Sun* (New York, 1938), pp. 137–39.

19. WHERE THERE'S SMOKE

1. *Herald*, Jan. 2 and 8, 1871. Sheriff O'Brien was also asked about his donations, and like Tweed was embarrassed by the subject. He was even more close-mouthed than Tweed. One reporter thought O'Brien expended about $120,000 during a four-year period for such purposes.
2. *Democrat*, Jan. 5, 6, 13 and 14, 1871; August Belmont to Tweed, Jan. 31, 1871, Tweed Misc. Mss., N.Y.H.S.L.
3. *Herald*, Jan. 8 and 21, 1871. The *Democrat*, as usual, Tweed's defender, found the tax levy gave the city a better tax rate than any other city in the country. It scoffed at newspapers constantly harping at "Ring" machinations. Jan. 19, March 1, 1871, Edward D. Durand, *The Finances of New York City* (New York, 1898), p. 132.
4. *Herald*, March 10, 12, 25 and 29, 1871; John D. Townsend, *New York in Bondage* (New York, 1901). Townsend, who became Tweed's lawyer in his last years, saw in the viaduct nothing but plunder for Tweed. His relationship with Tweed and his family was not good and ended in a lawsuit.

    Governor Hoffman vetoed a bill to allow construction of the Beach Pneumatic Tube Arcade Underground Railway Co. which had taken over Beach's Transit Co. The eccentric Alfred Beach, brother of Moses Beach, the *Sun* publisher, had in fact commenced work in 1870 for a short distance under the street, New York's first subway. The tunnel still exists, but the veto ended further construction of this and other undergrounds until the beginning of the twentieth century. *Herald*, April 1, 1871; Stokes, op. cit., VI, 544, 546. The viaduct scheme came in for special abuse during the July disclosures, as many, including A. T. Stewart, William B. Astor and Manton Marble, were castigated for robbing the city of $5 million a year. *Times*, July 27, 1871.
5. *Times*, March 5, 1871; *Herald*, March 5 and 29, April 13 and 19, 1871; *Tribune*, March 31, 1871; *Democrat*, March 24, 1871. Tweed also introduced a bill to repeal a law requiring the licensing of theaters. It was not passed. Stokes, op. cit., VI, 590.
6. Edward D. Durand, op cit., pp. 119–24, 372–81; *Herald*, April 14, 18–20, 1871; *Democrat*, Feb. 16, 1871.
7. Margaret Tweed to Anna Tweed, March 7, 1871, Tweed Family Papers.
8. Lucius S. Comstock to Cashier, Chemical Bank, Dec. 30, 1870, Continental National Bank to Comstock, Jan. 4, 1871, Manufacturers and Merchants Bank to Comstock, Jan. 4, 1871, Notes on Suspension Bridge and Erie Junction Railroad Co., Tilden Papers, New York Public Library.
9. *Times*, March 5 and 16, 1871. Later the *Times* suggested a weird vigil by "Tweed and Co." to make sure Watson said nothing to harm them. Sept. 26 and 29, 1871, Sept. 15, 1872.

10. William S. Copland, Sept. 9, 1872, Vouchers. Matthew J. O'Rourke, military editor of the *Times*, was an informant, as was A. B. Bishop. O'Rourke to Tilden, Nov. 22, 1871, A. B. Bishop to Tilden, Oct. 1876, Tilden Papers.

11. *Times*, July 1 and 3, 1871; Albert B. Paine, *Th. Nast: His Period and His Pictures* (New York, 1904), pp. 137, 153–58, 179–81. Although not a critical biography, some criticism of Nast does sneak in. See pp. 226–27. The *Herald* ran a satirical campaign against Nast asking for a relief fund for the "Blackbeard Martyr." *Herald*, Nov. 2 and 6, 1873. Donald B. Chidsey, *The Gentleman from New York: A Life of Roscoe Conkling* (New Haven, 1935), p. 249.

12. *Times*, July 5, 1871.

13. Ibid., July 11–15, 20–22, 1871; July Riots, Vouchers, 1871, Daniel Ullman Correspondence, N.Y.H.S.L.; Paine, op. cit., pp. 171–72.

20. BLACK HEADLINES

1. *Times*, July 8, 15, 22–24, 26 and 29, Aug. 2, 3, 6–10, 14 and 17, 1871; Elmer Davis, *History of the New York Times, 1851–1921* (New York, 1921), pp. 84, 121. Davis accepts rumors that Tweed wanted to buy the *Times*. On March 29, 1871, Jones wrote, "No money that could be offered me should induce me to dispose of a single share of my property to the Tammany faction . . ." Was an offer ever made? And, why in March?

   See also Roscoe Conkling to George Jones, July 28, 1871, George Jones Papers. N.Y.P.L.; Townsend, op. cit., pp. 65–72; Benjamin E. Buchman, *Samuel J. Tilden Unmasked* (New York, 1876). Buchman implies all sorts of chicanery on the part of Tilden, including helping Tweed's escape in exchange for a suppression of damaging information. This makes for interesting reading.

2. *Times*, July 8 and 10, Aug. 18–20 and 24, 1871; Taintor, Vouchers, 1871.

3. *Times*, Oct. 28 and 30, Sept. 3–5, 1871.

4. Committee of Arrangements to Tilden, Aug. 22, 1871, John A. Dix to Tilden, Sept. 2, 1871, H. A. Richmond to Tilden, Sept. 12 and 19, 1871, A. R. Flowers to Tilden, Sept. 9, 1871, Fitzwilliam Byrdsall to Tilden, Oct. 10, 1871, Belmont to Tilden, Nov. 1, 1871, Tilden Papers. There are also letters from William F. Havemeyer, S. M. Shaw, John Foley, Charles O'Conor and George Jones.

5. *Times* and *Herald*, Sept. 8 and 9, 1871. A few days before an attempt was made to prohibit payment of an iron bill for work on the courthouse by J. W. Cornell. Justice Josiah Sutherland, however, upheld the validity of the bill to the disgust of the *Times*. See issue of August 23, 1871.

6. *Times*, Sept. 10, 1871. There were earlier threats on Tweed's life. In April, a man by the name of George F. Tram delivered a speech while carrying a

pistol and threatening to put a quietus upon "Tweed, Sweeny & Co." *Democrat*, April 17, 1871.

7. *Herald* and *Times*, Sept. 12–19, 1871.

8. *Times*, Sept. 18 and 19, 1871; John Foord, *The Life and Public Services of Andrew Haswell Green* (New York, 1913), pp. 97–101; Alexander C. Flick, *Samuel Jones Tilden* (New York, 1939), p. 221.

9. *Herald*, Sept. 19, 20 and 22, 1871.

10. Ibid., Sept. 21–23, 1871.

21. "WHAT ARE YOU GOING TO DO ABOUT IT?"

1. *Herald*, Sept. 23, 24 and 30, Oct. 3–5 and 7, 1871; Philip C. Jessup, *Elihu Root* (New York, 1938), I, 78–93.

2. *Herald* and *Times*, Oct. 7, 10, 14, 18–22, 25 and 26, 1871.

3. *Evidence before the Grand Jury in the Case of A. Oakey Hall* (New York, 1871), a pamphlet.

4. *People of the State of New York* vs. *Tweed, Ingersoll, Woodward and Garvey*, motion filed Nov. 7, 1871, County Clerk's Office, New York City.

5. *Times* and *Herald*, Oct. 27–29, 1871.

6. *Herald*, Sept. 7 and 10, Oct. 1, 3–6, 12, 19–21, 23, 26 and 29, Nov. 3, 5, 6–10, 1871. See congratulations to Tilden on Tammany's defeat from Hamilton Fish, Nov. 8, 1871, Sandford E. Church, Nov. 9, 1871, Tilden Papers; Flick, op. cit., p. 225.

7. *Times* and *Herald*, Nov. 15, 16, 18, 19, 21, 24, 26, 27 and 30, Dec. 6, 10, 16, 17, 19, 27, 29–31, 1871. See also *People* vs. *William Tweed*, order to remove filed Dec. 15, 1871; *People* vs. *Elbert A. Woodward and William M. Tweed*, indictment filed Dec. 16, 1871; Tweed indictments, H.D.C.; *In the Matter of William Tweed*, Petition for a Writ of Habeas Corpus, filed Dec. 16, 1871, County Clerk's Office.

22. FIRST, THE JUSTICES

1. *Herald*, Jan. 1, 1872. Schell was officially elected Feb. 20, 1872. Though embarrassed by the Tweed affair, Tammanyites saw a ray of light, for the frauds were discovered by Democrats and were prosecuted by Democrats. At least, so said John Kelly. Feb. 20, March 9, 1872, Minutes of the Democratic-Republican General Committee, 1872–78, State Library, Albany.

2. *Herald*, Jan. 2, 4, 19, 20 and 30, Feb. 15, 1878. An unsuccessful attempt was also made to unseat Alexander Frear.

3. Swanberg, op. cit., pp. 260–78.

4. *Herald*, Jan. 2, 6, 13, Feb. 6, 11 and 18, 1872; Tweed indictments, County Clerk's Office. The Genet forgery charge was marked "Nolle Prosequi" in November 1873. Garvey's forgery charge was so marked in

January 1874, Woodward's in December 1876, Cook's on December 29, 1881, and Ingersoll's in March 1882. See indictments in the County Clerk's Office. Receipts of Catharine Bradley, Vouchers, 1872 and 1883; Gunning S. Bedford to Tilden, n.d., 1872, Tilden Papers. Hall appealed in vain to Tilden to stop the prosecution. Hall to Tilden, n.d., 1872, Tilden Papers.

5. Barlow to Tilden, Jan. 29, 1872, Tilden Papers; Barlow to C. P. Daly, Feb. 21, 1872, Algernon S. Sullivan to Daly, Feb, 21, 1872, Daly Papers.

6. *Herald* and *Times*, Sept. 21–23, 30 and 31, Nov. 1, 25 and 26, 1871; March 21 and 26, June 13 and 22, 1872. No one seemed to have really tried to examine the charred remains. One man suggested a method to try to recover the debris. R. Crook to Tilden, Sept. 21, 1871, Tilden Papers. Order Forms, May–Aug. 1870 in Vouchers, County Payroll, Aug.–Dec. 1870, in Vouchers, Charles Baulch Misc. Records, 1855–71, Vouchers. See also *People of the State of New York* vs. *Baulch and Haggerty*, General Sessions and Oyer and Terminer, 1871–72, H.D.C.

7. *Herald*, March 5, 8 and 9, 1871; Bowen, op. cit., pp. 156–66. Tilden had something on Hall. He had received information from the Tenth National Bank that Hall's account at the end of December 1870 stood at $170,549.52. Although he did not know where this money came from, he did not press the point. This is part of a strange accumulation of confused notes found in the Tilden Papers.

8. *Herald*, Sept. 4, 20 and 27, Oct. 10 and 18, 1872; Julius Chambers, *The Book of New York, Forty Years' Recollections of the American Metropolis* (New York, 1912), pp. 36–37.

9. *Herald*, June 5, July 17 and 18, Oct. 5, 10, 11, 16, 18, 23 and 24, 1872. See also Tweed indictments, 1872, County Clerk's Office; Bartlett to Tilden, Oct. 10, 1872, Tilden Papers; Jessup, op. cit., p. 81.

10. *Herald*, Oct. 24, 26, 29 and 31, Nov. 1, 1872; Bowen, op. cit., pp. 171–72, 190–97; Allan Pinkerton account, Jan. 16, 1873, Vouchers, 1873.

11. *Herald*, Aug. 11, Nov. 1, 1872; Ingersoll and Farrington indictments, 1872, County Clerk's Office.

12. *Herald*, Nov. 1, 15, 19 and 20, Dec. 3, 4, 6, 7, 11 and 12, 1872; Alexander, op. cit., III, 301; Tweed indictments, County Clerk's Office; Brady to C. P. Daly, Nov. 16, 1872, Daly Papers; Peckham to Tilden, Dec. 3, 1872, Tilden Papers.

13. *Strong Diary*, III, 116, 169, 233, 273, 413, 515, 544.

14. *Herald* and *Times*, Jan. 15, Feb. 3 and 16, March 10, 16, 19, 23 and 24, April 5, 7, 10 and 12, May 3, 11, 12, 22, 23 and 29, June 20 and 27, July 3, 4, 18, 26, 28, 30 and 31, Aug. 4, 6, 8, 15, 19, 20 and 22, 1872. Cardozo, of whom so little is known, deserves some study. Some of the cases he sat on were quite interesting, as were his decisions. *Herald*, May 12, 23 and 25, April 17, 1871.

15. *Strong Diary*, III, 433.

16. *Herald*, Feb. 9, March 6, 14 and 16, April 6, 1872.

23. THEN TWEED

1. For biographies of the various attorneys listed, see David McAdam et al., eds., *History of the Bench and Bar* (New York, 1897). For Davis, see II, 123, and for Peckham II, 304.
2. *Herald*, Jan. 1, 8–11, 14, 16–18, 21, 22, 24, 25, 28–31, Feb. 1 and 19, April 25, 1873; *People of the State of New York* vs. *William Tweed*, drawing of jury, County Clerk's Office; *Strong Diary*, III, 467; Alexander B. Callow, *The Tweed Ring* (New York, 1970), p. 288; Clinton, op. cit., pp. 442–43.
3. Tweed indictments, County Clerk's Office; *Herald*, Feb. 21 and 26, March 4 and 5, May 6 and 15, 1873.
4. *Herald*, Nov. 6–8, 11, 13, 16, 18–23, 25 and 30, Dec. 2; Peckham to Tilden, Nov. 2, 1873, Tilden Papers; Clinton, op. cit., pp. 443–68; *People of the State of New York* vs. *William Tweed, Proceedings Subsequent to Verdict* (New York, 1874), pp. 16–23. [Anon.], A Member of the Bar, *Judge Davis and Six Gentlemen of the New York Bar* (New York, 1874), *passim*.
5. *Herald*, Nov. 25, Dec. 5, 17–20, and 23, 1873; Jan. 9, 1874.
6. *Herald*, July 8, 1873; Correspondence between Margaret Tweed, William Tweed, Charles T. Rodgers, Sept.–Dec. 1873, Alfred Tweed to Mrs. Richard Tweed, various dates, 1873–75, Tweed Family Papers; Will of Eliza Tweed, Liber 215, p. 298, Wills, Surrogate's Court, New York County. Mrs. Richard Tweed's "genteel household furniture" was sold at auction on Oct. 13, 1873, at her home at 237 East Broadway, pamphlet, Tweed Family Papers.
7. C. G. Beach to Tilden, March 17, 1873, George Moss to Tilden, March 20, 1873, Tilden Papers; *Herald*, Feb. 12, 19, 23, 27 and 29, April 3, 6 and 22, 1873. It should be noted that Comptroller Andrew Green's arrest was ordered because of the "profligacy" with which public money was expended to influence the state legislature. He was released, but trial did not follow. Memories of "The Ring" were very clear. In July, there was a story circulated that due to the poor financial straits of the city, the paintings in City Hall would be sold. This too did not follow. *Herald*, July 3, 5 and 11, Oct. 9, 1873.

24. PRISON

1. Tweed to Margaret M. Tweed, March 21, 1874, Tweed Family Papers; *Herald*, Feb. 12 and 17, March 20 and 28, April 7, 16, and 24, May 30, June 18 and 20, Sept. 14, Dec. 1, 3, 16, 23, 26 and 30, 1874; *People* vs. *Tweed*, motion papers filed on various dates, County Clerk's Office.

25. SIX MILLION DOLLARS

1. *Herald*, Jan. 9, 12–15, 1871; *People* vs. *Tweed*, motion papers on file in county clerk's office. There were two other civil suits brought against Tweed. One was brought by the City against Edward Marrener and Tweed for $550,000, the other brought by G. S. Miller against Tweed. In both cases, Justice Abraham Lawrence decided on motion of Tweed's counsel that the plaintiffs had to supply a bill of particulars of their claim. Apparently unable to do so, both suits were dropped. *Times*, April 20, 1875.
2. *Herald* and *Times*, Jan. 17, Feb. 4 and April 19, 1875.
3. Ibid., April 3, 7 and 8, 1875; Flick., op. cit., p. 423.
4. Ibid., April 7, 8, 12 and 13. Among the properties attached were 439 Fifth Avenue, 17 East Forty-fourth Street, 10 East Thirteenth Street. Also included were stables on Forty-second Street, in whose "elegant rooms Tweed and favored friends met and had high revels over punch mixed in a wonderful and costly silver-punch bowl while many a plan was perfected there to plunder the City." It was a typical report that became history. *Times*, April 12, 1875; Alexander, op. cit., III, 244.

   A large number of persons who had bought property from Tweed now found that lis pendens had been filed against their property. They moved to cancel these lis pendens. These motions were usually successful, though not always. *Times*, July 17, Aug. 12, 1875; *People* vs. *Tweed*, petitions filed on various dates, County Clerk's Office; *People of the State of New York* vs. *William M. Tweed, Papers on Appeal for an Order Affirming Order Denying Motion to Vacate the Order of Arrest* (New York, 1875), pp. 185–86 (these papers contain a history of Tweed's real estate holdings).
5. Alfred Tweed to Margaret Tweed, Feb. 28 and April 11, 1875, Tweed Family Papers.
6. *Herald* and *Times*, April 29 and 30, May 2, June 1–3 and 16, 1875.
7. *Times*, June 16, 1875; Clinton, op. cit., pp. 469–92; Townsend, op. cit., pp. 110–11; O'Conor to Tilden, March 31, 1875.
8. *Times*, June 23, 24, 29 and 30, July 1 and 3, 1875; *Papers on Appeal*, cited in note 4.
9. *Times*, July 15, 17, 21 and 22, Aug. 1, 6, 7 and 24, Oct. 2, 7 and 9, 1875.
10. Ibid., Oct. 9, 13–16, 1875.
11. Ibid., Oct. 17, 28 and 30, Peckham to Daniel Pratt, Oct. 27, 1875, Tilden Papers.
12. *Times*, Oct. 29 and 30, Nov. 4, 7, 17, 18, 20, 21, 27 and 28, Dec. 7–9, 16, 29, 1875.

26. FATHER'S GONE

1. *Herald*, Dec. 9, 1874. An earlier and similar incident occurred a few days before. Ibid., Dec. 3, 1874.

2. Except where otherwise noted, the information regarding Tweed's escape comes from the December 5, 6, 7 and 9, 1875, issues of the *Times* and *Herald*.

3. Caleb Cushing to Hamilton Fish, Dec. 21, 1875, Charles L. Lawrence to George Bliss, May 29, 1876, Hamilton Fish Papers, Vol. III, Library of Congress. There are also a number of relevant letters to and from Lawrence in the same collection in volume 114.

4. Henry C. Hall to John L. Cadwalader, June 23, 1876, Robert Mason to A. D. Straus, Esq., July 12, 1876, Dispatches from United States Consuls in Havana, 1703–1906, T-20, Reel 76, National Archives. Except where otherwise noted all information on Tweed in Cuba is taken from these documents and on Tweed in Spain from Dispatches from United States Consuls in Spain, M-31.

5. Henry C. Hall to Hamilton Fish, July 28, 1876, Dispatches from Havana, Young telegram enclosed. See also Hamilton Fish to Benjamin K. Phelps, July 28, 1876, Tweed Misc. Mss., N.Y.P.L.

6. Allan Nevins, *Hamilton Fish, the Inner History of the Grant Administration* (New York, 1936), p. 841.

7. Entry, August 7, 1876, Hamilton Fish Diary, Library of Congress.

8. William Hunter to Hamilton Fish, Sept. 13, 1876, Fish Papers, 116; Adee to Fish and Collantes, Sept. 12, 16, 18 and 26, 1876, Dispatches from Spain.

9. Ulysses S. Grant to Fish, Sept. 13, 1876, Fish Papers, 116; Flick, op. cit., pp. 310–12.

10. *Times*, Oct. 21, Nov. 24, 1876; Fish to Commodore Howell, Sept. 20, 1876. Fish Papers, 116. The photographs were included in a message from Adee to Fish, Sept. 25, 1876, Dispatches from Spain.

11. Fish to John L. Cadwalader, Oct. 4, 1876, Fish Letter Books, 1876, Library of Congress; Cadwalader to Fish, Oct. 2 and 7, 1876, Fish Papers, 116.

12. Fish to Cadwalader, Oct. 6, 1876, Fish to Ulysses S. Grant, Oct. 6, 1876, Cadwalader to Fish, Oct. 7, 1876 (Cadwalader wanted luggage to be examined on the *Franklin*, since he felt customhouse officers were all thieves), Fish to George Robeson, undated, Fish Letter Books, 1876; Charles S. Fairchild to Fish, Sept. 19, 1876, Fish Papers, 116.

13. *Times*, Nov. 24, 1876, Cadwalader to Benjamin K. Phelps, Oct. 9, 1876, Tweed Misc. Mss., N.Y.P.L.

14. *Times*, Nov. 24, 1876.

15. Ibid., April 4 and 5, 1877. See Tweed's testimony at the aldermanic investigation in Chapter 29.
16. Townsend, op. cit., pp. 119–20.

27. SURRENDER

1. Peckham to Tilden, Jan. 20 and 21, Feb. 15, March 16, 1876, Tilden Papers. See also letter of Arthur E. Smith to Tilden, dated April 26, 1876, in the same collection requesting money for services rendered in giving testimony.

    A struck jury is a special jury where only a panel of forty-eight names is prepared, and the parties in turn strike off a certain number of names until the list is reduced to twelve.

2. Peckham to Tilden, Feb. 19 and 24, 1876; *Times*, Jan. 1, 4, 15 and 20, Feb. 1, 8, 9, 15, 18, 19 and 26, March 1–3, 7–9, 18 and 22, May 12 and 14, Oct. 21, Nov. 24, 1876.

    Charles Devlin, one of Tweed's bondsmen, brought suit against the city as well as Jackson S. Schultz, John H. Keyser, Andrew J. Garvey, Richard B. Connolly and James H. Ingersoll. Devlin's suit for an injunction prohibiting the city from releasing Keyser, Garvey, Connolly, Sweeny and Ingersoll from prosecution was brought under an act of the legislature of 1872 which gave citizens the right to sue officials in case of breach of authority. The suit represented the feeling of many in New York that the prosecution of Tweed alone was a miscarriage of justice. The injunction was not issued, all the suit did was cause discomfort or a moment of concern, at least, to Keyser. Keyser to Tilden, April 29, 1876, Tilden Papers; *Times*, Feb. 17, March 17, 1876.

3. *Times*, Sept. 1, Nov. 24, Dec. 12, 1876; Jan. 13, 1877.

4. There was a sputtering effort to try Sweeny. In May, Peckham and O'Conor wanted the matter to be put off to October. O'Conor because he was not feeling well enough, Peckham because a "good" jury was difficult to obtain, so many being out of town. Peckham to Tilden, May 29, 1876, Taintor to A. E. Smith, Sept. 30, 1876, Peckham to Tilden, Sept. 29, 1876, Tilden Papers. Had Sweeny's case come on, it would have been heard of Justice Westbrook. Again, he was Peckham's choice. Peckham to Tilden, Sept. 26, 1876, O'Conor to Tilden, Oct. 16, 1876, Tilden Papers; Townsend, op. cit., pp. 115–17. The city paid two detectives $182.40 for their expenses in returning Woodward from Chicago. Receipt of James Healy and George H. Dilks, dated Oct. 12, 1876, Vouchers, 1876.

5. O'Conor to Tilden, Dec. 16, 1876, Tilden Papers; Tweed to O'Conor, Dec. 6, 1876, O'Conor to Fairchild, Dec. 18, 1876, Fairchild Papers; Townsend, op. cit., pp. 119–20.

28. AN IMPLACABLE FOE

1. Townsend also assumed credit for leading the fight against Cardozo. Townsend, op. cit., pp. xi-xv, 18–19. This book is a rehash of stated evidence. He took Tweed as a client in an odd way. The agreement dated Feb. 12, 1877, was that he be paid $5,000 down, and $5,000 additional if Tweed were freed from prison. To secure the payment of the additional $5,000 were it to become due, he was given certain collateral by Benjamin P. Fairchild. After Tweed's death, Townsend was compelled to return the collateral to Fairchild, after the latter brought suit against him. *Times*, Nov. 13, 1878; Jan. 9, 1879.
2. *William M. Tweed* vs. *Mayor, etc.*, Judgment Roll, Dec. 1, 1877, Law Judgment M-473, County Clerk's Office.
3. Margaret Tweed to [W. M. Tweed], Jan. 7, 1877, Tweed Family Papers; Tweed to James H. Ingersoll, Jan. 10, 1877, Tweed Misc. Mss., N.Y.H.S.L.; Edith [Sands?] to Margaret Tweed, Jan. 14, 1877, Tweed to Lester Marquand, Nov. 3, 1877, Tweed Family Papers.
4. *Times*, Jan. 3 and 13, March 24, 1877; Peckham to C. S. Fairchild, April 17, 1877, W. C. Whitney to Fairchild, March 31, 1877, Peckham to Fairchild, April 17, 1877, Fairchild Papers. Tweed also lost another, though much smaller suit. In February 1877, John B. Marshall and William Fuller sued Tweed, Cornelius Carson, Richard M. Tweed and William E. King for $5,000. The plaintiffs had contracted with the Champlain Shore Iron Mountain Company to build a dock opposite the company's factory on Lake Champlain called Tweed's Bay. They received a judgment against the company in 1876, but when the judgment was not paid they sued Tweed and the others as stockholders in the company. They were, of course, successful in their suit, even though witnesses testified that much of the work contracted for was not done, and what was done, was done poorly. *Times*, Feb. 7, 1877.
5. Peckham to Townsend, Feb. 27, 1877, Fairchild Papers.
6. Whitney to Fairchild, March 31, 1877, Fairchild Papers; *Times*, Feb. 24, March 24, 27 and 29, April 6, 1877.
7. Townsend, op. cit., p. 129.
8. Folger to Fairchild, April 18, 1877, Townsend to Fairchild, April 18, 1877, Fairchild Papers; Townsend, op. cit., pp. 134–35; *Times*, April 17–20, 1877.
9. *Times*, April 22 and 25, May 1–3 and 11, 1877.
10. Peckham to Fairchild, May 3, 14 and 15, June 7 and 14, 1877, Whitney to Fairchild, May 25, 1877, John Foley to Fairchild, June 5, 1877, Townsend to Fairchild, June 6, 1877, Fairchild to Townsend, June 12, 1877, Fairchild Papers. Fairchild probably reasoned that to accept Tweed's evidence in the Sweeny case would not have helped to get money, but would have resulted in Tweed's freedom. Sweeny getting off "scot free

and Townsend earning a very pretty fee from each." Fairchild to Charles W. Carl, July 7, 1877, Fairchild Papers.

11. Townsend, op. cit., pp. 135–36, 138–42; *Times*, May 22, June 7 and 13, 1877; Fairchild to Peckham, July 7, 1877, Fairchild Papers.

12. *Times*, June 14, 1877, Fairchild to Townsend, June 12, 1877, Peckham to Fairchild, June 21, 1877, Fairchild Papers; Townsend, op. cit., pp. 136, 142–51.

13. Townsend, op. cit., pp. 129–35; *Times*, June 14, 16, 21, 22 and 29, July 7, 1877; Francis S. Barlow to Fairchild, June 25, 1877. For other letters of support for Fairchild's position, see letters to him written by F. F. Marberg, W. A. Beach and Sidney DeKay, all dated June 25, 1877, and George T. Curtis to Fairchild, July 5, 1877, Fairchild Papers.

14. *Times*, July 12, 18–21, 1877.

15. William C. Whitney to Fairchild, July 20, 1877, Tweed's statement, undated, signed by him, Fairchild Papers; *Herald*, Oct. 10 and 11, 1877; *Times*, Oct. 11–13, Nov. 2, 1877.

16. *Herald*, Nov. 16, Dec. 30, Feb. 9, 14 and 21, 1877. One suit not connected with Tweed, but with the times, was one brought by the City against Henry Starkweather for extracting fees illegally while collector of assessments. Starkweather's widow returned $23,866.07 to the city. *Times*, Feb. 7, 1878.

29. ALDERMEN AGAIN

1. *Times*, July 20, Aug. 12 and 31, Sept. 4, 1877.

2. Ibid., Sept. 7, 1877.

3. Ibid., Sept. 13 and 16, 1877.

4. Ibid., Sept. 16 and 19, 1877. In answer to inquiries from Taintor in 1872, O. P. Quintard, Secretary of the New York Bridge Company, wrote that Tweed, Sweeny, Smith, and Connolly were stockholders, and that each had bought stock amounting to $42,000. Each had paid four installments of 10 per cent each, and they owed two installments of 10 per cent each which they were unable to pay due to their "troubles." Payments were made by personal checks except in the case of Sweeny, whose share was paid for by his brother. Hall did not own shares in the company. O. P. Quintard to Taintor, Jan. 25, 1872, Tilden Papers.

5. *Times*, Sept. 16 and 19, 1877.

6. Ibid., Sept. 22, Dec. 13, 1877.

7. Ibid., Sept. 30, Oct. 7, 1877.

8. Ibid., Oct. 12 and 18, 1877.

9. Ibid., Oct. 21, 25, 28, 30 and 31, Nov. 4, 1877. Townsend estimated the city collected a total of over $1.3 million as follows: Watson's estate, $558,000; Sweeny, $395,000; Woodward, $150,000; Starkweather, $23,-000; National Broadway Bank, $291,000. From this counsel fees of $232,000 were subtracted. See pp. 150–51 of Townsend's book. Fair-

child's total comes to about the same, but with variations. Watson's estate, $590,000; Woodward, $150,000; Sweeny, $200,000; John H. Bradley, $200,000. Peckham received $12,249.52 from the Watson settlement. Attorney General in Account with City and County of New York, 1874–77, Wheeler H. Peckham Account, Nov. 1877, Fairchild Papers.

10. *Times*, Dec. 25, 1877.
11. Ibid., Nov. 22, 23, 27–29, Dec. 4 and 6, 1877.
12. Ibid., Jan. 5, 1878; Feb. 9 and 27, March 27, April 2, 1878; Townsend, op. cit., p. 151.

30. FINAL ESCAPE

1. For accounts of his death and funeral, as well as some background material which must be used with caution, see *Times* and *Herald*, April 11, 13–15 and 18, 1878.
2. *Times*, May 13 and 14, 1878, March 4, June 14, 1879.

Bibliography

A word about bibliography and historiography. There is heavy reliance in the writing of this work on newspapers, especially the *Times* and *Herald*, and to a lesser extent on journals like the *Tribune* or *Transcript*. These are especially valuable since there are very few papers left by members of "The Ring" or of those around them. There are no letters of any consequence extant, at least as of this writing, of Hall, Connolly, Sweeny, Watson, Keyser, Ingersoll and the rest. Fellow councilmen, supervisors, congressmen, members of the Board of Education have seemingly left nothing that relates to Tweed, or in most instances to anyone else. There are few if any Elijah Purdy letters, none of John Cochrane, or of Oscar Sturtevant or others who were intimate with Tweed. His lawyers, David D. Field or Elihu Root, left nothing and said nothing about their client. Some like William Edelstein promised that they would write a "true story," but they never did. Of Tweed himself, there are but a handful of letters, only some of any value, and these dealt mostly with his early life. The great bulk of his correspondence is missing. There are legends about mysterious trunks containing accounts, letters and similar material, but nothing has been found. Also, he is mentioned by few of his contemporaries in existing manuscripts, and then only at the height of his fame. No one seems to have asked details about his early life, his escape or political experience. When he decided to tell about the machinations of "The Ring," no one was really interested, feeling that the story would be just that, a story—told by a thief and escaped criminal anxious to save his life. It was seemingly so. There are, of course, a number of papers of prominent politicians available, particularly those of Samuel J. Tilden and Charles S. Fairchild. These collections have had "derogatory" material, especially in the Tilden case, removed by heirs. Still, these are valuable sources, though oddly neglected. Use has also been made of biographies and contemporary accounts, but as with so much else, these must be taken with a grain of salt. Matthew P. Breen's "Reflections" were published twenty years after Tweed's death and like so much else published about Tweed meant to fit the public image and market.

So much of the contemporary accounts are cut from similar cloth. E. L.

Godkin's articles in the *Nation*, Charles Nordhoff's and Charles Wingate's works in the *North American Review* are long on rhetoric and short on evidence. They too served to inflate the balloon. They are delightful reading but so too is *Treasure Island*.

While there is a paucity of certain kinds of materials, letters, diaries and the like, there is and does exist a large quantity of other records all practically untapped. What is available and what has been consulted are the voluminous State Department papers in the National Archives, Washington, D.C., essential to a study of Tweed's escape; city records, such as Board of Supervisors journals, comptroller's vouchers, warrants and bills. The latter luckily were saved from destruction ordered by officials, just prior to this writing, and were extensively used, as were voluminous trial records, most of which have heretofore been almost entirely overlooked.

SECONDARY SOURCES

Albion, Robert G. *The Rise of New York Port, 1815–1860*. New York, 1970.

Alexander, De Alva S. *A Political History of the State of New York*. New York, 1906–23. 4 vols.

Asbury, Herbert. *The Gangs of New York, An Informal History of the Underworld*. New York, 1929.

Bales, William A. *Tiger in the Streets*. New York, 1962.

Barrett, Walter. *The Old Merchants of New York City*. New York, 1885. 5 vols.

Berger, Meyer. *The Story of The New York Times*. New York, 1951.

Bigelow, John. *The Life of Samuel J. Tilden*. New York, 1895.

Bishop, Joseph B. *The Chronicles of One Hundred and Fifty Years of the Chamber of Commerce, State of New York, 1768–1918*. New York, 1918.

Blair, Jr., Francis P. *The Life and Public Services of Horatio Seymour*. New York, 1868.

Blake, E. Vale. *History of the Tammany Society*. New York, 1901.

Booth, Mary L. *History of the City of New York*. New York, 1860.

Bowen, Clarence L., ed. *History of the Centennial of the Inauguration of George Washington*. New York, 1892.

Bowen, Croswell. *The Elegant Oakey*. New York, 1956.

Brace, Charles L. *The Dangerous Classes of New York and Twenty Years' Work Among Them*. New York, 1872.

Breen, Matthew P. *Thirty Years of New York Politics Up-to-date*. New York, 1899.

Broun, Heywood, and Leech, Margaret. *Anthony Comstock, Roundsman of the Lord*. New York, 1927.

Brown, Francis. *Raymond of the Times*. New York, 1951.

Brown, Henry C., ed. *Valentine's Manual*. New York, 1916–28. 12 vols.

Bryce, James. *The American Commonwealth*. New York, 1970. 2 vols.

Buchman, Benjamin E. *Samuel J. Tilden Unmasked*. New York, 1876.

Callow, Jr., Alexander B. *The Tweed Ring*. New York, 1970.

Carman, Harry James. *The Street Surface Railway Franchises of New York City*. New York, 1919.

Chambers, Julius. *The Book of New York, Forty Years' Recollection of the American Metropolis*. New York, 1912.

Chester, Alden. *Legal and Judicial History of New York*. New York, 1911. 3 vols.

Chidsey, Donald B. *The Gentleman from New York: A Life of Roscoe Conkling*. New Haven, 1935.

Clark, Col. Emmons. *History of the Seventh Regiment of New York 1806–1889*. New York, 1890. 2 vols.

Clews, Henry. *Fifty Years in Wall Street*. New York, 1908.

Clinton, Henry L. *Celebrated Trials*. New York, 1897.

Coleman, Terry. *Going to America*. New York, 1972.

Collins, Frederick L. *Consolidated Gas Company of New York*. New York, 1934.

Cook, Adrian. *Armies in the Street*. Lexington, 1974.

Cook, Theodore. *The Life and Public Services of Hon. Samuel J. Tilden*. New York, 1876.

Costello, A[ugustine] E. *Our Firemen*. New York, 1887.

———. *Our Police Protectors*. New York, 1885.

Davis, Elmer. *History of the New York Times 1851–1921*. New York, 1921.

Dunshee, Kenneth A. *As You Pass By*. New York, 1952.

Durand, Edward D. *The Finances of New York City*. New York, 1898.

Emmet, Thomas A. *Incidents of My Life*. New York, 1911.

Ernst, Robert. *Immigrant Life in New York City*. New York, 1949.

Fairchild, Francis G. *The Clubs of New York*. New York, 1873.

Fiske, Stephen. *Off-Hand Portraits of Prominent New Yorkers*. New York, 1884.

Flick, Alexander C., ed. *History of the State of New York*. New York, 1933. 10 vols.

———. *Samuel Jones Tilden, A Study in Political Sagacity*. New York, 1939.

Foord, John. *The Life and Public Services of Andrew Haswell Green*. New York, 1913.

Fowler, William W. *Ten Years in Wall Street*. Hartford, 1870.

Franklin, Allan. *The Trial of the Tammany Tiger, 1789–1928*. New York, 1928.

Fuller, Robert H. *Jubilee Jim, The Life of Col. James Fisk, Jr*. New York, 1928.

Genung, Abram P. *The Frauds of New York City Government Exposed . . .* New York, 1871.

Greenleaf, Jonathan. *A History of the Churches of All Denominations in the City of New York*. New York, 1846.

Halpine, Charles. *The Life and Adventures, Songs, Services and Speeches of Private Miles O'Reilly*. New York, 1864.

Harlow, Alan F. *Old Bowery Days*. New York, 1931.

Haswell, Charles H. *Reminiscences of an Octogenarian of the City of New York (1816 to 1860)*. New York, 1896.

Headley, Joel T. *Pen and Pencil Sketches of the Great Riots*. New York, 1882.

Hellman, George S. *Benjamin N. Cardozo, American Judge*. New York, 1940.

Hemstreet, Charles. *When Old New York Was Young*. New York, 1902.

Hirsch, Mark D. *William C. Whitney, Modern Warwick*. New York, 1948.

Holmes, Anne Middleton. *Algernon Sydney Sullivan*. New York, 1929.

Huntington, Bishop. *Restell's Secret Life*. Philadelphia, 1897.

Jenkins, Stephen. *The Greatest Street in the World. The Story of Broadway, Old and New from Bowling Green to Albany*. New York, 1911.

Jessup, Philip C. *Elihu Root*. New York, 1938. 2 vols.

July, Robert W. *The Essential New Yorker, Gulian Crommelin Verplanck*. Durham, 1951.

Katz, Irving. *August Belmont, a Political Biography*. New York, 1968.

Keep, Austin B. *History of the New York Society Library*. New York, 1908.

Keller, Morton. *The Art and Politics of Thomas Nast*. New York, 1968.

Kernan, J. Frank. *Reminiscences of the Old Fire Laddies*. New York, 1885.

Kouwenhoven, John. *The Columbia Historical Portrait of New York*. New York, 1953.

Krout, John A. *The Origins of Prohibition*. New York, 1925.

Lamb, Martha J. *History of the City of New York*. New York, 1880. 2 vols.

Lanman, Charles. *The Dictionary of the United States Congress*. Philadelphia, 1859.

Leonard, John W. *History of the City of New York*. New York, 1910.

Lewis, Alfred H. *Richard Croker*. New York, 1901.

Limpus, Lowell M. *History of the New York Fire Department*. New York, 1940.

Lynch, Denis T. *"Boss" Tweed, The Story of a Grim Generation*. New York, 1927.

McAdam, David, et al., eds. *History of the Bench and Bar of New York*. New York, 1897. 2 vols.

McCabe, Jr., James D. *Lights and Shadows of New York Life or the Sights and Sensations of the Great City* . . . Philadelphia, 1872.

———. *New York by Sunshine and Gaslight*. New York, 1881.

McGuire, James K., ed. *The Democratic Party of the State of New York*. New York, 1905. 3 vols.

McJimsey, George T. *Genteel Partisan: Manton Marble 1834–1917*. Ames, 1971.

Mack, Edward C. *Peter Cooper, Citizen of New York*. New York, 1949.

Mandelbaum, Seymour J. *Boss Tweed's New York*. New York, 1965.

Maverick, Augustus. *Henry J. Raymond and the New York Press for Thirty Years*. Hartford, 1870.

Miller, Peyton F. *A Group of Great Lawyers of Columbia County, New York.* New York, 1904.

Mines, John F. *A Tour Around New York and My Summer Acre being the Recreations of Mr. Felix Oldboy.* New York, 1893.

Mitchell, Stewart. *Horatio Seymour of New York.* Cambridge, 1938.

Morris, Lloyd. *Incredible New York.* New York, 1951.

Mushkat, Jerome. *Tammany, The Evolution of a Political Machine, 1789–1865.* Syracuse, 1971.

Myers, Gustavus. *The History of Tammany Hall.* New York, 1901.

———. *History of the Great American Fortunes.* Chicago, 1911. 3 vols.

Nevins, Allan. *The Evening Post, A Century of Journalism.* New York, 1922.

———. *Hamilton Fish, The Inner History of the Great Administration.* New York, 1936.

Paine, Albert B. *Th. Nast: His Period and His Pictures.* New York, 1904.

Palmer, A. Emerson. *The New York Public School.* New York, 1905.

Peck, H. C., and Bliss, Theodore. *Kossuth and the Hungarian War.* New Haven, 1852.

Peel, Roy V. *The Political Clubs of New York City.* New York, 1935.

Peterson, Arthur Everett, and Edwards, George William. *New York as an Eighteenth Century Municipality.* New York, 1917.

Pinchon, Edgcumb. *Dan Sickles, Hero of Gettysburg and "Yankee King of Spain."* New York, 1945.

Pleasants, Samuel Augustus. *Fernando Wood of New York.* New York, 1948.

Ravitch, Diane. *The Great School Wars, New York City 1805–1973: A History of the Public Schools as Battlefield of Social Change.* New York, 1974.

Richmond, J. F. *New York and Its Institutions.* New York, 1872.

Rosenwaike, Ira. *Population History of New York City.* Syracuse, 1972.

Ross, Ishbel. *Crusades and Crinolines.* New York, 1963.

Scisco, Louis Dow. *Political Nativism in New York State.* New York, 1901.

Seitz, Don C. *Horace Greeley—Founder of New York Tribune.* Indianapolis, 1926.

Sheldon, George W. *The Story of the Volunteer Fire Department of the City of New York.* New York, 1882.

Silliman, B., and Goodrich, C. R., eds. *The World of Science, Art and Industry Illustrated from Examples in the New York Exhibition 1853–1854.* New York, 1854.

Smith, Matthew H. *Bulls and Bears of New York.* Hartford, 1875.

Smith, Ray B., ed. *History of New York State.* Syracuse, 1922. 6 vols.

Spatz, Marshall. "New York City Public Schools and the Emergence of Bureaucracy, 1868–1917." Unpublished doctoral dissertation, City University of New York.

Stebbins, Homer Adolph. *A Political History of the State of New York, 1865–1869.* New York, 1913.

Still, Bayrd. *Mirror for Gotham.* New York, 1956.

Stone, Candace. *Dana and the Sun*. New York, 1938.

Stone, William L. *History of New York City*. New York, 1872.

Swanberg, W. A. *Jim Fisk: The Career of an Improbable Rascal*. New York, 1959.

Syrett, Harold C. *The City of Brooklyn, 1865–1898*. New York, 1944.

Taft, Henry W. *A Century and a Half at the New York Bar*. New York, 1938.

Thomas, Lately. *Delmonico's, A Century of Splendor*. Boston, 1967.

Tilden, Samuel J. *The New York City "Ring," Its Origin, Maturity and Fall Discussed in a Reply to the New York Times*. New York, 1873.

Townsend, John D. *New York in Bondage*. New York, 1901.

Vanderpoel, Ambrose E., ed. *Personal Memoirs of Edwin A. Ely*. New York, 1926.

Van Deusen, Glyndon G. *Thurlow Weed: Wizard of the Lobby*. New York, 1947.

Van Pelt, Daniel. *Leslie's History of Greater New York*. New York, 1898. 3 vols.

Warren, John H. *Thirty Years Battle with Crime*. New York, 1874.

Watterson, Henry. *History of the Manhattan Club*. New York, 1915.

Werner, M. R. *Tammany Hall*. New York, 1928.

Wilson, James Grant. *The Memorial History of the City of New York*. New York, 1893. 4 vols.

Wilson, Rufus R. *New York: Old and New, Its Story, Streets and Landmarks*. Philadelphia, 1902. 2 vols.

ARTICLES

Chalmers, Leonard. "Tammany Hall, Fernando Wood, and the Struggle to Control New York City, 1857–1859." *The New-York Historical Society Quarterly*, April 1969, pp. 7–33.

Edwards, E. J. "The Rise and Overthrow of the Tweed Ring," *McClure's*, July 1895, pp. 132–43.

Godkin, E. L. "The Boss's Rule," *The Nation*, Oct. 12, 1871.

———. "Christmas and Thieves," *The Nation*, Nov. 2, 1871.

———. "Moral Career of Tweed," *The Nation*, April 18, 1878.

———. "Overthrow of Tweed," *The Nation*, Nov. 27, 1873.

———. "Rising against the Ring," *The Nation*, Nov. 9, 1871.

Hawley, Walter. "What New York Owes to Tweed." *Munsey's Magazine*, April 1907, pp. 616–20.

Hirsh, Mark. "More Light on Boss Tweed." *Political Science Quarterly*, June 1945, pp. 267–78.

Joline, Adrian Hoffman. "John Thompson Hoffman," *New York Genealogical and Biographical Record*, April 1911, pp. 111–28.

Myers, Gustavus. "The History of Public Franchises in New York City," *Municipal Affairs*, March 1900.

Nordhoff, Charles. "The Misgovernment of New York," *North American Review*, Oct. 1871.

Parton, James. "The Government of New York City," *North American Review*, Oct. 1866.

Pratt, John W. "Boss Tweed's Public Welfare Program." *The New-York Historical Society Quarterly*. Oct. 1961, pp. 396–411.

"Printing of the Records of the City of New York in the Days of William M. Tweed by the 'Ring.'" *The New-York Historical Society Quarterly*, Oct. 1923, pp. 88–89.

Wingate, Charles. "An Episode in Municipal Government," *North American Review*, Oct. 1874; Jan., July 1875; Oct. 1876.

PAMPHLETS

[Anon.]. A Member of the Bar. *Judge Davis and Six Gentlemen of the New York Bar*. New York, 1874.

———. *How New York is Governed. Frauds of the Tammany Democrats* (published by New York *Times*, 1871).

———. *The House that Tweed Built*. New York, 1871.

Citizens Association. *Address of the Citizens' Association of New York to the Public: History of Its Work—The Department of Docks—The Department of Health—The Fire Department*. New York, 1871.

———. *Address to the People of the City of New York by the Citizens' Association of New York*. May 6, 1870.

———. *An Appeal by the Citizens' Association of New York against the Abuses in the Local Government, to the Legislature of the State of New York, and to the Public*. New York, 1865.

———. *City Finances, Items of Expenditure for Stationery, Printing, etc.* New York, 1864.

———. *How the Money Goes. Letter from the Citizens' Association to Richard O'Gorman Relative to His Office*. New York, 1867.

———. *Important Reform Measures Passed by the Legislature of 1866*. New York, 1866.

———. *Items of Abuse in the Government of the City of New York: Taxpayers, Citizens, Read! Read! Read!* New York, 1866.

Citizens Committee. *Appeal to the People of the State of New York Adopted by the Executive Committee of Citizens and Taxpayers for the Financial Reform of the City and County of New York*. New York, 1871.

Clinton, Henry L. *Tammany Ring Exposed and Denounced*. New York, 1871.

Kilroe, Edwin P., et al., eds. *Tammany, 1786–1924, A Patriotic History*. New York, 1924.

Post, Eugene J. *The Wig and the Jimmy, or a Leaf in the Political History of New York*. New York, 1869.

Roosevelt, R[obert] B. *Political Corruption in New York*. New York, 1871.

St. John and Coffin. *The Downfall of Tammany Hall, No Fall at All, Not by A. Oakey Hall*. New York, 1871.

Sweeny, Peter B. *On the "Ring Frauds" and other Public Questions*. New York, 1894.

Tammany Society or Columbian Order. *Celebration of the Ninety-Fourth Anniversary of American Independence, at Tammany Hall, Monday, July 4, 1870*. New York, 1870.

——. *Celebration at Tammany Hall on Saturday, July 4, 1863*. New York, 1863.

——. *Proceedings of the Tammany Society on Laying the Corner-Stone of their New Hall in Fourteenth Street, and Celebrating the Ninety-first Anniversary of the Declaration of American Independence, July 4, 1867*. New York, 1867.

PRIMARY SOURCES

Manuscripts

New-York Historical Society Library
    James W. Beekman Papers
    Richard B. Connolly Papers
    Charles S. Fairchild Papers
    Andrew Haskell Green Papers and Diaries
    John Kelly Miscellaneous Manuscripts
    John D. Townsend Miscellaneous Manuscripts
    William M. Tweed Miscellaneous Manuscripts
    Daniel Ullman Papers
    George W. Wingate Miscellaneous Manuscripts
    George W. Wright Miscellaneous Manuscripts

New York Public Library
    John Bigelow Papers
    Abraham Oakey Hall Miscellaneous Manuscripts
    George E. Jones Papers
    W. E. D. Stokes Miscellaneous Manuscripts
    Samuel J. Tilden Papers
    William M. Tweed Miscellaneous Manuscripts
Hamilton Fish Papers, Diaries, and Letter-books, Library of Congress
Jones, George E., Papers, Historical Documents Collection
List of Membership in the Tammany Society, Edwin Patrick Kilroe Collection, Columbia University Library
Tammany Collection, State Library, Albany, New York
    Membership List, Society of Tammany or Columbian Order, 1834–80
    Minutes of the Democratic-Republican General Committee, 1840–41, 1837–78

Minutes of the Tammany Society or Columbian Order, 1863–74, 1874–81
Roll Book, 1789–97, 1808–16
Tweed Bible, Museum of the City of New York
Tweed, Richard M. Family Papers, Borger, Texas

Official Records

CENSUS

Census of the State of New York for 1845. Albany, 1846.
Hough, Franklin B., ed. *Census of the State of New York for 1855.* Albany, 1857.
Seaton, C. W., ed. *Census of the State of New York for 1875.* Albany, 1877.

COURT RECORDS

Court of Oyer and Terminer, General Sessions, 1871–78, indictments, Historical Documents Collection
Queens College, City University of New York, Flushing, New York
Evidence before the Grand Jury in the Case of A. Oakey Hall. New York, 1871.
Supreme Court, motions, indictments, pleadings, writs, trial records, 1871–78, County Clerk's Office, 31 Chambers Street, New York City

NEW YORK CITY

Board of Aldermen Documents, 1844–78
Board of Aldermen Proceedings, 1844–78
Board of Aldermen, Report of the Special Committee to Investigate the "Ring" Frauds . . . New York, 1878.
Board of Supervisors, Ledger A, County Treasury, 1859–74, Historical Documents Collection
Board of Supervisors, Journals, 1859–68, 1868–74, Historical Documents Collection
Board of Supervisors, Report of the Special Committee on New County Court House, June 6, 1863. New York, 1863.
Comptroller's Assignments, 1830–80. Historical Documents Collection
Tax Rolls, 1816–1840, Historical Documents Collection
Insolvency Assignments, 1850–90, Historical Documents Collection
Valentine, David T. *Obsequies of Abraham Lincoln in the City of New York.* New York, 1866.
———. *Report of the Committee of Arrangements of the Common Council of New York of the Obsequies in Memory of Henry Clay.* New York, 1852.
Wills, 1850–90, Historical Documents Collection (copies in Surrogate's Court, 31 Chambers Street, New York City)

NEW YORK STATE

Digest Special Statutes Relating to the City of New York 1778–1921. New York, 1922.

Hutchins, Stephen C., ed. *Civil List and Constitutional History of the State of New York.* New York, 1879.

Laws of the State of New York, 1850–78.

Assembly, *Charges of the Bar Association of New York against Hon. George G. Barnard and Hon. Albert Cardozo, Justices of the Supreme Court, and John H. McCunn, a Justice of the Superior Court of the City of New York.* New York, 1872. 3 vols.

Senate, *Journals of,* 1850–78.

UNITED STATES

Congressional Globe, 33rd Congress, 1853–1855. Washington, 1854–55.

Dispatches from United States Consuls in Havana, 1876, Reel T-20, National Archives

Dispatches from United States Consuls in Spain, 1876, Reels, M-17, and 31, National Archives

Directories, Guides, Atlases

[Anon.] *A Description of the Central Park.* New York, 1868.

[Anon.] *An Index to the Illustrations in the Manuals of the Corporation.* New York, 1900.

Bromley, George W. and Walter S. *Atlas of the Nineteenth and Twenty-Second Wards.* Philadelphia, 1880.

Butt Ender [pseud.]. *Prostitution Exposed or a Moral Reform Directory.* New York, 1839.

DeKock, Charles [old man of twenty-five, pseud.]. *Guide to the Harem or Directory to the Ladies of Fashion in New York and Various Other Cities.* New York, 1855.

Disturnell, John. *New York as It Is.* New York, 1833–76.

Doggett's New York City Directory. New York, 1842–52.

Hardy, John, ed. *Manual of the Corporation of the City of New York.* New York, 1870.

Longworth, David and Thomas. *New York City Directory.* New York, 1790–1843.

Miller, James. *New York as It Is.* New York, 1859–76.

Real Estate and Record Guide. New York, 1862–70.

Robinson, E., and Pidgeon, R. H. *Atlas of the City of New York.* New York, 1880–86.

Shannon, Joseph, ed. *Manual of the Corporation of the City of New York.* New York, 1868–69.

Stokes, I[saac], and Phelps, N. *The Iconography of Manhattan Island.* New York, 1915–28. 6 vols.

Trow, John F. *New York City Directory*. New York, 1852–78.
Valentine, David T., ed. *Manual of the Corporation of the City of New York*. New York, 1841–66.

Diaries

Nevins, Allan, ed. *Diary of Philip Hone 1828–1851*. New York, 1927. 2 vols.
Nevins, Allan, and Thomas, Milton H., eds. *Diary of George Templeton Strong*. New York, 1952. 4 vols.

Newspapers and Periodicals

NEW YORK CITY

Democrat, 1860–1871
Evening Post, 1851–1879
Harper's Weekly, 1866–1878
Herald, 1851–1879
Times, 1851–1879
Transcript, 1865–1871
Union, 1861
World, 1860–1871

ALBANY

Argus, 1877

Index